Artificial Intelligence and Machine Learning for Industry 4.0

Scrivener Publishing
100 Cummings Center, Suite 541J
Beverly, MA 01915-6106

Publishers at Scrivener
Martin Scrivener (martin@scrivenerpublishing.com)
Phillip Carmical (pcarmical@scrivenerpublishing.com)

Artificial Intelligence and Machine Learning for Industry 4.0

Edited by

M. Thirunavukkarasan

S. A. Sahaaya Arul Mary

Sathiyaraj. R

G. S. Pradeep Ghantasala

and

Mudassir Khan

Scrivener Publishing

WILEY

This edition first published 2025 by John Wiley & Sons, Inc., 111 River Street, Hoboken, NJ 07030, USA and Scrivener Publishing LLC, 100 Cummings Center, Suite 541J, Beverly, MA 01915, USA

For more information about Scrivener publications please visit www.scrivenerpublishing.com.

Wiley Global Headquarters
111 River Street, Hoboken, NJ 07030, USA

For details of our global editorial offices, customer services, and more information about Wiley products visit us at www.wiley.com.

Library of Congress Cataloging-in-Publication Data

ISBN 9781394275045

Front cover images supplied by Adobe Firefly
Cover design by Russell Richardson

Set in size of 11pt and Minion Pro by Manila Typesetting Company, Makati, Philippines

Printed in the USA

10 9 8 7 6 5 4 3 2 1

Contents

Preface

Intelligent automation is widely considered as the greatest potential of Industry 4.0 innovations for corporations. Artificial intelligence, defined as computational models that simulate behavioral intelligence, is set to unleash the coming era in technological revolution and provide businesses with an edge over its competitors. The significance of AI is not found in its computational models, but in how humans can use them. Industry things are increasingly being upgraded to machines with intelligence that can perceive, act, evolve, and interact in a particular environment. Artificial intelligence enables computer systems to learn from experience, adapt to new input data, and perform intelligent tasks. Consistently observing an equipment to keep it from malfunctioning is the procedure of predictive maintenance. Predictive maintenance anticipates an equipment failure in addition to typical equipment maintenance, which employs a periodic schedule rather than responding to equipment problems. In an Industry 4.0 context, data produced by sensor networks necessitates machine learning and data analysis tools. Industry 4.0 is enabling industrial facilities to convert into innovative factories by harnessing intelligent technologies. The primary drivers of this information-driven business shift are artificial intelligence and machine learning along with IoT. The confluence of Industry 4.0 technologies has led to an ideological shift in which the barriers between physical, electronic means, and biological are increasingly vanishing. The foundation of this technological convergence process, which will lead to the digitization of the business and the community at all the levels, represents a new era associated with hyperconnectivity and interoperability. This reveals precisely how AI and ML-based models are becoming more prevalent in various industries for smart functioning and greater productivity. The book aspires to emphasize technological developments that could have a greater influence on an industrial revolution. It also intends to present core technologies while imparting sophisticated strategies for strengthening the industrial sector.

The book anticipates to bring out the foundations of the AI/ML technologies in Industry 4.0 and pulls out the various intelligent algorithms, which can benefit the modern industrial needs. This book fosters contemporary technological advancements in the fields of AI and ML from an industry 4.0 perspective. It also looks at the prospects, obstacles, and potential applications of AI and ML in industry 4.0 research. Firstly, explores the foundation of technologies in Industrial real-time applications than presents an AI/ML based algorithms for predictive maintenance and improving the production effectively. Followed by providing the insights on how advanced technologies can support the industrial transformation and fulfill their requirements with smart techniques. Also, offers case studies to illustrate the necessitate of smart technologies in shifting the industries to next era.

The book titled *Artificial Intelligence and Machine Learning for Industry 4.0* is for AI and ML experts, industry professionals, entrepreneurs, data engineers, researchers, academicians and policy makers which provides the unique insights in the field of modern industrial revolution exploring the impact of AI, ML and advanced technologies on Intelligent systems. Additionally, the book provides the consideration and impact of technologies on smart and sustainable industries and case studies for stakeholders including industrialists and academicians, customers, government and policy makers for business empowerment. The secondary audiences are graduate students, researchers, and professionals in the fields of computer science and engineering, electronic engineering, and mechatronics engineering.

1

Industry 4.0 and the AI/ML Era: Revolutionizing Manufacturing

Balusamy Nachiappan[1], C. Viji[2], N. Rajkumar[2*], A. Mohanraj[3], N. Karthikeyan[4], Judeson Antony Kovilpillai J.[2] and Pellakuri Vidyullatha[5]

[1]Department of Information Technology, Prologis, Denver, USA
[2]Department of Computer Science & Engineering, Alliance College of Engineering and Design, Alliance University, Bengaluru, Karnataka, India
[3]Department of Computer Science & Engineering, Sri Eshwar College of Engineering, Coimbatore, Tamil Nadu, India
[4]Vellore Institute of Technology, Chennai, India
[5]Department of Computer Science and Engineering, Koneru Lakshmaiah Education Foundation, Vaddeswaram, Guntur, Andhra Pradesh, India

Abstract
The emergence of enterprise 4.0 signs a transformative era in manufacturing, wherein digital technology seamlessly merges with traditional business methods. This precis explores the profound impact of Industry 4.0, highlighting the synergy of the various Industrial Internet of Things (IoT) and its implications for clever production. At its core, business enterprise 4.0 allows the mixing of physical and virtual structures, fostering heightened interconnectivity and transparency. The IoT permits actual-time facts change among interconnected gadgets, supplying manufacturer with comprehensive insights into their production ecosystems. Decentralized selection-making, a key function of enterprise 4.0, is made viable with the aid of cyber-physical systems, empowering machines with independent choice-making capabilities and enhancing operational performance.

Even as AI is absent from the narrative, the point of interest stays at the transformative electricity of enterprise 4.0. Predictive preservation algorithms preemptively understand and prevent device failures, making sure ultimate performance and minimizing downtime. Actual-time quality manipulation mechanisms contribute to product consistency through early illness detection. The concept of

Corresponding author: nrajkumar84@gmail.com

M. Thirunavukkarasan, S. A. Sahaaya Arul Mary, Sathiyaraj. R, G. S. Pradeep Ghantasala and Mudassir Khan (eds.) Artificial Intelligence and Machine Learning for Industry 4.0, (1–28)

smart automation outcomes in adaptive and self-optimizing manufacturing strategies involves responding in real-time to changing conditions. Past the manufacturing facility, the strategic integration of the digital era optimizes delivery chain dynamics, facilitating smart forecasting, stock management, and logistics.

***Keywords*:** Business intelligence, big data analytics, industry 4.0, machine learning, artificial intelligence

1.1 Introduction

The roots of Industry 4.0 amplify deep into the annals of industrial history, with its emergence representing a natural evolution from prior revolutions. The first commercial revolution often characterized by the age of mechanization took flight within the late 18th century. Steam engines and mechanized textile manufacturing marked the transformative shift from manual labor to machine-driven strategies. This period laid the foundation for the next improvements, setting the degree for what might comply with.

As the 19th century unfolded, the second commercial enterprise revolution spread out with electrification at its center. The invention of the telegraph, the extraordinary adoption of power, and the development of assembly line production introduced approximately radical adjustments. Mass production became a truth, propelling industries into a new era of overall performance and scale. The sunrise of the 20th century noticed the onset of the third business revolution, characterized using the rise of computer systems and automation. This phase automatically guides duties, introducing programmable logic controllers and paving the manner for current production practices [1, 4, 5].

Against this ancient backdrop, industry 4.0 emerges as the 4th commercial revolution, fusing the virtual and physical domains extraordinarily. It represents a departure from the linear development of its predecessors, embracing a greater holistic and interconnected approach. The historical context serves as a crucial foundation for knowledge of the motivations at the back of enterprise 4.0.

At present, industry 4.0 is described via the convergence of numerous ground-breaking technologies. The creation of the net of factors (IoT) allows the interconnection of devices, enabling seamless conversation and record change. Cyber-physical systems integrate computational factors into physical approaches, blurring the strains between the digital and tangible worlds. Huge records analytics emerges as an effective tool, permitting groups to derive meaningful insights from the considerable quantities of records generated in actual time. Cloud computing presents scalable and

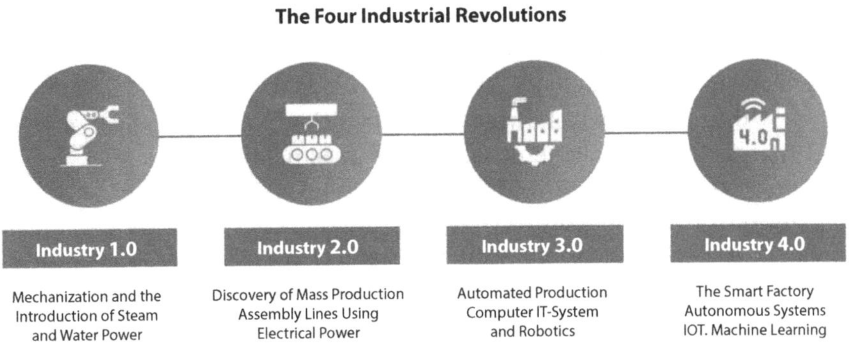

Figure 1.1 Industrial revolutions.

handy computational resources, fostering the improvement of advanced applications.

Figure 1.1 provides a clear depiction of the industrial revolutions. The historic trajectory predominant to Industry 4.0 underscores the non-stop quest for efficiency, productiveness, and innovation inside business approaches. Every revolution builds upon the achievements and demanding conditions of its forerunners, pushing the boundaries of what's feasible in manufacturing. Company 4.0, with its emphasis on smart automation, records-driven selection-making, and the mixture of modern-day technologies, represents the apex of this evolutionary journey.

As we delve deeper into the historical roots, it becomes obvious that Industry 4.0 isn't always simply a technological bounce but a holistic transformation in the manner of the industry's function. This revolution isn't constrained to isolated enhancements; it signifies a whole paradigm shift, ushering in a technology in which the virtual and bodily geographical regions coalesce to redefine the very essence of commercial company techniques.

1.1.1 Key Traits of Industry 4.0

Industry 4.0, the 4th commercial revolution, is defined through a set of transformative traits that distinguish it from its predecessors. Those key functions collectively form the landscape of present-day production, developing dynamic and interconnected surroundings. Figure 1.2 effectively illustrates the essential industry solutions.

➢ **Convergence of bodily and digital structures**

At the heart of Industry 4.0 is the seamless convergence of physical and virtual systems. In contrast to preceding commercial revolutions that predominantly focused on mechanization [2], electrification, and automation, enterprise 4.0 blurs the lines between the physical and virtual worlds. This convergence is facilitated by a complicated community of technology, along with the Internet of Things (IoT), which connects physical devices and enables them to talk and change facts in actual time.

➢ **Digitalization and connectivity**

Industry 4.0 is synonymous with the sizeable digitalization of commercial tactics. Analog methods are changed with the aid of virtual opposite numbers, growing a statistics-driven technique to production. This digital transformation is amplified by using considerable connectivity, permitting machines, structures, and people to communicate seamlessly. Cyber-physical structures, which combine computational abilities into physical processes, exemplify the fusion of the digital and bodily geographical regions.

➢ **Wise automation**

In comparison to preceding waves of automation, organization 4.0 introduces an emblem-new era of wise automation. Machines are not truly computerized however imbued with synthetic Intelligence (AI) and machine mastering (ML) abilities. These technologies empower machines to make selections, examine from information inputs, and adapt to changing conditions autonomously. The end result is a degree of automation that isn't always without a doubt green however, also responsive and adaptive.

➢ **Facts transparency and interoperability**

Enterprise 4.0 locations, a pinnacle class on information transparency and interoperability: The significant amount of data generated with the aid of way of interconnected gadgets and systems is made accessible and transparent all through the whole production chain. This transparency allows informed selection-making, as stakeholders have real time get admission to important facts. Moreover, interoperability ensures that several systems and technology can seamlessly put paintings together, fostering a greater integrated and cohesive production surroundings [3].

➢ **Decentralized selection-making**

In enterprise 4.0, choice-making is decentralized, and distributed during the network of intelligent devices and structures. This decentralization enhances the agility of manufacturing strategies, as choices may be made autonomously at various factors in the manufacturing chain [42, 43]. The functionality to make picks concerning the supply of records contributes to actual-time responsiveness and performance.

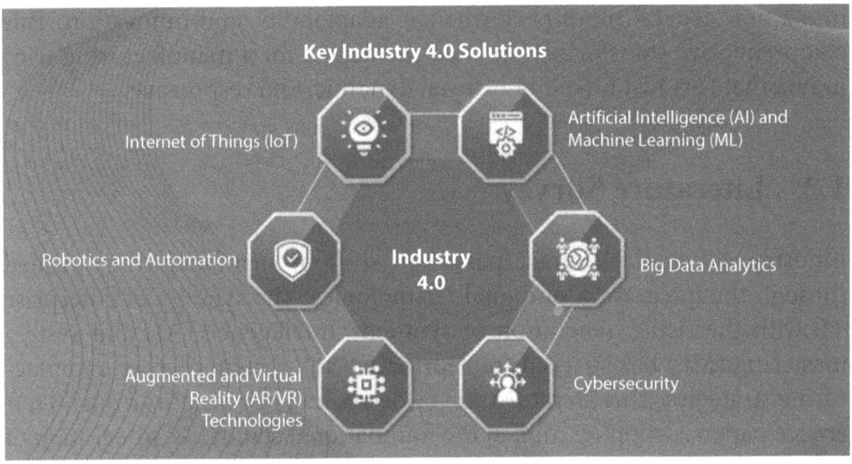

Figure 1.2 Key Industry 4.0 solutions.

➢ **Customization and flexibility**

One of the hallmark characteristics of Industry 4.0 is the emphasis on customization and flexibility. Traditional mass production models are giving way to more personalized and flexible manufacturing processes. Intelligent systems can adapt to different product specifications, allowing for more efficient and cost-effective production of customized goods.

➢ **Human-system collaboration**

Industry 4.0 acknowledges the importance of human-device collaboration. Rather than changing human people, advanced technologies are designed to paint along them. Augmented facts, collaborative robots, and clever gear permit a harmonious interaction between humans and machines. This collaboration enhances performance, reduces mistakes, and ensures a safer running environment.

➢ **Predictive maintenance**

Predictive upkeep is a cornerstone of Industry 4.0. AI and ML algorithms analyze statistics from sensors embedded in equipment to predict equipment screw-ups earlier than they occur. This proactive technique minimizes downtime, extends the lifespan of the system, and optimizes upkeep schedules [4, 5]. In precis, the important thing characteristics of industry 4.0 together redefine manufacturing processes. The convergence of bodily and digital systems, shrewd automation, records transparency, and decentralized decision-making form a powerful synergy that propels industries into a new generation of performance, adaptability, and innovation. This comprehensive transformation cited the degree for a manufacturing panorama that isn't just linked but clever, dynamic, and responsive.

1.2 Literature Survey

Industry 4.0 marks a great paradigm shift in manufacturing, pushed through the integration of digital technologies. The synergy of enterprise 4.0 with the rising generation of synthetic Intelligence (AI) and system mastering (ML) has sparked transformative adjustments across manufacturing strategies. This literature survey delves into key insights from 40 reference papers, dropping mild at the foundational standards, integration of AI/ML, clever automation, cognitive production, challenges, possibilities, and the symbiotic nexus of industry 4.0 and the AI/ML era. The impact of Industry 4.0 on library management systems has been profound, transforming various aspects of library operations, services, and user experiences [30–39].

1.2.1 Foundations of Industry 4.0

The adventure starts with the foundational works that laid the foundation for Industry 4.0. Lee *et al.* (2015) [14], delivered a cyber-physical systems architecture, emphasizing the interconnected nature of present-day production structures. Rüßmann *et al.* (2015), furnished strategic insights, highlighting the ability productivity and boom that Industry 4.0 may want to deliver to manufacturing industries [6–8]. This strategic angle framed the next discussions and paved the manner for complete expertise of the industry 4.0 panorama.

1.2.2 Integration of AI and ML

As enterprise 4.0 develops, the combination of AI and ML has become more and more prominent. Lu *et al.* (2017), surveyed technologies and packages within Industry 4.0, showcasing the various technological landscape. Chen *et al.* (2018), centered on modern-day enterprise 4.0, accentuating the function of AI. The key technologies in wise manufacturing had been explored by using Wang and Wang (2016), supplying a roadmap for the infusion of AI into manufacturing processes. These works collectively underscore the pivotal position of AI and ML in shaping the trajectory of Industry 4.0.

1.2.3 Smart Automation and Human-Robotic Collaboration

Improvements in smart automation and human-robotic collaboration symbolize an essential component of enterprise 4.0. Smith *et al.* (2022), explored the synergy between people and robots in smart factories, highlighting the transformative capability. Liu *et al.* (2017), investigated side computing in production, emphasizing the importance of decentralized intelligence. These studies together contribute to the know-how of how automation and collaboration are evolving within the context of Industry 4.0.

1.2.4 Cognitive Manufacturing

Tao and Cheng (2020), delved into records-pushed sensible production, showcasing the cognitive factors of current production approaches. Lu *et al.* (2018), supplied an enterprise method attitude on Industry 4.0, illuminating the cognitive packages that drive efficiency and innovation. These works make contributions to the evolving narrative of cognitive production as a quintessential element of enterprise 4.0.

1.2.5 Disturbing Situations and Opportunities

Expertise in the demanding conditions and opportunities furnished via the use of Business Enterprise 4.0 is critical for its successful implementation. Yu and Sarangi (2018), completed a whole literature examination, offering insights into the multifaceted landscape of Industry 4.0. Schumacher *et al.* (2016), proposed a maturity version for assessing enterprise 4.0 readiness, addressing traumatic conditions, and providing a dependent direction forward. The work collectively underscores the need for a nuanced understanding of the traumatic conditions and the large opportunities that Industry 4.0 offers.

The convergence of industry 4.0 with AI/ML era is a pivotal scenario, counted with wide variety explored in diverse dimensions. Zhou *et al.* (2019), provided a complete view of destiny industrial possibilities and traumatic conditions, emphasizing the symbiotic dating among industry 4.0 and AI/ML. Tao *et al.* (2019), brought the idea of a virtual dual maintain-ground, showcasing the mixing of AI and ML for clever manufacturing.

1.3 The AI/ML Era Within the Industrial Revolution

1.3.1 The Role of AI and ML

➢ **Foundations of AI and ML**

Gadget mastering, a subset of AI, includes the development of algorithms that permit pc structures to investigate from facts and make predictions or decisions [41–45]. The ideas of these generations rests on the idea of imparting machines with the capacity to analyze facts, take a look at them, and make clever alternatives.

➢ **Packages in production**

In the context of the economic panorama, AI and ML discover multifaceted packages. One of the key areas is predictive maintenance. Traditional protection techniques are reactive, responding to tool failures once they arise. With AI and ML, machines geared up with sensors observe facts and patterns to expect while preservation is needed, minimizing downtime, and optimizing operational performance [7, 47]. Great management in production methods moreover benefits notably from tool studying. AI algorithms can examine brilliant datasets in actual time, ensuring steady product best through a manner of identifying defects early in a manufacturing manner. This no longer reduces waste but moreover, complements the overall reliability of the producing method.

➢ **Deliver chain optimization**

The AIML era reshapes the dynamics of supply chain control. AI algorithms, powered by way of manner of device reading, convey predictive analytics to the vanguard. Through analyzing historical statistics, the algorithms can forecast demand more appropriately, optimizing inventory ranges and streamlining logistics. The result is a greater responsive and inexperienced supply chain, able to adapt to dynamic marketplace situations.

➢ **Clever automation**

Clever automation, a trademark of the AI/ML technology, represents a departure from conventional automation. In traditional automation, machines perform based totally on pre-programmed instructions. Within the AI/ML technology, automation turns into smart. Machines geared up with AI and ML competencies can adapt their operations based on actual-time information inputs and evolving situations. This level of adaptability enhances performance and responsiveness in production methods [8, 44, 48].

➢ **Cognitive production**

Cognitive technologies, a subset of AI, introduce a new dimension to production—cognitive manufacturing. This involves machines with the capacity to mimic human idea strategies. These cognitive systems could make complicated choices, remedy elaborate problems, and interact in dynamic problem-solving [10]. The integration of cognitive manufacturing elevates the decision-making abilities of machines to a level previously unseen in traditional manufacturing.

➢ **Human-robotic collaboration**

The AI/ML era fosters today's technology of collaboration among people and robots. In preference to viewing AI and robots as replacements for human labor, industries understand the capacity for collaboration. AI enables seamless coordination among human people and robot systems. This collaboration complements performance, as responsibilities are allotted based on the strengths of each human contributing instinct and adaptability, while robots carry precision and pace.

➢ **Statistics analytics and AI**

Huge facts analytics, empowered by using AI, play a pivotal position inside the AI/ML generation. The sheer volume of data generated in modern production methods can be overwhelming. AI algorithms sift through these records, extracting precious insights that are probably otherwise tough to discover. This information-driven technique permits knowledgeable decision-making at every degree of the economic workflow [9]. In essence, the function of AI and ML inside the AI/ML era transcends mere automation. It represents a shift during wise selection-making, adaptability, and a more nuanced approach to trouble-fixing within the industrial vicinity. The technology brings about a transformation that isn't most effective technically but moreover culturally, fostering collaborative and sensible surroundings in the production landscape. The mixture of enterprise 4.0 and the AI/ML era into the commercial panorama brings forth several traumatic conditions and possibilities, shaping the trajectory of modern-day manufacturing.

➢ **Statistics safety and privacy concerns**

The inflow of facts in Industry 4.0 increases large issues about records protection and privacy. The interconnected nature of systems creates vulnerabilities, and safeguarding touchy facts becomes paramount. Ensuring sturdy cybersecurity measures and addressing privacy troubles are pressing traumatic conditions that industries must navigate [10, 46].

➢ **Assignment displacement and personnel reskilling**

The advent of clever automation and AI technologies turns on concerns approximately pastime displacement. As machines deal with habitual obligations, there may be a capability effect on employment. Reskilling the team of workers to conform to new roles that complement clever technology becomes critical. Balancing technological improvements with a frame of people's dreams poses a touchy mission.

➢ **Interoperability issues**

Achieving seamless interoperability among diverse systems and technology is a chronic task. In employer 4.0, wherein a mess of gadgets and systems collaborate, ensuring compatibility and green conversation is complicated. Standardizing protocols and fostering collaboration for the duration of industries are ongoing annoying situations.

➢ **Excessive initial investments**

The transition to enterprise 4.0 frequently calls for large initial investments in superior technologies, infrastructure, and group of workers schooling. For small and medium-sized companies (SMEs), these upfront expenses can be a barrier to adoption. Placing stability among price problems and the lengthy period of advantages of technological integration poses a challenge.

➢ **Resistance to alternate**

Human resistance to change is a perennial challenge in any transformative tool. The introduction of cutting-edge technologies especially the ones as disruptive as industry 4.0 and AI, can also moreover encounter resistance from personnel accustomed to standard strategies. Overcoming this resistance requires effective exchange control strategies.

➢ **Ethical concerns**

Using AI in choice-making strategies increases ethical troubles. Questions about bias in algorithms, transparency, and responsibility have to be addressed. Setting up ethical frameworks and tips for the accountable use of AI in production is an ongoing mission.

1.3.2 Opportunities

➢ **Fee savings and performance profits**

Industry 4.0 offers massive opportunities for price financial savings and multiplied operational performance. Predictive upkeep reduces downtime, optimizing assets and increasing the lifespan of the system. Real-time records analytics enables faster and more informed choice-making, streamlining processes, and lowering charges [11].

➢ **Increased competitiveness**
Businesses embracing industry 4.0 technologies gain a competitive side. The capability to conform to market needs unexpectedly, supply custom-designed merchandise efficaciously, and preserve superb requirements positions agencies as leaders in their industries. Superior competitiveness opens doorways to new markets and commercial enterprise possibilities.

➢ **Innovation capability**
The convergence of Industry 4.0 and the AI/ML era sparks innovation. New enterprise models, merchandise, and offerings become a result of sensible automation, statistics analytics, and interconnected systems. Corporations that leverage those improvements' role themselves at the leading edge of technological improvements.

➢ **Progressed first-rate and customization**
The software of AI and ML in manufacturing tactics contributes to the step forward product nicely. Satisfactory manipulation measures turn out to be more sophisticated, reducing defects and ensuring consistency. Additionally, the flexibility of Industry 4.0 allows for extended customization, catering to various patron demands.

➢ **Supply chain optimization**
Industry 4.0 revolutionizes supply chain control, providing opportunities for optimization. Predictive analytics allows correct calls for forecasting, minimizing extra stock, and reducing expenses. Green delivery chains bring about faster delivery instances and progressed client delight.

➢ **Task advent in new fields**
While worries about job displacement exist, enterprise 4.0 additionally creates possibilities for process introduction in new fields. Roles related to records analysis, AI programming, cybersecurity, and maintenance of advanced structures turn out to be more and more essential. Personnel reskilling packages can channel exertions into these emerging sectors.

1.4 The Nexus of Industry 4.0 and the AI/ML Era: A Symbiotic Evolution

The confluence of enterprise 4.0 and the AIML generation ushers in a transformative symbiotic evolution that redefines the very material of present-day manufacturing. This nexus is going past the mere integration of technology; it forges a dynamic dating in which each factor complements and enhances the opposite, growing a genuinely interconnected and intelligent commercial ecosystem [12].

➢ **Interconnected improvements**

At the nexus of Industry 4.0 and the AI/ML generation, advancements are not remote but interconnected, forming a cohesive technological panorama. For instance, the statistics generated by using shrewd automation structures become the fuel for device getting-to-know algorithms. As machines research from these facts, they turn out to be greater adept at predicting, adapting, and optimizing processes in actual time. This interconnectedness amplifies the effect of individual improvements, creating a holistic and synergistic method of smart production.

➢ **Information-driven decision-making**

Imperative to this symbiotic evolution is the prominence of records-driven decision-making. Enterprise 4.0, with its array of sensors and interconnected gadgets, generates full-size amounts of records. System learning algorithms examine these statistics, extracting meaningful insights that tell selection-making at every degree of the producing method. The symbiosis ensures that choices aren't arbitrary but grounded in actual-time, statistics-driven intelligence.

➢ **Collaborative human-gadget dynamics**

The nexus emphasizes collaborative human-device dynamics, acknowledging that the future of producing lies in the synergy between human instinct and machine precision. In cognitive manufacturing, machines with AI abilities mimic human concept strategies, most important to a harmonious collaboration. Human beings contribute creativity, adaptability, and complex trouble-fixing, at the same time as machines control precision, automation, and facts evaluation. This collaboration creates an extra efficient and powerful production surrounding [13].

➢ **Average overall performance through predictive technologies**

Predictive generation has grown to be a cornerstone of the symbiotic evolution, optimizing primary performance at some stage within the production spectrum. Predictive safety, driven by way of AI algorithms, anticipates device screw-United States of America earlier than they occur, minimizing downtime and maximizing operational performance. Deliver chain optimization makes use of predictive analytics to forecast calls efficaciously, making sure that inventory degrees are optimized, and logistics streamlined. Splendid control blessings from actual-time statistics evaluation, lowering defects and improving everyday product extraordinarily well.

➢ **Dynamic adaptability**

The symbiotic evolution empowers production techniques with dynamic adaptability. Clever automation systems, guided via the use of system reading algorithms, adapt to converting situations in real time. Whether or not now, or no longer it is adjusting manufacturing schedules is primarily based on calls for fluctuations or optimizing electricity consumption in reaction to variable factors; the interconnected generation makes certain a degree of adaptability, critical in the fast-paced and ever-converting commercial company landscape.

➢ **Human-centric smart production**

At the nexus, the point of interest shifts in the direction of human-centric clever production. Even as machines manage repetitive duties and difficult techniques, people make a contribution to irreplaceable tendencies collectively with creativity, crucial wondering, and emotional intelligence. The collaborative environment guarantees that technology enhances human talents in preference to converting them. This shift within the course of a human-centric approach creates an administrative center wherein the strengths of all people and gadget are harnessed to their fullest ability.

➢ **Optimizing the entire value chain**

The symbiotic evolution optimizes the whole price chain, from raw material procurement to give up-product delivery. Every degree of the manufacturing system profits from interconnected generation. Predictive protection ensures the fitness of system, supply chain optimization minimizes waste and maximizes performance, and cognitive manufacturing complements preference-making throughout the fee chain. The end result is an unbroken, included, and optimized production technique from start to finish [14].

In essence, the nexus of industry 4.0 and the AI/ML era aren't always only a technological merger; it's a symbiotic evolution that elevates manufacturing to unparalleled degrees of intelligence, adaptability, and efficiency. The collaborative merge among statistics-pushed technology and human ingenuity creates a manufacturing ecosystem that isn't always the best interconnected but also capable of navigating the complexities of the modern commercial landscape with wonderful precision and agility.

1.5 Challenges and Opportunities in the Integration of Industry 4.0 and the AI/ML Era

The aggregate of Industry 4.0 and the AIML (synthetic intelligence and system studying) generation into the economic landscape brings forth a myriad of worrying conditions and possibilities. This transformative union, while promising tremendous performance and innovation, isn't without its complexities. Figure 1.3 clearly depicts the integration of Industry 4.0 concepts.

➢ **Facts safety and privateness issues**

The huge influx of records generated with the useful resource of interconnected devices in Industry 4.0 increases widespread worries regarding

Figure 1.3 Integration of Industry 4.0.

records protection and privacy [15]. With the ever-increasing assault floor, ensuring the confidentiality, integrity, and availability of touchy information is paramount. Unauthorized right of entry to and records breaches pose extreme threats, requiring sturdy cybersecurity measures and vigilance.

➢ **Task displacement and body of workers reskilling**

As industries embody clever automation and AI technology, there is a legitimate challenge approximately activity displacement. The automation of habitual responsibilities may cause a shift in job necessities, potentially rendering certain roles obsolete. Body of workers reskilling turns into a crucial task to make sure that employees own the talents and have to navigate the evolving technological landscape.

➢ **Interoperability problems**

Accomplishing seamless interoperability between numerous systems and technologies is a continual undertaking. In the interconnected world of enterprise 4.0, in which numerous gadgets, sensors, and structures want to talk effectively [16], ensuring compatibility becomes complicated. Standardizing protocols and fostering collaboration throughout industries are ongoing challenges to creating a cohesive and interoperable ecosystem.

➢ **Excessive preliminary investments**

The transition to Industry 4.0 regularly demands well-sized prematurely investments in superior technologies, infrastructure, and staff education. For small and medium-sized enterprises (SMEs), those prices may be prohibitive, potentially due to a virtual division where larger enterprises gain the benefits of advanced technologies while smaller players struggle to adopt them.

➢ **Resistance to change**

Human resistance to alternate is a perennial challenge in any transformative manner. The advent of new eras, especially those as disruptive as Industry 4.0 and AI, can also additionally encounter resistance from personnel accustomed to standard strategies. Overcoming this resistance calls for powerful trade manage strategies, which include conversation, education, and concerning personnel inside the transition machine [17].

➢ **Ethical issues**

Using AI in decision-making processes increases ethical issues. Bias in algorithms, loss of transparency, and duty problems are critical moral considerations. Putting a balance between the benefits of automation and the moral implications, which consist of fairness and privacy, remains an ongoing venture that industries want to navigate responsibly.

- **Value financial savings and performance income**

One of the primary opportunities provided through Industry 4.0 and the AI/ML era is the capability for considerable cost financial savings and improved operational overall performance [18]. Predictive maintenance, powered through AI algorithms, reduces downtime and maintenance expenses using foreseeing tool failures. Actual-time records analytics enhances choice-making, streamlining strategies, and optimizing useful resource usage, leading to tangible fee monetary savings.

- **Extended competitiveness**

Organizations embracing Industry 4.0 technology gain a significant competitive edge. The potential to conform to market needs rapidly, supply customized products effectively, and hold fantastic standards positions organizations as leaders of their industries. Stronger competitiveness opens doors to new markets and enterprise opportunities, fostering sustainable increase.

- **Innovation potential**

The combination of Industry 4.0 and the AI/ML era sparks innovation throughout industries. New enterprise fashions, merchandise, and offerings end up a result of clever automation, facts analytics, and interconnected systems. Corporations that leverage these improvements' position themselves at the forefront of technological improvements, riding enterprise-extensive innovation.

- **Advanced first-class and customization**

The application of AI and ML in production strategies enhances the quality of products. Advanced quality control measures become more sophisticated, reducing defects and ensuring consistency. Moreover, the ability of Industry 4.0 permits elevated customization, catering to numerous client needs [19]. This not only enhances client pride but additionally opens avenues for top-rate pricing and brand loyalty.

- **Supply chain optimization**

Business Industry 4.0 revolutionizes supply chain manipulation, presenting possibilities for optimization. Predictive analytics allows correct demand forecasting, minimizing greater inventory and reducing costs. Green supply chains result in quicker delivery times, superior client pride, and an aggressive advantage inside the market.

➢ **Mission advent in new fields**

While concerns about activity displacement exist, enterprise 4.0 moreover creates possibilities for job introduction in new fields. Roles related to data analysis, AI programming, cybersecurity, and renovation of superior structures turn out to be increasingly essential. A group of worker's reskilling programs can channel labor into those emerging sectors, fostering employment possibilities inside the evolving technological landscape [49].

➢ **Environmental sustainability**

Industry 4.0 offers opportunities for more appropriate environmental sustainability. Clever technology allows more green use of belongings, decreasing waste and power consumption [50]. Predictive preservation prevents needless replacements and maintenance, contributing to a greater sustainable and green production method.

1.6 Implementation Techniques

➢ **Integration of cyber-physical systems (CPS)**

The aggregate of cyber-physical systems form the backbone of enterprise 4.0, facilitating seamless conversation and collaboration among bodily and virtual components. To implement CPS successfully, organizations need to invest in strong connectivity infrastructure, ensuring that sensors, machines, and structures can talk in real time [20]. This integration lays the foundation for sensible choice-making, predictive analytics, and adaptive manufacturing tactics.

➢ **Strategic avenue mapping**

Strategic road mapping is a dynamic technique that involves developing a clear, phased plan for the adoption of Industry 4.0 technologies. It encompasses technology adoption, body of workers improvement, and technique optimization. Agencies must continuously revisit and alter their roadmaps, taking into consideration technological improvements, marketplace dynamics, and inner competencies [21]. This strategic technique guarantees that Industry 4.0 implementation aligns with overarching enterprise goals.

➢ **Statistics-pushed selection-making**

The emphasis on records as a strategic asset underscores the need for advanced analytics and system-gaining knowledge of fashions. Implementing data-driven decision-making includes establishing a records infrastructure that might capture, store, and process big volumes of information. Groups want to invest in analytics devices, records scientists, and AI specialists to extract meaningful insights. This strategy empowers producers to make informed choices, optimize techniques, and discover hidden styles inside their operations.

➢ **Human-robot collaboration**

The evolution toward human-robot collaboration requires a thoughtful method of employee integration. Groups must spend money on training programs to upskill employees and familiarize them with running alongside clever robot structures. Human-robotic collaboration can beautify flexibility and performance at the manufacturing facility ground, permitting people and machines to complement every exceptional strength. This approach moreover consists of designing painting environments that facilitate seamless interaction between people and robots [22, 23].

➢ **Agile and adaptive tactics**

Implementing agile and adaptive techniques necessitates a cultural shift within businesses. This includes fostering a mindset that embraces trade, encourages experimentation, and values continuous improvement. Agile methodologies, which consist of Scrum or Kanban, can be executed to manufacturing strategies, permitting agencies to respond rapidly to changing requirements and market conditions. This technique guarantees that agencies remain agile in the face of evolving Industry 4.0 technology.

1.6.1 Future Suggestions

➢ **AI-pushed predictive safety**

The future of Industry 4.0 lies in the optimization of predictive protection using artificial intelligence. Implementing AI-driven predictive upkeep includes deploying tools for studying algorithms that could examine device overall performance information and expect ability disasters [23, 45]. This proactive approach minimizes downtime, reduces upkeep fees, and extends the lifespan of equipment. Companies must invest in the sensor era, IoT gadgets, and AI structures to completely leverage the advantages of predictive renovation.

➢ **Blockchain for delivery chain transparency**

As Industry 4.0 is primarily based on interconnected delivery chains, the destiny direction involves integrating blockchain for improved transparency. Blockchain technology gives an immutable and decentralized ledger, ensuring facts integrity throughout the supply chain. Groups should explore blockchain applications in tracking and verifying the glide of merchandise, making sure of authenticity, and mitigating risks that consist of counterfeit merchandise [24–26]. This method helps build awareness among stakeholders and strengthening the integrity of the supply chain.

➢ **Region computing optimization**

The proliferation of region computing in Industry 4.0 necessitates ongoing optimization efforts. Final suggestions comprise growing realistic algorithms that may carry out efficiently at the brink, reducing latency and improving actual-time choice-making. Businesses must discover area computing frameworks that permit distributed intelligence, allowing fact processing to occur inside the direction of the delivery. This optimization technique enhances the general typical overall performance and responsiveness of Industry 4.0 systems [25, 26].

➢ **Human-centric AI packages**

The aggregate of AI into production approaches wants to prioritize human-centric applications. Future directions include designing AI structures that decorate the talents of humans in place of converting them. This method consists of growing consumer-tremendous interfaces, enforcing an AI-pushed system that resources choice-making, and fostering collaborative surroundings among humans and AI. Human-centric AI programs contribute to a harmonious integration of the era in people's lives.

➢ **Digital twin evolution**

Virtual dual technology will continue to evolve, encompassing a broader scope of internal production techniques. Future commands contain improving the accuracy and real-time simulation talents of digital twins. Organizations must discover the mixture of virtual twins during the complete product lifecycle, from layout and prototyping to manufacturing and renovation. This evolution contributes to a holistic and interconnected digital illustration of bodily assets, permitting higher desire-making and optimization [27].

- **Smart factories**

Industry 4.0 introduces the idea of smart factories in which machines and systems are interconnected, allowing real-time conversation and statistics exchange. AI and machine mastering algorithms play a vital position in optimizing production strategies, predicting protection desires, and improving common operational average performance.

- **Predictive safety**

AI and tool learning algorithms can test historical facts and sensor facts to predict expected device disasters before they arise. This allows for proactive protection, lowering downtime and stopping high-priced breakdowns. This predictive method improves common device effectiveness and extends the lifespan of the system.

- **Supply chain optimization**

AI technology facilitates advanced analytics and predictive modeling in delivery chain control. This consists of names for forecasting, inventory manipulation, and logistics optimization. Producers can limit fees, lessen lead instances, and enhance normal supply chain resilience.

- **Smart management and inspection**

AI-powered picture popularity and system-studying algorithms decorate exquisite management strategies. Computerized inspection structures can pick out defects and anomalies in real-time, ensuring that fine wonderful merchandise acquires the market. This results in stepped-forward customer satisfaction and logo recognition.

- **Customization and versatility**

Industry 4.0 permits customization in manufacturing processes. AI-pushed structures can adapt rapidly to adjustments in product specifications, permitting mass customization with minimum downtime. This flexibility is critical in assembling the wishes of a suddenly converting market.

- **Human-machine Collaboration**

The integration of AI and machine learning in production does not replace human beings but enhances their skills. Collaborative robots, or robots, work alongside humans, handling repetitive or hazardous tasks, while human workers focus on more complex and creative aspects of manufacturing [28].

➢ **Energy efficiency**

AI algorithms can optimize strength intake in production strategies with the aid of studying patterns and adjusting parameters in real time. This not only reduces operational prices but also contributes to sustainability desires by minimizing environmental impact.

➢ **Statistics safety and privacy**

As the manufacturing organization becomes more associated, ensuring the security and privacy of information becomes paramount. AI may be employed for advanced cybersecurity measures, together with anomaly detection, hazard identification, and encryption, to defend touchy statistics.

➢ **Non-stop improvement**

AI and gadget analyzing allow non-stop improvement through records-driven insights. Manufacturers can use analytics to identify regions for optimization, innovation, and price reduction, making sure that methods evolve dynamically through the years.

➢ **Talent development**

The adoption of Industry 4.0 era calls for employees with the right competencies. Destiny possibilities lie in making funding in education and education packages to equip people with the data needed to feature and keep superior manufacturing structures.

➢ **Digital twins**

The idea of virtual twins includes growing virtual replicas of physical belongings or systems. In production, AI-driven digital twins permit real-time tracking and simulation of manufacturing techniques. This period permits producers to optimize operations, select out potential problems, and test with technique enhancements in advance than implementing them inside the physical environment.

➢ **Location Computing**

Industry 4.0 leverages area computing to method statistics closer to the supply, decreasing latency and improving actual-time desire-making. AI algorithms deployed at the edge permit faster assessment of records from sensors and devices on the producing unit ground, improving regular responsiveness and overall performance.

➢ **Blockchain in deliver chain**

Integrating blockchain generation with AI complements transparency and traceability in the supply chain. Producers can use blockchain for comfortable and apparent file preservation, ensuring the authenticity of merchandise and stopping counterfeit objects. This is crucial in industries in which product provenance is critical.

➢ **Augmented reality (AR) and virtual fact (VR):** The AR and VR era are increasing being implemented in production for education, maintenance, and faraway help. AI algorithms enhance the reviews by way of manner of presenting contextual records, recognizing gadgets, and facilitating more immersive and green interactions for personnel [29].

➢ **Collaborative ecosystems:** Industry 4.0 fosters collaborative ecosystems wherein producers, companies, and different stakeholders' share statistics and insights. AI allows the mixture and evaluation of diverse facts gadgets, leading to extra knowledgeable choice-making across the entire fee chain.

➢ **Regulatory compliance and safety:** AI performs a vital characteristic in ensuring regulatory compliance and administrative center protection in manufacturing. Gadget getting to know algorithms can have a look at vast quantities of records to understand capability risks, advise safety measures, and make certain that operations adhere to company policies and standards.

➢ **Robotic process automation (RPA)**

RPA, blended with AI, automates ordinary and rule-based duties, which include facts get right of entry to and processing. This not only reduces human errors but also allows employees to focus on more complex and value-added activities, thereby boosting productivity.

➢ **Records monetization**

Manufacturers can discover new revenue streams by leveraging the facts generated from connected devices and strategies. AI permits extracting of precious insights from these statistics, which may be monetized through numerous manners, together with promoting statistics analytics offerings or growing new, facts-driven merchandise.

➢ **Worldwide connectivity and some distance off operations**
Industry 4.0 allows worldwide connectivity, permitting producers to reveal and control operations remotely. AI-driven analytics offer actual-time insights, taking into consideration prompt preference-making, even for centers positioned in distinctive components of the arena [30–35].

➢ **Moral AI in manufacturing**
As AI will become more protected in production tactics, there is a developing emphasis on ensuring ethical AI practices. This includes addressing biases in algorithms, maintaining transparency, and imposing accountable AI to construct beliefs among clients, employees, and regulatory bodies.

1.7 Conclusion

The advent of industry 4.0 and the proliferation of AI/ML generation have heralded a transformative technology in production, characterized with the aid of remarkable levels of performance, precision, and innovation. This revolution is not simply an enhancement of present methods but an essential overhaul of producing paradigms, driving the industry toward greater interconnectedness, intelligence, and sustainability. Industry 4.0 technology has appreciably boosted operational performance and productivity. The mixing of AI and ML into manufacturing approaches allows predictive upkeep, optimizing tool overall performance, and reducing downtime. Superior analytics provide insights into production records, facilitating actual-time decision-making and non-stop improvement. The automation of repetitive obligations through robotics and AI frees up human resources for extra complicated and revolutionary endeavors, improving ordinary productivity. The generation of mass production is giving way to mass customization, driven thru AI/ML technologies. Producers can now reply to man or woman patron selections with extraordinary speed and accuracy. Superior algorithms take a look at client records to expect tendencies and tailor products to unique needs. This flexibility now not nice meets market desires greater correctly however also reduces waste and improves useful resource usage, aligning with sustainable manufacturing practices.

First-rate manage has been revolutionized via AI-driven inspection structures, which discover defects with a precision that surpasses human abilities. Device studying algorithms continuously have a look at from manufacturing information, identifying styles and anomalies that propose capacity amazing issues. This proactive approach ensures better product super and reduces the charge associated with remembers and redesign. Supply chain control has additionally been converted with the aid of enterprise 4.0 technology. AI and ML optimize logistics, forecast call for extra appropriately, and manipulate inventory more correctly. The transparency and traceability presented by using blockchain technology in addition beautify deliver chain integrity, making sure that merchandise meet regulatory necessities and customer expectancies. The mixing of AI and ML into production techniques fosters innovation through manner of permitting the speedy improvement and trying out of new merchandise and techniques. Digital twins, simulations, and superior modeling techniques permit producers to test in virtual environments, reducing the time and value related to bodily prototyping. This improved innovation cycle gives an excellent competitive advantage in an unexpectedly evolving market.

Employer 4.0 and AI/ML technology make contributions to more sustainable production practices. Through using optimizing useful resource use, lowering waste, and enhancing electricity efficiency, those era help restrict the environmental footprint of manufacturing sports. Predictive analytics and smart grids aid the integration of renewable power assets, in addition selling sustainability. Irrespective of the giant potential of corporation 4.0, demanding situations continue to be [36–40]. The combination of AI and ML technology requires tremendous funding in infrastructure, abilities, and cybersecurity. Making sure information privacy and addressing moral problems around AI deployment are crucial problems. Furthermore, the transition to a fully digitized manufacturing environment necessitates a cultural shift and non-stop studying to hold pace with technological improvements. Finally, industry 4.0 and the AI/ML generation constitute a seismic shift in production, using the industry toward a destiny characterized thru performance, customization, wonderful, innovation, and sustainability. As producers encompass this technology, they unlock new possibilities and possibilities, paving the way for a better, more resilient, and more sustainable business panorama. The adventure closer to absolutely realizing the capability of enterprise 4.0 is ongoing, however, the trajectory is apparent: the destiny of manufacturing is wise, interconnected, and transformative.

References

1. Smith, J., *Smart Manufacturing: A Roadmap for Industry 4.0 Implementation*, Springer, Cham, Switzerland, 2022.
2. Wang, Q., Artificial Intelligence in Manufacturing: A Comprehensive Review. *IEEE Trans. Ind. Inf.*, 17, 6, 3972–3983, 2021.
3. Kim, S., *Cyber-Physical Systems for Smart Factories*, Procedia CIRP, 2020.

4. Chen, L., Data Analytics and Machine Learning for Predictive Maintenance in Industry 4.0. *J. Manuf. Syst.*, 62, 93–103, 2023.
5. Gupta, R., Blockchain Applications in Supply Chain Management: A Review. *Int. J. Prod. Econ.*, 233, 107–123, 2021.
6. Zhang, H., Human-Robot Collaboration in Smart Manufacturing. *Rob. Comput. Integr. Manuf.*, 75, 111–120, 2022.
7. Li, X., Digital Twin Technologies in Industry 4.0: A State-of-the-Art Review. *Comput. Ind.*, 132, 1–13, 2021.
8. Patel, Edge Computing Optimization for Real-Time Decision-Making. *Future Gener. Comput. Syst.*, 129, 357–368, 2023.
9. Nguyen, T., Augmented Reality in Human-Machine Interaction: A Survey. *Comput. Graphics*, 99, 77–90, 2022.
10. Kim, Y., Energy-Efficient Manufacturing in Industry 4.0: Challenges and Opportunities. *J. Clean. Prod.*, 278, 1–15, 2021.
11. Chen, W., Sustainable Practices in Industry 4.0: A Systematic Literature Review. *Sustainability*, 15, 2514–2536, 2023.
12. Singh, R., Security Measures in Industry 4.0: A Comprehensive Analysis. *Int. J. Inf. Secur.*, 51, 123–145, 2022.
13. Park, J., Smart Sensors for Condition Monitoring in Industry 4.0. *Sensors*, 21, 1132–1145, 2021.
14. Lee, S., Collaborative Robotics in Smart Factories: A Review. *J. Manuf. Processes*, 59, 45–56, 2023.
15. Wang, L., AI-Driven Predictive Maintenance: A Case Study in the Automotive Industry. *J. Manuf. Sci. Eng.*, 144, 111–120, 2022.
16. Kim, H., Challenges and Opportunities in Implementing Industry 4.0: A Global Perspective. *Technol. Forecast. Soc. Change*, 168, 120–135, 2021.
17. Wu, Q., The Role of 5G in Enabling Industry 4.0 Applications. *IEEE Trans. Ind. Inf.*, 69, 1803–1812, 2023.
18. Lim, Y., Optimizing Edge Computing for Smart Manufacturing. *J. Manuf. Syst.*, 63, 51–60, 2022.
19. Zhou, K., Blockchain-Enabled Smart Contracts in Supply Chain Management. *Comput. Ind.*, 132, 57–67, 2021.
20. Yang, C., Human-Centric AI Applications in Manufacturing Operations. *Rob. Comput. Integr. Manuf.*, 78, 213–220, 2023.
21. Liu, M., Towards Sustainable Practices in Industry 4.0: A Systematic Review. *Sustain. Prod. Consum.*, 27, 101–118, 2022.
22. Xu, L., Machine Learning Applications for Quality Control in Smart Factories. *J. Manuf. Processes*, 63, 88–99, 2021.
23. Wang, Y., The Impact of Industry 4.0 on Workforce Skills: A Global Survey. *Int. J. Adv. Manuf. Technol.*, 124, 789–800, 2023.
24. Nguyen, H., Digital Twin Evolution: From Concept to Practical Implementation. *J. Comput. Des. Eng.*, 9, 45–60, 2022.
25. Zhang, Y., Advancements in Cognitive Manufacturing: A Review. *CIRP Ann. Manuf. Technol.*, 70, 1–16, 2021.

26. Park, J., AI Applications for Sustainable Manufacturing Practices. *J. Clean. Prod.*, 330, 1–12, 2023.
27. Chen, X., The Evolution of Robotics in Industry 4.0. *Int. J. Adv. Rob. Syst.*, 19, 1–10, 2022.
28. Wang, Z., Integrating Sustainability into Industry 4.0 Practices. *Sustainability*, 13, 4157–4170, 2021.
29. Kim, G., IoT-enabled Smart Sensors for Real-Time Monitoring in Manufacturing. *J. Manuf. Syst.*, 63, 25–35, 2023.
30. Li, J., AI-Driven Innovation in the Automotive Industry. *Comput. Oper. Res.*, 37, 22–35, 2022.
31. Viji, C., Najmusher, H., Rajkumar, N., Mohanraj, A., Nachiappan, B., Neelakandan, C., Jagajeevan, R., Intelligent Library Management Using Radio Frequency Identification, in: *AI-Assisted Library Reconstruction*, pp. 126–143, IGI Global, Hershey, PA, USA, 2024.
32. Kumar, N., Antoniraj, S., Jayanthi, S., Mirdula, S., Saravanakumar, S., Rajkumar, N., Senthilkumar, K.R., Educational Technology and Libraries Supporting Online Learning, in: *AI-Assisted Library Reconstruction*, pp. 209–237, IGI Global, Hershey, PA, USA, 2024.
33. Mohanraj, A., Viji, C., Varadarajan, M.N., Kalpana, C., Shankar, B., Jayavadivel, R., Rajkumar, N., Jagajeevan, R., Privacy and Security in Digital Libraries, in: *AI-Assisted Library Reconstruction*, pp. 104–125, IGI Global, Hershey, PA, USA, 2024.
34. Rajkumar, N., Tabassum, H., Muthulingam, S., Mohanraj, A., Viji, C., Kumar, N., Senthilkumar, K.R., Anticipated requirements and expectations in the digital library, in: *AI-Assisted Library Reconstruction*, pp. 1–20, IGI Global, Hershey, PA, USA, 2024.
35. Jayavadivel, R., Arunachalam, M., Nagarajan, G., Shankar, B.P., Viji, C., Rajkumar, N., Senthilkumar, K.R., Historical Overview of AI Adoption in Libraries, in: *AI-Assisted Library Reconstruction*, pp. 267–289, IGI Global, Hershey, PA, USA, 2024.
36. Rajkumar, N., Viji, C., Mohanraj, A., Senthilkumar, K.R., Jagajeevan, R., Kovilpillai, J.A., Ethical Considerations of AI Implementation in the Library Era, in: *Improving Library Systems with AI: Applications, Approaches, and Bibliometric Insights*, pp. 85–106, IGI Global, Hershey, PA, USA, 2024.
37. Lalitha, B., Ramalakshmi, K., Gunasekaran, H., Murugesan, P., Saminasri, P., Rajkumar, N., Anticipating AI Impact on Library Services: Future Opportunities and Evolutionary Prospects, in: *Improving Library Systems with AI: Applications, Approaches, and Bibliometric Insights*, pp. 195–213, IGI Global, Hershey, PA, USA, 2024.
38. Nachiappan, B., Emerging and Innovative AI Technologies for Resource Management, in: *Improving Library Systems with AI: Applications, Approaches, and Bibliometric Insights*, pp. 115–133, IGI Global, Hershey, PA, USA, 2024.

39. Nachiappan, B., E-Resources Content Recommendation System Using AI, in: *Improving Library Systems with AI: Applications, Approaches, and Bibliometric Insights*, pp. 155–177, 2024.
40. Ramana, T.V., Ghantasala, G.S., Sathiyaraj, R., Khan, M. (Eds.), *Artificial Intelligence and Machine Learning for Smart Community: Concepts and Applications*, CRC Press, Boca Raton, 2024.
41. Ghantasala, G.P., Hung, B.T., Chakrabarti, P., Pellakuri, V., Artificial intelligence based machine learning algorithm for prediction of cancer in female anatomy. *Multimed. Tools Appl.*, 1–27, 2024.
42. Mohanty, A., Rahamathunnisa, U., Sudhakar, K., Sathiyaraj, R., Age of Computational AI for Autonomous Vehicles. *Artif. Intell. Auton. Veh.*, 25–54, 2024.
43. Rajendran, S., Sabharwal, M., Hu, Y.C., Balusamy, B. (Eds.), *Artificial Intelligence for Autonomous Vehicles: The Future of Driverless Technology*, John Wiley & Sons, Hoboken, NJ, USA, 2024.
44. Rajendran, S., Sabharwal, M., Ghinea, G., Dhanaraj, R.K., Balusamy, B. (Eds.), *IoT and Big Data Analytics for Smart Cities: A Global Perspective*, CRC Press, Boca Raton, FL, USA, 2022.
45. Arora, J., Singh, S., Sethi, M., Kaur, G., Ghantasala, G.P., Securing cloud data exchange related to IoT devices: key challenges and its machine learning solutions. *Hybrid Inf. Systems Non-Linear Optim. Strategies Artif. Intell.*, 177, 177–200, 2024.
46. Ramisetty, S., Ghantasala, G.P., Gupta, G., Prevention of Security Attacks at Wireless Network Layers using Machine Learning Techniques, in: *2024 11th International Conference on Computing for Sustainable Global Development (INDIACom)*, pp. 1787–1791, IEEE, New York, NY, USA, 2024, February.
47. Sharma, O., Ghantasala, G.P., Ioannou, I., Vassiliou, V., Advancing pneumonia virus drug discovery with virtual screening: A cutting-edge fast and resource efficient machine learning framework for predictive analysis. *Inf. Med. Unlocked*, *47*, 101471, 2024.
48. Dilip, K., Ghantasala, G.P., Rathee, M., Kallam, S., Bathla, P., A Brief Comparative Study of Metaheuristic Approaches for Hyperparameter Optimization of Machine Learning Model, in: *International Conference on Computer Science and Emerging Technologies (CSET)2023*, pp. 1–5, IEEE, New York, NY, USA, 2023, October.
49. Reddy, A., Ramaiah, V.S., Ayyappa, R.M.K., Ghantasala, G.P., Kurra, M., Bathla, P., An Empirical Brief Analysis of Novelistic Approaches for Detection Of Bone Marrow Cancer Health Monitoring Through DL MODEL, in: *2024 IEEE International Conference on Computing, Power and Communication Technologies (IC2PCT)*, vol. 5, IEEE, pp. 1211–1214, 2024, February.
50. Sharma, O., Lamba, V., Ghantasala, G.G.S., Mohapatra, S., Analysing optimal environment for the text classification in deep learning, in: *AIP Conference Proceedings*, vol. 2760, AIP Publishing, 2023, June.

2

Business Intelligence and Big Data Analytics for Industry 4.0

N. Rajkumar[1]*, C. Viji[1], Balusamy Nachiappan[2], A. Mohanraj[3], N. Karthikeyan[4], Judeson Antony Kovilpillai J.[1] and Sathiyaraj. R[5]

[1]*Department of Computer Science & Engineering, Alliance College of Engineering and Design, Alliance University, Bengaluru, Karnataka, India*
[2]*Department of Information Technology, Prologis, Denver, USA*
[3]*Department of Computer Science & Engineering, Sri Eshwar College of Engineering, Coimbatore, Tamil Nadu, India*
[4]*Vellore Institute of Technology, School of Computer Science and Engineering, Chennai, India*
[5]*GITAM School of Technology, GITAM University, Bangalore, India*

Abstract

Industry 4.0 industries are experiencing extensive changes pushed by way of statistics-pushed choices, new technologies, and connectivity. This looks at and explores how the complexity of Industry 4.0 is typically driven by business intelligence (BI) and large records analytics. We live in a generation packed with large amounts of dynamic and diverse statistics because of the convergence of cyber-bodily systems, smart devices, and the net of factors (IoT). For organizations to efficaciously leverage those large quantities of information, commercial business intelligence (BI) and statistics analytics are essential technologies. Business intelligence normally entails the collection, evaluation, and presentation of corporation information, forming the premise for knowledgeable selection-making. Business intelligence (BI) in Industry 4.0 consists of real-time analytics and predictive insights that move beyond widespread reporting. To this leap forward, agencies can now leverage insights gleaned from the considerable amounts of statistics generated by using connected devices and processes. Huge statistical analytics, however, is essential to studying large amounts of data and finding interesting patterns. Due to the volume, velocity, and style of data produced through Industry

**Corresponding author*: nrajkumar84@gmail.com

M. Thirunavukkarasan, S. A. Sahaaya Arul Mary, Sathiyaraj. R, G. S. Pradeep Ghantasala and Mudassir Khan (eds.) Artificial Intelligence and Machine Learning for Industry 4.0, (29–54)

4.0, advanced analytical methods which include machine-gaining knowledge of artificial intelligence are required. By the usage of these strategies, corporations can expect new traits, locate previously ignored connections, and significantly enhance their operations.

Keywords**:** Industry 4.0, business intelligence, big data analytics, machine learning, artificial intelligence

2.1 Introduction

Industry 4.0 is changing the way organizations manufacture, enhance, and distribute their supplies. Figure 2.1 truly defines the economic revolution; Industrialists are combining new technologies, together with the Internet of Things (IoT), Cloud Computing, Big Data Analytics, and AI and structures studying their manufacturing hubs and throughout their methods. Those clever industrial devices are organized with embedded software, advanced sensors, and robotics that accumulate and check out records and allow for better choice-making [49, 54]. An even higher cost is created while statistics from commercial operations are mixed with operational information from ERP, supply chain, customer support, and distinct company structures to create completely new tiers of visibility and insight from formerly siloed facts. This digital technology caused greater automation, predictive protection, self-optimization of approach enhancements, and, specifically, a new level of overall performance and responsiveness to customers that turned into now not formerly possible.

Industry 4.0 is the combining of physical and virtual nation-states, representing a digital revolution characterized by the aid of the use of massive

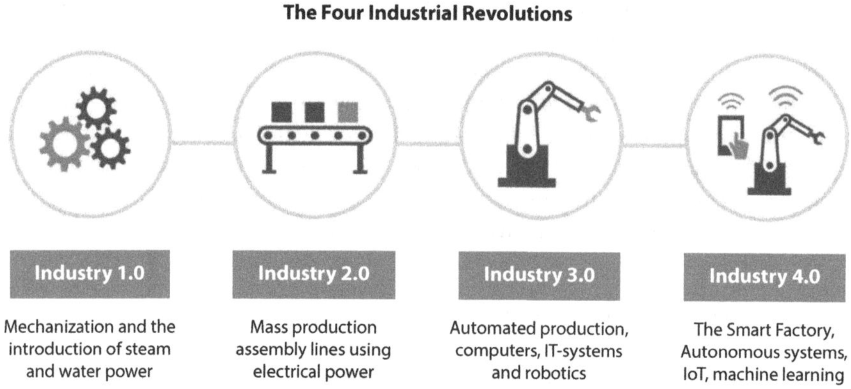

Figure 2.1 Industrial revolutions.

information and synthetic Intelligence (AI) to facilitate the improvement of self-mastering systems. Industry 4.0, a transformative industrial revolution, is being created through the seamless integration of automation, sensible systems, and digital generation. Corporations are offered both opportunities and issues by the splendid upward push in statistics gathering delivered via this paradigm trade. In this scenario, combining business intelligence (BI) with huge statistics analytics (BDA) turns into an important facilitator for reaching Industry 4.0's large capacity. Via the integration of virtual and physical generation, Industry 4.0 has essentially modified traditional production and running settings. Due to the increasing usage of networked gadgets, sensors, and machinery, statistics are increasing hastily. With the right use, the wealth of information to be had right here may provide a plethora of insights that may drastically improve selection-making and operational effectiveness. The middle underpinning for this facts-centric environment is supplied via Industry intelligence, which helps the collection, organization, and presentation of dependent data. Similarly, large facts analytics helps companies to pick out traits, styles, and conclusions internal big, unstructured databases. To efficaciously navigate Industry 4.0, BI and BDA collaborate to transform unstructured statistics into extensive insights and foster a way of life of record-driven choice-making.

This chapter is ambitious to study the intricate connection between Industry 4.0 and commercial Industry Intelligence/massive information Analytics. It'll look at the fundamental components of both BDA and BI, studying their personal and blended capacities. The research will even study real-global case research and situations to illustrate how corporations throughout several industries make use of BI and BDA to boost innovation, streamline operations, and gain a competitive gain. As we dig further, it becomes obvious that BI and BDA integration is a strategic want for groups seeking to thrive inside the continuously shifting, statistics-wealthy panorama of industry 4.0, in place of merely a technological one. Inside the framework of the 4th industrial revolution, the intricacies of BI and BDA could be explored within the following sections, in addition to their combined implications on choice-making, operational excellence, and sustainable increase [50].

Table 2.1 shows growth in Industry 4.0 in different aspects like technology adoption, data analytics, etc. This research examines the beneficial courting that exists among large facts analytics and company intelligence within the context of Industry 4.0. While BDA employs advanced analytics to sensation upon noteworthy patterns and developments, business intelligence (BI) substances the muse for organizing and offering records. While incorporated, those technologies allow organizations to make selections with actuality, optimize processes, and gain an aggressive area inside the

Table 2.1 Growth in Industry 4.0.

Aspect	Growth in Industry 4.0
Technology adoption	Increasing incorporation of IoT, AI, ML, and robotics
Connectivity	Expansion in 5G and edge computing technologies
Data analytics	Surge in the utilization of big data analytics applications
Automation	Widening application of autonomous systems
Cybersecurity	Heightened focus on securing digital processes
Smart manufacturing	Integration of intelligent technologies in manufacturing
Interoperability	Prioritizing seamless integration of systems
Supply chain	Enhanced efficiency through the digitization of supply chains
Skills development	Increasing demand for expertise in data science, AI, etc.
Environmental impact	Commitment to sustainable and environmentally friendly tech

unexpectedly evolving industry 4.0 market. Further to real-time tracking and predictive evaluation, combining BI with BDA enables proactive Industry operations. This paper goes into superb intensity on the important thing components of BI and BDA, which include statistics series, storage, processing, and visualization. Moreover, it highlights the want for adaptable and scalable answers by outlining the demanding situations and opportunities related to implementing BI and BDA inside the context of Industry 4.0. Through some case studies and examples from various sectors, it is proven how BI and BDA are revolutionizing decision-making strategies, aid allocation, and ordinary operational efficiency. This study also addresses the implications of privacy and facts safety while dealing with full-size volumes of sensitive records. The item emphasizes the need for Industry intelligence and huge facts analytics in navigating the challenges of Industry 4.0. The aggregate of BI and BDA will propel corporations inside the fourth commercial revolution in the direction of virtual transformation, agility, and creative, lengthy-time period success.

2.1.1 The Biggest Challenge of Industry 4.0

Figure 2.2 highlights the challenges in Industry 4.0 and its technologies have many benefits, but producers and service carriers are dealing with extremely demanding situations that should be considered and resolved for the powerful adoption of 4.0. From a loss of organizational culture and training, and a shortage of capabilities to the implementation of innovative Industry and sales models that take gain of digital transformation possibilities and conduct studies, the excellent and maximum viable solution must be determined. Parent 6 represents the respondents' minds on future limitations and challenges with a couple of picks. 79% of provider providers and manufacturers suppose that the maximum critical obstruction to implementing Industry 4.0 in their groups is obtaining seed investment. 54% of members said that they're engaged in dealing with other important demanding situations inside the organization and have no plans for 4.0. Similarly, the lack of employees educated in Industry 4.0 is every other hassle, preventing 48 % of producers and service providers from adopting 4.0, and 25% of them feel that they cannot use the suitable system and software program required by India [53]. 15% of participants mentioned different obstacles to I4.0, such as challenges in convincing decision-makers approximately the feasibility and significance of Industry 4.0, insufficient

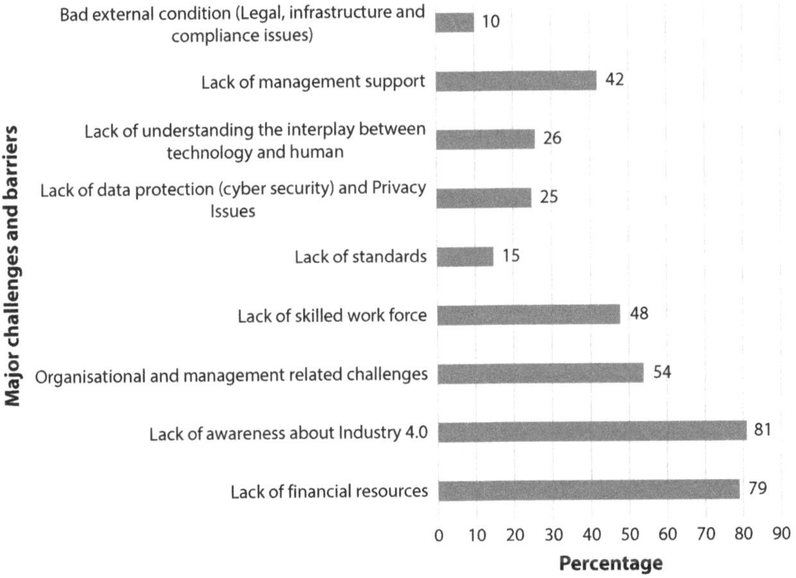

Figure 2.2 Challenges in Industry 4.0.

potential to integrate into the modern-day scope of operations, and lack of expertise approximately I4.0.

2.2 Literature Review

Cegielski *et al.*, [1] state that providers of textiles and apparel (T&A) are facing increased competition from the perspective of Industry 4.0. The division is facing difficulties including shorter order-to-delivery lead times, rising labor and raw material prices, and declining profit margins. Fast fashion's quick launch and the ensuing demand for quick order revisions led to a great deal of disruption and several systemic alterations. Loshin [2], claims that the T&A Corporation improved customer service by optimizing manufacturing schedules, maintaining inventory levels, and better-coordinating retail and delivery sites. But as Chongwatpol [3] pointed out, manufacturing timetables frequently deviate from what clients anticipate. Demand fluctuations and production delays might result in either too high or too low stock levels for items.

T&A businesses embrace the practice of producing items in a large range of sizes, shapes, colors, and styles to appeal to a large spectrum of prospective customers. In the textile and apparel production business, accessorizing jewelry, shoes, purses, and cosmetics is a common procedure [4]. This strategy seeks to accommodate the shifting customer tastes and the dynamic nature of market needs in the T&A industry.

According to Sodero *et al.*, [5] product designs are often modified by the Textile and Apparel (T&A) industry to conform to seasonal fluctuations. As opposed to the T&A sector, sectors such as the production of office and household appliances find it relatively easy to match supply with demand. T&A companies are thus recommended to take the required precautions to lessen the possibility of significant income loss because of out-of-date clothing supply, especially during quick seasonal transitions.

Since T&A goods are seasonal, it is difficult to accurately predict future product sales due to their scarcity [6]. Complicating matters further are factors related to the volume and interval of shipments. Real sales data must serve as the foundation for decisions about production volume and timing, which are critical for satisfying market needs [7]. Merchandise' transport to distribution centers, warehouses, and retail locations is vital to the T&A region since it facilitates inventory control and guards in opposition to shortages and surpluses [8]. Preserving operational effectiveness and quick and efficiently gratifying marketplace expectancies rely on this logistical issue.

Conduct has a major effect on environmental awareness, and environmental consciousness has a large effect on behavior. According to the studies, instrumental value has an extra effect on behavioral intentions and environmental consciousness than does terminal value. The examination also discovers that the link between instrumental/final price and behavioral intentions is somewhat mediated with the aid of environmental recognition. Full-size variations exist in the emotional loyalty scores of Generations Y and Z, which add complexity to the suggested paradigm. In step with the observation, judgments on what to shop for—particularly about eco-modern merchandise—are closely motivated by way of perceived marketplace impact and individualistic standards. Particularly in the placing of converged network offerings (CNS), client-independent judgment making (CIJM) and novelty-looking for behavior does not now undoubtedly impact customers' decisions to shop for green garb.

The outcomes of this examination highlight the importance of effectively conveying the environmental advantages of wearing inexperienced garments which can be of extraordinary use to entrepreneurs, environmentalists, and manufacturers of green clothing. Furthermore, the studies indicate that utilizing contemporary style tendencies for clothing, styles, substances, and designs may increase the benefits of wearing environmentally conscious attire. Word that the examiner's recognition changed into applying diagnostic and descriptive analytics techniques [10]. Nikolic [11], investigated many predictive upkeep structures and examined predictive analytics within the framework of Industry 4.0. [12], as compared to the benefits and downsides of using digital twins and huge records from each standard and information perspectives inside the production quarter. To add the fee to Industry models, Uhlmann *et al.* [12], reviewed the literature on the improvement of smart manufacturing systems for a duration of time. Xu and Hua [13], conducted a complete overview and evaluation of the contemporary nation of business large facts evaluation studies in clever factories. Within the framework of Industry 4.0 answers, Calabrese *et al.* [14], provided a comprehensive evaluation of synthetic intelligence (AI) in three-D portray for figuring out broken gadgets, with an emphasis on predictive analytics processes. Bordeleau *et al.* [15], evaluated the literature on business intelligence (BI) approximately Industry 4.0.

Many well-set up textile and apparel (T&A) businesses have used state-of-the-art software answers for manufacturing, control, and different middle business operations, in keeping with Hair [16]. "Industry 4.0" refers to a group of modern technologies that encompass mobile computing, RFID, cloud computing, large statistics, and the net of things (IoT). In step with [17], the muse of Industry 4.0 is the improvement of cyber-bodily systems using the net of factors and the iPhone working device (iOS), setting into exercise-wise networks like the ones supported by the Human Rights Council (HRC).

Companies that want to be on the top in their Industry, in the end, need to take complete gain of the possibilities these technological advancements bring. Successful organizations need to be flexible enough to react speedily to converting marketplace situations in addition to having a consistent pursuit of understanding [18]. Smartphone apps are taking on the travel and vacationer industry, particularly within the retail and layout sectors, because of the ability and agility of mobile cloud computing.

The increasing utilization of cellular devices is driving a wave of modern technological advancements in the tour and tourism area. The tourism industry is being pressured to regulate the new opportunities and hazards brought about by way of technological upgrades as capsules and smartphones turn out to be extra common in the administrative center.

Industry 4.0 aims to combine virtual infrastructure with brand-new production approaches so that corporations might also use advanced gear for analytics, modeling, tracking, and simulation to produce, accumulate, store, and share data [19]. By combining contemporary manufacturing techniques with digital infrastructure, businesses can also completely utilize the rising generation to reinforce productivity and competitiveness. Sharda *et al.* [20], claim that those kinds of technologies not handiest produce tremendous amounts of statistics, which might be called massive information, but in addition, they force organizations to reevaluate their organizational structures, which means they must ruin faraway from conventional assembly-line manufacturing and hierarchical organization. Large facts provide a major hassle for the textile and garb (T&A) business in terms of decision-monitoring at retail and distribution warehouse places, patron product transit, and different logistical obligations. Industry 4.0 has significantly impacted library management systems by integrating advanced technologies that enhance efficiency, accessibility, and user experience [40–48].

Predictive analytics' major purpose, in keeping with Basu and Sondhi [25], is to foresee destiny occurrences. This has looked at making use of numerous methodologies, along with extra present-day strategies on occasion referred to as "data mining" as well as traditional statistical methods. Using strategies like credit score threat exams, purchase conduct, and anticipated responses to provide, those fashions are looking to expect the activities of clients in the future. Various categorization algorithms, together with neural networks and selection tree fashions, function examples of the range of strategies reachable for developing analytical packages with predictive strength. Classification strategies, for instance, can be used to forecast movie receipts.

Bradlow *et al.* [26], declare that clustering techniques may be used successfully to categorize customers representing focused marketing. Since association mining techniques are available, educated guesses on possible relationships among distinctive types of client conduct can be hooked up. When a consumer buys whatever, they provide traders with useful statistics that facilitate them to estimate what different products would possibly catch their eye. Shops can also enhance their move-promoting and upselling strategies with the help of these statistics. The practical use of those algorithms can be seen, for example, while a consumer searches for an item on Amazon.com and the website offers different comparable matters. Prescriptive analytics revolves around imparting a solution to the problem of what ought to be accomplished now and in the future. Generally, the principal aim of this technique is to boost machine performance, a subject that has been very well researched in the domains of operational research and management technological know-how. In this case, having clear conclusions or a set of policies to move through is helpful.

2.3 Business Intelligence

A collection of techniques and tools used by businesses to evaluate company data is known as business intelligence (BI). Information must be gathered, arranged, analyzed, shared, and tracked as part of business intelligence. Converting data into useful insights that guide business choices is the aim of business intelligence (BI). A set of technologies known as "Industry 4.0" is what organizations rent to inspire innovation and reply immediately to changing market conditions. The desires of Industry 4.0 consist of extended flexibility, performance, and manufacturing. In manufacturing and supply chain management, it also helps with higher-knowledgeable selection-making and personalization. Both Figure 2.3 and Table 2.2 provide a comparison between business intelligence and traditional information systems.

In Industry 4.0, Industry intelligence (BI) is important for using facts analytics, and technology breakthroughs for properly informed choice-making and operational performance [37]. Via the aggregate of gadget learning algorithms, IoT devices, and real-time facts tracking, groups can also get essential insights from the big quantities of records produced with the aid of networked systems and strategies. Corporations may estimate costs, assume ability necessities, and find out patron calls for styles with the usage of those analytics. Groups can also acquire an aggressive edge with the aid of applying BI tools and techniques to reinforce industrial production performance via gaining thorough information on their operations, finding bottlenecks or inefficiencies, and making facts-driven selections.

Inside the context of Industry 4.0, BI also allows for the enhancement of cloth and product coping, optimization of warehouse management, doing away with errors greater quickly, and establishing better maintenance practices. For organizations to use records and analytics to improve performance, competitiveness, and performance, business intelligence (BI) is important within the circumstances of Industry 4.0 [24, 39]. Fink [27], highlights that BI has a history of improving choice-making in a diffusion of situations to bolster this. Nonetheless, the fourth industrial Revolution is changing the field [34], and main scholars are analyzing how it will affect production firms (Acknowledgment by the World Economic Forum, 2016). Economic considerations, technology forces, and shifting consumer demands are highlighted in several studies [28–32, 35, 36] as important reasons to comprehend these developments. Lee [28], stated Industry 4.0's smart factories produce enormous amounts of industrial data quickly, necessitating efficient integration and automated analysis to provide insightful information.

Businesses in the manufacturing sector are using data analysis more and more to improve their decision-making procedures [29]. However, a thorough literature assessment carried out in this research highlights that value generation from data consumption has not gotten a similar emphasis. The evaluation places a strong emphasis on integrating large amounts of unstructured data and real-time applications. Notably, as most studies focus on the technological components of Industry 4.0, there are shortages in business-related factors, such as value generation and business model change. In summary, business intelligence plays a pivotal role in facilitating Industry 4.0 by enabling the industry to leverage data and analytics for optimizing performance and gaining a competitive edge. A comprehensive comprehension of technical and commercial factors is necessary for the effective deployment and generation of value in the ever-changing market. Figure 2.3 and Table 2.2 compare Business intelligence vs Traditional information systems.

2.3.1 Challenges of Business Intelligence in Industry 4.0

- **Facts integration complexity**

Task: Industry 4.0 entails a mess of interconnected devices and systems, resulting to numerous statistics codecs and sources. Integrating these disparate records into a unified and coherent format for evaluation can be a great challenge.

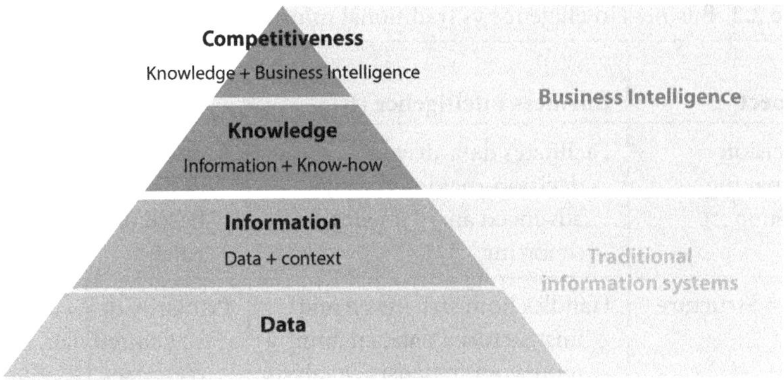

Figure 2.3 Business intelligence vs traditional information system.

Table 2.2 Business intelligence vs traditional information system.

Aspect	Business intelligence (BI)	Traditional information system
Focus	Analyzing and interpreting data for strategic decision-making	Managing and processing operational transactions
Data Source	Integrates data from various sources, internal and external	Primarily relies on structured data from internal sources
Purpose	Provides insights, trends, and patterns for proactive decision-making	Supports routine operational processes and transactions
Time Horizon	Often focuses on historical and actual data for predictive and prescriptive analytics	Emphasizes current and past data for transaction processing
User Interface	User-friendly interfaces with interactive dashboards, visualizations, and ad-hoc reporting	Standardized interfaces for data entry and retrieval

(Continued)

Table 2.2 Business intelligence vs traditional information system. (*Continued*)

Aspect	Business intelligence (BI)	Traditional information system
Decision-making Support	Facilitates data-driven decision-making through advanced analytics and reporting	Supports routine decision-making based on predefined rules
Data Structure	Handles both structured and unstructured data, enabling a more comprehensive analysis	Primarily deals with structured data in databases
Flexibility	Adaptable to changing business needs with agile reporting and dynamic analytics	Tends to be more rigid, designed for specific processes
Scope	Focuses on strategic, tactical, and operational levels, providing a holistic view	Primarily concentrates on operational and transactional data
Response Time	Can provide real-time or near-real-time insights, enabling quick responses to changes	Response time may vary and is typically optimized for routine transactions
Integration of Technologies	Integrates with emerging technologies like IoT, machine learning, and big data	May not seamlessly integrate with newer technologies
Costs	May require a higher initial investment but offers long-term value through insights	Generally, more cost-effective for routine transaction processing
Competitive Advantage	Provides a competitive edge through data-driven decision-making and innovation	Essential for operational efficiency but may not directly contribute to strategic advantage

Impact: Incomplete or inaccurate records integration can restrict the accuracy and reliability of BI insights.

- **Security issues**

Task: The extended connectivity and records sharing in Industry 4.0 improve protection issues. Protective sensitive commercial Industry intelligence records from cyber threats and unauthorized admission become paramount.

Impact: Protection breaches can compromise the integrity of BI outcomes and erode consideration in facts-pushed choice-making.

- **Scalability issues**

Task: As companies amplify their IoT networks and contain extra information sources, the scalability of BI answers turns into a challenge [38]. Traditional BI equipment may fail to handle the volume and velocity of facts generated in Industry 4.0.

Impact: Lack of ability to scale can bring about slower processing instances and degraded performance.

- **Ability hole:**

Task: Industry 4.0 technology frequently requires specialized talents in records science, machine mastering, and IoT. Corporations may additionally face demanding situations in acquiring and keeping personnel with important information [34, 35].

Impact: A lack of skilled experts can hinder the powerful implementation and utilization of BI equipment.

- **Actual-time analytics:**

Task: Industry 4.0 demands real-time analytics to reply rapidly to changing situations. However, traditional BI structures might also conflict with providing immediate insights due to latency issues.

Impact: Behind-schedule insights can restrict proactive choice-making and responsiveness to dynamic production tactics.

2.4 Big Data Analytics

Making use of contemporary laptop equipment on good-sized quantities of facts, large data analytics seeks to pick out important connections, styles, developments, and alternatives that help corporations make greater informed picks. Industry 4.0 uses large information analytics in numerous unique contexts, collectively with clever factories, wherein sensor records from production machines are examined to forecast while upkeep and upkeep may be required. Manufacturers may also benefit from manufacturing overall performance, recognize their real-time records with self-provider answers, optimize predictive protection, and automate manufacturing control with the aid of setting it to use. Big records analytics facilitates companies to see patterns and tendencies in big amounts of records approximately customers, which allows them to make higher agency choices.

The 4th industrial revolution has laid the inspiration for massive upgrades in how manufacturing are completed practically. The primary business revolution turned into steam engines being added. Currently, in this period, computing technology has produced large quantities of data. we've many sensors inside the industry 4.0 technology which includes imaginative and prescient sensors, and vibration sensors, and the records that these sensors generate can be analyzed to discover styles related to the health of the device and other associated tasks including patron cause evaluation (online purchasing), and more [9, 21–23, 55].

As we can truly see information is the new oil, it has a prime component to play in remodeling groups to fulfill industry 4.0 requirements. Big data is capable of being defined using 5 Vs – Volume, Velocity, Veracity, Value, and Variety.

2.4.1 Five Pillars of Big Data

Big information is a time period that encapsulates the tremendous volumes of information generated via numerous sources, the speed at which these records are produced and processed, and the numerous forms of facts to be had. Figure 2.4 illustrates the 5V's of Big Data. To correctly harness the potential of large records, it's urgently important to understand its foundational pillars, generally called the five Vs:

Volume: The most obvious factor of massive records is its sheer volume. The number of records being generated each 2nd is awesome, stemming from resources like social media, sensors, transactions, and others. Dealing with and storing this huge quantity of records calls for scalable storage solutions and progressive statistics control techniques.

Velocity: Velocity refers to the rate at which facts are generated, processed, and analyzed. In masses of conditions, statistics streams in real-time or close to-real-time, necessitating brief response times and actual-time analytics. Technologies which include streaming analytics structures and in-memory computing are crucial to address this speedy inflow of data.

Variety: Massive information is to be had in several forms, which incorporates based, unstructured, and semi-primarily based information. This range includes textual content, pics, motion snap shots, social media posts, sensor statistics, and more. Powerful information management and assessment require the capacity to way and integrate those various information sorts right into a coherent analytical framework.

Veracity: Veracity pertains to the trustworthiness and top notch of the data. With the considerable portions of records generated, no longer all of it is far accurate or reliable. Making sure records integrity, consistency, and accuracy are critical for making knowledgeable picks. Strategies collectively with records cleansing, validation, and sturdy information governance practices are essential to address veracity problems [51].

Value: In the long run, the fee pillar specializes in extracting significant insights and price from huge information. The genuine power of large facts lies in its capability to generate actionable insights that stress strategic choices, optimize operations, and create new opportunities. Advanced analytics, machine reading, and synthetic intelligence are pivotal in remodeling raw facts into precious insights that can be leveraged for competitive benefit.

2.4.2 Big Data to the Rescue

Businesses venturing into Industry 4.0 are using huge statistics as it could be finished with the use of commodity hardware because it rates effectiveness.

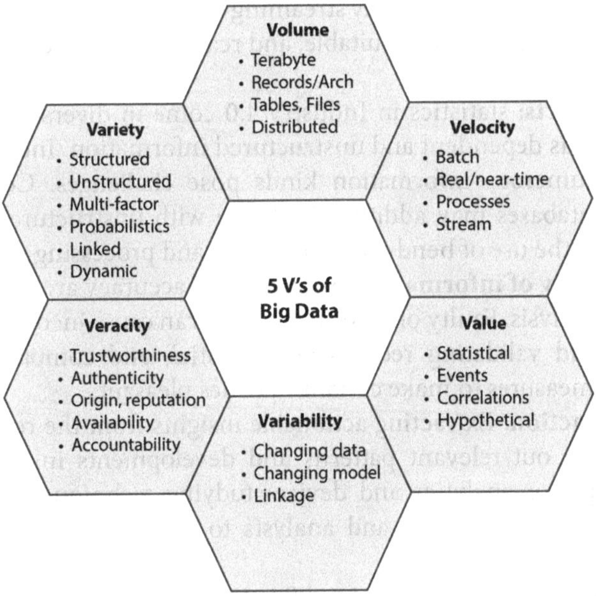

Figure 2.4 5V's of big data.

Hadoop was invented by way of Yahoo Inc., and it broke all benchmarks. Huge records have also made viable analytics, scalable, and accurate. Big records run on a disbursed architecture that is both horizontally and vertically scalable. The information this is generated can be mined to anticipate patterns that have been previously impossible to come across. The availability of massive data has moreover helped mitigate assaults on networks with the useful resource of hackers. There have been many times when companies efficiently mitigated big attacks using ways of analyzing community log files.

Aggregating the information can result in growing expressive dashboards which can offer valuable insights. Large records can manage terabytes/petabytes of statistics. Businesses have used big data to enhance their supply chain manipulation and relax big networks. Huge statistics aid in making essential choices as the insights that they generate can be useful resources for the whole business industry in enhancing its techniques. PC hardware has advanced appreciably during the last decade in layout, and this has made huge records evaluation more insightful.

2.4.3 Challenges in Big Data Analytics for Industry 4.0

- **Velocity of data:** Data is generated at an unprecedented speed in Industry 4.0, particularly in real-time processes. Analyzing and extracting meaningful insights from rapidly streaming data is challenging. Traditional batch processing may not be suitable, and real-time analytics solutions are needed.
- **Kind of facts:** statistics in Industry 4.0 come in diverse formats and brands, such as dependent and unstructured information. Integrating and analyzing numerous information kinds pose challenges. Conventional relational databases may additionally battle with unstructured statistics, necessitating the use of bendy records garage and processing solutions.
- **The veracity of information:** Statistics and accuracy are important for significant analysis. Faulty or incomplete facts can cause incorrect insights. Cleansing and validating records are essential, and companies should implement measures to make certain statistics pleasant.
- **Fee Extraction:** Extracting actionable insights from the records is the aim. Figuring out relevant patterns and developments inside the facts requires superior analytics and device-studying techniques. Companies want skilled facts scientists and analysts to interpret the statistics and derive treasured insights.
- **Security and privacy:** Industry 4.0 entails the trade of sensitive statistics, and protection is a paramount problem. Ensuring the confidentiality

and integrity of information is essential. Enforcing robust security measures, consisting of encryption, and getting entry to controls, are crucial to shield against cyber threats.

- **Interoperability:** In Industry 4.0, structures from exceptional vendors want to work together seamlessly. Making sure there is interoperability between numerous devices, systems, and structures is a venture. Requirements and protocols ought to be set up to facilitate easy information alternate.
- **Scalability:** Because the extent of facts grows, the analytics infrastructure must be scalable to address accelerated processing needs. Corporations must design their records architecture and analytics platforms with scalability in thoughts to accommodate the growing needs of Industry 4.0.
- **Price control:** Enforcing and retaining a sturdy massive data analytics infrastructure may be costly. Organizations need to control expenses effectively, considering elements that include hardware, software programs, and skilled employees. Cloud-based total answers can offer an extra flexible cost model.
- **Cultural shift:** Embracing a data-driven culture may require a significant shift in organizational mindset. Employees and stakeholders need to understand the value of data-driven decision-making.

2.4.4 Advantage in Big Data Analysis for Industry 4.0

Large information analysis plays an essential position in Industry 4.0, which represents the fourth business revolution characterized by way of the integration of virtual technology into production processes. Right here are some benefits of using large information evaluation in Industry 4.0:

- **Records-driven:** decision-making big records analytics allows agencies to make informed selections based on big volumes of facts. That is especially valuable in Industry 4.0, wherein actual-time facts from various sources may be analyzed to optimize production processes, supply chain management, and other operational components.
- **Predictive upkeep:** huge facts analytics facilitate in predicting system disasters and scheduling renovation sports before breakdowns arise. This proactive approach reduces downtime, extends the lifespan of machinery, and enhances universal operational efficiency.
- **Procedure optimization:** big facts analytics allows for the evaluation of big datasets generated through sensors and

other connected gadgets within the manufacturing environment. This helps in optimizing production procedures, improving performance, and decreasing waste.

- **Supply chain optimization:** massive information analytics presents insights into the entire delivery chain, from uncooked fabric sourcing to distribution. This optimization can lead to lower prices, better inventory management, and better coordination between suppliers, manufacturers, and distributors.
- **Refined management:** Examining large datasets can help identify patterns and anomalies in your production process that may indicate serious problems. This allows for early intervention and ensures that products meet the highest standards, reducing defects and increasing consumer pride.
- **Customization and personalization:** Big data analysis enables customization of products based on customer features and needs. This level of personalization is especially true in industries where customers are looking for specific, customized solutions.
- **Power efficiency:** reading strength consumption patterns through huge information can lead to sizeable strength financial savings. With the aid of figuring out regions of inefficiency, agencies can put in force changes to lessen electricity intake and, therefore, their environmental footprint.
- **Actual-time monitoring:** Industry 4.0 relies on real-time information monitoring and analysis. Large information technologies provide the capability to display and respond to events as they show up, making an allowance for agile selection and speedy adjustments to changing conditions [33].
- **Records safety and compliance:** As Industry 4.0 involves the alternative of touchy facts, big records analytics can be hired to enhance cybersecurity measures, making sure that statistics are included from unauthorized get entry [52]. It also enables ensuring compliance with Industry regulations and requirements.
- **Competitive gain:** groups that efficiently harness massive records analytics in Industry 4.0 gain a competitive side. The capability to conform quickly, optimize methods, and deliver awesome, custom-designed products positions corporations for achievement within the rapidly evolving industrial panorama.

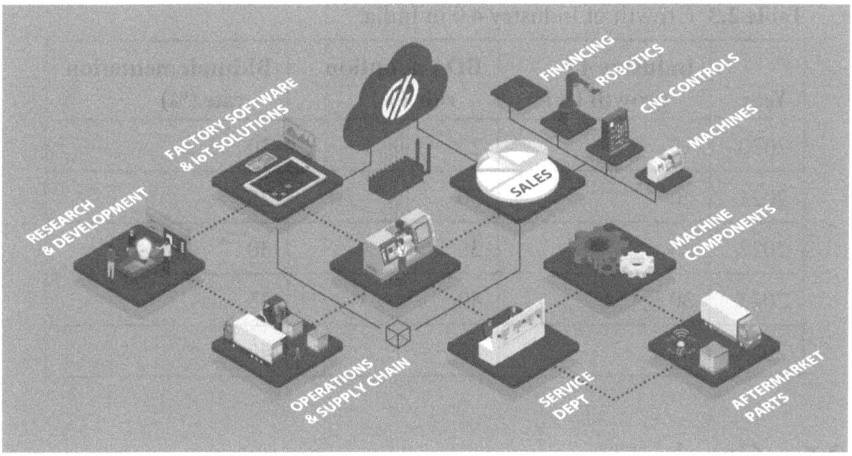

Figure 2.5 A fully connected industrial operation leverages Industry 4.0 technology.

Figure 2.5 depicts a fully connected industrial operation that leverages Industry 4.0 technology. In precis, huge statistics evaluation in Industry 4.0 brings approximately stepped forward performance, fee savings, and strategic advantages by harnessing the strength of statistics to drive decision-making and innovation.

2.5 Result and Discussion

The integration of BI and BDA has led to more informed decision-making processes. Real-time data analysis enables faster responses to market changes and operational challenges in Industry 4.0. The integration of BI tools has streamlined processes and reduced operating costs. BDA has played a crucial role in optimizing production processes and supply chain management. The use of BDA in Industry 4.0 has facilitated predictive maintenance by analyzing plant data. BI tools provide actionable insights into maintenance schedules and minimize downtime. BI and BDA have driven innovation by uncovering patterns and trends in huge data sets. The insights gained with these technologies contribute to the development of new products and services. Continuous monitoring of BI helps maintains and improve product quality standards. BDA detects potential quality issues early on and prevents errors in the manufacturing process. Table 2.3 summarizes the growth of Industry 4.0 through Big Data Analytics (BDA) and Business Intelligence (BI) in India.

Table 2.3 Growth of Industry 4.0 in India.

Year	Industry 4.0 growth (%)	BDA adoption rate (%)	BI implementation rate (%)
2020	15	25	20
2021	20	30	25
2022	25	35	30
2023	30	40	35
2024	35	45	40

2.6 Conclusion

In summary, the aggregate of Business Intelligence (BI) and massive records Analytics (BDA) in Industry 4.0 is developing transformative pressures that are reshaping the way agencies operate, make selections, and live competitively in contemporary monetary surroundings. It is described as representing those technology paintings synergistically to provide companies with many advantages that drive innovation, performance, and strategic insight. Business intelligence acts as a lens through which corporations take advantage of treasured insights from the past and gift facts. It enables reporting, visualizing data, and tracking normal overall performance, offering complete records approximately industrial business procedures. Seamlessly integrated with big information Analytics, which excels at handling big and numerous datasets, organizations can derive predictive and prescriptive insights and make fact-based total choices in actual time.

The feel of BI and BDA in Industry 4.0 is diverse. From predictive preservation and technique optimization to delivering chain overall performance and custom-designed product delivery, those technologies assist in accelerating operational excellence and competitiveness. The potential to review, analyze, and act on facts in real-time enhances decision-making, but also enables proactive responses to hard conditions, reduces downtime, and improves standard productivity. Moreover, the mixture of BI and mass records evaluation performs a key function in using innovation. This allows agencies become aware of upward developments, recognize patron conduct, and quickly adapt to market tendencies. In Industry 4.0, this pliability is important; agility and responsiveness are key to gaining an advantage in hastily evolving situations.

However, it's far more important to understand the demanding situations and issues related to enforcing BI and big statistics analytics in Industry 4.0. Those include statistical privacy problems, protection risks, and the need for a specialized group of workers. To acquire the overall performance blessings, agencies must invest in developing strong infrastructure, cybersecurity measures, and understanding. Essentially, the convergence of Business intelligence and large truth analysis in Industry 4.0 now not only successfully transforms statistics into actionable insights, but also puts groups at the vanguard of innovation. As industries end up extra virtual, organizations that properly utilize BI and complete statistical analysis will not only effectively live on, but thrive in a generation characterized by the aid of truth-based choice selections and technological advances.

References

1. Cegielski, C.G. and Jones-Farmer, L.A., Knowledge, skills, and abilities for entry-level business analytics positions: a multi-method study: knowledge, skills, and abilities for entry-level business analytics positions. *Decis. Sci. J. Innov. Educ.*, 14, 1, 91–118, 2016.
2. Loshin, D., *Business Intelligence: The Savvy Manager's Guide*, vol. 1, p. 12, Newnes, Burlington, MA, USA, 2012, doi: 10.1016/C2010-0-67240.
3. Chongwatpol, J., Managing big data in coal-fired power plants: a business intelligence framework. *Ind. Manage. Data Syst.*, 116, 8, 1779–1799, 2016.
4. Waller, M.A. and Fawcett, S.E., Data science, predictive analytics, and big data: a revolution that will transform supply chain design and management. *J. Bus. Logist.*, 34, 2, 77–84, 2013.
5. Sodero, A., Jin, Y.H., Barratt, M., The social process of Big Data and predictive analytics use for logistics and supply chain management. *Int. J. Phys. Distrib. Logist. Manage.*, 49, 7, 706–726, 2019.
6. Shmueli, G., Patel, N.R., Bruce, P.C., *Data mining for Business Intelligence: Concepts, Techniques, and Applications in Microsoft Office Excel with XLMiner*, vol. 2, pp. 23–25, John Wiley and Sons, Hoboken, NJ, 2011.
7. He, L., Liu, S., Shen, Z.-J.M., Smart urban transport and logistics: a business analytics perspective. *Prod. Oper. Manage.*, 31, 10, 3771–3787, 2022.
8. Larson, D. and Chang, V., A review and future direction of agile, business intelligence, analytics, and data science. *Int. J. Inf. Manage.*, 36, 5, 700–710, 2016.
9. O'Donovan, P., Leahy, K., Bruton, K., O'Sullivan, D.T.J., Big data in manufacturing: a systematic mapping study. *J. Big Data*, 2, 1, 20, 2015.

10. Nikolic, B., Ignjatic, J., Suzic, N., Stevanov, B., Rikalovic, A., Predictive manufacturing systems in industry 4.0: trends, benefits and challenges. *DAAAM Proceedings, DAAAM International Vienna*, pp. 0796–0802, 2017.
11. Qi, Q. and Tao, F., Digital twin and big data towards smart manufacturing and industry 4.0: 360-degree comparison. *IEEE Access: Pract. Innov. Open Solutions*, 6, 3585–3593, 2018.
12. Uhlmann, E., Hohwieler, E., Geisert, C., Intelligent production systems in the era of Industrie 4.0-changing mindsets and business models. *J. Mach. Eng.*, 17, 5–24, 2017.
13. Xu, X. and Hua, Q., Industrial big data analysis in smart factory: current status and research strategies. *IEEE Access: Pract. Innov. Open Solutions*, 5, 17543–17551, 2017.
14. Calabrese, M., Cimmino, M., Fiume, F., Manfrin, M., Romeo, L., Ceccacci, S., Paolanti, M., Toscano, G., Ciandrini, G., Carrotta, A., Mengoni, M., Frontoni, E., Kapetis, D., SOPHIA: an event-based IoT and machine learning architecture for predictive maintenance in industry 4.0. *Information (Basel)*, 11, 4, 202, 2020, doi: 10.3390/info11040202.
15. Bordeleau, F.-È., Mosconi, E., Santa-Eulalia, L.A., Business intelligence in industry 4.0: state of the art and research opportunities. *Proceedings of the 51st Hawaii International Conference on System SciencesHawaii International Conference on System Sciences*, 2018.
16. Hair, J.F., Knowledge creation in marketing: the role of predictive analytics. *Eur. Bus. Rev.*, 19, 4, 303–315, 2007.
17. Tiwari, S., Wee, H.M., Daryanto, Y., Big data analytics in supply chain management between 2010 and 2016: insights to industries. *Comput. Ind. Eng.*, 115, 319–330, 2018.
18. Delen, D., *Real-World Data Mining: Applied Business Analytics and Decision Making*, Pearson, Upper Saddle River, NJ, 2014.
19. Loureiro, A.L.D., Miguéis, V.L., da Silva, L.F.M., Exploring the use of deep neural networks for sales forecasting in fashion retail. *Decis. Support Syst.*, 114, 81–93, 2018.
20. Sharda, R., Asamoah, D.A., Ponna, N., Research and pedagogy in business analytics: opportunities and illustrative examples. *J. Comput. Inf. Technol.*, 21, 3, 171, 2013.
21. Rane, S.B. and Mishra, N., Roadmap for business analytics implementation using DIPPS model for sustainable business excellence: case studies from the multiple fields. *Int. J. Bus. Excell.*, 15, 3, 308, 2018.
22. Appelbaum, D., Kogan, A., Vasarhelyi, M., Yan, Z., Impact of business analytics and Industry systems on managerial accounting. *Int. J. Account. Inf. Syst.*, 25, 29–44, 2017.
23. Wong, E. and Wei, Y., Customer online shopping experience data analytics: integrated customer segmentation and customised services prediction model. *Int. J. Retail Distrib. Manage.*, 46, 4, 406–420, 2018.

24. Chen, J.-S., Le, T.-T., Florence, D., Usability and responsiveness of artificial intelligence chatbot on online customer experience in e-retailing. *Int. J. Retail Distrib. Manage.*, 49, 11, 1512–1531, 2021.
25. Basu, R. and Sondhi, N., Online versus offline: preferred retail choice for premium brand purchase. *Int. J. Retail Distrib. Manage.*, 49, 10, 1447–1463, 2021.
26. Bradlow, E.T., Gangwar, M., Kopalle, P., Voleti, S., The role of big data and predictive analytics in retailing. *J. Retail.*, 93, 1, 79–95, 2017.
27. Fink, L., Yogev, N., Even, A., Business intelligence and organizational learning: An empirical investigation of value creation processes. *Inf. Manage.*, 54, 1, 38–56, 2017.
28. Bagheri, B., Yang, S., Kao, H.-A., Lee, J., Cyber-physical systems architecture for self-aware machines in industry 4.0 environment. *IFAC-Papers Online*, 28, 3, 1622–1627, 2015.
29. Chien, C.-F., Hsu, C.-Y., Chen, P.-N., Semiconductor fault detection and classification for yield enhancement and manufacturing intelligence. *Flexible Serv. Manuf. J.*, 25, 3, 367–388, 2013.
30. Dai, Q., Zhong, R., Huang, G.Q., Qu, T., Zhang, T., Luo, T.Y., Radio frequency identification-enabled real-time manufacturing execution system: a case study in an automotive part manufacturer. *Int. J. Computer Integr. Manuf.*, 25, 1, 51–65, 2012.
31. Gröger, C., Kassner, L., Hoos, E., *et al.*, The data-driven factory leveraging big industrial data for agile, learning and human-centric manufacturing, pp. 40–52, 2016.
32. Lee, J., Bagheri, B., Kao, H.-A., A Cyber-Physical Systems architecture for Industry 4.0-based manufacturing systems. *Manuf. Lett.*, 3, 18–23, 2015.
33. Eiskop, T., Snatkin, A., Kõrgesaar, K., Søren, J., Development and application of a holistic production monitoring system, pp. 85–91, 2014.
34. Schwab, K., *The fourth industrial revolution*, Crown Business, New York, 2016.
35. Monostori, L., Cyber-physical production systems: Roots, expectations, and R&D challenges. *Procedia CIRP*, vol. 17, pp. 9–13, 2014.
36. Lee, J., Kao, H.-A., Yang, S., Service Innovation and Smart Analytics for Industry 4.0 and Big Data Environment. *Prod. Serv. Syst. Value Creation. Proc. 6th CIRP Conf. Ind. Product-Service Syst.*, 16, 3–8, 2014.
37. Hoerlsberger, M., Innovation management in a digital world. *J. Manuf. Technol. Manage.*, 30, 8, 1117–1126, 2019, https://doi.org/10.1108/JMTM-12-2019-461.
38. Varadarajan, M.N., Viji, C., Rajkumar, N., Mohanraj, A., Integration of AI and IoT for Smart Home Automation. *SSRG Int. J. Electron. Commun. Eng.*, 11, 5, 37–43, 2024.
39. Revathi, S., Babu, M., Rajkumar, N., Meti Vinod Kumar, V., Ratna, K.S., Sampath, B., Unleashing the Future Potential of 4D Printing: Exploring

Applications in Wearable Technology, Robotics, Energy, Transportation, and Fashion, in: *Human-Centered Approaches in Industry 5.0: Human-Machine Interaction, Virtual Reality Training, and Customer Sentiment Analysis*, pp. 131–153, IGI Global, Hershey, PA, USA, 2024.

40. Viji, C., Najmusher, H., Rajkumar, N., Mohanraj, A., Nachiappan, B., Neelakandan, C., Jagajeevan, R., Intelligent Library Management Using Radio Frequency Identification, in: *AI-Assisted Library Reconstruction*, pp. 126–143, IGI Global, Hershey, PA, USA, 2024.
41. Kumar, N., Antoniraj, S., Jayanthi, S., Mirdula, S., Saravanakumar, S., Rajkumar, N., Senthilkumar, K.R., Educational Technology and Libraries Supporting Online Learning, in: *AI-Assisted Library Reconstruction*, pp. 209–237, IGI Global, Hershey, PA, USA, 2024.
42. Mohanraj, A., Viji, C., Varadarajan, M.N., Kalpana, C., Shankar, B., Jayavadivel, R., Rajkumar, N., Jagajeevan, R., Privacy and Security in Digital Libraries, in: *AI-Assisted Library Reconstruction*, pp. 104–125, IGI Global, Hershey, PA, USA, 2024.
43. Rajkumar, N., Tabassum, H., Muthulingam, S., Mohanraj, A., Viji, C., Kumar, N., Senthilkumar, K.R., Anticipated requirements and expectations in the digital library, in: *AI-Assisted Library Reconstruction*, pp. 1–20, IGI Global, Hershey, PA, USA, 2024.
44. Jayavadivel, R., Arunachalam, M., Nagarajan, G., Shankar, B.P., Viji, C., Rajkumar, N., Senthilkumar, K.R., Historical Overview of AI Adoption in Libraries, in: *AI-Assisted Library Reconstruction*, pp. 267–289, IGI Global, Hershey, PA, USA, 2024.
45. Rajkumar, N., Viji, C., Mohanraj, A., Senthilkumar, K.R., Jagajeevan, R., Kovilpillai, J.A., Ethical Considerations of AI Implementation in the Library Era, in: *Improving Library Systems with AI: Applications, Approaches, and Bibliometric Insights*, pp. 85–106, IGI Global, Hershey, PA, USA, 2024.
46. Lalitha, B., Ramalakshmi, K., Gunasekaran, H., Murugesan, P., Saminasri, P., Rajkumar, N., Anticipating AI Impact on Library Services: Future Opportunities and Evolutionary Prospects, in: *Improving Library Systems with AI: Applications, Approaches, and Bibliometric Insights*, pp. 195–213, IGI Global, Hershey, PA, USA, 2024.
47. Nachiappan, B., Emerging and Innovative AI Technologies for Resource Management, in: *Improving Library Systems with AI: Applications, Approaches, and Bibliometric Insights*, pp. 115–133, IGI Global, Hershey, PA, USA, 2024.
48. Nachiappan, B., E-Resources Content Recommendation System Using AI, in: *Improving Library Systems with AI: Applications, Approaches, and Bibliometric Insights*, pp. 155–177, IGI Global, Hershey, PA, USA, 2024.
49. Arora, J., Singh, S., Sethi, M., Kaur, G., Ghantasala, G.P., Securing cloud data exchange related to IoT devices: key challenges and its machine learning solutions, in: *Hybrid Information Systems: Non-Linear Optimization Strategies with Artificial Intelligence*, p. 177, 2024.

50. Ghantasala, G.P., Hung, B.T., Chakrabarti, P., Pellakuri, V., Artificial intelligence based machine learning algorithm for prediction of cancer in female anatomy. *Multimed. Tools Appl.*, 1–27, 2024, https://doi.org/10.1007/s11042-024-19655-1.
51. Sravanthi, J., Reddy, C.S., Mahendar, A., Kumar, V.R., Buragadda, S., Ghantasala, G.P., Gupta, G., Improve Accuracy in Healthcare Data Analysis using Competitive Ensemble Deep Learning Model, in: *2024 11th International Conference on Computing for Sustainable Global Development (INDIACom)*, pp. 1792–1797, IEEE, 2024, February.
52. Ramisetty, S., Ghantasala, G.P., Gupta, G., Prevention of Security Attacks at Wireless Network Layers using Machine Learning Techniques, in: *2024 11th International Conference on Computing for Sustainable Global Development (INDIACom)*, pp. 1787–1791, IEEE, 2024, February.
53. Tamilarasi, R., Kumar, P.S., Ghantasala, G.P., Rao, D.N., Bathla, P., Gupta, G., Machine Learning Challenges of E-government Models of Cloud Computing in Developing Countries, in: *2024 11th International Conference on Computing for Sustainable Global Development (INDIACom)*, pp. 1804–1809, IEEE, 2024, February.
54. Ghantasala, G.P., Kunchala, A., Vidyullatha, P., Banu, S.R., Bhaumik, A., Banu, S.B., Gupta, G., Tech-Enabled Banking Revolt: The Transformational Era of IT in the Financial Sector, in: *2023 Seventh International Conference on Image Information Processing (ICIIP)*, pp. 133–136, IEEE, 2023, November.
55. Guruguntla, V., Lal, M., Ghantasala, G.P., Vidyullatha, P., Alqahtani, M.S., Alsubaie, N., Soufiene, B.O., Ride comfort and segmental vibration transmissibility analysis of an automobile passenger model under whole body vibration. *Sci. Rep.*, *13*, 1, 11619, 2023.

3

"AI-Powered Mental Health Innovations": Handling the Effects of Industry 4.0 on Health

U Ananthanagu* **and Pooja Agarwal**

Department of Computer Science and Engineering, PES University, Bengaluru, India

Abstract

Industry 4.0 innovations—which include the use of digitalization, artificial intelligence (AI), customer response data, and cutting-edge technologies—are causing a revolution in the medical services sector. By using proactive therapy, especially for early disease identification and control, this change seeks to improve patient comfort. Healthcare delivery is being revolutionized by technologies like VR- Virtual Reality, AI, IoT-Internet of Things and Big Data. The current epidemic has brought even more attention to the problems facing the mental health systems of today, including a lack of psychiatrists, lengthy wait periods, and stigma. These issues underline the necessity for digital change. AI's ability to improve mental health has been proved by the growth of online treatment, which has also made distant therapy more practical. Information and communication technology (ICT) applications for mental therapy and different medical diagnoses. The basis of Industry 4.0, which includes IoT, cloud computing, big data, remote internet, 5G, augmented/virtual reality, and AI, offers an intelligent, patient-centered healthcare system that is more sustainable and efficient overall. The chapter examines how new technologies, by providing creative answers to contemporary problems, can transform mental health care.

Keywords: AI-artificial intelligence, Industry 4.0, and information and communication technology (ICT), mental health

**Corresponding author*: nagu.anantha@gmail.com

M. Thirunavukkarasan, S. A. Sahaaya Arul Mary, Sathiyaraj. R, G. S. Pradeep Ghantasala and Mudassir Khan (eds.) Artificial Intelligence and Machine Learning for Industry 4.0, (55–86)

3.1 Introduction

Healthcare is changing because of digitization, artificial intelligence (AI), and 5G connectivity—a phenomenon known as Industry 4.0. This revolution is a response to manufacturing companies' mounting need for higher levels of efficiency and production. Industry 4.0, also called "the fourth industrial revolution," is the method of integrating new technology to reduce expenses and increase income [1]. The idea started at the 2011 CeBIT Discussion Meeting and has since spread to portray the utilization of distributed computing, digital actual frameworks, 3D printing, robots, large information, and AI, among other web-based innovations. The medical services area has changed decisively throughout the past 100 years, with new techniques and instruments being created consistently. This study [2], takes a gander at what Industry 4.0 means for medical care frameworks. Specifically, man-made reasoning changes existing frameworks and is basic to upgrading the arrangement of medical care administrations. Medical organizations and establishments have amassed enormous data sets containing information about claims, socio-economics, pay, schooling, and instruction as well as data about well-being testing and clinical preliminaries. Man-made reasoning (AI) frameworks can examine this tremendous measure of information and find examples and experiences that are unimaginable to people. Finding a specialist with a particular subject matter can be testing since medicines in the conventional medical services framework are much of the time in view of the patient's current condition. By giving mastery in a couple of medical services regions, including solution research, diagnostics, patient observing, and care frameworks, simulated intelligence resolves this issue. It further develops medical services frameworks by resolving the issue of doctors' deficient comprehension of sicknesses. Man-made intelligence is being used to upgrade medical care administrations, including the determination and therapy of diseases. Man-made brainpower (artificial intelligence) calculations influence information from computerized well-being records to enhance past information assortment for further developed sickness anticipation and therapy. This application exhibits how man-made consciousness (Artificial Intelligence) can possibly thoroughly adjust the medical services area by using information from earlier years to convey more powerful and modified patient consideration [3]. Industry 4.0 is introducing another time in medical care, by which propels in innovation like man-made brainpower is changing outdated medical services frameworks. Simulated intelligence in medical care resolves issues including a deficiency of specialists and an absence of information about sicknesses as well as improving administration and conveyance. The capacity of simulated intelligence frameworks to dissect enormous datasets and produce significant experiences further develops determination, patient consideration, and clinical exploration. As we explore this mechanical change, the ramifications of Industry 4.0 on medical services are yet being felt, however, they guarantee expanded viability, modified care, and a change in perspective in the way we approach and convey medical services administrations.

3.1.1 An Overview of Industry 4.0's Development in Healthcare Over Time

The development of medical services has been a surprising excursion set apart by tons of mechanical progressions inside the setting of Industry 4.0. Figure 3.1, which shows the transient movement from the early utilization of digitalization to anticipated future headings, mirrors an emotional change in medical care ideal models.

Early reception of digitalization during the 2000s: A simpler and more effective method for overseeing information was made conceivable by the beginning of the digitalization of medical care during the 2000s. During this time, there was a significant shift towards the digitization of patient

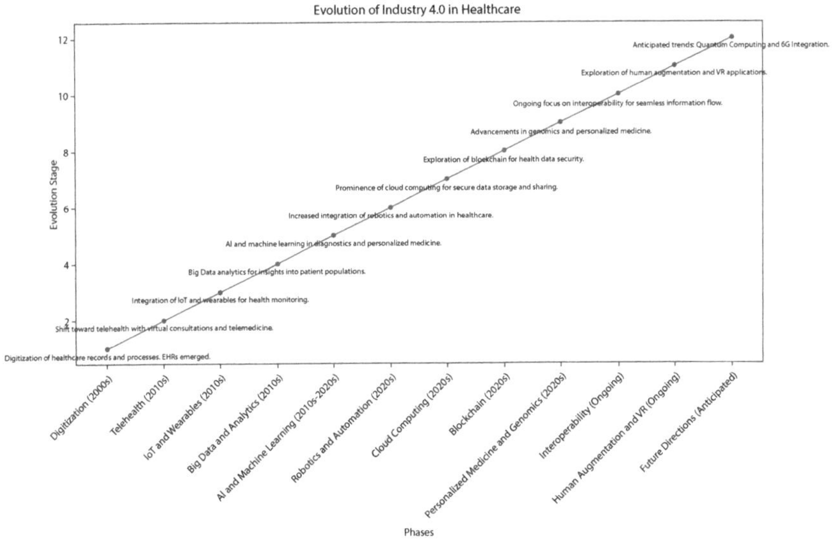

Figure 3.1 Healthcare's use of Industry 4.0 evolution.

information and regulatory methods with the presentation of EHRs-Electronic Health Records.

The appearance of telehealth during the 2010s: In the ten years that followed, the attention moved toward telehealth choices during the 2010s. The development of telemedicine, virtual counsels, and remote checking has altered the patient-supplier dynamic and incredibly further developed admittance to medical care administrations. The way healthcare services were sourced and provided underwent significant change as a result of this shift.

The ascent of wearables and IoT during the 2010s: The Web of Things (IoT) and wearable advancements consolidated to set out new open doors for wellbeing observing during the 2010s. The limit of individuals to track and trade constant well-being information with medical services suppliers through wellness trackers and smartwatches advanced a more cooperative and information driven way to deal with medical care.

Integration of Big Data and Analytics (2010s): At the same time, big data investigation developed and became essential, empowering the handling of monstrous datasets and the extraction of significant data. This scientific capacity offered a more profound cognizance of patient groupings, treatment results, and patterns in deterrent consideration utilizing predictive analytics.

The Rise of man-made intelligence and AI (2010s-2020s): Ensuing headways presented Machine Learning and AI to the medical care area. Diagnostics, individualized medication, and predictive modeling are now possible; thanks to these technologies. At the point when Artificial intelligence frameworks began to help clinical experts in the examination of convoluted clinical information, another period in information driven navigation was conceived.

Advanced mechanics and Robotization's Development during the 2020s: In medical services settings, computerization and advanced mechanics have become more common during the 2020s. These applications, which went from exoskeletons in restoration to mechanical cycle mechanization and careful robots, showed the wide and progressive capability of computerization in numerous medical services areas.

Future of Healthcare Cloud Computing: To address stresses with respect to get information handling, sharing, and putting away in the medical care area, distributed computing arrangements acquired fame during the 2020s. Cloud stages empowered cooperation among medical care partners, yet additionally reinforced the versatility of advanced well-being administrations.

Blockchain for Wellbeing Information Security (2020s): Right now, clinical records were believed to be possibly safeguarded by utilizing blockchain innovation. Trust and integrity in data processing were promoted by its decentralized and impenetrable nature, which addressed significant privacy and security concerns in healthcare transactions.

Personalized Medicine and Genomics 2020s: Industry 4.0 made a substantial contribution to the advancements in genomics and personalized medicine in the fields of personalized medicine and genomics. AI and genetic data combined to provide more precise diagnosis, and customized treatment regimens, which marked a paradigm change in the direction of personalized healthcare.

Sustaining the Focus on Interoperability: The process of progress is a testament to the importance of interoperability, which is essential to accelerating the smooth interchange of data among several healthcare systems and devices. To create a coherent and integrated healthcare ecosystem, ongoing standardization efforts are intended to improve communication and collaboration.

Virtual Reality and Human Augmentation (Ongoing): Research into virtual reality applications and human augmentation technology is simultaneously changing patient experiences, therapy, and training. The quality and efficiency of healthcare services are being improved by the rising use of virtual reality in surgical planning, medical education, and mental health therapies.

Prospects for the Future: Quantum Computing and 6G (EXPECTED): Anticipated future developments include the application of 6G telecommunications and the investigation of quantum computing for sophisticated healthcare simulations. It is anticipated that these developments will push the limits of what is possible in healthcare by enabling faster, more dependable communication for medical equipment [4].

3.1.2 The Advancement of AI in Mental Health

Artificial intelligence (AI) in psychological health is a fast-developing topic that has the capability to significantly alter how mental health illnesses are identified, addressed, and supported for those who need them. Figure 3.2 provides an abstract of the key stages in the development of AI in psychological health.

First Entries (2010-2011): From the beginning, computer-based intelligence was utilized to psychological wellness through chatbots and virtual

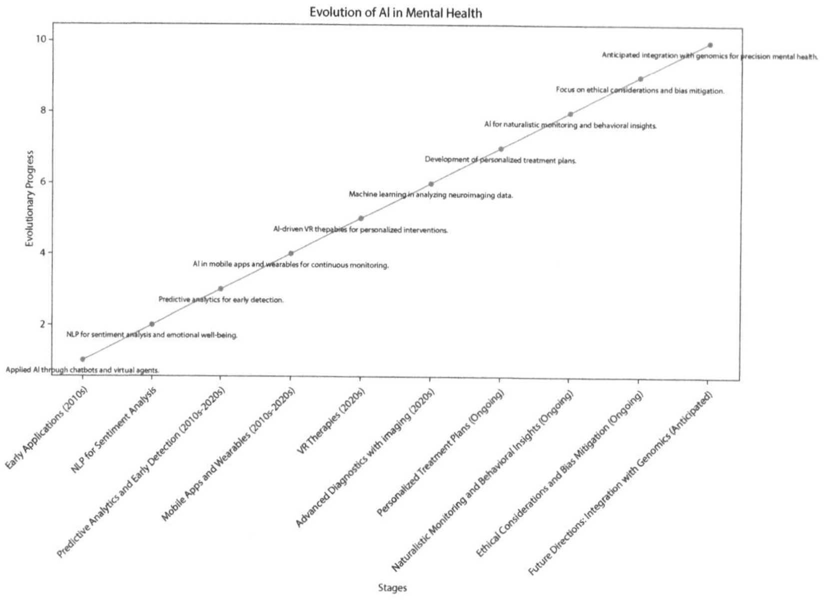

Figure 3.2 Evolution of AI in mental health.

specialists, which gave direction, support, and simple restorative collaborations. The purpose of these apps was to provide users who were dealing with common mental health issues with some basic support.

NLP and sentiment analysis: As Artificial Intelligence innovation progressed, NLP's importance in sentiment analysis developed. While trying to recognize designs that could highlight emotional well-being, artificial intelligence (AI) systems began looking at textual data, such as posts on social media. This considered a more profound comprehension of individuals' psychological states.

2010–2020: Early identification and predictive analytics algorithms for artificial intelligence (AI) have been utilized to dissect information from different sources, including behavioral patterns, biometric data, and electronic health information. Predictive analytics makes it possible to distinguish early indications of emotional wellness issues, empowering proactive mediation and tweaked treatment plans.

Cell phone Applications and Wearables (2010s-2020s): The reconciliation of artificial intelligence (AI) into portable applications and wearable innovation has extended admittance to psychological well-being administrations. Wearables and apps powered by AI encouraged a more adaptable and user-focused approach to mental health by providing continuous monitoring, real-time feedback, and tailored interventions.

2020s: VR (virtual reality) treatments: During the 2020s, computer generated reality (VR) treatments controlled by simulated intelligence originally surfaced. These immersive activities were intended to look like remedial conditions and integrate openness treatment, care activities, and unwinding procedures. To expand the adequacy of intercessions, AI systems tailored the VR experience based on each user's response.

High level Diagnostics utilizing Imaging (2020s): ML and other AI technologies became increasingly important for the processing of neuroimaging data. High level analytic devices controlled by computerized reasoning that analyze designs in cerebrum movement and construction could be helpful in the early recognition of conditions including nervousness, depression, and neuro-developmental issues.

Modified Treatment Plans (Ongoing): The essential objective of late progressions in AI is the advancement of customized treatment plans. Based on each individual's unique qualities, feelings, and preferences, machine learning algorithms look at large-scale datasets to determine the most effective qualities. By tailoring interventions to each patient's specific requirements, this strategy aims to improve therapeutic outcomes.

Continuous Exploration: Lifelike behavior, speech patterns, and other logical variables are being checked by artificial intelligence. Through the examination of everyday interactions, artificial intelligence (AI) innovation can give insightful data on a person's emotional wellness status, in this way adding to additional complete and careful appraisals.

Concerns about integrity and reducing bias: As AI in psychological well-being keeps on creating, it is more vital than at any time in recent memory to address moral worries and decrease biases. Guaranteeing decency, straightforwardness, and assurance of client protection are urgent components in carrying out man-made intelligence reasonable for emotional wellness applications.

Anticipated mix of Genomics and Bioinformatics: Later on, the investigation of psychological well-being might require more incorporation of AI with hereditary qualities and bioinformatics. Understanding the hereditary and sub-atomic elements impacting psychological wellness issues might introduce another period of accurate emotional well-being treatment. With this information, mediation could be more designated and powerful [4].

3.2 Related Work

3.2.1 Recognizing AI's Place in Healthcare

AI has arisen as an incredible asset in the clinical field, assisting with early illness identification, better figuring out the course of sickness improvement, optimizing prescription dosages, and creating novel therapy approaches. One of Artificial intelligence's essential advantages is its capacity to rapidly break down massive datasets and work with pattern recognition. Among the clinical claims to fame that have effectively integrated artificial intelligence are radiography, ophthalmology, and malignant growth diagnostics. Artificial intelligence calculations have shown that with regards to spotting irregularities or nuances that the natural eye can neglect while concentrating on clinical pictures, they can either coordinate or outperform qualified clinical experts. One such model is the capacity to decide a patient's gender from retinal scans.

Though it is unlikely that intelligent systems will replace doctors entirely, they are being employed more and more to support clinical decision-making. Artificial intelligence (AI)-enabled technologies, in contrast to human learning, which is constrained by learning capacity, availability to knowledge sources, and lived experiences, can swiftly synthesize data from an unlimited range of health data sources. Utilizing enormous datasets—like EHRs, that can be computationally processed to reveal relationships pertaining to human behaviors, trends and patterns is necessary to optimize the potential of AI. This computational analysis is crucial because it frequently provides insights that would be difficult for humans to get by hand. Essentially, the use of AI in medicine is a paradigm shift that will improve the skills of medical practitioners and completely change how medical diagnosis and decision-making are approached [5].

3.2.2 Comprehending AI's Impact on Mental Health

AI is gaining ground in the arena of physical health applications in the context of Industry 4.0, but its adoption in the field of psychological well-being has been slower. Interpersonal skills are crucial for psychological healthiness consultants, who are known for their patient-centered and hands-on approach. They establish connections with patients and closely observe their behaviors and feelings. In the field of psychological condition, written notes and subjective, qualitative patient remarks are frequently used as clinical data, which presents its own set of difficulties.

In the framework of Industry 4.0, there is unrealized potential for AI technology to transform the diagnosis and understanding of mental diseases, despite the unique features of mental health practice. Understanding an individual's bio-psycho-social profile in its whole is essential to understanding mental health; nevertheless, our current comprehension of the complex interplay among psychological, biological and social systems is still somewhat limited. There is a great deal of variability in the pathophysiology of mental illnesses, and the discovery of biomarkers may lead to more precise and impartial classifications of these disorders.

By utilizing AI approaches in the context of Industry 4.0, it is possible to create sophisticated risk models and pre-diagnosis screening tools. These models can help identify a person's susceptibility to or likelihood of acquiring mental illness. In the context of Industry 4.0, to achieve the long-term objective of individualized mental health care, we must leverage computational methods that are best adapted to managing large datasets, or "big data." We are positioned to usher in a new era of diagnoses and individualized care by strategically integrating AI in mental health inside the industry 4.0 paradigm, addressing the complexities of mental health with never-before-seen precision and insight [6–8].

3.3 Machine Learning in Healthcare

An approach to AI called Machine Learning (ML) uses a diversity of methods to make an algorithm capable of learning.

3.3.1 SML-Supervised Machine Learning

The algorithm's goal is to create relationships between input features that are taken from several data streams and include clinical, physiological, and socio-demographic information. Its main objective is to learn from pre-labeled data, where labels denote states such as the absence of depression or major depressive disorder (MDD), to maximize predictions [9, 10]. To enable machine learning (SML), the labels serve as a guiding force, telling the computer how to label the data during the learning process. It supports categorical labels (MDD or not) as well as continuous labels (a continuum of severity). During a learning phase, the algorithm learns to correlate labels with particular attributes. After training on a significant amount of categorized training data, the model is evaluated using unlabeled test data to determine its accuracy in classifying the target variable, such as MDD.

The model's performance is closely examined to prevent overfitting, which is the process of discovering bogus patterns. If the model's precision or any other parameter declines in relation to the test data, it is deemed overfit and incapable of being applied to outside, independent samples. While certain methods, like logistic regression and linear regression, are specially designed for support vector machines (SML), others, like support vector machines (SVM), are taken straight from traditional statistics [11].

3.3.2 Unsupervised Machine Learning (UML)

UML function without labels, which allows them to find patterns and basic structures in the input features. These algorithms, however, do not directly associate features with predefined labels [12]. Clustering algorithms such as Kmeans, Hierarchical, and Principal Component Analysis are used in Unsupervised Machine Learning (UML) to identify key components in a dataset by organizing and classifying data into patterns [13]. The data generated must be interpreted by subject-matter experts for it to be considered valuable. When labels are absent, UML becomes more difficult to use, but it is excellent for displaying a dataset's underlying structure free from bias.

3.3.3 Deep Learning (DL)

By gaining from raw information, Deep Learning (DL) algorithms enjoy the benefit of consequently uncovering inactive relationships without requiring human cooperation [14]. These algorithms utilize Artificial Neural Networks (ANNs), which mimic how the human brain functions, to explore complex raw information through different "hidden layers" [15]. It's interesting to take note of that Deep Learning (DL) has been portrayed as less mechanical than common AI (ML) and has been contrasted with human mental cycles. To be thought of "deep," an ANN should have more than one hidden layer [16].

The layer comprises of nodes that change the impact of information on the result by applying a bunch of coefficients or weights. DL succeeds at distinguishing complex designs while working with high-layered information, for example, clinical and non-clinical information given by patients or doctor notes in electronic well-being records [14]. Practitioners of deep learning need to be cautious with the "black box" phenomenon, which refers to the potential difficulty in interpreting the output of ANNs with buried layers. It's frequently no longer clear how the algorithm arrived at a specific conclusion [17].

3.3.4 NLP - Natural Language Processing

NLP is a branch of artificial intelligence that deals with unstructured text and uses algorithmic methods to process and analyze human language on computers. This covers jobs like language translation, information extraction, and semantic understanding [18]. Before introducing other AI technologies, mental health practices will significantly rely on natural language processing (NLP) as a fundamental step because to the quantity of raw input data in the form of text (e.g., clinical notes) and talk (e.g., counseling sessions) [17, 19, 20]. Notwithstanding the complexities of human language, it is an impressive technological achievement for computer software to be able to automatically interpret the meanings of underlying words. Applications in mental healthcare greatly benefit from this capability [21].

3.4 Genetics and Machine Learning for Understanding and Prediction of Complicated Illnesses

The field of Genetic Information and Technologies has experienced a notable surge since 2008, posing difficulties in handling the rapidly growing volume of data. Technologies such as next-generation sequencing (NGS) have been crucial in accelerating the sequencing of whole human genomes at a significantly lower cost. It is yet unknown how to decipher the intricate instructions included in the human genome, a complex structure that contains information on traits and development. Understanding gene interactions is made more difficult by individual genetic variation. Large human genome samples have been the focus of health programs to find statistically significant trends across various populations. About 20,000 genes are stored on the 23 chromosomes of the human genome, which are essential for protein coding during cell development [22]. Estimates, however, point to differing numbers of genes—some speculating as many as 25,000 or as few as 19,000 [23, 24]. Genetic dark matter, often referred to as missing heritability, is a substantial percentage of genetic information that does not appear to have a protein-coding function but may affect gene expression levels, and therefore, influence health. A useful technique for spotting patterns and trends in genetic data is machine learning. Through the analysis of large genomic datasets, this technology can forecast the risks of various diseases, such as cancer and Alzheimer's. Machine learning is also being used to investigate genetic connections to mental disorders including bipolar disorder and schizophrenia, which may provide information on inherited tendencies. The amalgamation of machine learning with genetic research has the potential for enhanced illness prediction and a more precise comprehension of intricate genomic relationships [25].

3.5 AI-Driven Virtual Healthcare Support for Patient Care

Innovative solutions are involved in the context of Industry 4.0 to meet the growing demands on healthcare services with limited resources. With AI-powered apps, chatbots, and interfaces, virtual health assistants (VHAs) are emerging as revolutionary solutions that support healthcare workers by mimicking human communication and providing individualized patient care. These digital assistants are essential to patient care; they help with everything from diagnosing symptoms to giving advice on medicine, scheduling appointments, reminding patients to take their meds, and monitoring vital signs. Virtual assistants improve patient outcomes by reducing the strain of human healthcare practitioners and enhancing patient care by effectively gathering daily health information and transmitting reports to designated physicians [26].

Virtual assistants' round-the-clock accessibility guarantees patients easy access to healthcare, completely changing the way healthcare is delivered. Artificial Intelligence (AI)-powered phone apps, like those utilized by the National Health Service (NHS), enable patient triaging based on entered symptoms, providing a more streamlined and effective substitute for conventional non-emergency hotlines. Furthermore, the market's introduction of intelligent speakers is especially helpful for chronically ill and elderly people who might have trouble using smartphone apps. In the context of Industry 4.0, Virtual health aides have probably and substantially raise the bar for healthcare delivery in terms of quality, effectiveness, and cost. These technologies provide a critical step in optimizing healthcare in the face of changing problems and resource constraints by raising patient participation and offering an improved overall experience [27–30].

3.6 AI's Advantages for Mental Health Treatment

AI-driven developments are revolutionizing mental health treatment in Industry 4.0 in a few important ways. AI uses data analysis to identify patterns in language and behavior, which greatly improves early mental health issue diagnosis and fits in with the speed and accuracy of Industry 4.0 technologies. Machine learning's ability to handle large information efficiently not only helps with diagnosis but also makes individualized treatment choices easier to give, which fits in well with Industry 4.0's data-driven and agile philosophy. By ensuring timely mental health assistance and eliminating wait periods, the combination of AI-powered chatbots and virtual therapists improves accessibility to treatment and allows people to reflect on themselves in the changing environment of Industry 4.0.

Patient-data-driven predictive modeling aligns with Industry 4.0's data-driven paradigm by enabling continuous adjustments to treatment plans for enhanced effectiveness and personalization. Furthermore, AI-powered screening tools enable more effective assessments, actively reducing the stigma associated with seeking help and promoting a proactive approach to managing mental health in the progressive framework of Industry 4.0 [25]. When compared to usual diagnostic methods, the use of AI technologies to medical diagnostics in the era of Industry 4.0 holds significant promise for increasing accuracy, reducing costs, and saving time. Notably, AI can generate faster, more accurate responses while lowering the likelihood of human error. Artificial intelligence (AI) innovation can possibly assume a huge part later on in supporting doctors during their dynamic cycle by offering them constant help and experiences. The numerous uses of AI in clinical finding and treatment, including the examination of CT, X-ray, and X-ray pictures, are as yet being explored. Artificial intelligence (AI) can find abnormalities, find issues like growths and cracks, and give quantitative estimations to analyze clinical problems quickly and really by using AI (ML) methods [31]. Artificial intelligence can possibly change clinical research center testing, an essential part of contemporary medical services. Artificial Intelligence holds an extraordinary guarantee to change clinical diagnostics by further developing research center tasks' speed, accuracy, and effectiveness. This could prompt better clinical navigation and work on patient safety. Eminently, with the making of AI (ML) frameworks expected to recognize, distinguish, and measure microorganisms, order illnesses, and figure clinical results, artificial intelligence's importance in clinical microbial science is growing rapidly. Inside the setting of Industry 4.0, these frameworks use different information sources, for example, quality sequencing, genomic information, metagenomic sequencing results, and minute imaging, featuring the intricate impacts of AI on further developing clinical diagnostics [32].

3.7 AI's Predictive Capabilities: Revolutionizing Mental Health Treatment

We look at the progressive meaning of AI computer-based intelligence in radiology and pathology-related early illness determination. We'll take a gander at the diagnostic tools that are fueled by AI (man-made intelligence) now and how they significantly impact patient outcomes.

AI in Radioscopy: Radiology is driving how in Industry 4.0's reconciliation of AI, getting a groundbreaking time for clinical diagnostics. The investigation of radiology, which use imaging to recognize illnesses, has embraced Artificial Intelligence algorithms that can decipher complex examples found in images from diagnostic tests like X-rays, CT scans, and X-rays. AI in radiology changes the worldview by giving specialists apparatuses to analyze oddities all the more rapidly and precisely. Artificial intelligence is being utilized in radiology for different purposes, showing how the field is altering medical care. A couple of these applications incorporate working on heart imaging, classifying brain tumors, recognizing vertebral cracks, distinguishing Alzheimer's illness, smoothing out detailing and information related undertakings, and early bosom disease location. One such algorithm is IBM's Medical Sieve, intended to improve clinical dynamic in cardiology and radiology. This method shows how AI could upgrade diagnostic capacities by quickly and definitively recognizing issues in radiology images. Proceeding with this pattern, Stanford scientists have fostered an AI machine learning algorithm that, in several seconds, incredibly well diagnoses chest X-rays for 14 unique circumstances. This is an excellent illustration of the synergy between advanced AI technology and radiological techniques to deliver rapid, accurate insights necessary for timely medical interventions. The merging of AI and radiology in the Industry 4.0 landscape is bringing in a new era of precision and efficiency in medical imaging, which not only speeds up diagnostic operations but also drastically changes the capabilities of healthcare staff [33].

Artificial Intelligence (AI) in Pathology: In the age of Industry 4.0, the study of diseases at the microscopic level, or pathology, is undergoing a major transition as a result of the incorporation of AI. Pathology is being revolutionized by artificial intelligence (AI) systems that possess the ability to analyze digital slide images and learn from them. Pathologists may concentrate on more complex diagnostic duties because of this technological synergy, which not only speeds up the diagnostic procedure but also guarantees the accuracy of the results. AI improves our understanding of the complex story that each individual cell tells, much like having an interpreter for them.

Applications of AI in pathology are numerous and include forecasting, pathology training, image analysis, instrument automation, result interpretation, forecasting, test utilization, error detection, genomics, pandemic prevention, rare event detection, and education, image analysis, rare event detection, and many more. AI's adaptability in pathology demonstrates how it could transform the medical industry in a few ways, in line with Industry 4.0 ideas. Professor Nira Jha of Princeton University is an expert in electrical and computer engineering. He has led AI efforts in pathology, with an emphasis on the field that has grown since the coronavirus outbreak. This demonstrates how AI technologies can adapt quickly to changing healthcare needs. Furthermore, since 2018, the Biomedical Semantic Understanding Group at Xi'an Jiaotong University has been actively involved in the field of digital pathology by creating and managing the OpenHI platform. These projects provide as an excellent example of how academia and business may work together to leverage AI to develop pathology practices in the context of Industry 4.0, which will ultimately result in more effective, precise, and significant disease diagnosis and treatment [33].

AI-Powered Diagnostic Instruments: Unquestionably, AI has an impact on healthcare outcomes. This is especially true with AI-driven diagnostic tools. One example is Google DeepMind, which uses machine learning to distinguish between healthy and malignant tissues in mammography screening for accurate breast cancer detection. Sensely is a platform that is leading the way in Virtual Primary Care, or VPC, and it symbolizes a progressive approach to healthcare. Furthermore, Accelerated Access Collaborative (AAC) support 38 innovative initiatives, including an AI-guided tool that improves healthcare workers' accuracy in diagnosing heart attacks and an algorithm that expedites the identification of lung cancer. Within the context of Industry 4.0, these examples highlight the revolutionary impact of AI in healthcare by highlighting developments that lead to more accurate diagnoses and creative solutions [33].

3.8 AI's Limitations and Research on Mental Health

AI as it exists now is still far from being able to diagnose mental illnesses accurately, and it will not be able to do so anytime soon. Beyond technical difficulties, the true issue for AI-based mental disease diagnosis lies in our general understanding of mental problems. The absence of impartiality in diagnosing mental diseases makes AI diagnoses desirable. However, there are now challenges with AI diagnosis, including data-related problems like dataset capacity limits and training dataset ecological validity. Technological developments may be able to help with these technical challenges.

A more basic problem, though, stems from the difficulties in detecting mental illness itself, since low-level data is the main source of AI training data, and current diagnostic criteria are subjective and qualitative. Early in the creation of AI systems, there may be a mistaken understanding of mental illnesses. The ability of artificial intelligence to recognize depressive disorders is dependent on the caliber of the samples and the annotations made for them in the datasets. Generalization and result comparability are further hampered by heterogeneity in data collection, scanning parameters, and processing techniques. The accuracy of automatic diagnosis could be improved by including multimodal data [34].

3.9 Ethical Issues and Difficulties with AI-Powered Mental Health

Ensuring the privacy and security of sensitive mental health data is critical and necessitates stringent compliance with data protection laws, strong encryption protocols, and safe storage procedures. A clear description of how AI algorithms manage patient information is one of the significant parts of transparency and informed consent for the ethical application of artificial intelligence in emotional wellness. Empowering people to grasp and uninhibitedly agree to computer-based intelligence-driven mediations is essential for cultivating patient confidence through autonomous consent.

Biases in AI innovation is difficult to keep away from, particularly when demographic and cultural factors are thought about. Developers should be proactive in recognizing and eliminating bias to guarantee that these advances are utilized fairly. The subject of responsibility in AI-driven emotional well-being choices is as yet being examined to keep away from mistakes and handle algorithmic responsibility. Exploring the obstacles of AI in mental health requires finding some kind of harmony between the responsibilities of architects, clinical professionals, and clients. Algorithm consistency requires progressing audits and adjustments to keep up with validity. Human administration is at this point significant, highlighting the way that simulated intelligence in emotional well-being care should help human judgment rather than having its spot. As to Industry 4.0, interdisciplinary support between ethicists, administrators, specialists, and information researchers becomes crucial for the ethical utilization of PC-based knowledge close to home wellbeing. request to foster capable and proficient computer-based intelligence applications in psychological wellness care, this helpful technique guarantees that moral issues, strategy suggestions, clinical ability, and information science bits of knowledge all meet up.

3.10 Healthcare AI Governance

Ethical and regulatory governance — which handles concerns like bias, transparency, privacy, safety, and liability — becomes significant as AI turns out to be increasingly more incorporated into medical care. Laura Craft, VP Analyst at Gartner, features the significance of artificial intelligence governance, particularly for applications in the medical care industry. She points out the absence of uniform guidelines that help organizations in executing novel artificial intelligence strategies. The World Health Organization (WHO) facilitated the arrangement of the "Ethics & Governance of Artificial Intelligence for Health" record with experts in ethics, technology, law, and human rights. The review frames six agreement standards: advancing human security, developing responsibility, ensuring straightforwardness, maintaining value, and helping with harmless to the ecosystem and versatile innovation. The rules set forth by the WHO plan to expand artificial intelligence's possible in medical care while keeping up with clinical staff responsibility and local area responsiveness. With an emphasis on keeping up with autonomy, advancing security, transparency, responsibility, value, and long-haul responsiveness, the review features that it is so critical to have an extensive moral structure to direct computer-based intelligence applications to guarantee that the innovation is utilized for the benefit of the public [35].

3.11 Artificial Intelligence in Augmented and Virtual Reality (AR & VR)

In the system of Industry 4.0, the assembly of Artificial Intelligence (AI) and Virtual Reality (VR) holds extraordinary potential for significant change in the medical services area. These state-of-the-art advances are changing patient considerations, clinical training, and general medical services tasks with their immersive and interactive experiences. AR and VR offer practical realistic simulations that empower clinical experts to direct medical procedures, therapies, and diagnostics in a protected virtual environment when it comes to medical education and training.

AI upgrades individual execution through custom-fitted development, progressing criticism, and adaptable preparation modules. AR soothes out activities without unnecessary interferences by superimposing basic clinical information onto experts' perspectives while they are chipping away at tasks. By utilizing VR to make 3D models utilizing imaging information, the pre-usable arrangement is incredibly helpful. AI-controlled VR applications, like openness treatment, consider the personalization of encounters according to patients' reactions, supporting clinical decisions, treatment, and online discussions for exhaustive patient education. Virtual reality (VR) is particularly helpful during situations involving global health since it enables remote consultations in virtual environments. Exercises done in virtual reality (VR) help with physical therapy and recovery, and AI algorithms personalize programs according to each person's progress. In addition, virtual reality (VR) environments powered by artificial intelligence (AI) enable detailed visualization and analysis of complex medical data, promoting a deep comprehension of complex patterns and relationships. AR also provides real-time overlays for medical professionals during procedures. Through the introduction of innovative methods to patient care, medical education, and treatments, Industry 4.0 and AI have the potential to alter the healthcare industry [36–39].

3.12 Methodology

The goal of selecting depression as a focal area for AI and machine learning research, among other mental illnesses, is to apply computational techniques to comprehend the intricacies of this prevalent mental health problem. Several AI/ML approaches, including AdaBoost, Bayesian Networks, Deep Learning, and Support Vector Machines, can be applied to assess complex datasets about depression in different ways. With the aid of these algorithms, researchers may identify patterns, identify predictive traits, and develop models that advance our knowledge of the underlying causes, variety of presentations, and effective therapies for depression. The decision to focus on depression within the context of various mental disorders is in line with the prospective benefits of AI/ML, which include improved diagnostic precision, customized therapies, and the establishment of individualized mental health services. This strategic goal could lead to advancements in computational psychiatry and, in turn, more efficacious approaches to early detection, tailored therapies, and better results for depressed individuals.

Details of the research and performance indicators that were employed: Based on the type of predictive variables the AI systems are fed. Each study's setting and population, main objective, predictors, sample size used as input data, kind of AI algorithm and validation, top-performing outcomes, and a succinct conclusion are listed. The most often reported performance measures across research were: The curve for the receiver operating characteristic (ROC): Plotting the true positive rate (TPR) on the y-axis and the false positive rate (FPR) on the x-axis represents the area under the ROC curve, or AUC [40, 56, 57]. An AUC=1 denotes excellent capacity to discriminate between classes, an AUC=0 indicates poor ability to classify (illness vs. no disease, for example).

Accuracy percentage (%): The percentage of accurate predictions is known as percent accuracy, and it is calculated by dividing the total number of observations (FPs + FNs) by the number of correct predictions (TPs + TNs).

Sensitivity: Measures the ratio of TPs that are correctly detected (TPs/(TPs+FNs)), is corresponding to the TPR and "recall" (R). Specificity, which is the same as TNR, is the proportion of correctly identified TNs to total number of TNs (TNs/(TNs+FPs)). Specificity and sensitivity are frequently inversely correlated.

F1 scores and precision, also known as positive predictive value, or PPV. Precision is the proportion of affirmative detections (e.g., actuality of MDD) that the algorithm (TPs/(TPs + FPs)) correctly classifies.

A wide range of Artificial Intelligence (AI) and Machine Learning (ML) approaches, statistical approaches, and related data formats used in depression-focused mental health research. AdaBoost, Bayes, Bayesian Networks (BN), Classification, Clustering, Deep Learning, Decision Trees (DT), Epistasis Network Centrality Analysis, Evaporative Cooling Feature Selection, FURIA, Gaussian Processes, Genetic Algorithm, Gradient Boosting, Hierarchical Clustering, JRIP, k-means clustering, k-Nearest Neighbors (kNN), Multivariate Classification, N, Neural Networks (NN), Principal Component Analysis (PCA), Regression, Random Forest (RF), Naive Bayes (NB), Linear Discriminant Analysis (LDA), Searchlight, Semi-supervised Topic Modeling Over Time, Sentiment Analysis, and Support Vector Machines (SVM).

Numerous data types are involved with this, such as biological, audio, electronic health records, clinical notes, imaging, mobile/wearable sensors, social media, surveys, video/photo, and electronic health assessment. The multidisciplinary nature of research in this crucial field is emphasized by this compilation, which highlights the flexibility of computational approaches and the adaptability of data modalities in the field of depression research within mental health. In the context of depression, the citations show how common and important these methods and data kinds are in a variety of applications, from imaging, social media, and wearable sensor data to clinical evaluations and electronic health records [47, 48].

3.13 Results and Discussions

The features of the predictor variables that were used as input data, include the use of inventive monitoring systems, brain imaging data, electronic health records (EHRs), social media platforms, and mood evaluation scales, The most common mental illness that was studied was mood disorder, or depression.

3.13.1 Synopsis of AI Research in Mental Health

The utmost used AI method was SML (Supervised Machine Learning), while several studies also employed NLP before using ML. Although most studies employed cross-validation techniques, a few also tested the algorithm in an external validation sample or on a held-available subsample that wasn't used for exercise. The results that were reported in different studies varied greatly. The range of accuracy values for depression prediction was low (62 percent from smartphone data and 63 percent from posts on social media [40]) to high (98 percent from clinical measures of physical function, BMI, cholesterol, etc.) and high (97 percent from sociodemographic variables and physical comorbidities [41, 43]). Furthermore, ML approaches were able to predict treatment responses to routinely prescribed antidepressants like citalopram (65% accuracy) and identify factors such as education that were related with placebo versus medication responses. NLP algorithms identified indicators of severe mental illness from EHR data with 90% accuracy and 85% recall [44]. 87% of fMRI features correctly classified schizophrenia (as opposed to controls) [46], and 63-61% of brain MRI features correctly identified neuroanatomical subtypes of schizophrenia [45, 53]. Compared to adjusted directly observed therapy (72%), an AI platform resulted in a better success rate of drug

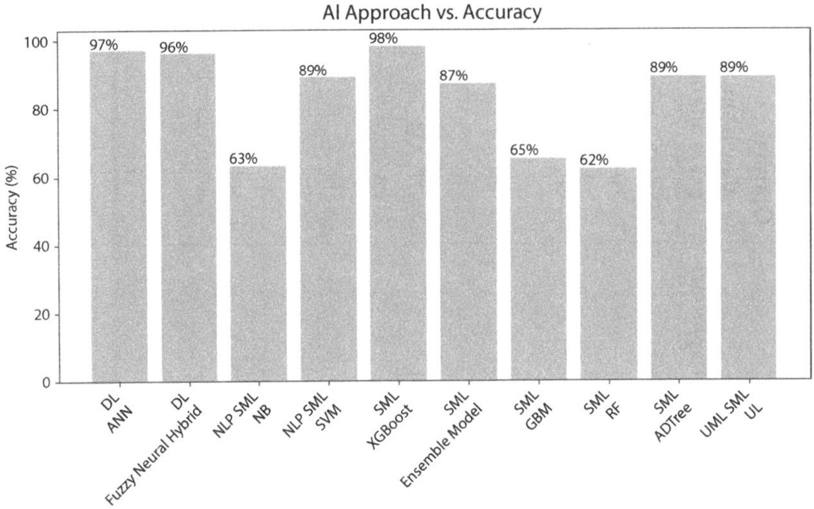

Figure 3.3 AI approaches and their corresponding performance metrics.

adherence (90%) for patients with schizophrenia. Health insurance records (AUC=0.69) [42], survey and text message data (sensitivity=0.76; specificity=0.62), and electronic health records contributed to the prediction of suicidal ideation and attempts. Figure 3.3 displays AI techniques together with the performance indicators that go along with them.

Various artificial intelligence (AI) techniques have been used in several research to address mental health issues. The Summary of Research on AI and Mental Health in Depression is provided in Table 3.1.

3.13.2 AI-Driven Intervention as the Future of Mental Healthcare

As stated by the World Health Organization (WHO), "a state of complete physical, mental, and social well-being and not merely the absence of disease or infirmity" constitutes health. Modern technology makes it possible to track people's unique bio-psycho-social profiles over an extended period, which has a substantial impact on their mental health. The massive volume of complex, multimodal data generated is too much for humans to handle, which is why artificial intelligence (AI) is best suited for the task. Beyond the existing DSM-5 (Diagnostic and Statistical Manual of Mental Disorders) categorization system, additional objective diagnoses of mental diseases could be established as AI approaches advance. This development

Table 3.1 A synopsis of research on artificial intelligence and depression mental health.

Written by	Principal objective	Study designing	Sample size (n)	AI approach	Optimal algorithmic/ performance
Arun *et al.*, [4]	Utilizing hospital EHR data, forecast depression using the Euro-Depression Inventory	CSI Holdworth Memorial Hospital in Mysuru, the South India Research Unit, Mysuru	270 patient records	SML	XGBoost: 98% accuracy SN=98%, SP= 94%
Sau & Bhakta [50]	Predict depression with clinical information and sociodemographic traits	Kolkata, India Bagbazar Urban Health & Training Centre	105	DL	ANN: AUC=0.99 Accuracy= 97%
Kalmady *et al.*, [45]	Identify Schizophrenia based on FMRI (Functional magnetic resonance imaging) data	National Institute of Mental Health & Neurosciences (NIMHANS, India)	Brain Imaging	SML	Ensemble model: Accuracy= 87%

(*Continued*)

Table 3.1 A synopsis of research on artificial intelligence and depression mental health. (*Continued*)

Written by	**Principal objective**	**Study designing**	**Sample size (n)**	**AI approach**	**Optimal algorithmic/ performance**
`Chattopadhyay [51]	Model mathematically the clinical perception and diagnosis of depressive conditions by psychiatrists	India Hospital	Brain Imaging-302 depression 50 HC	DL	Fuzzy neural hybrid model: accuracy= 96%
Chekroud *et al.*, [52]	Estimate if individuals with depression who take citalopram for 12 weeks will experience a clinical remission.	Combining Medicines to Improve Depression Outcomes	Mood rating scales	SML	GBM: Accuracy of training = 65% AUC = 0.70
Patel *et al.*, [54]	Utilizing network-based characteristics and multi-modal imaging, forecast late-life MDD (Major Depressive Disorder) diagnosis	Pittsburgh, PA, USA MRI laboratory	68 Depression	SML	ADTree: Accuracy= 87%

(*Continued*)

Table 3.1 A synopsis of research on artificial intelligence and depression mental health. (*Continued*)

Written by	Principal objective	Study designing	Sample size (n)	AI approach	Optimal algorithmic/ performance
Wahle *et al.*, [55]	Use smartphone data to identify individuals who have clinically significant depression.	Zürich, Switzerland Community smart-phone usage over 4 weeks	Novel monitoring system- Smartphone usage, accelerometer, Wi-Fi, & GPS data	SML	RF Accuracy= 62%
Aldarwish & Ahmed [40]	Determine which social media users are depressed by looking at their postings.	Saudi Arabia	Social Media- Training set= 6773 posts	NLP SML	NB: Recall= 58% Accuracy= 63% precision= 100%
Deshpande *et al.*, [56]	Sort tweets that show Symptoms of emotional instability and sadness from those that don't.	Twitter API platform	Social Media- 10,000 Tweets	NLP SML	NB: Precision= 0.836 Accuracy= 83%

(*Continued*)

Table 3.1 A synopsis of research on artificial intelligence and depression mental health. (*Continued*)

Written by	Principal objective	Study designing	Sample size (n)	AI approach	Optimal algorithmic/ performance
Mowery *et al.*, 2016 [57]	Determine the type of depression and whether a tweet exhibits signs of depression.	Depressive Symptoms & Psychosocial Stressors Associated with Depression (SAD) dataset	Social Media- 9,300 tweets queried using a subset of the LIWC	SML NLP	SVM: F1 score=52

**ANN-Artificial Neural Network, NB-Naive Bayes Classifier, GBM-Gradient Boosting Machine, RF-Random Forest, SVM-Support Vector Machine, UML-Unsupervised Machine Learning, ADTree-Alternating Decision tree, UL-Unsupervised Learning, SN-Sensitivity SP-Specificity, LIWC-Linguistic Inquiry Word Count, SAD-Stressors Associated with Depression.*

could make it easier to diagnose mental diseases early on or at the prodromal stage, resulting in more successful treatments. AI has taken huge steps in the diagnosis and treatment of psychological well-being problems by having the option to tailor recommended medicines because of the extraordinary attributes of every person. Broad, high-quality datasets are important to investigate the associations between hidden variables and mental illnesses. Notwithstanding, admittance to these profoundly phenotype datasets remains a significant obstruction to emotional wellness research, underlining the significance of cooperative endeavors. As the amount and complexity of these datasets rise, Deep Learning (DL) approaches become increasingly significant, outflanking traditional supervised machine learning (SML) techniques. Notwithstanding, the interpretability of these DL models is a significant thought, and it is exhorted that the field moves past the "black box" worldview. The most common way of adapting algorithms intended for one reason to another, known as transfer learning (TL), is one method for creating AI (ML) models and improving their performance. Transfer Learning is turning out to be more famous in the field of psychological well-being research and is, as of now, broadly utilized in image-centric fields like pathology and radiology.

3.14 Conclusion

Artificial Intelligence (AI) addresses a profoundly encouraging space for making critical headways in the domain of psychological well-being, mental health research and treatment methodologies. The healthcare industry is sincerely embracing the Fourth Industrial Revolution. Related to changing healthcare, the coming of Industry 4.0 has made ready novel ways to deal with and address psychological wellness problems like depression. Artificial intelligence is generally perceived as a vital part of digital medicine, exhibiting a significant sure impact on mental healthcare potential. A wide cluster of specialists — including scientists, doctors, controllers, and patients — should participate in cooperative endeavors to completely gain the advantages presented by this drive. The dynamic investment of the mental health community, which advocates for a sympathetic and complete way to deal with mental health treatment, is fundamental for the ethical and effective integration of AI into clinical care. The field of medication is nearly a huge change, as shown by conversations encompassing the "Fifth Industrial Revolution" and ideas, for example, "Hospital 4.0" and "Medicine 4.0." This cycle highlights the meaning of secure administration of well-being information, enveloping electronic clinical records, computerized well-being records, clinical information storehouses, and well-being data trades, especially in the domain of emotional well-being. Future examination will investigate a different scope of advances that add to the digitalization of medication and medical care in the post-fourth Industrial Revolution. These advances envelop organic added substance production, online protection innovative work, virtual and VR trials, and a huge scope of information investigation for anticipating pandemics. The direction of medical services development in this powerful setting will be essentially impacted by continuous cooperation and proactive commitment of all stakeholders, all things considered, with a particular spotlight on tending to and moderating psychological wellness challenges in contemporary times.

References

1. Popov, V.V., Kudryavtseva, E.V., Kumar Katiyar, N., Shishkin, A., Stepanov, S.I., Goel, S., Industry 4.0 and Digitalisation in Healthcare. *Materials (Basel, Switzerland), 15*, 6, 2140, 2022, https://doi.org/10.3390/ma15062140.
2. Ahsan, M.M. and Siddique, Z., Industry 4.0 in Healthcare: A systematic review. *Int. J. Inf. Manage. Data Insights*, 2, 1, 100079, 2022, ISSN 2667-0968, https://doi.org/10.1016/j.jjimei.2022.100079.
3. Rajput, S., Bhanodia, P., Sethi, K.K., Rathore, N.P.S., The Impact of Artificial Intelligence on Healthcare, in: *Industry 4.0 and Healthcare*. Advanced Technologies and Societal Change, A. Mishra and J.C.W. Lin (Eds.), Springer, Singapore, 2023, https://doi.org/10.1007/978-981-99-1949-9_4.
4. https://chat.openai.com/
5. Panwar, A., Malhotra, N., Malhotra, D., INDUSTRY 4.0: A Comprehensive Review of Artificial Intelligence, Machine Learning, Big Data and IoT in Psychiatric Health Care, in: *Proceedings of 3rd International Conference on Computing Informatics and Networks*. Lecture Notes in Networks and Systems, vol. 167, A. Abraham, O. Castillo, D. Virmani (Eds.), Springer, Singapore, 2021, https://doi.org/10.1007/978-981-15-9712-1_42.
6. Jiang, F., Jiang, Y., Zhi, H., Dong, Y., Li, H., Ma, S., *et al.*, Artificial intelligence in healthcare: past, present and future. *Stroke Vasc. Neurol.*, 2, 4, 230–43, 2017, https://doi.org/10.1136/svn-2017-000101.
7. Graham, S., Depp, C., Lee, E.E., *et al.*, Artificial Intelligence for Mental Health and Mental Illnesses: an Overview. *Curr. Psychiatry Rep.*, **21**, 116, 2019, https://doi.org/10.1007/s11920-019-1094-0.
8. Miller, D.D., Facp, C.M., Brown, E.W., Artificial intelligence in medical practice: the question to the answer? *Am. J. Med.*, 131, 2, 129–33, 2018, https://doi.org/10.1016/j.amjmed.2017.10.035.
9. Bzdok, D., Krzywinski, M., Altman, N., Machine learning: supervised methods. *Nat. Methods*, 15, 1, 5–6, 2018, https://doi.org/10.1038/nmeth.4551.

10. Fabris, F., de Magalhães, J.P., Freitas, A.A., A review of supervised machine learning applied to ageing research. *Biogerontology*, 18, 2, 171–88, 2017, https://doi.org/10.1007/s10522-017-9683-y.
11. Kotsiantis, S.B., Zaharakis, I., Pintelas, P., Supervised machine learning: a review of classification techniques. *Emerg. Artif. Intell. Appl. Comput. Eng.*, 160, 3–24, 2007.
12. Miotto, R., Li, L., Kidd, B.A., Dudley, J.T., Deep patient: an unsupervised representation to predict the future of patients from the electronic health records. *Sci. Rep.*, 6, 26094, 1–10, 2016, https://doi.org/10.1038/srep26094.
13. Dy, J.G. and Brodley, C.E., Feature selection for unsupervised learning. *J. Mach. Learn. Res.*, 5, 845–89, 2004, Retrieved from: http://www.jmlr.org/papers/volume5/dy04a/dy04a.pdf.
14. Shickel, B., Tighe, P.J., Bihorac, A., Rashidi, P., Deep EHR: A survey of recent advances in deep learning techniques for electronic health record (EHR) analysis. *IEEE J. Biomed. Heal. Inf.*, 22, 5, 1589–1604, 2018, DOI: https://doi.org/10.1109/JBHI.2017.2767063.
15. Faust, O., Hagiwara, Y., Hong, T.J., Lih, O.S., Acharya, U.R., Deep learning for healthcare applications based on physiological signals: a review. *Comput. Methods Prog. Biomed.*, 161, April, 1–13, 2018, https://doi.org/10.1016/j.cmpb.2018.04.005.
16. LeCun, Y., Bengio, Y., Hinton, G., Deep learning. *Nat. Methods*, 521, 7553, 436–44, 2015, https://doi.org/10.1038/nature14539.
17. Samek, W., Wiegand, T., Müller, K.-R., Explainable artificial intelligence: understanding, visualizing and interpreting deep learning models, arXiv Prepr arXiv., 2017, 1708.08296. Available from: http://arxiv.org/abs/1708.08296.
18. Calvo, R.A., Milne, D.N., Hussain, M.S., Christensen, H., Natural language processing in mental health applications using non-clinical texts. *Nat. Lang. Eng.*, 23, 05, 649–85, 2017, https://doi.org/10.1017/S1351324916000383.
19. Hirschberg, J. and Manning, C.D., Advances in natural language processing. *Sci. Mag.*, 349, 6245, 261–6, 2015, https://doi.org/10.1126/science.aaa8685.
20. Demner-Fushman, D., Chapman, W.W., McDonald, C.J., What can natural language processing do for clinical decision support? *J. Biomed. Inform.*, 42, 5, 760–72, 2009, https://doi.org/10.1016/j. jbi.2009.08.007.
21. Cambria, E. and White, B., Jumping NLP curves: a review of natural language processing research. *IEEE Comput. Intell. Mag.*, 9, 2, 48–57, 2014, https://doi.org/10.1109/MCI.2014.2307227.
22. Collins, F.S., Lander, E.S., Rogers, J., Waterson, R.H., Finishing the euchromatic sequence of the human genome. *Nature*, 431, 7011, 931–945, 2004.
23. Willyard, C., Expanded human gene tally reignites debate. *Nature*, 558, 354–355, 2018, Online: Published 19 June 2018.
24. Ezkurdia, I., Juan, D., Rodriguez, J.M., Frankish, A., Diekhans, M., Harrow, J., *et al.*, Multiple evidence strands suggest that there may be as few as 19000 human protein-coding genes. *Hum. Mol. Genet.*, 23, 22, 5866–5878, 2014.

25. Sanghvi, T., AI's Role in Detecting Mental Health Patterns: Revolutionizing Early Intervention, https://syndelltech.com/impact-of-ai-in-mental-healthcare/.
26. Buch, V.H., Ahmed, I., Maruthappu, M., Artificial intelligence in medicine: current trends and future possibilities. *Br. J. Gen. Pract.*, 68, 668, 143–4, 2018, https://doi.org/10.3399/bjgp18X695213.
27. Curtis, R.G., Bartel, B., Ferguson, T., Blake, H.T., Northcott, C., Virgara, R., *et al.*, Improving user experience of virtual Health Assistants: scoping review. *J. Med. Internet Res.*, 23, 12, e31737, 2021, https://doi.org/10.2196/31737. Ghosh, P.K., Jain, P., Wankhede, S., Preethi, M., Kannan, M.K., Virtual nursing Assistant. *J. Geog. Sci.*, 8, 279–85, 2021, 20.18001.GSJ.2021.V8I3.21.36690.
28. Burgess, M., The NHS is trialling an AI chatbot to answer your medical questions, Wired, 2017, Jan 5, http://www.wired.co.uk/article/babylon-nhschat-bot-app. Accessed 20 June 2023.
29. Jiřík, P., Inspiring Applications of Digital Virtual Assistants in Healthcare, July 22, 2022, https://www.phonexia.com/blog/inspiring-applications-ofdig-ital-virtual-assistants-in-healthcare/. Accessed 20 June 2023.
30. Kim, J.W., Jones, K.L., D'Angelo, E., How to prepare prospective psychiatrists in the era of Artificial Intelligence. *Acad. Psychiatry*, 43, 3, 337–9, 2019, https://doi. org/10.1007/s40596-019-01025-x.
31. Undru, T.R., Uday, U., Lakshmi, J.T., *et al.*, Integrating Artificial Intelligence for Clinical and Laboratory diagnosis - a review. *Maedica (Bucur)*, 17, 2, 420–6, 2022, https://doi.org/10.26574/maedica.2022.17.2.420.
32. Peiffer-Smadja, N., Dellière, S., Rodriguez, C., Birgand, G., Lescure, F.X., Fourati, S., *et al.*, Machine learning in the clinical microbiology laboratory: has the time come for routine practice? *Clin. Microbiol. Infect.*, 26, 10, 1300–9, 2020, https://doi.org/10.1016/j.cmi.2020.02.006.
33. Mekonnen, A.M., AI: The Game-Changer in Diagnostics and Early Detection, Digital Health Digest.
34. Yan, W.-J., Ruan, Q.-N., Jiang, K., Challenges for Artificial Intelligence in Recognizing Mental Disorders. *Diagnostics*, 13, 1, 2–2, 2022, doi: 10.3390/diagnostics13010002.
35. The benefits of AI in healthcare, https://www.ibm.com/blog/the-benefits-of-ai-in-healthcare/.
36. Marino, E., Barbieri, L., Colacino, B., Fleri, A.K., Bruno, F., An Augmented Reality inspection tool to support workers in Industry 4.0 environments. *Comput. Ind.*, 127, 103412, 2021.
37. Sherry, J., Grand View Research Healthcare Augmented & Virtual Reality Market Worth $5.1 Billion by 2025, 2017, Available online: http://www.grandviewresearch.com.
38. MED-TECH Innovation News First Spinal Surgery with Augmented Reality Headset Takes Place, Available online: https://www.med-technews.com/news/Digital-in-Healthcare-News/first-spinal-surgery-with-augmented-reality-headset-takes-pl/ (accessed on 8 January 2022).

39. Karami, B., Koushki, R., Arabgol, F., Rahmani, M., Vahabie, A.-H., Effectiveness of Virtual/Augmented Reality–Based Therapeutic Interventions on Individuals with Autism Spectrum Disorder: A Comprehensive Meta-Analysis. *Front. Psychiatry*, 12, 887, 2021, [CrossRef].
40. Aldarwish, M.M. and Ahmad, H.F., Predicting Depression Levels Using Social Media Posts. *Proc - 2017 IEEE 13th Int Symp Auton Decentralized Syst ISADS 2017*, pp. 277–80, 2017, DOI: 10.1109/ISADS.2017.41.
41. Deshpande, M. and Rao, V., Depression detection using emotion artificial intelligence. *Proc Int Conf Intell Sustain Syst ICISS 2017*, pp. 858–62, 2017, DOI: 10.1109/ISS1.2017.8389299.
42. Choi, S.B., Lee, W., Yoon, J.H., Won, J.U., Kim, D.W., Ten-year prediction of suicide death using Cox regression and machine learning in a nationwide retrospective cohort study in South Korea. *J. Affect. Disord.*, 231, 1, 8–14, 2018, DOI: 10.1016/j.jad.2018.01.019 [PubMed: 29408160].
43. Fernandes, A.C., Dutta, R., Velupillai, S., Sanyal, J., Stewart, R., Chandran, D., Identifying Suicide Ideation and Suicidal Attempts in a Psychiatric Clinical Research Database using Natural Language Processing. *Sci. Rep.*, 8, 1, 7426, 2018, DOI: 10.1038/s41598-018-25773-2 [PubMed: 29743531].
44. Jackson, R.G., Patel, R., Jayatilleke, N., Kolliakou, A., Ball, M., Gorrell, G., *et al.*, Natural language processing to extract symptoms of severe mental illness from clinical text: The Clinical Record Interactive Search Comprehensive Data Extraction (CRIS-CODE) project. *BMJ Open*, 7, 1, e012012, 2017, DOI: 10.1136/bmjopen-2016-012012.
45. Kalmady, S.V., Greiner, R., Agrawal, R., Shivakumar, V., Narayanaswamy, J.C., Brown, M.R.G., *et al.*, Towards artificial intelligence in mental health by improving schizophrenia prediction with multiple brain parcellation ensemble-learning. *npj Schizophr.*, 5, 1, 2, 2019, DOI: 10.1038/s41537-018-0070-8 [PubMed: 30659193.
46. Dwyer, D.B., Cabral, C., Kambeitz-Ilankovic, L., Sanfelici, R., Kambeitz, J., Calhoun, V., *et al.*, Brain subtyping enhances the neuroanatomical discrimination of schizophrenia. *Schizophr. Bull.*, 44, 5, 1060–9, 2018, DOI: 10.1093/schbul/sby008 [PubMed: 29529270] This study used both unsupervised and supervised machine learning with structural MRI data and suggested that sMRI-based subtyping enhances neuroanatomical discrimination of schizophrenia by identifying generalizable brain patterns that align with a clinical staging model of the disorder.
47. Ananthanagu, U. and Agarwal, P., A Systematic Review and Future Perspective of Mental Illness Detection Using Artificial Intelligence on Multimodal Digital Media, in: *Intelligent Sustainable Systems*. Lecture Notes in Networks and Systems, vol. 578, A.K. Nagar, D. Singh Jat, D.K. Mishra, A. Joshi (Eds.), Springer, Singapore, 2023, https://doi.org/10.1007/978-981-19-7660-5_4.
48. Ananthanagu, U., Ebin, P.M., Mathkunti, N.M., FFO-ABC DepressioGuard: A Hybrid Classification Framework for Social Media Depression Detection.

Procedia Comput. Sci., 230, 138–149, 2023, ISSN 1877-0509, https://doi.org/10.1016/j.procs.2023.12.069.
49. Arun, V., Prajwal, V., Krishna, M., Arunkumar, B.V., Padma, S.K., Shyam, V., A Boosted Machine Learning Approach for Detection of Depression. *Proc 2018 IEEE Symp Ser Comput Intell SSCI 2018*, pp. 41–7, 2018, DOI: 10.1109/SSCI.2018.8628945.
50. Sau, A. and Bhakta, I., Artificial neural network (ANN) model to predict depression among geriatric population at a slum in Kolkata, India. *J. Clin. Diagn. Res.*, 11, 5, VC01–4, 2017, DOI: 10.7860/JCDR/2017/23656.9762.
51. Chattopadhyay, S., A Fuzzy Approach for the Diagnosis of Depression. *Appl. Comput. Inf.*, 13, 1, 10–8, 2018, DOI: 10.1016/j.aci.2014.01.001.
52. Chekroud, A.M., Zotti, R.J., Shehzad, Z., Gueorguieva, R., Johnson, M.K., Trivedi, M.H., *et al.*, Cross-trial prediction of treatment outcome in depression: A machine learning approach. *Lancet Psychiatry*, 3, 3, 243–50, 2016, DOI: 10.1016/S2215-0366(15)00471-X.
53. Drysdale, A.T., Grosenick, L., Downar, J., Dunlop, K., Mansouri, F., Meng, Y., *et al.*, Resting-state connectivity biomarkers define neurophysiological subtypes of depression. *Nat. Med.*, 23, 1, 28–38, 1878, DOI: 10.1038/nm.4246.
54. Patel, M.J., Andreescu, C., Price, J.C., Edelman, K.L., Reynolds, C.F., Aizenstein, H.J., Machine learning approaches for integrating clinical and imaging features in late-life depression classification and response prediction. *Int. J. Geriatr. Psychiatry*, 30, 10, 1056–67, 2015, DOI: 10.1002/gps.4262.
55. Wahle, F., Kowatsch, T., Fleisch, E., Rufer, M., Weidt, S., Mobile Sensing and Support for People With Depression: A Pilot Trial in the Wild. *JMIR mHealth uHealth*, 4, 3, e111, 2016, DOI: 10.2196/mhealth.5960.
56. Landeiro Dos Reis, V. and Culotta, A., Using Matched Samples to Estimate the Effects of Exercise on Mental Health from Twitter. *Proc Twenty-Ninth AAAI Conf Artif Intell*, pp. 182–8, 2015.
57. Mowery, D., Park, A., Conway, M., Bryan, C., Towards Automatically Classifying Depressive Symptoms from Twitter Data for Population Health. *Proc Work Comput Model People's Opin Personal Emot Soc Media*, pp. 182–91, 2016.

4

AI ML Empowered Smart Buildings and Factories

Akey Sungheetha[1]*, Rajesh Sharma R.[1], R. Chinnaiyan[2] and G. S. Pradeep Ghantasala[1]

[1]*Department of Computer Science and Engineering, Alliance University, Bangalore, India*
[2]*Department of Computer Science and Engineering, Lingayas Vidyapeeth University, Faridabad, Haryana, India*

Abstract
This chapter examines machine learning's important role in automating numerous tasks. In "intelligent" buildings, the use of mobile devices and computers may greatly simplify tasks like monitoring security, regulating the interior climate, and carrying out routine maintenance. The World Wide Web or Internet of Things is used by intelligent buildings to create connections between the various parts that comprise the building. The chapter also covers the development of artificial intelligence at smart buildings, with a focus on global issues. Specifically, energy conservation and consumption pose the biggest obstacles for all industries, but particularly for the home and industrial sectors. The foundation of Production 4.0 is founded by an innovative knowledge termed the internet of everything (IoeT). The IoT makes it possible for mechanisms and devices to communicate seamlessly.

In the context of building engineering and construction industry 4.0, the chapter explores in detail the claims made by the domains of computing (artificial intelligence), informed machine learning techniques (ML), as well as deep learning algorithms (DL). It also looks at the idea of intelligent manufacturing for smart cities. These applications comprise architectural enterprise besides picturing, structural analysis and plan, material design in addition to optimization, off-site manufacturing while automation, construction supervision and progress tracking, longevity, life cycle assessment, smart functioning, building administration, and the circular economy are all included. Insights into the Smart building

**Corresponding author*: akey.sungheetha@alliance.edu.in

M. Thirunavukkarasan, S. A. Sahaaya Arul Mary, Sathiyaraj. R, G. S. Pradeep Ghantasala and Mudassir Khan (eds.) Artificial Intelligence and Machine Learning for Industry 4.0, (87–106)

technology is based on the integration of devices, large information, with AI. To support smart building applications, a thorough examination and categorization of machine learning approaches are provided. A new era in city energy efficiency may result from this. Artificial intelligence (AI) can be used in intelligent structures to improve control, automation, and dependability—all of which will lead to a decrease in energy usage.

Within the broader architecture, technology, and construction sector, the chapter highlights how IoT, big data, through artificial intelligence have become more integrated; thanks to the quick advancement of technology, which has been fueled by machine learning as well as IoT. Innovation besides technological advancement in the manufacturing have accelerated due to this convergence. This book chapter gives a thorough overview of how "smart" manufacturing is becoming the norm and how the traditional production-oriented manufacturing environment is soon to give way to one that is more data-oriented, automated, and smart.

Keywords: IoT, sensors, data, energy, smart buildings

4.1 Introduction

By combining many different kinds of city infrastructure and persuading bureaucracy to cooperate, the merging of AI in addition to intelligent learning is revolutionizing keen cooperatives and buildings and fostering a smarter urban environment. In this case, smart ports would not make sense outside of smart houses due to their dense reliance on them [4]. People living in smart homes may feel secure in the knowledge that AI along with the IoT have taken care of their security. IoT smart homes employ sensor data to minimize energy consumption and improve functionality [19–21].

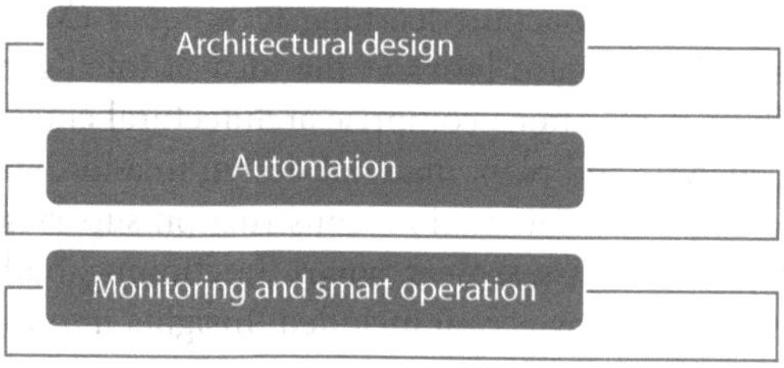

Figure 4.1 AI application in three segments for building construction.

4.1.1 An Account of How Machine Learning Contributes to Task Automation

Machine learning makes it possible to automate tasks in smart buildings and factories by analyzing data patterns to predict and enhance operations. The architectural segments continue to perform automation, progress monitoring and smart operation are as shown in Figures 4.1 to 4.3.

With its all-encompassing platform, the Digital Twin technology quickly evaluates the collected data and keeps an eye on the devices, from edge connectivity to client-facing web-based business applications. Using industry-standard protocols, CONTACT Elements on IoT presents this data as a visual dashboard and message queuing telemetry transport

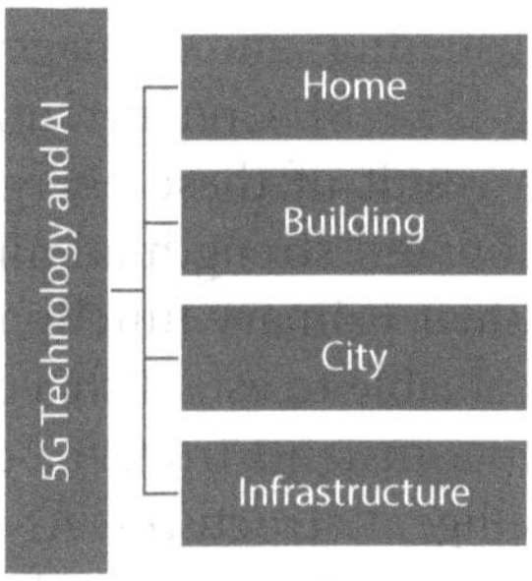

Figure 4.2 Demands for 5G in AI and smart building.

Figure 4.3 Measures to improve energy efficiency.

(MQTT) protocols, following processing by a range of signal analysis and machine learning techniques [2]. In an effort to save money, time, and material consumption associated with extensive testing, researchers [3, 23] investigated the application of models based on machine learning to predict mechanical properties.

After observing a given set of data, a computer applies the artificial intelligence field of machine learning to build a model that can be utilized to solve problems. In Figure 4.4, we see that profound knowledge of deep learning represents a subclass of learning techniques. Artificial neural networks along with related machine learning techniques, which all have multiple hidden layers, are explored and understood in this context [3]. The introduction of smart buildings is the most promising use of AI for urban strength arrangements. Many sensors, subsystems, and controllers are included in smart constructions, and their many sophisticated industrial listening, and management tools may be used for strength-conditioning [25–28]. Concurrently, greenhouse vapor diffusions are reduced as a result of these energy-use reductions. While automation in construction and strength administrative orders are useful in certain situations, their primary functions are alerting and listening. It is now extremely valuable to establish a centralized analytics hub, enabling us to derive deeper insights from the combined data; thanks to the blending various intelligent structures. AI is now firmly positioned as the main force behind the present-day evolution of humanity, thanks to its remarkable progress that has led to the development of big data, robotics, IoT, self-driving cars, and robotics.

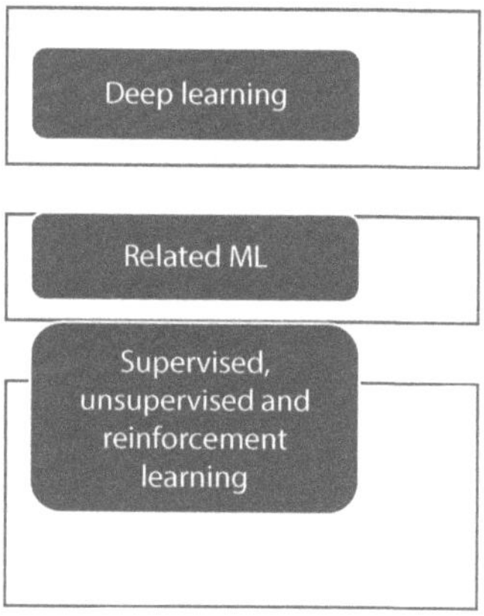

Figure 4.4 DL and related ML categories.

4.1.2 A Description of How Mobile Phones and Computers Facilitate the Completion of Tasks in Intelligent Buildings

Computers and mobile phones are vital parts of intelligent factories and buildings because they can automate, monitor, and control a wide range of systems remotely. A new era of innovation has been ushered in by these state-of-the-art technologies, which have completely transformed the construction sector. The industry has accepted the digital revolution, moving away from antiquated procedures and toward wise and sustainable ones. Building on the strengths of Construction 4.0—which stood out for its seamless automation and integration—Construction 5.0 is centered on sustainability, environmental awareness, and the circular economy. IoT is a wide variety of physically linked objects that can gather, share, and evaluate data on its own. These objects are outfitted with sensors, software, and connectivity. The Internet of Things (IoT) has numerous applications in the architecture as well as engineering fields, from intelligent structures and building sites to sustainable infrastructure projects. IoT devices improve smart building automation systems, making it possible to manage and control a variety of building functions with ease. Residents can customize the climate, lighting, and security in the building by interacting with its frameworks through the use of their phones or tablets. Beyond automating different development processes, AI has enhanced the preciseness and precision of task planning and execution. In the AEC industry, the use of AI-driven predictive diagnostics and machine learning algorithms has greatly improved risk management, assessments, and security procedures.

As a result, more astute and adaptable frameworks have been developed, addressing growing social needs and advancing goals for economically viable progress.

4.1.3 Intelligent Buildings as well as IoT

Through the automation and linking of multiple systems made possible by the Internet of Things, interconnected buildings enable maintenance teams to anticipate problems by reacting proactively to information gathered by sensors incorporated into lighting, elevator, and HVAC systems. AI and IoT integration also make it easier to create intelligent structures with adaptable features. To design buildings that are both occupant-focused and energy-efficient, sensors must monitor activity sequences, desired lighting, and temperature modifications.

4.1.4 Utilizing the Ubiquitous Internet of Things Plus the Global Web to Link Buildings

The wide range of applications promises to fundamentally alter the conception, execution, and upkeep of AEC projects. Infrastructure monitoring and smart buildings are two examples. Smart buildings have sensors that monitor environmental factors, energy consumption, and occupancy. These sensors allow the buildings to dynamically change settings to optimize energy efficiency and occupant comfort. Engineers can benefit greatly from IoT sensors that provide real-time monitoring of infrastructure and buildings' structural integrity. This information allows for preventive maintenance and reduces the likelihood of sudden events. By utilizing continuous tracking via Internet existing things sensors, engineers can reduce the likelihood of unplanned failures and make proactive maintenance decisions. This is because IoT sensors provide engineers with invaluable insights into the underlying condition of structures and infrastructure. The integration of artificial intelligence (AI) into structural analysis has improved simulation efficiency and accuracy, enabling engineers to design infrastructures that are both resistant and performance optimized. Energy management: Artificial intelligence (AI) systems analyze Internet of Things sensor data to maximize building energy consumption. Smart lighting controls, energy storage solutions, and HVAC systems reduce operating costs and advance sustainability goals by dynamically adapting to occupancy patterns, the climate, and energy pricing [6, 22].

4.2 The Advancement of Computational Intelligence within Smart Building Technology and Its Worldwide Consequences

The development of intelligent computing in smart building technological advances, which is driven by Standard building can be affordably converted into smart buildings through the use of sensor devices, big data analytics, computer networks, and machine learning (ML). There are definite benefits to implementing these technologies and making use of fresh innovations as shown in Figure 4.5. The applications will improve the organized smart functionalities and for a user friendly environment.

Additionally, alarm and fire prevention schemes involve industries hooked on to extremely complex system applications that incorporate techniques for detecting the fire besides tragedy on using essential components

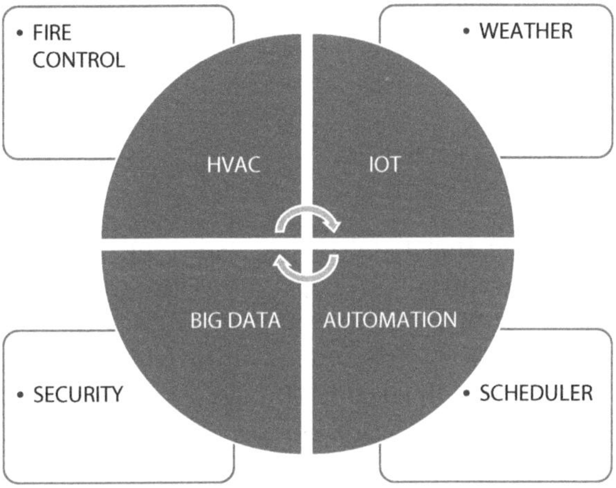

Figure 4.5 Systems for smart buildings driven by AI.

of the complete system. There are still many barriers to energy conservation in smart buildings, despite the fact that the idea of smart buildings can now be put into practice because of recent developments in machine learning algorithms [7].

4.2.1 Industrial 4.0 Along with IoT

With IoT integration, Industrial 4.0 revolutionizes manufacturing by tying systems and machines together for data-driven decision-making. Automation of processes, increased productivity, and smart building and factory integration are made possible by AI and ML technologies. The

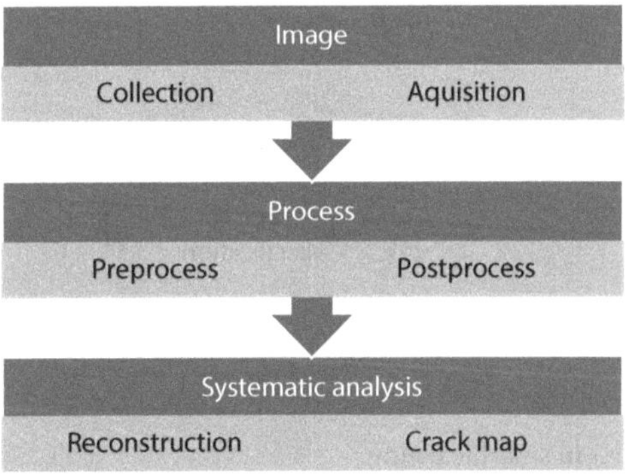

Figure 4.6 Smart buildings infrastructure.

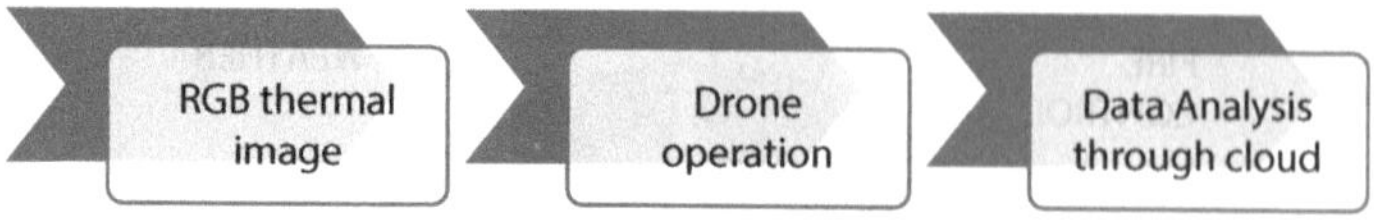

Figure 4.7 Smart buildings infrastructure.

digital transformation that is occurring makes predictive maintenance, real-time monitoring, and adaptive operations possible, and it is also making the industrial sector more innovative and competitive. Establishing a Facade Assessment System with Drones with AI-Powered 5G Technology Systems for Artificial intelligence (AI) is used in smart building maintenance to carry out effective façade checks. Construction management in the modern era integrates intelligent infrastructure, as shown by the construction sector's 4.0 framework (Figure 4.6 and Figure 4.7).

The aim is building an operational demonstration for UAV based building checkup scheme capable of taking quality definition, real-time video and picture capture. After authorization, footage or pictures are sent to the scanner for review which is vulnerable. The blended learning state involving the VR and 5G is shown in Figure 4.8.

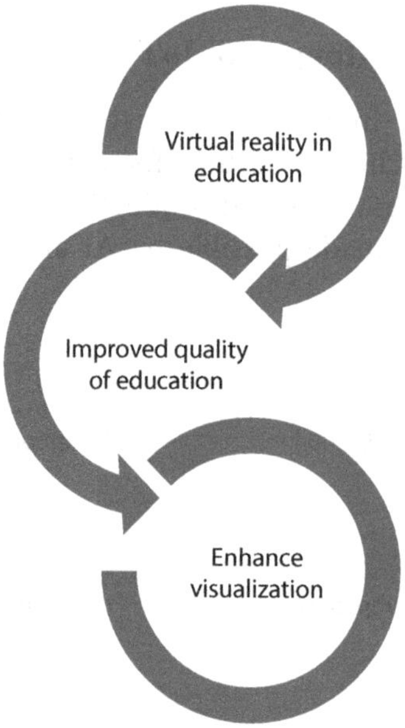

Figure 4.8 VR and 5G in smart learning.

In light of these particulars, this artefact inspects the present worldwide developments, popular 5G besides AI bids in keen building technologies, along with the studies, development, as well as testing being conducted in 5G labs. What we took for granted are eight keen outline dimensions. This idea is considered important enough by the engineering standard to be included in the suggested architecture for intelligent structures [1].

This data collection uses 255 sensors to record the steps required to prepare musical pieces in 51 different locations over the course of 4 floors of Sutardja Dai Auditorium at UC Berkeley. It could be applied to look for trends in a range's material belongings. Additionally, it can be used for second-hand experiments related to occasion-order tasks, sensor combination networks, or the Internet of Things (IoT). This dataset is suitable for two education tasks, one alone (assembling) and the other together guided (categorization and reversion).

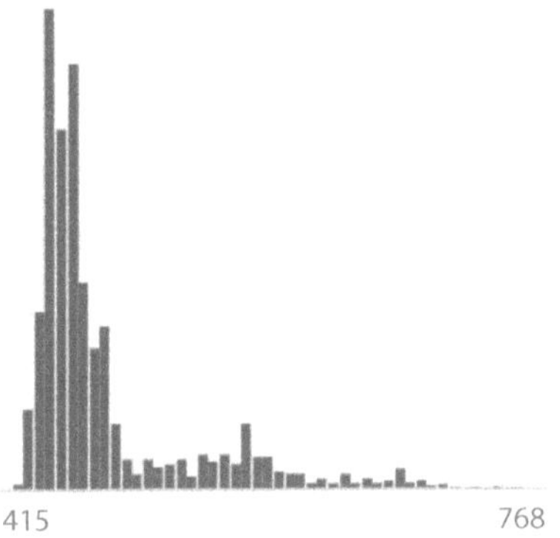

Valid	131k	100%
Mismatched	0	0%
Missing	0	0%
Mean	485	
Std. Deviation	58.1	
Quantiles	415	Min
	448	25%
	463	50%
	487	75%
	768	Max

Figure 4.9 CO_2.

Five different sorts of calculations are included in each range: CO_2 collection, which includes air moisture, humidity, luminosity, and PIR motion sensors data. These calculations are made over the course of a single, concluding period that runs from Friday afternoon, August 23, 2013, to a Saturday August 31, 2013. Ten seconds are spent sampling the PIR motion sensor, and five seconds are spent sampling the staying sensors. The timestamps and the actual sensor readings are stored in each file, both in Unix Epoch Time. The soulless color associated with blood sensors (PIR sensor) is a photoelectric sensor that detects the proximity of objects in an allure visual field by measuring the shade that resembles such infrared light scattering. One can see that the range is busy because about 6% of the total PIR dossier

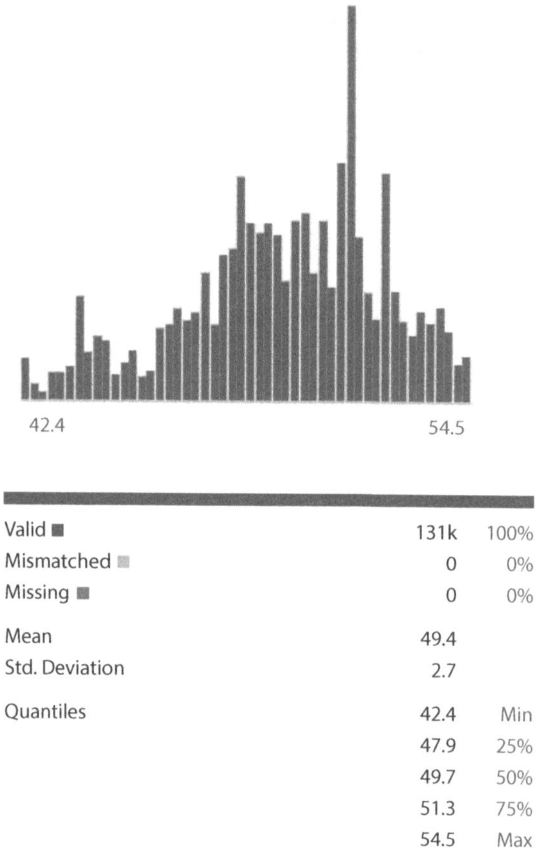

Figure 4.10 Humidity.

contains nothing at all. The extra 94% of the PIR dossier shows an empty range and is nothing. Figures 4.9 to 4.13 represents CO_2, humidity, light, PIR and temperature respectively.

4.2.2 An Exploration of the Web of Things and Its Role in Making 4.0

The Internet of Things' capabilities are expanded by the Web of Things (WoT), which standardizes device communication and interoperability. Making 4.0 data exchange and automation are enhanced by cyberattacks will undoubtedly become more frequent due to 5G connections' faster speed. Hackers will find it simpler to target a greater number of internet-connected devices due to the unstable connections between devices.

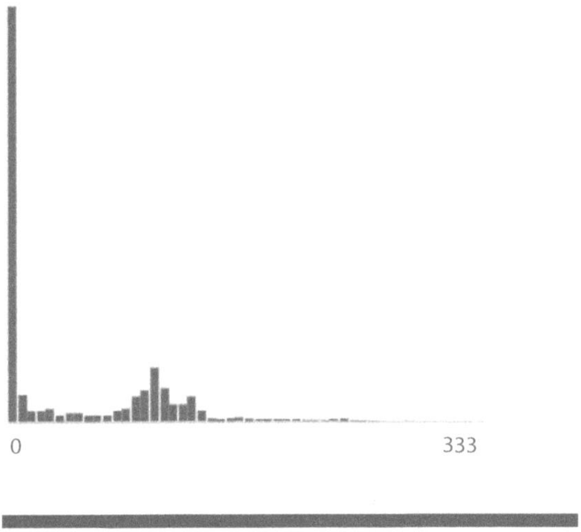

Valid	131k	100%
Mismatched	0	0%
Missing	0	0%
Mean	53.7	
Std. Deviation	62.4	
Quantiles	0	Min
	4	25%
	9	50%
	103	75%
	333	Max

Figure 4.11 Light.

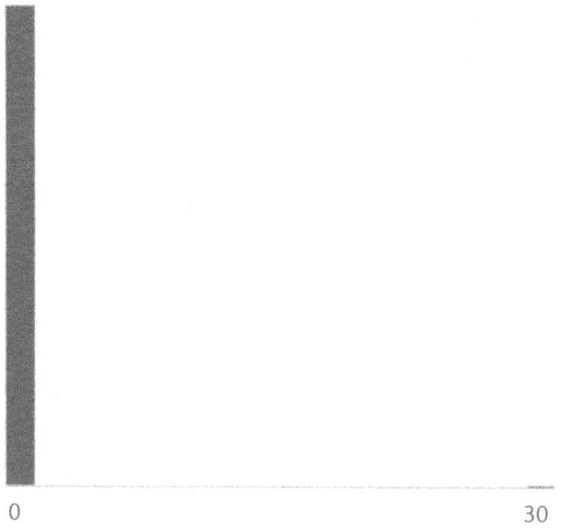

Valid ■	72.2k	100%
Mismatched ■	0	0%
Missing ■	0	0%
Mean	0.46	
Std. Deviation	3.3	
Quantiles	0	Min
	0	25%
	0	50%
	0	75%
	30	Max

Figure 4.12 PIR.

With 5G, there will likely be more IoT device availability, but there will also probably be more risk. Management becomes more difficult as the number of Internet of Things gadgets increases and poses more security risks. Hackers may be able to access and extract data, including personal information, from a device connected to a 5G network far more quickly than they could in the past [8].

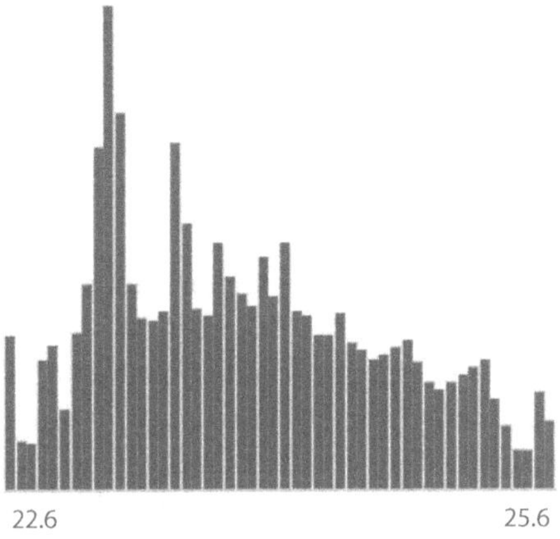

Valid ■	131k	100%
Mismatched ■	0	0%
Missing ■	0	0%
Mean	23.9	
Std. Deviation	0.75	
Quantiles	22.6	Min
	23.3	25%
	23.8	50%
	24.5	75%
	25.6	Max

Figure 4.13 Temperature.

4.3 An Examination on ML, DL and AI Algorithms Used for Engineering and Construction

In terms of academics' and businesses' perceptions of the possible benefits of 5G technology, the construction sector, like other sectors, has demonstrated itself to be more resilient in its application of the technology during the past two years. Take the manufacturing and sales of smart buildings by IBM and Intel, which demonstrate the viability and competitiveness of 5G [9].

The investigations inspect numerous representations based on AI related methodologies which have accelerated the rebound on building 4.0 including corresponding effects on risk management, project scheduling, and design optimization. The creation of resilient, accessible, and socially sound sustainable infrastructure would also be made possible by endowed AI solutions used within the structures of Construction 5.0 as well as Society 5.0 [10].

4.3.1 Utilization in Intelligent Structures

4G The most typical data transfer rate for the previous generation of technology is a download speed of no more than 100 M bit/s. However, as 5G advances, it will be feasible to use more intelligent, sophisticated equipment. A 5G network's primary function is to make it simple for users to communicate with one another. To ensure that the proper control for each situation is enforced, 5G can also be changed quickly in real-time. 5th Generation may be implemented quickly in several industries to provide quick data [11].

The construction phase is inherently intricate, requiring a large number of steps, skilled labor, and intricate supply chains. Processes are optimized by big data electronics by offering legally enforceable insights derived from multiple datasets. Distribution of resources, a significant challenge, is enhanced by Big Data analytics assessing historical and present project dossiers, ensuring effective material and labor customization. Logical analysis predictive science, driven by big data, predict bottlenecks, permit enthusiastic problem solving, timeline upkeep, and expense growth. In addition, building generates a lot of waste. Smart construction sites are made possible by big data and Internet of Things (IoT) strategies. A certain-opportunity document on habit, tear and damage, and environmental environments is collected by embedded sensors found in explanation supplies and fabrics. By reducing material usage and energy use, this dossier analysis reduces waste. For instance, sensors track humidity and temperature to ensure that the right conditions are met for things like factual information and fewer errors.

4.3.2 A Few Examples of the Numerous Uses in Smart Buildings are Automation, Material Efficiency, Off-Site Production, Designing Buildings, and the Combination of Big Data

In the past two years, 5G technology gained significant popularity in the construction industry, and academics and entrepreneurs have been exploring the potential benefits of 5G technology. Additionally, some companies, like IBM and Intel, have developed and sold smart buildings, representing one of the competitive advantages of 5G and its promising future [12].

Adopted by industrial automatic control systems, the data transmission technology is incredibly dependable. Hubs, switches, and Ethernet are some well-known, dependable wired communication technologies that are in widespread use. Channel coding is the technique employed by 5 G networks for data validation. Even if data weren't transmitted at all or were transmitted incorrectly, 5 G technologies can detect this information and possibly even self-correct [1].

Building intelligent, strong, and occupant-responsive structures is now possible; thanks to IoT science and architecture. Sensors integrated into various building schemes, including those for safety, Data on occupancy patterns, physical environment, and building usage are continuously gathered by the lighting and air conditioning, ventilation, and heating systems. Then, with this information, expenses are reduced, energy efficiency is increased, and occupant comfort is raised. For instance, energy-saving automated lighting may dim or consequently off lights in vacant spaces, and occupancy-based smart thermostats can change the temperature. The construction, architecture, and engineering industry's creative and building processes undergo a transformation when the IoT is integrated with supplementary AR along with VR technologies.

Creators besides architects can captivate us with their building and site models. These models are powered by real-time data from IoT sensors, which allow clients and architects see how their building will communicate with its surroundings. For example, these data allow architects to plan their buildings with knowledge of how different parts of the structure will receive natural light during the day.

As a result of AR and VR technologies, stakeholders are more cooperative and are able to virtually complete rehearsal houses before they are built, which improves the accuracy and skill of design modifications and approvals. The construction phase is inherently intricate, requiring a large number of steps, skilled labor, and intricate supply chains. Processes are optimized by big data electronics by offering legally enforceable insights derived from multiple datasets. Distribution of resources, a significant challenge, is enhanced by large information analysis evaluating past in addition to present scheme dossiers, safeguarding effective component customization. Logical analysis prognostic science, driven through large information, predict holdups, permit enthusiastic problem solving, timeline upkeep, and expense growth. In addition, building generates a lot of waste. Smart construction sites are made possible by large data in addition to IoT strategies. A certain-opportunity document on habit, tear and damage, and environmental environments is collected by embedded sensors found in explanation supplies and fabrics. By reducing material usage and energy use, this dossier analysis reduces waste. For instance, sensors track humidity and temperature to ensure that the right conditions are met for things like factual information and fewer errors [5].

4.3.3 Detectors, and Computational AI Enabling Intelligent Management and Energy Efficiency

The only fire alarm systems that can precisely pinpoint the offset location of a fire are ultimate advance fire control systems. Apps, the internet, and devices with wireless connectivity can all aid in the prevention of fires in smart construction. Temperature sensors that have the ability to trigger cigarette alarms and incite bureaucracy when required urgently in situation which pointedly recover and protect in smart constructions. Highly sophisticated computing networks that include orders for crisis ideas and fire discovery manage the flow of new fire supervision and alarm orders [13, 14, 24].

A useful IoT-based smart house was suggested for informed strength-conditional [15]. In this case, motion detection in the surveillance camcorder may be used to trigger or deactivate the lights, heating, and cooling system when a resident leaves or enters the house. Light and HVAC management strategies may also be used in conjunction with the camcorder. To perform monitoring from the remote power specifically for birthplaces and buildings, a smart strength administration model that is aware of power use in real-time through netting and traveling devices has been imported [16].

By increasing the pace of strength savings, facilitating on-scene generation, identifying and recognizing movement transgressions, controlling and ensuring sustained strength savings, AI can assist in overcoming the difficulties in developing strength-efficient homes [17].

LiDAR sensors use light rays to calculate distance and create accurate three-dimensional (3D) models of their surroundings. LiDAR sensor integration with building appliances and AEC busses enhances mapping and navigation [18].

4.4 Conclusion

Machine learning, the Internet of Things, and artificial intelligence are reshaping the AEC industry to become increasingly data-driven, automated, and intelligent manufacturing.

The development and widespread application of new science has made it possible for fifth-generation electronics to build more functional cities, towns, and constructions. The combination of machine learning (ML) and artificial intelligence (AI) techniques has increased the standard important, which includes rule-distinguishing language acquisition, as there is concern that these approaches may become obsolete in smart downtowns employing 5G science.

Additionally, the study underscored how crucial AI models and methodologies are to the advancement of AEC manufacturing. An array of mechanical construction techniques, as well as the precision and consistency of project planning and execution, have all benefited from artificial intelligence. The construction industry has advanced significantly in meeting its obligations for risk management, quality control, and security by utilizing AI-driven forecasting information along with predictive machine learning algorithms. As a result, to meet the evolving demands of society and facilitate reasonable incident objectives, the foundation has developed into a more sophisticated and flexible entity.

4.5 Future Advances in Urban Energy Efficiency and Smart Building Technologies

The major advantages of innovative city electronics are available to large capitals. The idea of a creative city is gaining popularity all over the world, which has increased interest in the topic of affordable downtown planning and construction. The utilization of renewable energy solutions is expected to ensure the ongoing sustainability of regional endeavors and control the limited supply of energy that is not renewable. Because of this, the incident involving a reserved and technological method revealed AI and 5G as additional research areas that are susceptible to incidents in the future.

Additionally, the study looked into the innovative uses of blockchain, when AI and IoT are combined to produce AEC goods, transaction reliability is increased and partner trust is fostered. Using blockchain technology into creative endeavors has strengthened accountability, freedom, and transparency. This has expedited rational cooperation amongst project shareholders, simplified supply chain management, and minimized dishonest activities. As a result, it has created an environment within the AEC subdivision that values frequent and moral behavior. The adaptation of these technical advancements in tandem with the goals for sustainable development is a crucial point emphasized in this research.

References

1. Mazhar, T., *et al.*, The role of ML, AI and 5G technology in smart energy and smart building management. *Electronics*, 11, 23, 3960, 2022.
2. Baduge, S.K., *et al.*, Artificial intelligence and smart vision for building and construction 4.0: Machine and deep learning methods and applications. *Autom. Constr.*, 141, 1044405, 2022.
3. Güçlüer, K., *et al.*, A comparative investigation using machine learning methods for concrete compressive strength estimation. *Mater. Today Commun.*, 27, 1022785, 2021.
4. Farzaneh, H., *et al.*, Artificial intelligence evolution in smart buildings for energy efficiency. *Appl. Sci.*, 11, 2, 763, 2021.
5. Rane, N., Integrating leading-edge artificial intelligence (AI), internet of things (IOT), and big data technologies for smart and sustainable architecture, engineering and construction (AEC) industry: Challenges and future directions. Engineering and Construction (AEC) Industry: Challenges and Future Directions, September 24, 2023.
6. Rane, N., Choudhary, S., Rane, J., Artificial Intelligence (AI) and Internet of Things (IoT)-based sensors for monitoring and controlling in architecture, engineering, and construction: applications, challenges, and opportunities. 4642197, 1–22, 2023, Available at SSRN 4642197.
7. Shah, S.F.A., *et al.*, The role of machine learning and the internet of things in smart buildings for energy efficiency. *Appl. Sci.*, 12, 15, 7882, 2022.
8. O'Dwyer, E., Pan, I., Acha, S., Shah, N., Smart energy systems for sustainable smart cities: Current developments, trends and future directions. *Appl. Energy*, *237*, 581–597, 2019.
9. Jia, M., *et al.*, Adopting Internet of Things for the development of smart buildings: A review of enabling technologies and applications. *Autom. Constr.*, 101, 111–1265, 2019.
10. Blanco, J.L., *et al.*, Artificial intelligence: Construction technology's next frontier. *Build. Econ.*, Sep 2018, 7–13, 2018.
11. Rao, S.K. and Prasad, R., Impact of 5G technologies on smart city implementation. *Wireless Pers. Commun.*, 100, 161–176, 2018.
12. Magruk, A., The most important aspects of uncertainty in the Internet of Things field–context of smart buildings. *Procedia Eng.*, 122, 220–227, 2015.
13. Barmpoutis, P., *et al.*, A review on early forest fire detection systems using optical remote sensing. *Sensors*, 20, 22, 6442, 2020.
14. Wahab, F., *et al.*, Design and implementation of real-time object detection system based on single-shoot detector and OpenCV. *Front. Psychol.*, 13, 10396455, 2022.
15. Salman, L., Salman, S., Jahangirian, S., Abraham, M., German, F., Blair, C., Krenz, P., Energy efficient IoT-based smart home, in: *Proceedings of the 2016 IEEE 3rd World Forum on Internet of Things (WF-IoT)*, Reston, VA, USA, pp. 526–529, 12–14 December 2016.

16. Kim, W.H., Lee, S., Hwang, J., Real-time energy monitoring and controlling system based on Zigbee sensor networks. *Procedia Comput. Sci.*, 5, 794–797, 2011.
17. GrueneichDian, M., The next level of energy efficiency: the five challenges ahead. *Electr. J.*, 28, 7, 44–56, 2015.
18. Razali, M.I., *et al.*, Quality Assessment of 3D Point Clouds on the Different Surface Materials Generated from iPhone LiDAR Sensor. *Int. J. Geoinformatics*, 18, 4, 51–58, 2022.
19. Kiran, C., *et al.*, Cyber Physical System Centred Protective Laboratory for Industries. *International Conference on Microelectronics, Electromagnetics and Telecommunication*, Springer Nature Singapore, Singapore, 2023.
20. Tilahun, E., *et al.*, Culture Reflecting Artistic Fashion Design using Deep Learning and Assisting Custom Algorithm. *2023 International Conference on New Frontiers in Communication, Automation, Management and Security (ICCAMS)*, 1, IEEE, 2023.
21. Menon, S., *et al.*, Insight Importance of Supply Chain Management of Vaccines in India During Covid Pandemic. *2023 International Conference on New Frontiers in Communication, Automation, Management and Security (ICCAMS)*, 1, IEEE, 2023.
22. Ghantasala, G.P., Hung, B.T., Chakrabarti, P., Pellakuri, V., Artificial intelligence based machine learning algorithm for prediction of cancer in female anatomy. *Multimed. Tools Appl.*, 25, 1–27, 2024.
23. Pushpa Rani, K., Vidyullatha, P., Srinivas Rao, K., An optimized topic modeling question answering system for web-based questions. *Multimed. Tools Appl.*, 83, 1–19, 2024.
24. Vidyullatha, P., Prapulla, S.T., Saran, A.P., Ramya, P., Machine Vision based Object Detection using Deep Learning Techniques, in: *2023 3rd International Conference on Smart Data Intelligence (ICSMDI)*, IEEE, pp. 466–470, 2023, March.
25. Ramana, T.V., Ghantasala, G.S., Sathiyaraj, R., Khan, M. (Eds.), *Artificial Intelligence and Machine Learning for Smart Community: Concepts and Applications*, CRC Press, 2024.
26. Parameswaran, T., Reddy, Y.P., Nagaveni, V., Sathiyaraj, R., Era of Computational Big Data Analytics and IoT Techniques in Smart City Applications, in: *IoT and Big Data Analytics for Smart Cities*, pp. 1–22, 2022.
27. Sathiyaraj, R., Bharathi, A., Khan, S., Kiren, T., Khan, I.U., Fayaz, M., A genetic predictive model approach for smart traffic prediction and congestion avoidance for urban transportation. *Wireless Commun. Mobile Comput.*, *2022*, 1, 5938411, 2022.
28. Reddy, Y.P., Parameswaran, T., Sathiyaraj, R., A smart environment monitoring framework using big data and IoT, in: *2021 IEEE Mysore Sub Section International Conference (MysuruCon)*, pp. 399–404, IEEE, 2021, October.

5

Applications of Artificial Intelligence and Machine Learning in Industry 4.0

Tina Babu[1*], Rekha R. Nair[1] and Kishore S.[2]

[1]Department of Computer Science and Engineering, Alliance College of Engineering and Design Alliance University, Bengaluru, India
[2]Department of Computer Applications, Nitte Institute of Professional Education, Nitte University, Mangalore, India

Abstract
Industry 4.0, sometimes referred to as the fourth industrial revolution, has brought about a major transformation in the manufacturing processes through the use of smart technologies for innovation, including artificial intelligence, machine learning, and the internet of things. This chapter covers various aspects of using AI and ML in managing complex and reformed operations with emphasis on smart manufacturing, prediction in maintenance, supply chain, quality, robotics and automation, data analytics, cyber-security, human centric operations and energy efficiency as well as sustainable industry 4.0. The chapter also looks at the application of these technologies in synergy where the convergence of the technologies leads to predictive maintenance, proper planning of production, identification of flaws and moreover the formulation of intelligent decision support systems. The chapter also explores future developments and innovation areas that can apprehend AI and ML in AM, digital twin, and cyber-security. In addition, it stresses the imperative to adopt the sustainable principles in Industry 4. For its part, the IT industry considers zero value parts of frameworks, such as energy efficiency, renewable energy integration, and circular economy principles. In conclusion, this chapter seems to offer valuable pieces of knowledge about the use of AI and ML in industry, potential changes in its functions, increased efficiency, and environmentally friendly endeavors within the paradigm of Industry 4.0.

Keywords: Industry 4.0, artificial intelligence, machine learning, smart manufacturing, predictive maintenance, sustainable practices

**Corresponding author*: tinababup@gmail.com

M. Thirunavukkarasan, S. A. Sahaaya Arul Mary, Sathiyaraj. R, G. S. Pradeep Ghantasala and Mudassir Khan (eds.) Artificial Intelligence and Machine Learning for Industry 4.0, (107–144)

5.1 Introduction

The fourth revolution in industry, known as Industry 4.0, is a cyber-physical system with intelligent full automation at its heart. AI and ML are especially well-situated to take charge of the process. Despite being pioneers in this regard, they have the power to transform and will definitely do so. AI awards higher cognitive functions of sight, logic, learning, and decision support to apparatuses to fully revolutionize industrial processes. AI with related computer vision systems can scan products or observing operations with enhanced accuracy and efficiency. AI embedded predictive analytics can predict demand, determine the right time to produce goods, and avoid expensive breakdown of equipment [1]. AI even powers intelligent robotics systems combining perception, decision-making, and control.

Advantaged with this adaptive intelligence, manufacturing operations will drive smarter process control, more dynamic scheduling, and intelligent maintenance, among much more. These technologies also enable remarkable developments such as lights out flexible manufacturing, mass customization, self-optimizing supply chain logistics and, ultimately, the self-designing and self-constructing products of our imaginations. They may be as boundless as our creativity and nerve in embracing these powerful technologies. This chapter examines how AI and ML are currently affecting industrial production and projects how important a role they will play in the next several decades [2]. Those who effectively leverage these innovations will lead the revolution powered by Industry 4.0. They may be as boundless as our creativity and nerve in embracing these powerful technologies. This chapter explores the current impact of AI and ML in industrial manufacturing, and it provides a prognostication of their pivotal role in the coming decades. Those who effectively leverage these innovations will lead the revolution powered by Industry 4.0.

5.1.1 Overview of Industry 4.0

The Fourth Industrial Revolution, or Industry 4.0, is a profound shift that is altering business and industry as we know it. It's like the rebirth of digitalization, transforming our factories and production lines into something completely different. Imagine if our traditional workplaces would transform and become smart digital spaces. There was a time when mechanical precision was important on the factory assembly line. They rely on the function and characteristic that it is a dynamic, connected ecosystem which makes use of the myriad opportunities presented by having the capacity to adapt to the technological possibilities of change [1]. These are not just factories, but also known as water sources of new ideas and products, connected to the most advanced, cutting-edge digital solutions that define business pressure in a world defined by competition [3].

Consider what this means to you; it is equivalent to growing from a mere use of a phone to that of a smart phone! Strengthening its position in digitization with the help of such technologies as the Internet of Things (IoT), automation, and artificial intelligence (AI). Thus, it could be regarded as a significant component of Industry 4.0. This is an outstanding revolution of machines talking to each other, fast data acquisition, and analysis of flight data and even the aspect of making decisions [4].

Industry 4.0 Key Strategies for People's Quest for Smart, Fast and Efficient Business Development. By integrating Industry 4.0, principles, businesses can adapt to the business changes, enhance timely decision making with the real time information, and sustain in the modern cut throat global business environment. Imagine a factory where machines have the capacity to predict maintenance requirements before they happen by use of AI-powered predictive analytics [5]. Alternately, conceive a tightly regulated assembly line where each part communicates seamlessly with the internet, fostering smooth communication and synchronization throughout several manufacturing stages. Industry 4.0 promises that it goes beyond production only to build an environment characterized by better quality, faster pace, and more intelligence, as shown in Figure 5.1 [6].

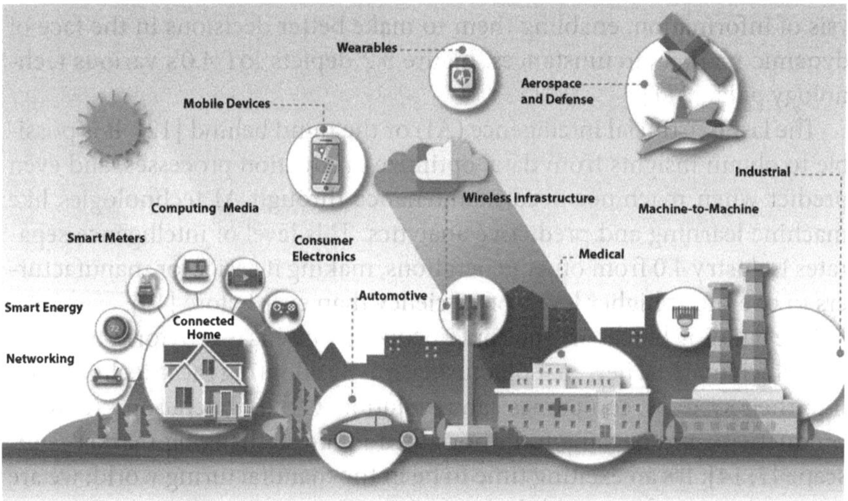

Figure 5.1 Various applications of IoT [6].

Industry 4.0 is more than just a buzzword; it is a transformative way of thinking about industry and manufacturing [7, 8]. It is about adopting technology for innovation, optimizing production processes, and eventually having a better and more competitive world for businesses globally. Industry 4.0, therefore, provides an exciting opportunity to re-invent your business regardless of whether you are a small-scale manufacturer or a multi-national corporation in the modern digital era.

5.1.2 Key Components and Technologies

Some of the key ingredients and technologies defining Industry 4.0 define its success. First of all, there are cyber-physical systems that can in some ways be considered as control centers [2]. These systems incorporate both hardware tools and software to monitor and manage production line and process in real time manner [8, 9]. For example, it will be possible to closely observe machine productivity on the manufacturing floor or make some changes to a production plan within a few mouse-clicks. Secondly, the IoT system is like the nervous system that helps facilitate Industry 4.0. Thus, the IoT enables the collection of data from within production ecosystem; thus, the exchange between connected devices and sensors becomes applicable. This connectivity opens up several avenues for, for instance, monitoring stock, or improving supply chain processes [10].

Industry 4.0 rests on cloud computing, which provides storage and processing capabilities for handling immense amounts of data from intelligent factories. The cloud facilitates manufacturers' real-time access to and analysis of information, enabling them to make better decisions in the face of dynamic market circumstances. Figure 5.2 depicts IoT 4.0's various technology pillars [11].

The last is artificial intelligence (AI) or the mind behind [12]. It is possible to obtain insights from data, optimize production processes, and even predict when machines need maintenance through AI technologies like machine learning and predictive analytics. This level of intelligence separates Industry 4.0 from other generations, making it easier for manufacturers to operate at higher levels of efficiency than ever before [13].

The building blocks are thus put up together in this way to form Industry 4.0, which marks a new manufacturing era. By adopting these technologies into their systems, companies can revolutionize their operations, increase productivity and become future-oriented in a fast-changing market landscape [7, 14]. It's an exciting time to be in the manufacturing world; we are moving into the future with Industry 4.0.

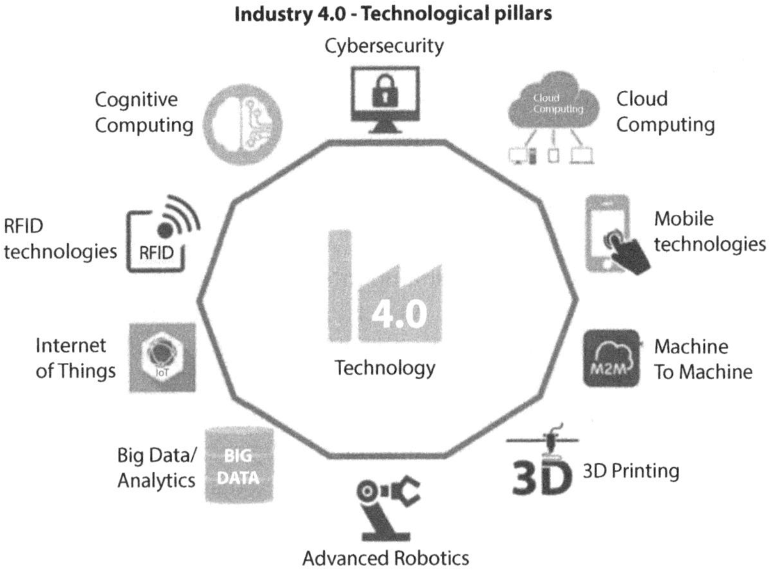

Figure 5.2 Various technological components of IoT 4.0 [11].

5.2 Smart Manufacturing and Predictive Maintenance

Smart manufacturing corresponds to a magician in your factory, which involves using cool super technology to run things smoothly [15]. Imagine if machines could talk to other machines, collect data and then make decisions on their own is like they have their own minds. Predictive Maintenance: It works like a seer who can predict what will happen to our machines in the future. With sophisticated sensors and smart devices, we can monitor our equipment and know when something may go wrong before it happens. It's as if we have a crystal ball that shows us when exactly we should fix them so that they do not break down without warning.

Therefore, fusing smart manufacturing with predictive maintenance in IoT 4.0 equates to fielding the ultimate dream team for your factory. They collaborate with the aim of ensuring everything goes well, averting accidents even before they occur, and remaining ahead of others always [16]. In short, it combines technology (i.e., science) and enchantment (i.e., magic), resulting in improved lives through improved factories – the best of both worlds.

5.2.1 Integration of AI/ML in Manufacturing Process

If we integrate AI and ML into the manufacturing process, it is like having a "super-smart assistant" who can tell exactly what needs to be done to optimize production. These technologies bring intelligence to another level on the factory floor, making operations smoother, more efficient, and cost-effective [17, 18]. What if machines could learn from past experiences and adjust their behavior accordingly? That is precisely what we get with AI and ML! The systems can process vast amounts of data instantly, while humans may not spot patterns or trends. As per Figure 5.3, this means fewer mistakes, shorter times of production, and better-quality products [19].

However, it's not just about crunching numbers – AI and ML also enable predictive maintenance by anticipating when equipment might fail before they do. This method saves time and money because it does not require much time. There is also good management. Actually, machine learning (ML) and artificial intelligence (AI) techniques are able to identify product flaws and problems, guaranteeing that only appropriate products are put through the production process [15]. Thus, incorporating machine learning and artificial intelligence into the production process will revolutionize the industry. Delivering quality work is like having a team of experts

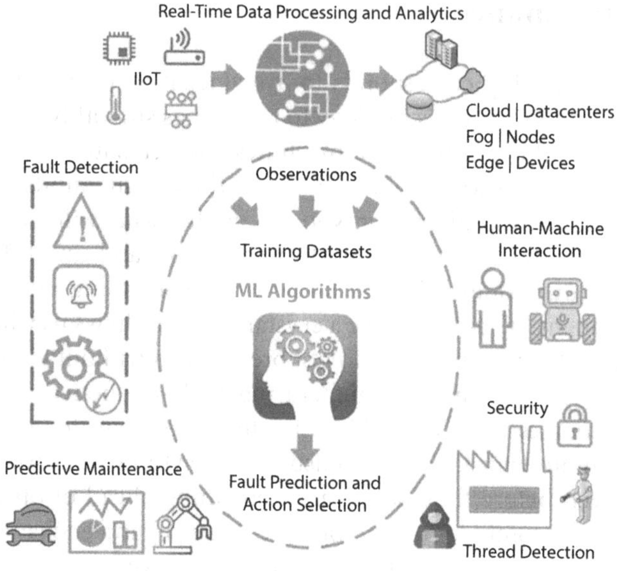

Figure 5.3 Various AI/ML integration into the manufacturing process [19].

to identify areas for improvement and drive innovation. This technology offers us endless opportunities, and the future of manufacturing has never been brighter.

5.2.2 Predictive Maintenance Strategies

Intelligent factory monitoring systems are made possible by AI and ML. Imagine a bustling company with many machines, each with its own function. Instead of waiting for failure, artificial intelligence and machine learning are stepping in like superheroes to predict and prevent problems [20]. Thanks to this technology, we can predict when equipment will need maintenance before it breaks down. They analyze sensor and machine data for patterns and inconsistencies to help us understand what repairs may be necessary in the future. We have experts mining the evidence to predict when the machine will need maintenance [19].

But they have many responsibilities beyond this. Additionally, AI and machine learning help us improve maintenance times, reducing the time and resources spent on necessary repairs. They crunch the numbers and determine the best time to perform maintenance tasks, maximizing efficiency and minimizing production disruptions. Additionally, our predictive management strategies are becoming more sophisticated with artificial intelligence and machine learning support. It means that they keep on modifying their approaches based on outcomes of previous incidents which is kind of like fine-tuning a computer program to make it more accurate [75].

Whether it is with regards to identifying that bearings are tired before failure or when seeking to fine tune for increased efficiency, then it is ML and AI that are propelling the success of intelligent design in the aspect of predictive maintenance. It observes the ordinary workers of the factory, making sure that everything is in order, novices who prevent something undesirable from happening.

5.3 Supply Chain Optimization

Integrated logistics management in IoT 4.0 refers to the leverage of Internet of Things (IoT) technologies for enhancing and enhancing products. This is like the supply chain that has been digitalized and where IoT devices, sensors and connections are tools of this change [1]. All these technologies acquire real-time data at various supply chain points so that organizations can obtain the right information they require to fix inefficiencies.

For instance, through installing sensors on the products, packaging as well as vehicles, firms acquire a rich stream of information about the product's movements and event from the devices [21]. This continuous data allows them to identify inefficiencies, predict potential outages, and take critical steps to improve performance.

5.3.1 AI/ML for Supply Chain Management

Data management is evolving as a result of AI and ML, which make new techniques possible. Strategies to increase efficiency, improve processes, and risk management are shown in Figure 5.4 [22]. Let's see how AI/machine learning applications are changing many aspects of supply chain management:

- Predicting Demand: By processing historical sales data, tracking business models, and combining factors, AI and machine learning algorithms are better at predicting future needs [23]. This means making better product-level decisions, reducing disruptions, and investing less in bulk products.
- Keeping Inventory in Check: AI-powered systems monitor inventory levels, identify demand patterns, and order more products when necessary. Machine learning algorithms fine-tune the art of restocking, ensuring shelves are stocked

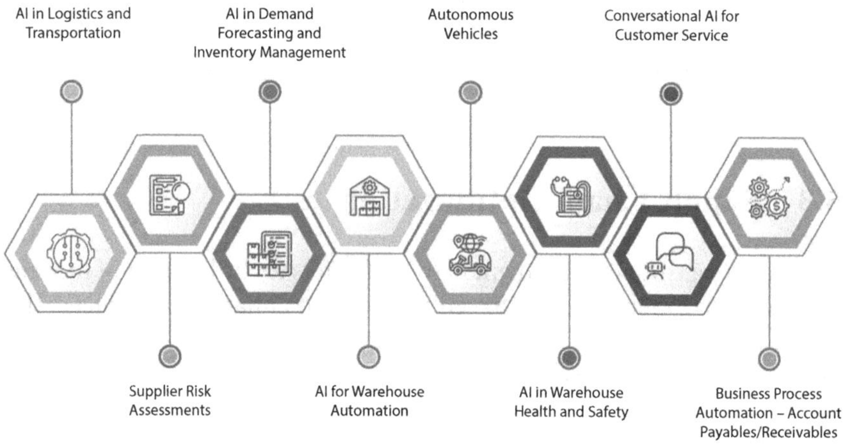

Figure 5.4 Various supply chain management uses of AI and ML [22].

enough to meet demand but not cluttered with unnecessary products.

- Navigating Logistics: Artificial intelligence algorithms, such as GPS for trucks, calculate the most suitable fuel. Good performance, schedule the delivery at the right time, and ensure the trucks are suitable. Machine learning-based analytics predict potential problems and instantly resend shipments to ensure packages arrive on time and within budget.
- Mastering Warehousing: AI warehouse systems control inventory, identification, packaging, and delivery. Machine learning algorithms optimize layout and storage and speed up the shipping process.
- Strengthening Supplier Bonds: AI tools closely monitor product performance, looking for problems or signs of improvement. ML algorithms evaluate reliability, track shipments, and select the best suppliers to ensure the efficient operation of the supply chain [24].
- Quality Assurance and Upkeep: AI/ML solution to track damaged or quality products. Business tools. They can detect defects when they occur and predict when machines need to be adjusted, reducing downtime and increasing efficiency.
- Shedding Light on the Supply Chain: The support from the AI solutions enables real-time value-added detail from the point of sale, through the warehouse and to delivery. To remedy this, there are issues where machine learning algorithms can search large data sets, find issues, make tasks easier, and improve items.

Using AI and machine learning, businesses can optimize processes, production, and logistics and improve security measures. Be ahead in the game in the constantly changing business environment we face today.

5.3.2 Optimizing Logistics and Inventory

Thus, AI and ML have contributed to a new age of business chain modernization and optimization as they have revolutionized the logistics and product management processes [23]. Contemporary automatons provide a number of answers to numerous challenges characteristic to contemporary items and equipment. Determining the paths that products to be delivered will follow is one of the main uses of ML and AI in logistics. Applying artificial intelligence, it is possible to create vehicles of the highest quality using the data of previous traffic, analysis of the traffic flow, and the impact of the climate [25]. This helps in cutting the expenses on fuel while at the same time catering for delivery and satisfying the customers. In addition, the accurate demand should be forecasted with the help of artificial intelligence to manage stock effectively. Machine learning models pay attention to the data of previous sales movements, business strategies, and many factors that ultimately help to forecast future demands promptly and correctly. It restricts spending on inventories and their related costs at the same time as it helps companies to have better control over inventory and avoid stock-outs.

Another revolution in the shipping and inventory management is the maintenance forecasting through Artificial Intelligence. Real-time monitoring of equipment and tools as well as analyzing sensor data machine learning algorithm makes it easier for persons to predict failure that may occur on the equipment thus leading to prevention of maintenance and reduction of on equipment downtime. Thus, it guarantees that the field of logistics is linked with no issues emerging in it. Furthermore, there ought to be the use of an artificial intelligence enabled warehouse management system also for inventory and returns. Employing machine learning techniques, demand history images, storage capability, and inventory status data are utilized to find the most suitable storage place for the product. This cuts down the time of selecting and packaging, help order correctly, and consequently make the best out of household products.

However, it is noteworthy that AI and ML are beneficial more and in terms of product delivery and optimization; costs are noticeably lower and productivity is increased alongside customer satisfaction. These technologies depict strategies through which organizations can have control on how they can fasten or strategize to cope with the current business world.

5.4 Quality Control and Defect Detection

In IoT 4.0, ensuring a good product is like sending a careful inspection team to the production floor but doing it with a high-tech approach. Image sensors, actuators, and other IoT devices are scattered throughout the production line, carefully monitoring everything from temperature and humidity to pressure and vibration [26]. Like a little detective on duty, he constantly feeds production-related information to the central brain.

Defect testing, however, focuses on detecting and correcting defects or deficiencies in products or processes before they cause defects. IoT-enabled defect inspection systems use sensors, cameras, and imaging technology to detect product defects, specification deviations, or other quality issues. For example, vision systems can take pictures of an object and examine and check it for any sort of defects that can be in form of scratches, cracks, blemishes among others. Likewise, acoustic sensors can sense that there are flaws that would suggest that a machine or equipment is faulty or is malfunctioning.

5.4.1 AI/ML for Quality Assurance

ML and AI are used to improve standard applications in the context of the IoT, which is the linking of physical things to the Internet system 4.0. In questions of how different technologies are transforming business industry for the IoT connected world, it is crucial to mention the shift from predictive maintenance to error detection, these technologies are revolutionizing how quality and reliability of products is ensured [27].

Security is well defined in context with IoT 4. One of the most notable examples AI and ML in practice, it is ranked at 0. Since, real-time data can be received from the various sensors installed in systems or equipment, intelligent algorithms present the possibility of predicting equipment which require repairs and break-downs. This approach also minimizes time and in turn, grants business-time and money by avoiding downtimes [28]. Also, defect detection is facilitated through artificial intelligence and machine learning. These systems employ the abilities of machine learning which enables the systems to analyze images and sensor data to identify production defects. From inspecting a batch of parts in a supermarket for scratches to checking for variations from the set standards, these intelligent machines are of help to companies aiming to adhere to high standards besides minimizing on wastage [87, 88].

Effective management, backed by intelligent systems, plays a crucial role in enabling high-level monitoring and real-time analysis of production processes. They are always pre-processing data collected from IoT sensors and identifying inadequacies or problems in the process. They can then personally suggest immediate corrective measures to improve product quality. Also, these intelligent systems are the building blocks of complex advanced analytics, since they assimilate data from various inputs and analyze them for patterns. By doing this, they can get to the bottom of issues, enabling organizations to get it right the next time without the problem reoccurring.

By using smart solutions and information, organization is able to get deep insight into its functioning, monitoring productivity, efficiency and maintain high standard of quality control at every stage of production.

The following approach makes it possible for the organizations to improve service and product delivery as well as increase efficiency in the consumption of resources. Thus, intelligent systems are gradually becoming an essential tool that allows companies to stay ahead and adapt to the constantly shifting needs and expectations of the market in the globally connected and the rapidly developing digital environment.

5.4.2 Automated Defect Detection System

The element of quality assurance is an essential aspect that is vital in the emerging field of design. ICT advancements like AI, ML and other advance technologies are redesigning the future of IoT 4. From the current study, there is zero percent vulnerability detection and mitigation. In this way, this technology guarantees that products are uniform, performant, and capable of adapting to changes [29, 80].

Modeling on the other hand, involves using ML and AI in image processing for the purpose of identifying errors. Some of the AI techniques that have been developed to be adopted by the manufacturers include CNN and deep learning that enable the analysis of images captured by cameras mounted on the production lines [81–85, 89]. These algorithms are capable of inspecting and evaluating even the most flawed ones like a scratch, dent or no color on the surface to make certain that the final packaging delivered to a customer is absolutely perfect. Troubleshooting in machines and devices is another bright area of artificial intelligence and machine learning. By analyzing data from artificial objects such as vibration or acoustic sensors, AI algorithms can detect unusual patterns that could lead to defects, malfunctions or disruptions in the chain. For example, changes in vibration patterns or sudden, strange machine sounds can be early indicators of impending issues [30]—and catching these early enough can nip problems in the bud before they have profound, more costly implications.

Also, artificial intelligence and machine learning algorithms are good at learning from historical data to predict probability. These algorithms carefully analyze sensor data and IoT output, identifying trends and relationships that indicate increased risk. This vision allows companies to use preventive strategies, create good processes, and reduce costs. More importantly, new artificial intelligence and machine learning applications have taken the vulnerability detection system to new heights in IoT 4.0 [31]. By using this powerful technology, companies can maintain exceptional standards of quality, efficiency, and productivity to ensure their products best suit customers' needs.

5.5 Robotics and Automation

There is a wide range of industries that have seen their processes and workflows change as a result of automation and robotics.

5.5.1 Robotics in Smart Factories

Robotics plays a significant role in the conversion of traditional factories into smart, flexible and networked industrial environments. In today's dynamic industrial environment, companies that are clever can incorporate robots' technology for more efficiency, agility as well as better competitiveness [32]. The advent and operation of smart factories commonly known as Industry 4.0 or the fourth industrial revolution depend on robotics. Figure 5.5 shows robotically operated smart factories. By incorporating automated technologies into production lines, robotics in smart factories transform industrial processes [33]. These advanced solutions reduce costs while enhancing safety, efficiency accuracy, and adaptably.

Robotics is vital in transforming conventional factories into intelligent ones that are flexible, efficient and digitally connected to create modern manufacturing sectors for sustainability, innovation and global competitiveness. Modern technologies like robotics, automation, data analytics, and the IoT are used in "smart factories" to provide extremely flexible and effective production methods [34]. Smart industries leverage automation through robots. Robots equipped with sensors and AI algorithms for repetitive tasks can complete them quickly and precisely enhancing productivity levels thereby having consistent product quality [35]. When repetitive labor-intensive tasks are automated, human workers can involve themselves in more sophisticated jobs that add value. This encourages innovations and creativity in the organizations.

The use of smart manufacturing robotics enables real time data analysis and monitoring which also provides intelligence on performance measures and production metrics. Through this data driven strategy manufacturers can use the insights to estimate maintenance needs, identify areas of improvement as well as optimize production schedules, thus increasing productivity and resource utilization [36]. Smart manufacturing robotics has another important innovation called cobots or collaborative robots. These robots enhance safety and productivity by working closely with human operators. Force limiting sensors and vision systems are some of the contemporary advanced safety features that boost communicational security between these machines and people in communal

Figure 5.5 Robotics-operated smart factories [38].

work spaces [37]. They can be used in smart manufacturing as Automated Production, Collaborative Robotics (Cobots), Mobile Robots and AGVs, Flexible Manufacturing Systems, Predictive Maintenance, Quality Control, Inspection Systems Data Integration and Connectivity, Human-Robot Collaboration.

5.5.2 AI-Driven Automation Process

AI-driven automation procedures lower costs, minimize errors, and eliminate human labor while enabling businesses to improve productivity, flexibility, and creativity. Businesses may take advantage of new opportunities, promote growth, and maintain their competitiveness in the current digital era by utilizing AI technologies [39]. An example for AI-driven automation

Figure 5.6 An example for AI-driven automation process in factories [40].

process in factories is shown in Figure 5.6. An outline of how AI powers automation procedures is provided below:

1) Gathering and Analyzing Data:
   - AI algorithms can collect and analyze large amounts of data in real-time or almost real-time from a variety of sources, both organized and unorganized.
   - AI systems may find patterns, correlations, and insights in data by using machine learning (ML) and deep learning techniques. This provides useful information for making decisions.
2) Decision Making and Prediction:
   - AI models enable the automation of decision-making processes by generating predictions and judgments based on the data that has been evaluated.
   - Algorithms for predictive analytics project future patterns, actions, and results, assisting companies in anticipating needs, allocating resources optimally, and managing risks [41].
3) Natural Language Processing (NLP):
   - AI systems are able to understand and interpret both written and spoken human language.
   - Chatbots and virtual assistants replace human customer service representatives by automating interactions that involve answering questions, delivering information, and resolving problems.
4) Robotic Process Automation (RPA):
   - Artificial intelligence (AI) and robotic process automation (RPA) combine to automate rule-based, repetitive processes that are traditionally completed by humans [42].
   - Software robots do human tasks across a variety of applications and systems, including data entry, form filling, and data extraction.
5) Autonomous Systems:
   - With minimal assistance from humans, AI-driven autonomous systems are capable of making decisions and acting in unpredictable and dynamic contexts.
   - AI is used by robots, drones, and autonomous cars to facilitate automated transportation, surveillance, and

inspection duties by detecting objects, avoiding obstacles, and navigating [43, 86].

6) Personalization and Recommendation:
   - Recommendation engines with AI capabilities examine user preferences, actions, and past data to provide tailored content recommendations.
   - Recommendation algorithms are used by e-commerce sites, streaming services, and social media sites to improve user experience and increase interaction.
7) Process Optimization and Continuous Improvement:
   - Using historical data and real-time input, AI systems detect inefficiencies, bottlenecks, and places for improvement to optimize processes.
   - AI devices are prepared to continuously optimize processes for better performance and outcomes by utilizing approaches from reinforcement learning [39].
8) Risk Control and Fraud Identification:
   - To identify potential threats, fraudulent activity, and security issues, artificial intelligence (AI) systems examine trends and abnormalities in data [44].
   - In order to assist businesses, minimize financial losses and defend against cyber risks, fraud detection systems employ machine learning models to detect fraudulent transactions, behaviors, and patterns.

5.6 Data Analytics and Decision Support

Large datasets and predictive analytics as well as data analytics and decision support systems leverage AI-driven automation to extract insights and support informed decision making. These systems employ advanced algorithms to recognize patterns and trends and provide instantaneous insights into customer behavior, market dynamics, and operational performance [45]. By simplifying the process of data processing and analysis, AI-powered solutions enable businesses allocate resources more efficiently, reduce risks, to enhance productivity all of which drive innovation and competitive advantage in the data-driven business environment of today.

5.6.1 Big Data Analytics in Industry 4.0

It is predicated heavily on big data analytics, which allows manufacturers to use the vast quantities of data produced by networked devices, sensors, and systems to drive innovation, competitiveness and operational efficiency. By introducing IoT, AI and automation technologies to big data, it facilitates real-time monitoring, analysis and optimization of the manufacturing process [46].

Manufacturers can gather and analyze data from a range of sources, including supply chain systems, production equipment and customer feedback, to build a coherent view of production efficiency, product quality and predictive maintenance requirements [47]. As a result, they can locate bottlenecks, improve production plans, and take proactive measures to resolve problems before they have an adverse effect on output. A pictorial representation of big data in industry is shown in Figure 5.7.

Big data analytics facilitates predictive maintenance, where machine learning algorithms analyze historical and current data to predict equipment failure and maintenance needs. This extends the life of critical equipment, reduces maintenance costs and minimizes downtime [48]. Additionally, manufacturers can tailor their goods and services to the requirements and tastes of individual consumers with the aid of big data analytics. Manufacturers can adjust products, prices, and marketing based on customer data analysis (such as purchasing behavior, feedback, and chatter on social media), thereby increasing customer satisfaction and loyalty [49].

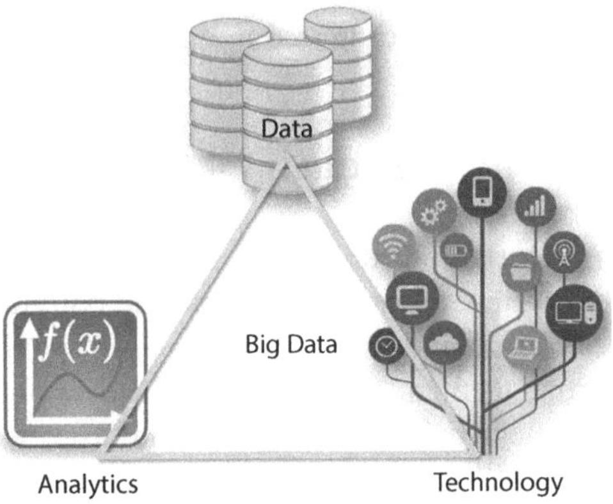

Figure 5.7 Pictorial representation of big data in industry [50].

5.6.2 Decision Support System with AI/ML

Decision support systems (DSS) developed with machine learning (ML) and artificial intelligence (AI) capabilities, using advanced analytics and automation. Nature can decide. When AI and machine learning are integrated into DSS, organizations can use unique capabilities to process, analyze, and extract insights from large amounts of complex data [51]. This method is especially good at prediction. They use machine learning (ML) algorithms to predict future patterns and outcomes based on existing data, enabling better risk management and decision-making [52].

In addition, the recommendation engine supported by artificial intelligence improves the decision-making process by providing users with information and suggestions that will help them make decisions. DSS's machine learning algorithms are very good at identifying patterns, relationships, anomalies, and hidden information that traditional analysis methods may not have [53]. AI optimization algorithms also simplify planning, resource allocation, and optimization by determining the best way to achieve specific goals.

AI-Enhanced DSS is known for its real-time decision-making that continuously analyzes input data to provide timely insights and recommendations. These are important for quick decision-making in a good environment [53]. Additionally, adaptive learning can make machine learning models more efficient when data and situations change, ensuring that decisions are made correctly and updated. Overall, thanks to the integration of ML and AI into DSS, companies can make faster and more informed decisions on various business and management issues, thus increasing efficiency and providing a competitive advantage.

5.7 Cybersecurity in Industry 4.0

Cyber security is essential to protect against changing threats in Industry 4.0. It requires encryption, access restrictions, and continuous monitoring to protect networks, endpoints, and data. Employee training, supply chain security, identity management and access are also important. Protecting digital assets in connected factories must create a cybersecurity culture and comply with the rules [54]. The characteristics of network security are shown in Figure 5.8.

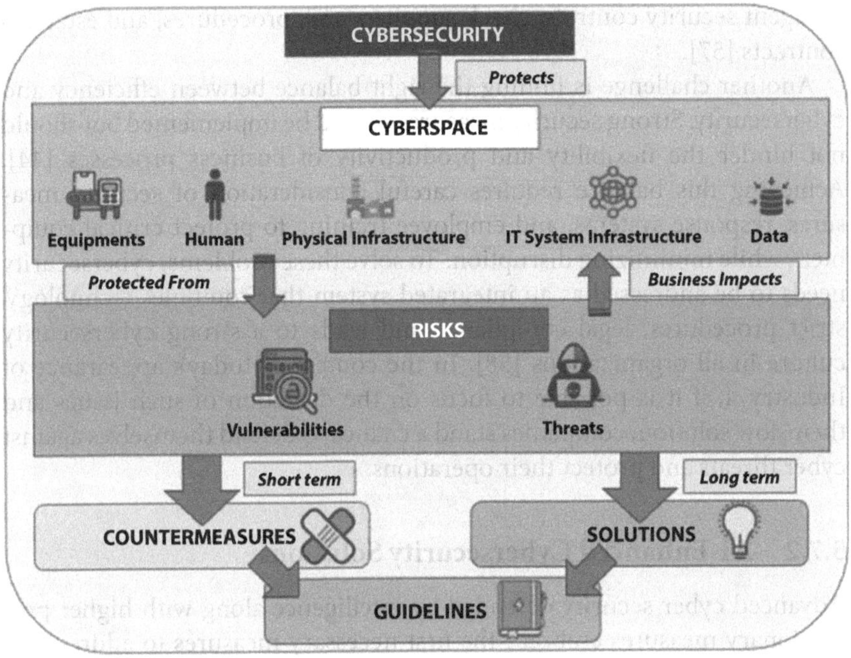

Figure 5.8 Cybersecurity technical characterization [54].

5.7.1 Challenges and Threats

Because digital systems are interconnected, cybersecurity in Industry 4.0 faces numerous risks and concerns. The prevalence of cyberthreats, such as ransomware, phishing, and malware attacks, which are always becoming more sophisticated and frequent, is one major obstacle. These attacks aim to compromise sensitive data and interfere with operations by targeting operational technology (OT) systems, IoT devices, and associated networks. They do this by taking advantage of security flaws [55].

Another big challenge is the difficulty of managing security across multiple networks. Cyber-attack comes into context and most of the sensors, devices and gadgets make up the business 4.0 environment. Each has its own security policy. To ensure the security of the ecosystem, access control, robust network segmentation, and vulnerability assessment to find and fix vulnerabilities are required [56]. Also, one of the biggest challenges of Industry 4.0 is ensuring the security of the supply chain for the entire system. Third-party vendors and partners often present additional cybersecurity risks; therefore, to reduce risk, organizations need to implement stringent security controls, check suppliers' risk procedures, and establish contracts [57].

Another challenge is finding the right balance between efficiency and cybersecurity. Strong security measures should be implemented but should not hinder the flexibility and productivity of business processes [44]. Achieving this balance requires careful consideration of security measures, response systems, and employee training to protect critical equipment while minimizing disruption. To solve these problems, cybersecurity needs to be addressed as an integrated system that combines technology, strict procedures, legal compliance and leads to a strong cybersecurity culture in all organizations [58]. In the context of today's appearance of Industry 4, if it is possible to focus on the detection of such issues and their slow solution, companies stand a chance to defend themselves against cyber threats and protect their operations.

5.7.2 AI-Enhanced Cybersecurity Solutions

Advanced cyber security defended by intelligence along with higher precautionary measures embrace the first necessary measures to address the constantly emerging and developing threats in the information age. These technologies use compact and strong ML and other advanced algorithms for accurate recognition and evaluation of cyber threats and their subsequent handling, which is quicker and less difficult than through conventional techniques. The strength of intelligence is that these solutions make it possible to analyze data in real-time, a factor that means huge data sets can be analyzed in short time, and key issues such as repeated patterns, anomalies, or risks can be detected which a human analyst will not notice. Thus, using intelligence technologies, regularly updated and adjusted to emerging threats, appropriate reaction time and improvement of detection rates can be achieved [59]. In addition, with the help of such solutions others can predict possible cyber security threats and actions should be taken against them can be taken. Before attacking an organization, the machine learning models can be used by organizations to detect the risks and frustrate the potential assaults. Cyber threats, then, may be forecast using historical data, user behavior, and models of networks by machine learning [60].

Thus, the AI can assist in human decision-making, the level of threat perception, and their response by faking suspicious actions and more. Security teams can redirect their concern to various tasks when wielding AI-based security systems for assessing security alerts and threats, as well as designing and implementing countermeasures including immobilizing hazardous incoming vehicles or quarantining infected instruments [61]. Anti-malware solutions backed up with AI makes it possible for the firms to share information easily about threats. Fusing and analyzing threat information AI offers big-picture global risk and attack trends data, that is otherwise challenging to assimilate. It also assists companies to build up their defenses and offer ability to respond to new threats [61].

Some of the challenges that have arisen as a result of integrating artificial intelligence in enhancing cybersecurity involve: failures in artificially intelligent systems, criminal-minded intentions to conduct more daring and intricate cyber-attacks, data protection and ethical issues [62]. Despite these challenges, it became clear that the use of artificial intelligence approaches could expand the range of cybersecurity measures and adapt to the rapidly growing cyber threat at the digital level and its internationalization.

5.8 Human-Machine Collaboration

5.8.1 Human-Centric AI Applications

Industry 4.0's human-centric AI applications focus on enhancing workplace safety, productivity, and user experience, as well as improving human-AI interactions [63]. Here are several examples:

- *Collaborative Robots (Cobots):* Socially assistive robots thus as designed to work and be situated right alongside people to assist with tasks that might require flexibility of movement, power, or to do tasks that entail repetitive cycles. These robots using Artificial Intelligence work along with humans, matching their movements to develop safe ways of working especially at industrial settings. It is possible to be integrated with a human crew performing tasks that are within immediate reach, such as assembling, packing or checking on faulty products.
- *Personalized Training and Assistance*: Smart learning systems can help deliver a more engaging training solution for employees, which can enable them to learn better, acquire new knowledge and work skill to meet Industry 4.0 technologies [64]. Such systems rely on the ML algorithm to determine learning preferences, styles, and performance of each user and delivers relative up-to-point training material and feedback. Moreover, intelligent VA can accompany the real personnel working on

the floor of the factory, giving them direction and support, in case of any questions, difficulties in finding information, means, or completing tasks.

- *Augmented Reality (AR) and Virtual Reality (VR):* By providing individuals with an opportunity to fully interact with machines through a holographic environment, AR and VR make human-machine interaction rich and stimulating [65]. It is within this context that the following technologies can be employed in Industry 4.0 for help from other departments such as the technical team for remote assistance, fixing, or even training. For example, augmented reality-based smart glasses enable the employee to project digital information onto real objects for guiding employees in intricate assembly or maintenance operations [20], while the virtuous reality application can depict dangerous and risky scenarios to let the employees practice safety measures in a safe mode.
- *Natural Language Processing (NLP):* Implementations of natural language involve the use of languages which are employable in conversing with machines like chatbots and voice commands. Opportunities of and barriers to using NLP applications in Industry 4. It is therefore apparent that the number 0 can be utilized for regulating operations in industries, as well as for data retrieval from databases and systems and to interact with intelligent assistances. Employees can call and report problems, ask questions on data, and get immediate responses from the embedded smart systems using voice or via a keyboard and screen, improving organizational efficiency.
- *Emotion Recognition and Sentiment Analysis:* Such technologies rely on AI to analyze the human emotion and probably the next action based on speech, or even hand movement and face expression. In Industry 4.0, it can be used to manage and supervise employees, to check on their state of mind and of health, to guarantee their security and well-being as well as contentment in the workplace [77–79]. On human eyes, it can identify workers who are dozing off, stressed or distracted and then act or take necessary measures to control accidents or increase output.
- *Ethical AI and Human-Centered Design*: Concerning, the implementation of AI in Industry 4.0, it is imperative to consider the principles of development and application of AI systems. To support such a finding when the value of 'x'

is equal to 0, it is necessary to underscore the importance of the human-centered design approach and ethical concerns. Specificity of introducing people-oriented artificial intelligence technologies: it is also necessary to involve value judgments of people, attitudes to the corresponding decisions, their openness, non-discrimination, and protection of people's rights. Thus, by engaging the workers in the development of the AI solutions, the organizations are able to build technologies that improve the quality of the people's lives and, at the same time, the organization's trust in the AI solutions and positive relationship between people and AI technologies in the workplace are facilitated.

5.8.2 Collaboration Interfaces in Smart Manufacturing

Collaboration interfaces are essential in smart industrial settings as they facilitate connections, communication, and coordination between individuals, machinery, and frameworks. These interfaces integrate a range of technologies, including wearables, touchscreen displays, VR and AR, to improve productivity and enable seamless communication in production contexts [66, 76]. Collaborative interfaces in smart manufacturing can look like these:

- *Augmented Reality (AR) and Mixed Reality (MR) Interfaces*: Augmented Reality (AR) projects digital data into the real world, giving workers real-time direction, instructions, and contextual data. AR glasses or headsets, for instance, can show detailed assembly instructions, identify parts, and show equipment maintenance processes. Through the integration of virtual and real-world aspects, mixed reality (MR) enables simultaneous interaction between people and digital and physical things. Multiple stakeholders can engage with 3D models and prototypes in real-time during collaborative design reviews, remote help, and immersive training simulations made possible by MR interfaces [67].
- *Virtual Reality (VR) Environments:* Users can explore and interact with completely immersive, computer-generated environments through virtual reality (VR) headgear or portable controllers. VR interfaces are used in smart manufacturing for planning industrial layouts, conducting simulation-based training exercises, and virtual prototyping. VR-based collaboration

platforms enable distributed teams to collaborate on design projects, conduct virtual meetings, and co-create digital prototypes regardless of their physical locations. Users can interact with 3D models, annotate designs, and make real-time modifications in shared virtual spaces.

- *Wearable Devices and Smart Tools:* Wearable devices, such as smart glasses, wristbands, and exoskeletons, provide hands-free access to information and assistance in manufacturing environments. These devices can display work instructions, monitor biometric data, and provide haptic feedback to guide users during manual tasks. Tools with sensors and networking capabilities allow for real-time tracking of production parameters, tool conditions, and equipment performance. When outfitted with safety measures and sensors, collaborative robots, or cobots, can operate alongside humans to help with jobs that call for strength, dexterity, or accuracy [68].
- *Touchscreen Displays and Interactive Dashboards:* Workstations, control panels, and factory floors all have touchscreens screens installed as user-friendly interfaces for obtaining production data, keeping an eye on process variables, and adjusting equipment settings. Real-time visibility into production schedules, maintenance warnings, and key performance indicators (KPIs) is possible with interactive dashboards.

5.9 Energy Efficiency and Sustainability

5.9.1 Role of AI ML in Energy Management

Industrial development is crucial for the power system's expansion, fortification, stability, technological progression, dependability, choice, and dynamic reaction. Billions of dollars are invested by governments and corporations on technology that convert, gather, adapt to changing demand and supply patterns, increase efficiency, and store energy [69]. The absence of analytics in these technologies prevents them from being used optimally. Here, the effects of AI are beginning to be felt in the energy sector. This research looked at seven different energetics systems and their many applications in light of the importance of artificial intelligence. These included: among the several disciplines that make up the energy sector are energy generation, power transmission, distribution networks, energy storage, energy-efficient technologies, innovative energy materials and devices, energy conservation strategies, and nanotechnology. It also includes economics and policy related to energy. Fuzzy logic systems, genetic algorithms, artificial neural networks, and expert systems are the four primary approaches utilized in contemporary artificial intelligence (AI) technology. These approaches are mostly responsible for advancements in this area. The power business in industrialized nations has started incorporating artificial intelligence (AI) into smart meters, smart grids, and Internet of Things (IoT) devices.

As the energy industry around the world changes to meet the decarbonization target, artificial intelligence, machine learning, and cutting-edge information technology integration have arisen to enable breakthroughs in energy transformation and administration. The integration of ML and AI into the energy transformation, preservation, and transmission domains has promising prospects for optimizing energy conversion processes and impacting both domestic and international energy markets. This integration is growing rapidly, exhibiting positive advancements and useful practical applications [70].

Numerous industries, including autonomous driving, robotic manipulators, analysis of images, computer vision, art production, natural language processing, time series analysis, target internet advertising, etc., are undergoing revolutions thanks to artificial intelligence (AI). AI includes knowledge representation, ML, neural networks, perception, and more. This is now possible due to the growing availability and storage of digital data. The amount of structured data tends to increase an algorithm's ability to perform better. The European Commission unveiled a plan of action in October 2022 to digitize the energy sector and build data centers, energy data spaces, and mechanisms for data sharing. As a result of these advancements, artificial intelligence algorithms and methods hold great promise for the modeling, forecasting, and optimization of energy conversion processes, which will increase the energy sectors' overall efficacy [71].

Here are some key ways AI and ML contribute to energy management:

- *Predictive Maintenance*: By analyzing prior information from energy systems, AI and ML algorithms can forecast when service is required, averting expensive breakdowns and maximizing equipment efficiency. This helps in reducing downtime and improving overall energy efficiency.
- *Energy Consumption Optimization*: Machine learning algorithms are able to detect inefficiencies and recommend improvements by examining trends in data related to energy usage. These systems

can adjust heating, cooling, and lighting based on occupancy patterns, optimizing energy consumption in buildings.

- *Demand Response Optimization*: Through complex analysis of existing data, one can forecast the trends of demand swings and, in response, ensure generating and distributing energy in a more optimal manner and at a lower cost.
- Renewable Energy Integration: This technology can predict spots of renewable energy production depending on climates and determine the correct blend of solar and wind power to feed into the grid to maintain stability and effectiveness.
- *Energy Trading*: Through the use of machine learning approaches whereby the tendencies in the markets are forecasted, the energy traders, producers, and consumers can be in a position to achieve more of their goals and requirements without incurring numerous costs.
- *Grid Management*: Experience from many areas can be used to employ AI for analysis of sensor data on equipment and areas of the grid for early detection of problems such as equipment faults or blackouts; this improves the reliability of the grid.
- *Smart Building Management*: Intelligent systems can manage energy demand inside a building space through the use of automation devices such as heating, cooling, lighting, as well as occupancy sensors that dictate usage rates to enhance comfort and reduce power consumption.
- *Energy Forecasting*: These are more reliable and efficient than traditional methods as they use data analytics, machine learning, and AI tools, which enable accurate forecasting of demand and supply.

5.9.2 Sustainable Practices in Industry 4.0

Industry 4.0 is concerned with the usage and implementation of IoT technologies in an industrial setting, offering a CPS that supports the ideas of smart factories and products, value extensions, vertical and horizontal integration, and end-to-end manufacturing [72].

These are known as the Fourth Industrial Revolution, or simply Industry 4.0, is a process of integrating digital technology into manufacturing value chain which enhances the level of automation and connectivity within manufacturing systems by incorporating real-time data within the production processes. In Industry 4.0, it is our responsibility to ensure that the resources available are-utilized efficiently and recycled appropriately to minimize their usage while safeguarding the environment for future generations and promoting sustainable economic growth. This systematic review's objective is to consider how sustainable manufacturing research contributes to the realization of Industry 4. To further advance the agenda 0 and aid in the development of the highly facilitated links among Industry 4.0 and sustainable manufacturing by expanding on previous research findings, creating a research plan, and identifying opportunities and gaps for additional study [73].

Here are some of the social responsibilities of Industry 4.0 and how they can be implemented to promote environmental conservation:

- *Energy Efficiency*: Energy efficiency is very plausible in manufacturing plants; this can be achieved with the adoption of technologies and processes that enhance energy efficiency. This also entails use of smart sensors in plants to control energy wastage as well as energy management plans to schedule production routines more efficiently.
- *Renewable Energy Integration*: In manufacturing processes, using renewable energy like solar, wind or hydro-electric power will assist in the decentralization of the dependency on fossil energy and aid in cutting down on emissions. Industry 4.0 technologies can enable the effective arranging and controlling and implementation of renewable power plants with industrial processes.
- *Resource Optimization*: Proper use of big data and other automated predictive maintenance techniques can enhance the efficient use of resources including materials, water, and chemicals. In this way, manufacturers are able to track the production processes in use and determine which problems can be solved by reusing resources more efficiently.
- *Circular Economy Practices:* Introducing circular economic concepts require systemic shifts to ensure the products are created with longevity, recyclability, and reusability in mind. Industry 4.0, for example, the use of 0 technologies like additive manufacturing (3D printing) for production can create products that are customizable and repairable while the usage of advanced analytics can make reverse logistics and material recovery possible.
- *Smart Supply Chain Management:* Such IoT devices along with blockchain and AI has a capability of providing a better vision to the supply chain. It also allows for improvement in

inventory and transportation impacts, as well as the ability to monitor more effectively the sustainable sourcing initiatives.

- *Green Manufacturing Technologies:* The implementation of environmentally sustainable technologies, including water-borne coatings, solventless and environmentally friendly inks and adhesives and use of environmentally friendly material can go a long-way in reducing pollution and the consequent overall impact on the earth during production [74].
- *Remote Monitoring and Maintenance:* Smart health monitoring solutions for equipment ensure that failure signs are noticed and addressed early so that they do not cause the system to waste resources when they fail. Regular and timely maintenance and recognition of resulting needs can help manufacturers increase the service time of the machines and decrease the demand for the spare parts.
- *Employee Training and Engagement:* By causing awareness on the issue of sustainability within the organization and making training programs for the employees, the company will be able to adapt to environmentally friendly culture. This is because when employees are allowed to participate in sustainability efforts and even give feedback, there could be new suggestions for enhancing the company's performance in environmental management.

5.10 Emerging Trends and Future Prospects

Industry 4.0 has been under a massive process of innovation due to increased research in ML and AI which is also influencing change in supply chain, new product development and manufacturing processes. Here are some of the key advances in the AI and ML fields that are most pertinent to Industry 4.0:

- *Predictive Maintenance:* To be more specific, AI and ML-based algorithms examine data from the machinery and gadgets to spot possible problems prior to their occurrence. This extends asset's life span; reduces time an asset is out of service and allows for predictive maintenance instead of being reactive.
- *Quality Control and Defect Detection:* When products are inspected through computer vision systems powered by artificial intelligence, the results are incredibly accurate detection

of defects. They, in turn, are always learning from newer data, and therefore, have very effective detecting skills in their work; and this in turn, ensures that the quality of the results produced is always constant.

- *Optimized Production Planning and Scheduling*: The resources in production are procured, scheduled and organized by the optimization of an artificial intelligence program that analyzes the factors such as the machine's availability, constraint resources, and the clients' requests. Fewer Production Delays: Machine learning models predict production disruptions and offer recommendations to increase efficiency.
- *Supply Chain Optimization*: AI and ML ensure efficient SC performance by predicting future demand, providing appropriate inventory management, and finding potential disruptions. It facilitates the method of ordering and using products such as inventory only when needed through technologies such as JIT and so cuts the cost of logistics and strengthens the chain of supply.
- *Autonomous Robots and AGVs*: The industrial application of AI includes the operation of robots and the AGVs that transport materials, assemble goods, and package them. Self-learning and adaptive capabilities of robots make it possible for the machines to adjust to changes, emulate human behavior, and improve performance in the long run based on the input from the ML algorithms.
- *Additive Manufacturing (3D Printing):* AI and ML algorithms affect 3D printing by predicting the fine parameters that would be most suitable for the job performed thus minimizing material wastage and thus the quality of the part to be produced. It is used to produce narrow pitches and small V's as well as bespoke pieces as these tools are more efficient.
- *Smart Maintenance and Servicing:* Digital twins employ the concept of artificial intelligence to produce a digital doppelgänger for real physical assets that can be used to monitor and evaluate their functioning in real time. Using ML algorithms of maintenance, digitals twins' data is used to determine the right time for maintenance, handling of some problems from a remote region and other enhancements of some equipment.
- *Energy Management and Sustainability*: These concepts offer accuracy in tracking energy patterns, increases efficiency of usage, and combines renewable energy options with

manufacturing facilities. These technologies endeavor to support sustainable development activities and minimize the effects of industries on the environment.

- *Human-Robot Collaboration:* AI systems exist to ensure that robots and their human counterparts can work side-by-side in a factory without fear of accidents or improper handling of objects. These methods entail sophisticated sensing and planning methods, where interactions are done more effectively, tasks are well-distributed, and productivity improved.
- Cybersecurity and Data Privacy: The cybersecurity solutions with AI included provide real-time identification and neutralization of cyber risks and safeguard industrial systems and data. The ML algorithms are also used in analyzing the traffic patterns and then detecting outcomes that could lead to security breaches within the network.

Conclusion

Machine thinking or artificial intellect and machine learning provide crucial support to the fourth revolution known as Industry 4.0. Many of these technologies have transformed conventional fabrication procedures by rendering them more efficient, automated, and integrated with decision-making processes; utilizing ML and AI in Industry 4.0 to forecast equipment and time utilization and consequently sustain performance. Businesses should thus draw out inclinations, and anticipate underperformance to bring out optimally planned maintenance schedules, reduce on losses due to machine breakdowns, and prolong asset lifespan. Also, it applies AI in quality control so that industries are able to provide products that appear to be similar but are very different as it detects faults with high precision.

Moreover, machine learning and artificial intelligence make it possible to develop robotic systems and autonomous systems that can accomplish some of the rigorous tasks that are only done by humans with a little help from the machines. Given the versatility of adapting to the environment, incorporating lessons learned from errors, and the improvement of function as time goes on, these systems can be beneficial in the aspect of lowering operating costs as well as increasing production. Additionally, supply chain, logistics, and inventory management have all benefited from increased efficiency; thanks to AI and ML. Thus, ways on products that customers are likely to buy, transportation and customers' behavior etc.

which can contribute large data sets that help improve on business solutions and even improve systematically the whole system performance.

In light of this, and given the context in which concepts like AI, ML, and Industry 4.0, this is mainly affecting to drive changes in production. As a result of this technology, it is smarter, efficient, data driven, and overall, it makes those holding businesses more competitive, stable, and profitable.

References

1. Manavalan, E. and Jayakrishna, K., A review of internet of things (iot) embedded sustainable supply chain for industry 4.0 requirements. *Comput. Ind. Eng.*, 127, 925–953, 2019.
2. Kim, J.H., A review of cyber-physical system research relevant to the emerging it trends: industry 4.0, iot, big data, and cloud computing. *J. Ind. Integr. Manage.*, 2, 03, 1750011, 2017.
3. Kalsoom, T., Ahmed, S., Rafi-ul-Shan, P.M., Azmat, M., Akhtar, P., Pervez, Z., Ur-Rehman, M., Impact of iot on manufacturing industry 4.0: A new triangular systematic review. *Sustainability*, 13, 22, 12506, 2021.
4. Krishnamoorthy, S., Dua, A., Gupta, S., Role of emerging technologies in future iot-driven healthcare 4.0 technologies: A survey, current challenges and future directions. *J. Ambient Intell. Hum. Comput.*, 14, 1, 361–407, 2023.
5. Christou, I.T., Kefalakis, N., Soldatos, J.K., Despotopoulou, A.M., End-to-end industrial iot platform for quality 4.0 applications. *Comput. Ind.*, 137, 103591, 2022.
6. Wesley, Maintenance, IoT and industry 4.0, onkey.com, https://www.onkey.com/maintenance-iot-industry-4-0/. [Accessed 05-06-2024].
7. Saravanan, G., Parkhe, S.S., Thakar, C.M., Kulkarni, V.V., Mishra, H.G., Gulothungan, G., Implementation of iot in production and manufacturing: An industry 4.0 approach. *Mater. Today Proc.*, 51, 2427–2430, 2022.
8. Aly, M., Khomh, F., Yacout, S., What do practitioners discuss about iot and industry 4.0 related technologies? characterization and identification of iot and industry 4.0 categories in stack overflow discussions. *Internet Things*, 14, 100364, 2021.
9. Duman, M.C. and Akdemir, B., A study to determine the effects of industry 4.0 technology components on organizational performance. *Technol. Forecasting Social Change*, 167, 120615, 2021.
10. Zawra, L.M., Mansour, H.A., Eldin, A.T., Messiha, N.W., Utilizing the internet of things (iot) technologies in the implementation of industry 4.0, in: *International Conference on Advanced Intelligent Systems and Informatics*, pp. 798–808, Springer, 2017.
11. Saturno, M., Pertel, V.M., Deschamps, F., Proposal of an automation solutions architecture for industry 4.0, in: *24th international conference on production research*, vol. 1, p. 2021, 2017.

12. Khan, I.H. and Javaid, M., Role of internet of things (iot) in adoption of industry 4.0. *J. Ind. Integr. Manage.*, 7, 04, 515–533, 2022.
13. Trappey, A.J., Trappey, C.V., Govindarajan, U.H., Chuang, A.C., Sun, J.J., A review of essential standards and patent landscapes for the internet of things: A key enabler for industry 4.0. *Adv. Eng. Inf.*, 33, 208–229, 2017.
14. Rath, K.C., Khang, A., Roy, D., The role of internet of things (iot) technology in industry 4.0 economy, in: *Advanced IoT Technologies and Applications in the Industry 4.0 Digital Economy*, pp. 1–28, CRC Press, Boca Raton, FL, 2024.
15. Pech, M., Vrchota, J., Bednář, J., Predictive maintenance and intelligent sensors in smart factory. *Sensors*, 21, 4, 1470, 2021.
16. Çınar, Z.M., Abdussalam Nuhu, A., Zeeshan, Q., Korhan, O., Asmael, M., Safaei, B., Machine learning in predictive maintenance towards sustainable smart manufacturing in industry 4.0. *Sustainability*, 12, 19, 8211, 2020.
17. Zonta, T., Da Costa, C.A., da Rosa Righi, R., de Lima, M.J., da Trindade, E.S., Li, G.P., Predictive maintenance in the industry 4.0: A systematic literature review. *Comput. Ind. Eng.*, 150, 106889, 2020.
18. Compare, M., Baraldi, P., Zio, E., Challenges to iot-enabled predictive maintenance for industry 4.0. *IEEE Internet Things J.*, 7, 5, 4585–4597, 2019.
19. Angelopoulos, A., Michailidis, E., Nomikos, N., Panagiotis, T., Hatziefremidis, A., Voliotis, S., Zahariadis, T., Tackling faults in the industry 4.0 era—a survey of machine-learning solutions and key aspects. *Sensors*, 20, 1, 109, 2019.
20. Abidi, M.H., Mohammed, M.K., Alkhalefah, H., Predictive maintenance planning for industry 4.0 using machine learning for sustainable manufacturing. *Sustainability*, 14, 6, 3387, 2022.
21. De Vass, T., Shee, H., Miah, S., Iot in supply chain management: Opportunities and challenges for businesses in early industry 4.0 context. *Oper. Supply Chain Manage.: Int. J.*, 14, 2, 148–161, 2021.
22. 8 Ways AI is Massively Transforming Supply Chain, Birlasoft, birlasoft.com, https://www.birlasoft.com/articles/eight-ways-ai-is-massively-transforming-supply-chain. [Accessed 05- 06-2024].
23. Matani, A.G., Industry 4.0 optimizing logistics processes and supply chain management in industries, in: *Decision Analytics Applications in Industry*, pp. 485–496, 2020.
24. Paksoy, T. and Garza-Reyes, J.A., The new challenge of industry 4.0: Sustainable supply chain network design with internet of things, in: *Logistics 4.0*, pp. 51–64, CRC Press, Boca Raton, FL, 2020.
25. Winkelhaus, S. and Grosse, E.H., Logistics 4.0: A systematic review towards a new logistics system. *Int. J. Prod. Res.*, 58, 1, 18–43, 2020.
26. Singh, J., Ahuja, I.S., Singh, H., Singh, A., Application of quality 4.0 (q4.0) and industrial internet of things (iiot) in agricultural manufacturing industry. *AgriEngineering*, 5, 1, 537–565, 2023.

27. Saihi, A., Awad, M., Ben-Daya, M., Quality 4.0: leveraging industry 4.0 technologies to improve quality management practices–a systematic review. *Int. J. Qual. Reliab. Manage.*, 40, 2, 628–650, 2023.
28. Sader, S., Husti, I., Daroczi, M., A review of quality 4.0: Definitions, features, technologies, applications, and challenges. *Total Qual. Manage. Bus. Excell.*, 33, 9-10, 1164–1182, 2022.
29. Shahbazi, Z. and Byun, Y.C., Integration of blockchain, iot and machine learning for multistage quality control and enhancing security in smart manufacturing. *Sensors*, 21, 4, 1467, 2021.
30. Rai, R., Tiwari, M.K., Ivanov, D., Dolgui, A., Machine learning in manufacturing and industry 4.0 applications. *Int. J. Prod. Res.*, 59, 16, 4812–4820, 2021.
31. Escobar, C.A., McGovern, M.E., Morales-Menendez, R., Quality 4.0: a review of big data challenges in manufacturing. *J. Intell. Manuf.*, 32, 8, 2319–2334, 2021.
32. Khang, A., Rath, K.C., Satapathy, S.K., Kumar, A., Das, S.R., Panda, M.R., Enabling the future of manufacturing: Integration of robotics and iot to smart factory infrastructure in industry 4.0, in: *Handbook of Research on AI-Based Technologies and Applications in the Era of the Metaverse*, pp. 25–50, IGI Global, Hershey, PA, 2023.
33. Makris, S., Michalos, G., Karagiannis, P., Digitalising smart factories. *Int. J. Computer Integr. Manuf.*, 36, 1, 1–2, 2023.
34. Nair, R.R., Babu, T., Kishore, S., Recent and emerging technologies in industrial iot, in: *Opportunities and Challenges of Industrial IoT in 5G and 6G Networks*, pp. 50–72, 2023.
35. Lins, R.G. and Givigi, S.N., Cooperative robotics and machine learning for smart manufacturing: platform design and trends within the context of industrial internet of things. *IEEE Access*, 9, 95444–95455, 2021.
36. Edvards, J., Building a smart factory with ai and robotics, Robotics Business Review, 2022.
37. Javaid, M., Haleem, A., Singh, R.P., Rab, S., Suman, R., Significant applications of cobots in the field of manufacturing. *Cognit. Rob.*, 2, 222–233, 2022.
38. Active Silicon news: Active Silicon's AI Series, part 5, activesilicon.com, https://www.activesilicon.com/news-media/news/active-silicons-ai-series-part-5-ai-and-co. [Accessed 05-06-2024].
39. Aldoseri, A., Al-Khalifa, K., Hamouda, A., A roadmap for integrating automation with process optimization for ai-powered digital transformation, 2023.
40. From Manual to Marvel: AI-Driven Automation in Manufacturing Processes, praxie.com, ai-driven-automation-in-manufacturing-processes/. [Accessed 05-06-2024].
41. Dixit, A.K., Nair, R.R., Babu, T., Analysis and classification of restaurants based on rating with xgboost model, in: *2022 3rd International Conference on*

Issues and Challenges in Intelligent Computing Techniques (ICICT), IEEE, pp. 1–6, 2022.
42. Benotsmane, R., Kovács, G., Dudás, L., Economic, social impacts and operation of smart factories in industry 4.0 focusing on simulation and artificial intelligence of collaborating robots. *Social Sci.*, 8, 5, 143, 2019.
43. Bathla, G., Bhadane, K., Singh, R.K., Kumar, R., Aluvalu, R., Krishnamurthi, R., Basheer, S., Autonomous vehicles and intelligent automation: Applications, challenges, and opportunities. *Mobile Inf. Syst.*, 2022, 1–36, 2022.
44. Bécue, A., Praça, I., Gama, J., Artificial intelligence, cyber-threats and industry 4.0: Challenges and opportunities. *Artif. Intell. Rev.*, 54, 5, 3849–3886, 2021.
45. Wang, J., Zhao, Y., Balamurugan, P., Selvaraj, P., Managerial decision support system using an integrated model of ai and big data analytics. *Ann. Oper. Res.*, 319, 1–18, 2022.
46. Nayyar, A. and Kumar, A., *A roadmap to industry 4.0: Smart production, sharp business and sustainable development*, Springer, Cham, Switzerland, 2020.
47. Gokalp, M.O., Kayabay, K., Akyol, M.A., Eren, P.E., Koçyiğit, A., Big data for industry 4.0: A conceptual framework, in: *2016 international conference on computational science and computational intelligence (CSCI)*, IEEE, pp. 431–434, 2016.
48. Santos, M.Y., Oliveira e Sá, J., Costa, C., Galvão, J., Andrade, C., Martinho, B., Costa, E., A big data analytics architecture for industry 4.0, in: *Recent Advances in Information Systems and Technologies*, vol. 2, pp. 175–184, Springer, Cham, Switzerland, 2017.
49. Duan, L. and Da Xu, L., Data analytics in industry 4.0: A survey. *Inf. Syst. Front.*, 23, 6, 1–17, 2021.
50. Reis, M.S. and Gins, G., Industrial process monitoring in the big data/industry 4.0 era: From detection, to diagnosis, to prognosis. *Processes*, 5, 3, 35, 2017.
51. Higgins, O., Short, B.L., Chalup, S.K., Wilson, R.L., Artificial intelligence (ai) and machine learning (ml) based decision support systems in mental health: An integrative review. *Int. J. Mental Health Nurs.*, 32, 4, 966–978, 2023.
52. Sachan, S., Yang, J.B., Xu, D.L., Benavides, D.E., Li, Y., An explainable ai decision-support-system to automate loan underwriting. *Expert Syst. Appl.*, 144, 113100, 2020.
53. Patalay, S. and Bandlamudi, M.R., Decision support system for stock portfolio selection using artificial intelligence and machine learning. *Ing. Syst. Inf.*, 26, 1, 87–93, 2021.
54. Mullet, V., Sondi, P., Ramat, E., A review of cybersecurity guide lines for manufacturing factories in industry 4.0. *IEEE Access*, 9, 23235–23263, 2021.
55. Humayun, M., Industry 4.0 and cyber security issues and challenges. *Turk. J. Comput. Math. Educ. (TURCOMAT)*, 12, 10, 2957–2971, 2021.

56. Tsochev, G., Trifonov, R., Nakov, O., Manolov, S., Pavlova, G., Cyber security: Threats and challenges, in: *2020 International Conference Automatics and Informatics (ICAI)*, IEEE, pp. 1–6, 2020.
57. Morris, D., Madzudzo, G., Garcia-Perez, A., Cybersecurity threats in the auto industry: Tensions in the knowledge environment. *Technol. Forecasting Social Change*, 157, 120102, 2020.
58. Culot, G., Fattori, F., Podrecca, M., Sartor, M., Addressing industry 4.0 cybersecurity challenges. *IEEE Eng. Manage. Rev.*, 47, 3, 79–86, 2019.
59. Markevych, M. and Dawson, M., A review of enhancing intrusion detection systems for cybersecurity using artificial intelligence (ai). *Int. Conf. Knowledge-Based Organ.*, 29, 30–37, 2023.
60. Vegesna, V.V., Comprehensive analysis of AI-enhanced defense systems in cyberspace. *Int. Numeric J. Mach. Learn. Rob.*, 7, 7, 298–312, 2023.
61. Thapa, P. and Arjunan, T., Ai-enhanced cybersecurity: Machine learning for anomaly detection in cloud computing. *Q. J. Emerging Technol. Innovations*, 9, 1, 25–37, 2024.
62. Kant, D. and Johannsen, A., Evaluation of ai-based use cases for enhancing the cyber security defense of small and medium-sized companies (smes). *Electron. Imaging*, 34, 1–8, 2022.
63. Horvatić, D. and Lipic, T., Human-centric ai: the symbiosis of human and artificial intelligence. *AI and Ethics*, 1, 4, 539–544, 2021.
64. Longo, F., Nicoletti, L., Padovano, A., New perspectives and results for smart operators in industry 4.0: A human-centered approach. *Comput. Ind. Eng.*, 163, 107824, 2022.
65. Machała, S., Chamier-Gliszczyński, N., Królikowski, T., Application of ar/vr technology in industry 4.0. *Procedia Comput. Sci.*, 207, 2990–2998, 2022.
66. Zheng, P., Wang, H., Sang, Z., Zhong, R.Y., Liu, Y., Liu, C., Xu, X., Smart manufacturing systems for industry 4.0: Conceptual framework, scenarios, and future perspectives. *Front. Mech. Eng.*, 13, 137–150, 2018.
67. Garcia, M.A.R., Rojas, R., Gualtieri, L., Rauch, E., Matt, D., A human-in-the-loop cyber-physical system for collaborative assembly in smart manufacturing. *Procedia CIRP*, 81, 600–605, 2019.
68. Kong, X.T., Luo, H., Huang, G.Q., Yang, X., Industrial wearable system: the human-centric empowering technology in industry 4.0. *J. Intell. Manuf.*, 30, 2853–2869, 2019.
69. Nutakki, M. and Mandava, S., Review on optimization techniques and role of artificial intelligence in home energy management systems. *Eng. Appl. Artif. Intell.*, 119, 105721, 2023.
70. Mazhar, T., Malik, M.A., Haq, I., Rozeela, I., Ullah, I., Khan, M.A., Hamam, H., The role of ml, ai and 5g technology in smart energy and smart building management. *Electronics*, 11, 23, 3960, 2022.
71. Cheng, L. and Yu, T., A new generation of ai: A review and perspective on machine learning technologies applied to smart energy and electric power systems. *Int. J. Energy Res.*, 43, 6, 1928–1973, 2019.

72. Jamwal, A., Agrawal, R., Sharma, M., Giallanza, A., Industry 4.0 technologies for manufacturing sustainability: A systematic review and future research directions. *Appl. Sci.*, 11, 12, 5725, 2021.
73. Javaid, M., Haleem, A., Singh, R.P., Suman, R., Gonzalez, E.S., Understanding the adoption of industry 4.0 technologies in improving environmental sustainability. *Sustainable Oper. Comput.*, 3, 203–217, 2022.
74. Vrchota, J., Pech, M., Rolinek, L., Bednář, J., Sustainability outcomes of green processes in relation to industry 4.0 in manufacturing: Systematic review. *Sustainability*, 12, 15, 5968, 2020.
75. Ghantasala, G.P., Hung, B.T., Chakrabarti, P., Pellakuri, V., Artificial intelligence based machine learning algorithm for prediction of cancer in female anatomy. *Multimedia Tools Appl.*, 83, 2, 1–27, 2024.
76. Narayana, M.V., Rao, J.N., Shrivastava, S., Ghantasala, G.S., Ioannou, I., Vassiliou, V., A framework for identification of brain tumors from MR images using progressive segmentation. *Health Technol.*, *14*, 3, 539–556, 2024.
77. Hariharan, D., Banerjee, S.K., Jinnah, A.M.A., Banu, S.B., Ghantasala, G.P., A Comparative Study Revealing the Behavioural Difference Between Autistic and Healthy Adults, in: *2024 10th International Conference on Communication and Signal Processing (ICCSP)*, IEEE, pp. 459–463, 2024, April.
78. Sravanthi, J., Reddy, C.S., Mahendar, A., Kumar, V.R., Buragadda, S., Ghantasala, G.P., Gupta, G., Improve Accuracy in Healthcare Data Analysis using Competitive Ensemble Deep Learning Model, in: *2024 11th International Conference on Computing for Sustainable Global Development (INDIACom)*, IEEE, pp. 1792–1797, 2024, February.
79. Reddy, A., Ramaiah, V.S., Ayyappa, R.M.K., Ghantasala, G.P., Kurra, M., Bathla, P., An Empirical Brief Analysis of Novelistic Approaches for Detection Of Bone Marrow Cancer Health Monitoring Through DL MODEL, in: *2024 IEEE International Conference on Computing, Power and Communication Technologies (IC2PCT)*, vol. 5, IEEE, pp. 1211–1214, 2024, February
80. Ramana, T.V., Ghantasala, G.S., Sathiyaraj, R., Khan, M. (Eds.), *Artificial Intelligence and Machine Learning for Smart Community: Concepts and Applications*, CRC Press, Boca Raton, FL, 2024.
81. Kiran, C.C., Vidyullatha, P., Ram, V.V., Manish, T., Gopichand, K., Ghantasala, P., Graph Based Big Data Analytics on Unsupervised Machine Learning Framework, in: *2023 International Conference on Advancement in Computation & Computer Technologies (InCACCT)*, IEEE, pp. 732–737, 2023, May.
82. Mounika, C., Poojitha, K.V.V.M., Supraja, P.D.L.S., Vidyullatha, P., Priya, P.K., Gantasala, G.P., Advanced Graph Analytics Algorithms On Genre Based Recommending System, in: *2023 International Conference on Advancement in Computation & Computer Technologies (InCACCT)*, IEEE, pp. 738–743, 2023, May.
83. Ghantasala, G.P., Hung, B.T., Chakrabarti, P., An approach for cervical and breast cancer classification using deep learning: a comprehensive survey, in:

2023 International Conference on Computer Communication and Informatics (ICCCI), IEEE, pp. 1–6, 2023, January.
84. Chandana, P., Ghantasala, G.P., Jeny, J.R.V., Sekaran, K., Deepika, N., Nam, Y., Kadry, S., An effective identification of crop diseases using faster region based convolutional neural network and expert systems. *Int. J. Electr. Comput. Eng. (IJECE)*, *10*, 6, 6531–6540, 2020.
85. Anand, D., Arulselvi, G., Balaji, G.N., Ghantasala, G.P., Deep Convolutional Extreme Learning Machine with AlexNet-Based Bone Cancer Classification Using Whole-Body Scan Images, in: *Digital Transformation: Industry 4.0 to Society 5.0*, pp. 307–325, Springer Nature Singapore, Singapore, 2024.
86. Rajendran, S., Sabharwal, M., Hu, Y.C., Balusamy, B. (Eds.), *Artificial Intelligence for Autonomous Vehicles: The Future of Driverless Technology*, John Wiley & Sons, Hoboken, NJ, 2024.
87. Rajendran, S., Sabharwal, M., Ghinea, G., Dhanaraj, R.K., Balusamy, B. (Eds.), *IoT and Big Data Analytics for Smart Cities: A Global Perspective*, CRC Press, Boca Raton, FL, 2022.
88. Pushpa Rani, K., Vidyullatha, P., Srinivas Rao, K., An Intelligent Tuned Topic Modelling Questing Answering System as Job Assistant. *Wireless Pers. Commun.*, *135*, 3, 1761–1782, 2024.
89. Vidyullatha, P., Reddy, V.D., Ram, K.D., Reddy, D.S., Shaik, A., Ramya, K.R., A Computer Vision based Facial Denoising Alignment using Convolution Neural Network Model, in: *2023 8th International Conference on Communication and Electronics Systems (ICCES)*, IEEE, pp. 841–848, 2023, June.

6

Application of Machine Learning in Moisture Content Prediction of Coffee Drying Process

Tuan M. Le[1], Thuy T. Tran[1], Hieu M. Tran[1] and Son V.T. Dao[1,2]*

[1]*School of Electrical Engineering, International University, Vietnam National University Ho Chi Minh City, HCMC, Vietnam*
[2]*School of Science, Engineering and Technology, RMIT University Vietnam, Ho Chi Minh City, Vietnam*

Abstract
Predicting humidity is not only essential for preserving product quality and shelf life, but it also presents a chance to reduce steam and energy consumption in drying technologies. Determining the predictive efficacy of machine learning (ML) approaches in the coffee production process is the aim of this research. The beverage company that specialized in coffee drying techniques provided the practical data for this research. Although they have invested a lot in their database, it has not yet been fully utilized in the investigation of the relationship between process parameters and moisture prediction. There are two supervised ML techniques: the Artificial Neural Network (ANN) and the Adaptive Network-based Fuzzy System (ANFIS) that are conducted, two transformation data techniques (Normalization and Standardization), two evaluation metrics Root Mean Square (RMSE) and Mean Absolute Error (MAE), and two feature selection techniques Mutual Information and Correlation. As a result, the ANFIS method shows a better performance in predictive food drying techniques.

Keywords: Drying technology, moisture prediction, ANFIS, feature selection, cross validation

**Corresponding author*: son.daovutruong@rmit.edu.vn; ORCID: 0000-0001-9281-4869

M. Thirunavukkarasan, S. A. Sahaaya Arul Mary, Sathiyaraj. R, G. S. Pradeep Ghantasala and Mudassir Khan (eds.) Artificial Intelligence and Machine Learning for Industry 4.0, (145–168)

6.1 Introduction

Nowadays, in the specific production of food and beverage (F&B) industry, the basic thermal physics, mechanics, and transport characteristics of food materials including specific heat capacity, thermal conductivity, and rigidity [1] are frequently picked as one of the critical factors in a study using mathematical modeling to control the product quality and developmental process during drying technology. To reduce energy consumption during food drying and improve product quality, it's vital to fine-tune drying steps and quality traits. Drying factors include heat level, air flow, air force, size, and shape of the item. The top qualities to watch are texture, looks (like color), and nutrition. The texture is a sensory feature that is made up of several textural properties such as geometrical, mechanical, and compositional [2]. For drying technology to match the requirements, it is crucial to comprehend and model each of the relationships in the F&B market. Determining how the outputs and inputs of a drying process relate is notably tough, often seen as daunting, through the use of math, numerical, and analytic methods [3].

In most leading companies in the food industry, the drying process is a crucial phase in the processing of coffee since the moisture content at the end of dehydration impacts numerous important aspects, including storability, the color of the coffee product, and sensory quality [4]. In addition, the stability and increase of humidity can save energy and steam in drying technology while maintaining product quality and shelf life.

In this research, we implement the ML model to determine the influencing factors to water availability within the coffee drying process in the Swiss water technique. Develop a model to predict the moisture content of coffee after extracting coffee in the decaffeinating coffee process and reduce the standard deviation of moisture results from 2.0% to 1.0% to increase the quality of coffee and optimize cost.

The structure of the chapter is presented as follows: literature reviews are given in section 6.2. Data preprocessing and research methodology are described in section 6.3, while section 6.4 presents the findings and additional recommendations. A final conclusion is presented in section 6.5.

6.2 Literature Reviews

6.2.1 Related Works

There are two most economically important varieties of coffee plants in Vietnam: Arabica and Robusta [5] which have their characteristics divided into intrinsic quality, specific character, undesirable flavor, and off-flavor. Drying coffee processes helps coffee reduce undesirable flavor (green grassy, baggy, hay, woody, papery, etc.) and off-flavors (chemical, fermented, earthy musty moldy, etc.), which are unacceptable characteristics in the finished coffee and could be affected during the manual drying, harvesting, postharvest and storage. Therefore, coffee drying techniques have developed significantly day by day. More and more advanced drying techniques are being developed to satisfy the needs of the premium coffee market.

Besides, Clydesdale [6] has stated that decaffeinated coffee is a type of coffee using some technology to decaffeinate green coffee such as direct solvent by methylene chloride, indirect solvent technology, supercritical carbon dioxide process, and Swiss water process. The cleanest and most advanced method for extracting caffeine from coffee using water is the Swiss water procedure.

In this case study, the decaffeinated coffee only applies the Swiss water decaf process, chemical-free could remove caffeine up to 99.9% and has a delicious flavor. Meanwhile, by using this water extraction technique, the moisture content of coffee is the decisive factor in the company's prices, which defeats other competitors. To say so, the more moisture content of coffee, the more economical the company gains.

6.2.2 Background of Machine Learning and Credit Risk Prediction Techniques

Machine learning (ML) is well-known as the most rapidly expanding branch of computer science, with extensive applications. This method refers to the automatic detection of meaningful data patterns. Machine learning is well adapted to the complexities of dealing with disparate data sources, a wide range of variables, and a large amount of data, where ML thrives on increasing datasets [7, 8]. The more data that is consumed into an ML structure, the more it can be trained, which leads to a higher value of insights. The classification task is a typical form of the supervised learning challenge: by exploring many input-output instances of the function, the learner must estimate the function's action, which sorts a vector into one of various classes. The act of deriving a set of guidelines from a set of examples is termed as inductive machine learning.

Drying, as a method of food preservation, pulls out water to prevent the formation of bacteria, yeasts, and molds [9, 10]. Thus, dry foods have become key in commerce, marking a major growth area in the farming sector. One of the biggest benefits of dried foods is that they require far less transportation and storage space than canned or frozen foods.There are many developed methods in drying technology such as hot air drying, freeze-drying, fluidized bed drying, etc. Convection or the most popular drying technique is drying by using hot air since it is the most straightforward. However, several issues such as extended drying durations, limited energy effectiveness, and compromised quality features are tied to this widely used drying method. Thus, possessing a deep comprehension of the drying process and enhancing the quality of the product is crucial. To overcome this situation, food processing has adopted a predictive strategy based on ML [11–13].

6.2.2.1 *Non-Linear Regression*

Linear regression constitutes a fundamental linear modeling technique within the statistical domain, employed to elucidate the relationship between a scalar dependent variable, denoted as y, and one or multiple explanatory variables, represented collectively as a vector x [14]. The core idea of nonlinear regression mirrors that of linear regression, differentiated by the prediction formula's nonlinear reliance on one or multiple unknown parameters. While linear regression often shapes purely data-driven models, nonlinear regression is generally applied when there's a physical basis to expect that the link between the outcome and the predictors adheres to a distinct functional form. G. Xanthopoulos *et al.* [15], used non-linear regression to prove that there are correlations between the drying conditions and the parameters of the model, which were determined to calculate moisture ratio to drying time.

6.2.2.2 *Artificial Neural Networks (ANN)*

ANN consists of nodes layers, encompassing an input layer, several hidden layers, and an output layer. Each node, acting as an artificial neuron, connects to others and carries its own weight and threshold within the model. When the output of a node surpasses its set threshold, it activates and transmits data to the subsequent layer. If not, the data doesn't advance to the next layer. Neural networks with merely two or three layers are regarded as basic neural networks. This description aims to simplify the complexity of ANNs for a scholarly audience while ensuring the use of straightforward language and maintaining the integrity of the original content's meaning. Additionally, a deep learning model or a deep neural network encompasses over three layers, encompassing both inputs and outputs.

Erenturk and Erenturk [14], reported that the Artificial Neural Networks methodology outperformed the revised page model to the mathematical modeling chosen and optimized by the Genetics Algorithm for forecasting the water content of carrot slices by using hot air to dry them. Woinaroschy *et al.* [16], used a simple multilayer perceptron ANN model to estimate and optimize the moisture levels of potassium persulfate while using a vibro fluidized bed dryer as a function of drying time and dryer operational parameters.

6.2.2.3 *Adaptive Network-Based Fuzzy Inference System (ANFIS)*

The neuro-fuzzy model merges a neural network [17] with a fuzzy inference system, employing neural networks to set the parameters of the fuzzy inference system [9]. It blends the advantages of fuzzy systems, which handle clear knowledge to easy to explain and understand, with the strengths of neural networks, which manage hidden knowledge that can be learned. This approach integrates the explicit handling of understandable knowledge through fuzzy systems with the implicit learning capabilities of neural networks.

Prakash and Kumar [18] analyzed three ANFIS methodologies with the model of numeric thermal for using the solar greenhouse to convectively dry the jaggery fruit naturally and forecast the product heat, and rate of drying. By comparing thermal modeling techniques, the outcomes of the ANFIS simulation and data were in satisfactory correlation. Lertworasirikul [19] demonstrated that the selected multilayer perceptron ANN outperformed thin-layer drying and the models ANFIS in forecasting the humidity ratio of unfinished cassava crackers during drying convectively. to calculate the duration of apple slices to dry by freezing, A new method that incorporates an ANFIS model and the approach of data scaling method depends on multiple outputs was created by Polat and Kirmaci [20]. When compared to the simple ANFIS model, the proposed hybrid method for simulating the drying routines of apple slices by freezing was proven to be reliable and effective. In conclusion, these researches demonstrated that ANNs might be more effective than conventional statistical methods.

6.3 Methodology

The design model outlines a process to use machine learning for predicting the moisture content of coffee beans, as shown in Figure 6.1. It starts with gathering data through the system. Next, the method of exploring data

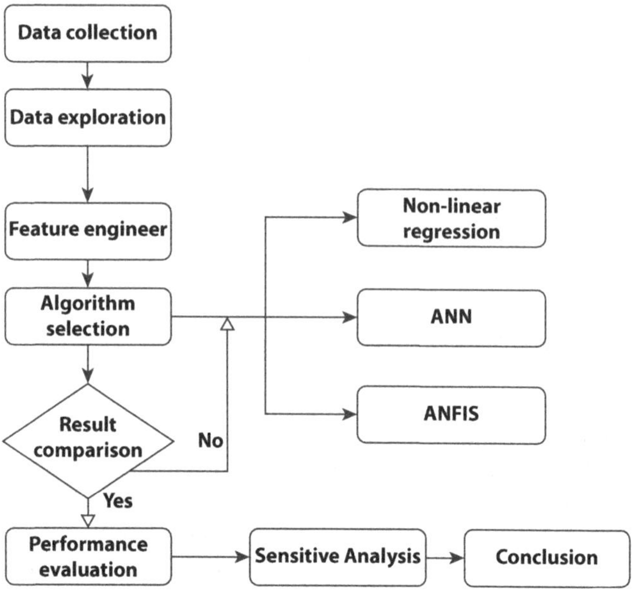

Figure 6.1 Overall framework [21].

helps in understanding the dataset and its features better. This approach enables a deep dive into the data's characteristics before applying machine learning techniques to estimate the moisture content accurately. From the extracted data set, this research utilizes feature engineering to evaluate and conduct the relationship of relevant inputs. Hereafter, three algorithms of Machine Learning, which are Non-linear regression, Artificial Neural Networks, and a system for adaptive fuzzy neural inference will be included to compare and evaluate the performance. The best methods can be chosen by error and then expanding the practice of this study by analyzing the sensitivity before concluding.

6.3.1 Data Collection

All data is obtained from the JQK Vietnam Company's Digital Manufacturing Operation system (DMO). This factory has presently operated three main production lines as below: Pure Soluble Coffee, Coffee Capsules, and Decaffeinated Coffee Beans. The main scope of this research is to implement the Decaffeinated Coffee Bean Plant, which provides 20000 tons of decaffeinated coffee for the company and the global market. In detail, after extracting caffeine out of green coffee beans with water, the product needs to be dried to reach a moisture of about 12.5%-14.5%.

The drying process of this company contains 11 drying decks. Coffee was dried by a system of four heaters using steam energy to create the hot temperature in the drying tower. The motivation of the atmosphere inside the deck comes from a system of six fans to circulate air and push it out of the environment. The detailed process is divided into seven groups: discharging, primary drying, secondary drying, tertiary drying, quaternary drying, cooling, and air exhausting. Especially, there is a sampling point for operations to record data and control the moisture in the eleventh deck. The coffee after getting the moisture standard from 12.5% to 14.5% could be delivered by a coffee pipe system to fill and pack in the filling station.

This dataset is about the primary factors in the process of coffee drying manufacturing, which seem to affect the moisture standard of coffee. It was recorded manually and tracked by operators in every drying batch to self-control moisture and support statistical process control purposes. This data set consists of 759 data points with each point containing 12 attributions. There are 11 attributions out of 12 that represent input columns,

Table 6.1 The characteristics of a dataset.

ID	Attribute	Description	Range	Unit
1	Bean batch	Number of bean batch	[1,758]	NA
2	Batch time	Drying time of coffee	[4574,5283]	second
3	Fill timer	Filling time	[680,720]	second
4	First sub-batch mass	The mass weight of the first sub-batch	[152,190]	kg
5	The last sub-batch mass	The mass weight of the last sub-batch	[670,845]	kg
6	Solid dosing	The mass weight of the liquid supply	[553,1095]	kg
7	$t°$ Heater 1	$t°$ of Heater 1	[105,125]	°C_
8	$t°$ Heater 2	$t°$ of Heater 2	[80,97]	°C_
9	$t°$ Heater 3	$t°$ of Heater 3	[65,79]	°C_
10	$t°$ Heater 4	$t°$ of Heater 4	[48,55]	°C_
11	Moisture	Moisture of bean batch	[12.5,14.5]	%

including bean batch, total mass, batch time, fill time, first sub-batch mass, last sub-batch mass, solid dosing, t° of Heater 1, t° of heater 2, t° of heater 3 and t° of heater 4, and the last column represents the output that the model is required to predict which here is the moisture of coffee beans. Table 6.1 presents the characteristics of a dataset.

6.3.2 Data Preprocessing

6.3.2.1 Missing Value Detection and Attribute Visualization

In the following, we use missing value detection to check which values are missing, which can be seen by using the IsNull() function. Besides, we also use duplicated() function to know if there are any duplicating data points.

Furthermore, we analyze the relationship between each attribute within our dataset through the use of the correlation function corr(). The correlation values will range from 0 to 1, where values nearing 1 denote a higher degree of linkage between the two parameters. Figure 6.2 illustrates the

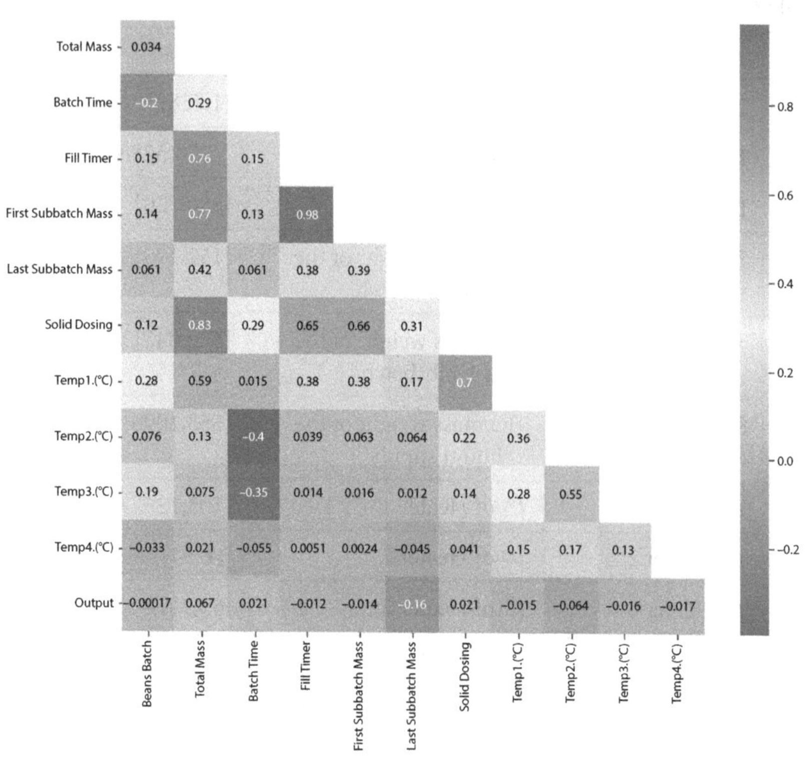

Figure 6.2 Overview of the characteristic relationships.

overall relation between those attributes. It can be observed that some features are related, such as first sub-batch mass and fill timer; solid dosing, and total mass. Indeed, these correlations are very influential to each other. For example, the first sub-batch mass is the decisive factor affecting the time to fill the coffee into the drying tower, so this correlation is up to 0.98.

6.3.2.2 *Normalization*

Normalization is a basic pre-processing step before training ML models, and it is used for standardizing the range of characteristics in the input dataset. When there is a significant difference in the ranges of characteristics in input data or unalignment in the measurement unit, data normalization can be applied. ML models are likely to be inefficient as a result of the disparities in the range of input features. As a result, data standardization approaches before implementing machine learning models to ensure that the ML model has the most effective learning ability.

Normalization and standardization are two major strategies for preparing data before ML models. In this case, the normalization technique will scale each input variable separately in the 0 - 1 range value domain, which is the value domain of the attribute where machine learning models often perform best.

During the normalization process, data is rescaled from its original range so that all values fall from 0 to 1. For normalization, the lowest and highest observable values must be known or precisely calculated. The following is how the formula is shown:

$$x = \frac{x - min}{\max - min} \tag{6.1}$$

6.3.2.3 *Standardization*

Scaling the dataset's distribution is necessary for standardization. Generally, the standard deviation is 1 and the mean of the values is 0. This is the same as centering the data or deducting the mean value. Similar to normalization, standardization can be helpful—and in some cases, necessary—in ML when the input data has a large range of values and is difficult to scale. The foundation of standardization is the presumption that the data have a well-behaved mean and standard deviation and fit into a Gaussian distribution.

Calculating the mean and standard deviation of observable variables is a prerequisite for standardization. Instead of using the complete dataset, it might be able to calculate those values by using data for training. The formula is presented as follows:

$$x = \frac{x - mean}{standard\ deviation} \tag{6.2}$$

6.3.2.4 Cross-Validation

I is a statistical method used in the domain of artificial intelligence to compare the outcome of ML models. This technique is simple to understand, and implement, and provides more reliable estimates than other methods. Cross-validation is a sampling method for evaluating ML models when data are scarce. This key parameter is k, which represents the number of slices into which the data will be divided.

6.3.3 Research Methodology

6.3.3.1 Multi-Layer Perceptron (MLP) Regression

Feedforward neural networks process data in a multidirectional pattern. It also implies that the activation signals will go ahead and never go back to the nodes they have already encountered throughout each training iteration. In addition, while employing feedforward neural networks, it is presumed that every input data scenario is independent of every other scenario. Put differently, every training labeled point is handled separately from every other labeled point.

There are three types of feedforward neural networks. The single-layer perceptron (SLP) [22], MLP [23], and extreme learning machine (ELM) [24]. The input and output layers of an MLP are separated by one or more hidden layers. The MLP can therefore learn non-linear problems. Nevertheless, the weight-update process also gets more complex as the model gets more sophisticated. The back-propagation algorithm is an effective method for updating weights.

6.3.3.2 Adaptive Neuro-Fuzzy Inference System – ANFIS

A fuzzy inference system that was trained using an algorithm from neural network theory serves as the foundation for the ANFIS model. Three-input,

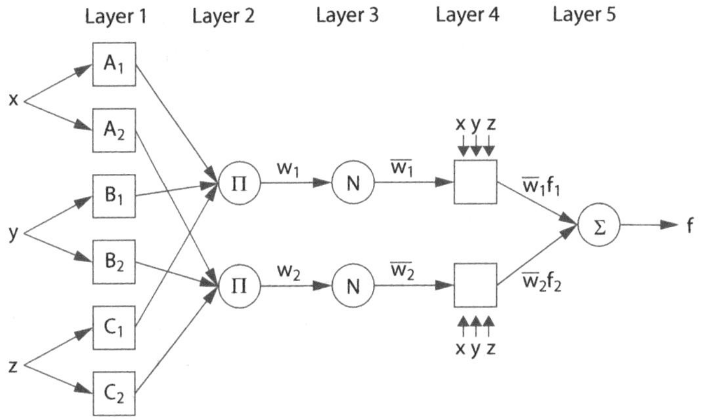

Figure 6.3 The structure of model ANFIS.

two-rule ANFIS Sugeno-type systems are shown in Figure 6.3. The transmitter direction is the connection between tuo nodes.

In Figure 6.3, there are three input variables, x, y, and z in the ANFIS model. Each input variable contains three membership functions (A1, A2), (B1, B2), (C1, C2) respectively. The Sugeno-type fuzzy rule for a linear output variable is set up as follows:

If x equals A_i, y equals B_i, and z equals C_i then:

$$f_i = p_i x + q_i y + r_i z + s_i \tag{6.3}$$

A_i, B_i, C_i: fuzzy sets (uniquely identified by the membership function)
f_i: output of new layers
p_i, q_i, r_i, s_i : training coefficients
Membership function Gaussian:

$$\mu_{z'}(x') = f(x', \sigma) = \exp\left(-\left(x' - \frac{c}{\sigma}\right)^2\right) \tag{6.4}$$

x': input value to node ith

c and σ (premise parameters): width of the Gaussian curve center of the corresponding set

- The first layer contains the adaptive node is represented by i and outputs are calculated with the function as:

$$O_{1.i} = \mu_{A_i}(x), i = 1,2 \tag{6.5}$$

μ: membership function

- The second layer ís the rule one. Each node in this layer has a circular shape. An output from a rule node represents the product of the input signal. The fire strength of each rule is represented by a node. The sum of all the incoming signals is the output.

$$O_{2.i} = w_i = \mu_{A_i}(x)\mu_{B_i}(y)\mu_{C_i}(z) \tag{6.6}$$

- The third layer contains a fixed node named Norm. The ith node calculates the proportion of the firing strength of the ith rule to the combined firing strength of all rules. Outputs (normalized firing strengths) are calculated below.

$$O_{3.i} = \overline{w_l} = \frac{w_i}{\sum w_i} \tag{6.7}$$

- A node function is present in every node of the fourth layer.

$$O_{4.i} = \overline{w_l} f_i = \frac{w_i}{\sum w_i}(p_i x + q_i y + r_i z + s_i) \tag{6.8}$$

- The summation layer or the fifth layer consists of one output node. In this layer, every fixed node is labeled sum using the total of all incoming signals:

$$O_{5.i} = \sum_{i=1}^{2} O_{4.i} = \sum_{i=1}^{2} \overline{w_l} f_i \tag{6.9}$$

The output value of f is described in the following equation:

$$(x, y, z) = \frac{w_1 f_1 + w_2 f_2}{w_1 + w_2}, \text{ f1 and f2 are functions with x, y and z.} \tag{6.10}$$

6.3.3.3 *Feature Selection Techniques*

Feature subset selection is one method for reducing the number of input variables and improving model performance. It can help to lower the computational expense of modeling and increases the model's efficacy. Moreover, feature selection is associated with dimensionality reduction strategies, since it endeavors to minimize the quantity of input variables inside a predictive model. Whereas feature selection chooses which features to retain in the dataset and which to discard, dimensionality reduction projects the data to generate new input features one at a time. Therefore, dimension reduction is an option to feature selection rather than a kind of feature selection.

6.3.3.3.1 Mutual Information (MI)

The mutual dependence between two random variables that are calculated simultaneously is measured by a quantity called mutual information. In particular, it quantifies the average amount of information that one random variable conveys about another. Given two random variables, X and Y, whose joint distribution is described by $P(X, Y)$, the definition of their mutual information is as follows:

$$I(X;Y) = \sum_{x \in \mathcal{X}} \sum_{y \in \mathcal{Y}} P(x,y) \log \frac{P(x,y)}{P(x)P(y)} \tag{6.11}$$

where P(x) and P(y) are the marginal distributions of x and y.

MI always has a value larger than or equal to zero, indicating a closer relationship between the two variables. In the event that the computed result is zero, the variables are independent. In general, mutual information is utilized as a sort of correlation coefficient to evaluate the dependence between random variables.

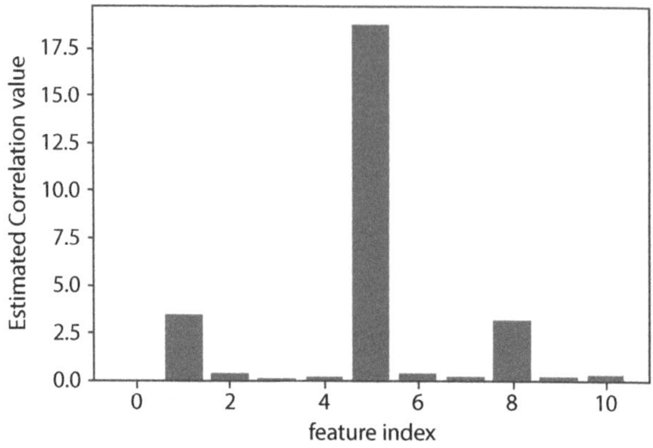

Figure 6.4 The plot of correlation metric feature selections.

6.3.3.3.2 Correlation (Pearson, Spearman)

The measure of the relationship between two variables changes is a correlation. The most common correlation measure is named Pearson's correlation, which computes the linear relationship between numerical variables under the assumption that each variable has a Gaussian distribution. This is done by calculating a correlation between the regressor and the target and compare with a critical value F and then a p-value is obtained to indicate the significance of the correlation.

- A correlation is calculated between each regressor and the target.
- It is transformed into a p-value and subsequently an F score.

Because of the 11 attributes in the experimental dataset, the research will examine the results of executing some loops to test the combinations of 2 to 11 attributes.

The estimated mutual information between every feature and the target variable is shown on the y-axis. We can determine that many features have clear relationships when compared to the correlation feature selection approach. This may be caused by statistical noise existing in the dataset. Based on Figure 6.4, by using the mutual information algorithm for feature selection, we can see that there is not much influence on the results from the first feature, whereas we can see the sixth feature expresses the relationship with the results clearly. Similarly, by using the correlation method as indicated in Figure 6.5.

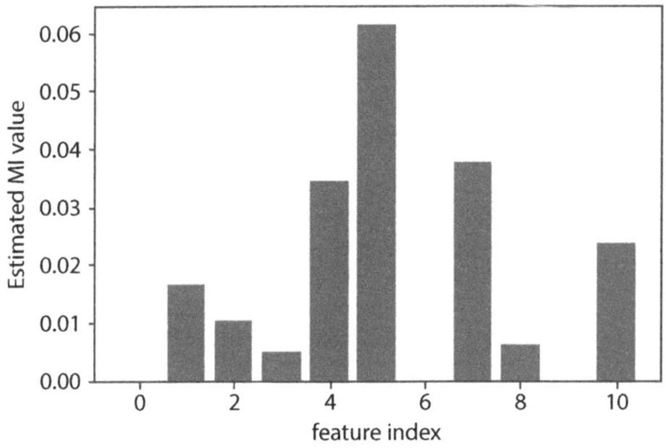

Figure 6.5 Feature selection plot of MI value.

6.4 Results and Analysis

6.4.1 Model Evaluation

To compare and evaluate the effectiveness of the models against each other, they can be used as the standard measures for the regression problem. This model is a machine-learning technique for figuring out how one independent variable and one dependent variable are related. In this research, we use the following metrics to assess:

MAE: a simple metric to calculate the absolute difference between the actual and predicted values of the model.
RMSE: a simple square root of mean squared error. The value represents the standard deviation of the residuals and shows how far from the regression line data points are.

6.4.2 Analysis Results

The result of the machine learning problem is combined with the knowledge of ANN and ANFIS models. It is evaluated the accuracy by MAE and RMSE can be shown below:

Tables 6.2 and 6.3 present the results of experiments according to each fold by methods ANN and ANFIS. This result was calculated by using the attributes of the dataset as input information for the models. The results are evaluated on measures such as MAE and RMSE. According to Tables 6.2 and 6.3, the ANFIS model generates better results than the ANN in almost

Table 6.2 Experimental results from the ANN model.

KFold	MAE	RMSE
Fold 1	0.4627	0.5682
Fold 2	0.3156	0.4294
Fold 3	0.3154	0.4843
Fold 4	0.2589	0.3300
Fold 5	0.4773	0.5682
Average	**0.3660**	**0.4760**

Table 6.3 Experimental results of the ANFIS model.

KFold	MAE	RMSE
Fold 1	0.2159	0.2956
Fold 2	0.2212	0.3051
Fold 3	0.2629	0.3650
Fold 4	0.2387	0.3083
Fold 5	0.2537	0.3439
Average	**0.2385**	**0.3236**

all values from both measures. Generally, the results also provide that the ANFIS model from two measures is much more efficient than the ANN model.

6.4.3 Analysis Results with Feature Selection

6.4.3.1 Feature Selection with ANN

In this part, two feature subset selection methods, Mutual Information (MI) and Correlation Feature Selection are investigated. The outcomes of the ANFIS model and the ANN model are shown in Tables 6.4 and 6.5, respectively. Experimental results are evaluated by 5 folds.

Table 6.4 Experimental results of ANN model combined with MI feature selection.

Feature selection	MAE	RMSE
2 features	0.2448	0.3342
3 features	0.2459	0.3399
4 features	0.2691	0.3588
5 features	0.2742	0.3651
6 features	0.2535	0.3412
7 features	0.2933	0.3917
8 features	0.3283	0.4257
9 features	0.3391	0.4447
10 features	0.3225	0.4379
11 features	0.3660	0.4760

Table 6.4 indicates the results of the ANN model combined with the MI-FS method based on a 5-fold evaluation. The results indicate that the ANN is an efficient model when selecting two features and generating the result of the MAE is 0.2448 and the result of RMSE of 0.3342. In addition, the model tends to reduce the results when increasing the number of selected features from eight or more. It demonstrates that numerous features lower the system's efficiency in a dataset.

Similarly, Table 6.5 presents the experimental results of the ANN network model with the feature selection method based on the combination of features. The difference between this feature selection model and the MI model is the combination of three features gives the best results with MAE being 0.2433 and RMSE being 0.3287. This result is higher than the result of the ANN model combined with the MI feature selection method. Specifically, by using the MAE measure, the ANN model combined with the Correlation feature selection method generates a higher result than the ANN model combined with the MI method about +0.0015.

Figure 6.6 presents a comparison chart of the ANN method combined with two feature selection methods on the MAE measure and the combination of different feature numbers. Generally, the correlation feature selection method generates better or worse results than the MI method depending on the feature selection combination. For instance, when the feature selection combination is two and three, the correlation method provides a better result or equal result to MI. Otherwise, the number of features is five, seven, and nine, the MI method gives better results than the correlation method.

Table 6.5 Experimental results of ANN model combined correlation feature selection (Pearson, Spearman).

Feature selection	MAE	RMSE
2 features	0.2487	0.3502
3 features	0.2433	0.3287
4 features	0.2687	0.3559
5 features	0.2498	0.3358
6 features	0.2560	0.3432
7 features	0.2847	0.3729
8 features	0.3457	0.4809
9 features	0.2976	0.3892
10 features	0.3333	0.4480
11 features	0.3660	0.4760

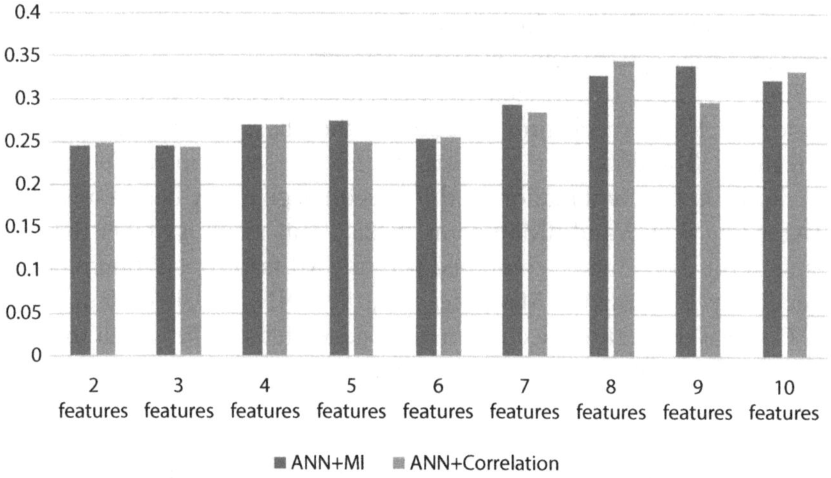

Figure 6.6 Comparison chart of ANN method combined with two feature selection methods on MAE measure.

Table 6.6 The experimental results of the ANFIS model combined MI feature selection.

Feature selection	MAE	RMSE
2 features	0.2356	0.3255
3 features	0.2358	0.3248
4 features	0.2805	0.3742
5 features	0.2956	0.3822
6 features	0.2388	0.3264
7 features	0.2972	0.3844
8 features	0.2382	0.3235
9 features	0.2586	0.3431
10 features	0.2379	0.3227
All features	0.2385	0.3236

Table 6.7 The experimental results of the ANFIS model combined correlation feature selection (Pearson, Spearman).

Feature selection	MAE	RMSE
2 features	0.2370	0.3254
3 features	0.3816	0.5035
4 features	0.2383	0.3231
5 features	0.2886	0.3554
6 features	0.2446	0.3258
7 features	0.2431	0.3268
8 features	0.2752	0.3623
9 features	0.2416	0.3252
10 features	0.2411	0.3271
All features	0.2385	0.3236

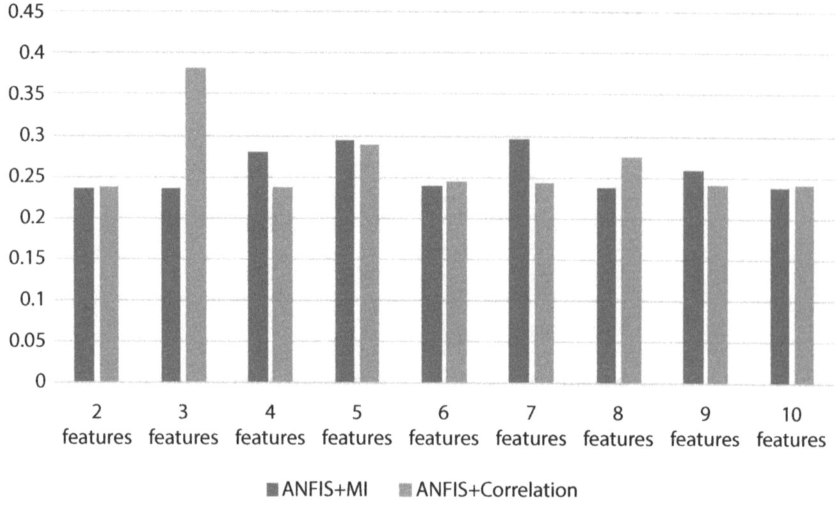

Figure 6.7 Comparison chart of ANFIS method combined with two feature selection methods on MAE measure.

6.4.3.2 *Feature Selection with ANFIS*

In this part, two methods of feature selection based on a combination of features when using the ANFIS model are researched and evaluated. The results are presented in Tables 6.6 and 6.7. Thereafter, the research concludes the results between the two models ANN and ANFIS when applied with the best feature selection method for each model. Figure 6.7 presents a comparison chart of the ANFIS method combined with two feature selection techniques, evaluating the MAE measure across different feature combinations.

6.5 Conclusion

This research aims to evaluate the prediction efficacy of machine learning models, as well as to deeply learn about the manufacturing process. The beverage company that specialized in coffee drying techniques provided the practical data for this research. Although they have invested a lot in their database, it has not yet been fully utilized in the investigation of the relationship between process parameters and moisture prediction. To arrive at the outcome, two supervised machine learning techniques (ANN and ANFIS) were conducted, two transformation data techniques (Normalization and Standardization), two evaluation measures (MAE and RMSE), and two feature selection techniques (Mutual Information and Correlation) were also conducted. The result, the ANFIS method shows a better performance in predictive food drying techniques, especially in coffee products. In practice, the ANFIS model could be used as a reliable technique in moisture prediction when the accuracy is approximately about 80%.

There is still big potential for development. The final percentages of precision and accuracy were both around 80%, but additional improvements could be made to raise it even higher. To provide a more contextualized picture of prediction, many attributes may be included. One of these could be the weather, or rain discharge that could dramatically affect the data that is currently available. If the inputs were better, there is practically no doubt that the results would be better.

In conclusion, there are still enormous ways this topic might be developed. However, any lack of increased results can be explained by the fact that we are in a satisficing situation. For instance, improving repetition may cause accuracy to fluctuate, indicating that no overall improvement is feasible. The outcome could be considered a compromise. Improved production quality management results from effective moisture and process parameter prediction, all of which are positive developments for the business. As a result, more effort should be put into quality prediction and process parameter optimization to allow rapid response times while operating production for new product trials or gain the loyalty of consumers.

References

1. Khan, Md.I.H., Sablani, S.S., Joardder, M.U.H., Karim, M.A., Application of machine learning-based approach in food drying: opportunities and challenges. *Dry. Technol.*, 40, 6, 1051–1067, May 2022, doi: 10.1080/07373937.2020.1853152.
2. Ansari, S., Maftoon-Azad, N., Farahnaky, A., Hosseini, E., Badii, F., Effect of moisture content on textural attributes of dried figs. *Int. Agrophys.*, 28, 403–412, 2014, https://doi.org/10.2478/intag-2014-0031.
3. Aghbashlo, M., Mobli, H., Rafiee, S., Madadlou, A., The use of artificial neural network to predict exergetic performance of spray drying process: A preliminary study. *Comput. Electron. Agric.*, 88, 32–43, Oct. 2012, doi: 10.1016/j.compag.2012.06.007.
4. Amaral, R., Andrade, E.T., Gomes, F.C., Borém, F.M., Lemos, I., Dias, C.A., Simulation of coffee fruit drying using computational fluid dynamics. *Coffee Sci.*, 13, 4, 477–488, 2018. ISSN 1984-3909, [S. l.].
5. Odeny, D.A., Chemininingwa, G.N., Shibairo, S.I., Biochemical Components of Shaded Coffee under Different Management Levels. *Adv. J. Food Sci. Technol.*, 12, 9, 9, 2016, doi: 10.19026/ajfst.12.3063.

6. How is caffeine removed to produce decaffeinated coffee?, Scientific American, Accessed: Mar. 18, 2024. [Online]. Available: https://www.scientificamerican.com/article/how-is-caffeine-removed-t/.
7. Angiulli, G. and Versaci, M., A Neuro-Fuzzy Network for the Design of Circular and Triangular Equilateral Microstrip Antennas. *Int. J. Infrared Millimeter Waves*, 23, 10, 1513–1520, Oct. 2002, doi: 10.1023/A:1020333704205.
8. Le, T.M., Vo, T.M., Pham, T.N., Dao, S.V.T., A Novel Wrapper–Based Feature Selection for Early Diabetes Prediction Enhanced With a Metaheuristic. *IEEE Access*, 9, 7869–7884, 2021, doi: 10.1109/ACCESS.2020.3047942.
9. Hussain, M.A. and Rahman, M.S., Thermal conductivity prediction of fruits and vegetables using neural networks. *Int. J. Food Prop.*, 2, 2, 121–137, Jul. 1999, doi: 10.1080/10942919909524596.
10. Karim, M.A. and Hawlader, M.N.A., Mathematical modelling and experimental investigation of tropical fruits drying. *Int. J. Heat Mass Transfer*, 48, 23, 4914–4925, Nov. 2005, doi: 10.1016/j.ijheatmasstransfer.2005.04.035.
11. Tran, H.M., Pham, K.T., Vo, T.M., Le, T.-H., Huynh, T.T.M., Dao, S.V.T., A New Approach for Estimation of Physical Properties of Irregular Shape Fruit. *IEEE Access*, 11, 46550–46560, 2023, doi: 10.1109/ACCESS.2023.3273777.
12. Huynh, T.T.M., Le, T.M., That, L.T., Tran, L.V., Dao, S.V.T., A Two-Stage Feature Selection Approach for Fruit Recognition Using Camera Images With Various Machine Learning Classifiers. *IEEE Access*, 10, 132260–132270, 2022, doi: 10.1109/ACCESS.2022.3227712.
13. Physical Characteristics Estimation for Irregularly Shaped Fruit Using Two Cameras, IEEE Conference Publication, IEEE Xplore, Accessed: Mar. 18, 2024. [Online]. Available: https://ieeexplore.ieee.org/document/10207992.
14. Erenturk, S. and Erenturk, K., Comparison of genetic algorithm and neural network approaches for the drying process of carrot. *J. Food Eng.*, 78, 3, 905–912, Feb. 2007, doi: 10.1016/j.jfoodeng.2005.11.031.
15. Li, H., Linear Regression, in: *Numerical Methods Using Java: For Data Science, Analysis, and Engineering*, H. Li (Ed.), pp. 915–978, Apress, Berkeley, CA, 2022, doi: 10.1007/978-1-4842-6797-4_14.
16. Woinaroschy, A., Jinescu, G., Tebrencu, C., Application of Neural Nets for Optimization of Vibro-Fluidization Drying. *Chem. Eng. Technol.*, 23, 2, 130–132, 2000, doi: 10.1002/(SICI)1521-4125(200002)23:2<130::AID-CEAT130>3.0.CO;2-B.
17. Osisanwo, F.Y., Akinsola, J.E.T., Awodele, O., Hinmikaiye, J.O., Olakanmi, O., Akinjobi, J., Supervised Machine Learning Algorithms: Classification and Comparison. *International Journal of Computer Trends and Technology (IJCTT)* 48, 3, 128–138, June 2017. ISSN:2231-2803. www.ijcttjournal.org.
18. Prakash, O., and Kumar, A. ANFIS modelling of a natural convection greenhouse drying system for jaggery: an experimental validation. *Int. J. Sustain. Energy*, 33, 2, 316–335, 2012, https://doi.org/10.1080/14786451.2012.724070

19. Lertworasirikul, S., Drying kinetics of semi-finished cassava crackers: A comparative study. *LWT Food Sci. Technol.*, 41, 8, 1360–1371, Nov. 2008, doi: 10.1016/j.lwt.2007.09.009.
20. Lertworasirikul, S. and Tipsuwan, Y., Moisture content and water activity prediction of semi-finished cassava crackers from drying process with artificial neural network. *J. Food Eng.*, 84, 1, 65–74, Jan. 2008, doi: 10.1016/j.jfoodeng.2007.04.019.
21. Sun, Q., Zhang, M., Mujumdar, A.S., Recent developments of artificial intelligence in drying of fresh food: A review. *Crit. Rev. Food Sci. Nutr.*, 59, 14, 2258–2275, Aug. 2019, doi: 10.1080/10408398.2018.1446900.
22. Macaluso, A., Orazi, F., Klusch, M., Lodi, S., Sartori, C., A Variational Algorithm for Quantum Single Layer Perceptron, in: *Machine Learning, Optimization, and Data Science*, G. Nicosia, V. Ojha, E. La Malfa, G. La Malfa, P. Pardalos, G. Di Fatta, G. Giuffrida, R. Umeton (Eds.), pp. 341–356, Springer Nature Switzerland, Cham, 2023, doi: 10.1007/978-3-031-25891-6_26.
23. Le, M.T., Thanh Vo, M., Mai, L., Dao, S.V.T., Predicting heart failure using deep neural network, in: *2020 International Conference on Advanced Technologies for Communications (ATC)*, Oct. 2020, pp. 221–225, doi: 10.1109/ATC50776.2020.9255445.
24. Pan, Z., Meng, Z., Chen, Z., Gao, W., Shi, Y., A two-stage method based on extreme learning machine for predicting the remaining useful life of rolling-element bearings. *Mech. Syst. Signal Process.*, 144, 106899, Oct. 2020, doi: 10.1016/j.ymssp.2020.106899.

7

Survivable AI for Defense Strategies in Industry 4.0

Anuradha Reddy[1]*, G. S. Pradeep Ghantasala[2], Ochin Sharma[3], Mamatha Kurra[1], Kumar Dilip[2] and Pellakuri Vidyullatha[4]

[1]*Department of Computer Science and Engineering, Malla Reddy Institute of Technology & Science, Maisammaguda, Secunderabad, Telangana, India*
[2]*Department of Computer Science and Engineering, Alliance College of Engineering and Design, Alliance University, Bangalore, Karnataka, India*
[3]*Department of Computer Science and Engineering, Chitkara Institute of Engineering and Technology, Chitkara University, Rajpura, Punjab, India*
[4]*Department of Computer Science and Engineering, Koneru Lakshmaiah Education Foundation, Vaddeswaram, Guntur, Andhra Pradesh, India*

Abstract

The rapid progression of Industry 4.0 brings forth new opportunities and defies the defense segment, dictating the expansion of survivable artificial intelligence (AI) schemes. These systems play a vital role in preserving security, protecting precarious infrastructure, and improving the adeptness and efficacy of defense operations. This chapter discusses the key considerations for building survivable AI schemes that can endure and adapt to various threats and disruptions within the defense strategies of Industry 4.0. Mobility stands as an essential quality of survivable AI systems, requiring the depiction of discharged contraptions, fault-tolerant designs, and dispersed contrivances to lower predilections and reduce the likelihood of errors. Security measures, including encryption, access control, and invasion recognition, are essential in preventing unauthorized access, tampering, and manipulation. Provocative heftiness is vital for protecting AI systems against malicious attacks. Practices such as refining training data and implementing anomaly detection help in fortifying AI models against adversarial tactics. Moreover, examination and situational attentiveness abilities are essential, authorizing unremitting valuation of device portrayal, real-time hitch recognition, and human clench of

**Corresponding author*: anuradhareddy.anu@gmail.com

M. Thirunavukkarasan, S. A. Sahaaya Arul Mary, Sathiyaraj. R, G. S. Pradeep Ghantasala and Mudassir Khan (eds.) Artificial Intelligence and Machine Learning for Industry 4.0, (169–196)

the device's enactment. Survivable AI arrangements should preserve the capability for ceaseless facts and change to revolve the self-encouraged nature of Industry 4.0 environs. This enmeshed leveraging reinforcement learning approaches, ceaseless learning agreements, and data-driven decision-making practices to acquaint imitations and approaches based mostly on developing instances.

Virtuous observations are prevailing, protection clarity; explicate skill, and detachment in AI decision-making. Mitigating preconceptions and discrimination, regarding isolation and records safety concords, and conforming to virtuous philosophies and actual instances are dangerous for responsible AI temperament. Severance and gridlock classifications play a massive role in making sure decisions of operations throughout gadget calamities, cyberattacks, or interruptions. Retentive discharged modules, dispersed strategies, and failover devices permit backup competencies and structure flexibility. The elaboration of survivable AI for safety strategies in Industry 4.0 compels interdisciplinary collaboration among AI specialists, cybersecurity experts, safety professionals, and ethicists. Together, they can address the progressing challenges and safeguard responsible and effective use of AI in security applications.

Keywords: Artificial intelligence (AI), machine learning (ML), industry 4.0, industrial automation, smart manufacturing, industrial IoT (I IoT), predictive maintenance, cyber-physical systems

7.1 Introduction

The initiation of Industry 4.0 [1], categorized by the amalgamation of progressive tools such as artificial intelligence (AI), Internet of Things (IoT), and big data analytics, has transfigured various segments, including defense. The protection diligence is leveraging these industrial progressions to improve effective adeptness, elevate resource portions, and reinforce retreat procedures. Conversely, as security systems become gradually consistent and contingent on AI, they also face a novel set of encounters associated with pliability, refuge, and malleability in the facade of evolving extortions. This has led to the advent of the idea of survivable AI for security tactics in Industry 4.0.

Survivable AI systems are intended to withstand and adapt to disruptions, attacks, and failures, ensuring the continuity and effectiveness of defense operations. In the context of Industry 4.0, survivable AI for protection strategies [2] takes on an essential role, safeguarding essential infrastructure, protecting touchy data, and allowing real-time decision-making in dynamic and complicated environments. These structures include superior technology and methodologies to improve protection structures against numerous threats, such as cyberattacks, hostile manipulations, and device failures.

This research discovers the implications and essential concerns for emergent survivable AI structures for protection strategies in Industry 4.0 [3]. It investigates the multidimensional sides of pliability, refuge, and malleability which might be critical for protecting the survivability of AI schemes in protection solicitations. Furthermore, decent deliberations and permissible outlines are deliberated, accentuating the accountable and decent practice of AI in security operations.

Furthermore, this investigation examines the scientific progressions and best practices essential for the erection of survivable AI systems. It refuges issues such as confrontational sturdiness, unceasing learning and reworking, observing and situational responsiveness, dismissal and conflict management systems, and alliance and evidence sharing. By investigating these aspects, we can gain insights into the complex scenario of survivable AI for security strategies in Industry 4.0 and comprehend the defies and prospects it presents.

7.2 Purpose

The goal of emerging survivable AI for defense tactics in Industry 4.0 is to safeguard the sturdiness, dependability, and flexibility of AI classifications used in defense bids within the milieu of the quarter trade upheaval. The initiation of Industry 4.0 conveys interrelated and intellectual systems, with AI, that can suggestively improve defense proficiencies. Nevertheless, as these classifications develop progressively intricate and interrelated, they also become further susceptible to several coercions and distractions.

The goal of survivable AI is to discourse these encounters and produce AI systems t that can endure accusatorial bouts, system fiascos, or other distractions without negotiating their capacity to achieve perilous defense roles. The expansion of survivable AI intentions to deliver the following assistance:

- Heftiness: Survivable AI systems are premeditated to withstand diverse types of outbreaks, counting accusatorial outbreaks, safeguarding that they can endure functioning effectually even in the occurrence of malicious ideas or efforts to deploy their behavior.
- Pliability: Survivable AI systems have the capability to acclimate to fluctuating environments and convalesce from commotions, such as system fiascos or communique outages. They can sustain their functionality and operative efficacy in the face of unpredicted actions.

- Safety: Survivable AI emphasizes building AI systems that are resilient to unauthorized access, data breaches, or other cybersecurity threats. This certifies that subtle defense-related evidence remains protected and confidential.
- Fidelity: By evolving survivable AI, a conviction can be recognized in the performance and steadfastness of AI schemes used in security. This is decisive in circumstances where verdicts made by AI schemes can have momentous significance and need to be reliable.
- Improved security competencies: Survivable AI permits security organizations to influence the benefits of AI technologies while sustaining operational effectiveness. AI schemes that are vigorous, resilient, and secure can sustain defense claims such as threat detection, decision support, autonomous systems, and cyber defense.

Overall, the resolution of survivable AI for security tactics in Industry 4.0 [4] is to bind the probable AI technologies while extenuating threats and ensuring the reliable performance of AI schemes in defense claims. By addressing challenges interrelated to heftiness, pliability, refuge, and fidelity, survivable AI purposes to afford security organizations with steadfast and operative tackles to improve their competencies in the contemporary epoch of combat and refuge.

7.3 Scope

The scope of survivable AI for security strategies in Industry 4.0 comprehends a wide range of features associated with the expansion, disposition, and application of AI schemes in security requests within the milieu of the fourth business upheaval. Some crucial expanses within this scope comprise the following:

- AI scheme strategy and architecture: This comprises the expansion of AI procedures, replicas, and designs that are resilient, vigorous, and protected. It encompasses conniving AI schemes with built-in devices to perceive and alleviate accusatorial bouts [5], knob qualms, and convalesce from fiascos or distractions.
- Antagonistic machine learning: This extent emphasizes perusing the susceptibilities of AI schemes to antagonistic

outbreaks, emerging procedures to perceive and guard against such outbreaks, and conniving procedures that are resilient to operation or exploitation.

- Cybersecurity and menace recognition: Survivable AI comprehends the expansion of AI-powered systems for sleuthing, analyzing, and retorting to cyber threats in defense systems and substructures. This comprises glitch recognition, invasion recognition, and real-time monitoring of system circulation to detect probable cyber coercions.
- Resilient autonomous systems: The scope covers the development of autonomous systems, such as unmanned aerial vehicles (UAVs) [6, 35, 36], autonomous ground vehicles, or robotic systems, that rely on AI for decision-making and situational awareness. These systems should be able to operate in dynamic and unpredictable environments, adapting to changing conditions and recovering from failures or disruptions.
- Data confidentiality and security: This extent discourses the fortification of delicate defense-related information and the expansion of privacy-preserving AI procedures. It encompasses certifying that AI schemes operate within authorized and principled limitations, shielding distinct discretion civil liberties and averting unlawful access or drip of penetrating evidence.
- Human-AI rapport and decision sustenance: Survivable AI reconnoiters the amalgamation of AI technologies with social machinists in security scenarios. This comprises emerging AI schemes that deliver decision support, enhance social competencies, and permit actual alliance between humans and AI.
- Principled contemplations and strategic agendas: The opportunity asylums investigate the principled insinuations of using AI in security, creating procedure agendas, and strategies for accountable AI positioning. It comprises contemplations such as human control, accountability, transparency, and faithfulness to universal benevolent decrees [7].
- Canons and accreditation: Survivable AI comprises the creation of canons, accreditations, and supervisory agendas to guarantee the fidelity, steadfastness, and fortification of AI structures used in security bids. This encompasses estimating and authenticating acquiescence with precise conditions associated with refuge, pliability, and concert.

- Training and edification: The scope also comprises drill security employees in the use, maneuverer, and supervision of AI schemes, as well as hovering awareness about the probable threats, encounters, and best practices allied with survivable AI in security.
- Alliance and information allocation: Given the intricate and sprouting fauna of survivable AI, alliance among security organizations, universities, businesses, and supervisory frames is decisive. This possibility comprises nurturing alliances, easing info allocation, and endorsing investigative and expansion enterprises to advance survivable AI for security tactics in Business 4.0.

It is significant to note that the choice of survivable AI for security strategies in Industry 4.0 is active and subject to enduring improvements and incipient challenges in AI technology, defense necessities, and cybersecurity scenario.

7.4 History of AI for Defense Strategies in Industry 4.0

The history of AI for security tactics in Industry 4.0 is thoroughly tangled with the wider expansion of AI technologies and their application in the security segment. Here is an outline of vital advances:

Initial espousal of AI in security AI technologies began creating their way into the security segment as early as the 1950s. The emphasis during this retro was on using AI for decision support schemes and premature procedures of proficient systems to aid military forecasting [8] and investigation. Improvements in machine learning in the 1980s and 1990s and machine learning practices, such as neural networks and arithmetical modeling, expanded eminence. This empowered security bids to influence data-driven tactics for errands like pattern appreciation, prime target identification, and glitch recognition.

Autonomous systems and Automation: The advent of autonomous systems and automation in the twilight of the 20th century had a philosophical impression on security strategies. UAVs, unmanned robots, and autonomous vehicles were instigated to be deployed for investigation, exploration, and logistics operations. Amalgamation of Cyber-Physical Schemes [8]: The intensification of Industry 4.0 in the initial 21st century brought about the amalgamation of AI and cyber-physical schemes in security. This encompassed the use of interrelated strategies, radars, and grids to empower real-time communique and society among corporeal resources.

AI machineries have played a decisive part in emerging intellectual command and control (C2) [9] schemes for security. These schemes ease supervisory, situational awareness, and harmonization of military services in intricate functioning environment. AI-powered prognostic analytics have been used in security to evaluate threats, anticipate threats, and enhance resource distribution. Machine learning procedures analyze hefty volumes of information to categorize designs, tendencies, and probable safety hazards [10]. As replicated coercions become progressively intelligent, AI has been employed for intellectual refuge and imitation protection.

AI schemes can perceive and respond to cyberattacks in instantaneous, categorize susceptibilities, and improve the pliability of perilous security setups. The practice of AI in security strategies has impelled deliberations around conscience, accountability, transparency, and permissible agendas. Apprehensions over sovereign missiles, predisposition in AI procedures, and the accountable use of AI have designed strategy negotiations and principles.

Human-Machine Team-up [11]: Industry 4.0 and AI have simplified the advancement of human-machine teaming perceptions in security. Collaborative environment, where people and AI schemes work together, improve decision-making, speed, and operational efficacy. The perception of survivable AI has gained significance in security tactics within Industry 4.0. Vigorous AI schemes that can survive accusatorial outbreaks, culpabilities, and interruptions are crucial for preserving operative proficiencies and undertaking endurance.

In summary, the history of survivable AI for security strategies in Industry 4.0 is categorized by developments in AI technologies, the incorporation of autonomous systems, the advent of Industry 4.0, and the emphasis on emerging resilient and vigorous AI schemes to discourse safety challenges in the contemporary security scenario. Generally, the history of AI for security strategies in Industry 4.0 is marked by the embracing of AI technologies athwart several security fields, the amalgamation of cyber-physical schemes, the progression of independent schemes, and the emphasis on sturdiness, pliability [12], and accountable use of AI in the security segment.

Figure 7.1 illustrates the evolution of industry from Industry 1.0 to Industry 4.0, showing the key technological advancements and shifts in manufacturing processes over time. Industry 1.0 marks the introduction of mechanization powered by steam engines, while Industry 2.0 represents the rise of mass production with electricity and assembly lines. Industry

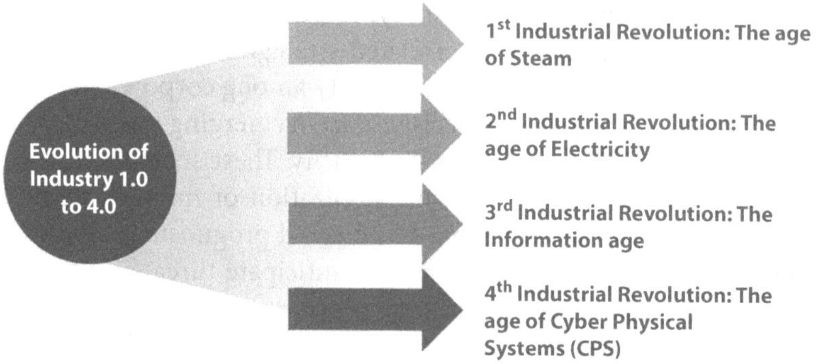

Figure 7.1 Evolution of Industry 1.0 to Industry 4.0.

3.0 highlights the integration of computers and automation, which allowed for greater efficiency and precision. Finally, Industry 4.0, depicted in this figure, encompasses the digital transformation with cyber-physical systems, IoT (Internet of Things), AI (artificial intelligence), and data analytics, leading to smarter, more connected production systems.

7.4.1 AI in Defense

AI has turned out to be progressively significant in the security segment, transfiguring various aspects of military operations. Here are some vital areas where AI is actually exploited in defense:

Autonomous Systems: AI permits the expansion of autonomous systems, including UAVs, unmanned robots, and autonomous vehicles. These classifications can accomplish errands such as investigation, scouting, and logistics operations without unswerving human control. Intelligence, Surveillance, and Reconnaissance (ISR) [13]: AI systems like machine learning and computer vision improve ISR proficiencies by inevitably analyzing large capacities of radar information, categorizing things of curiosity, and sleuthing incongruities. This empowers sooner and more precise management on the turf. Command and Control (C2): AI supports command and control systems by providing real-time information analysis, situational awareness, and decision support. AI procedures can process and infer complex data, abetting military commanders-in-chief in scheduling, organizing, and performing actions.

Cyber Defense: AI is contributory in sleuthing and retorting to replicate threats [14]. AI procedures can analyze system circulation patterns, recognize mistrustful events, and unconventionally retort to alleviate

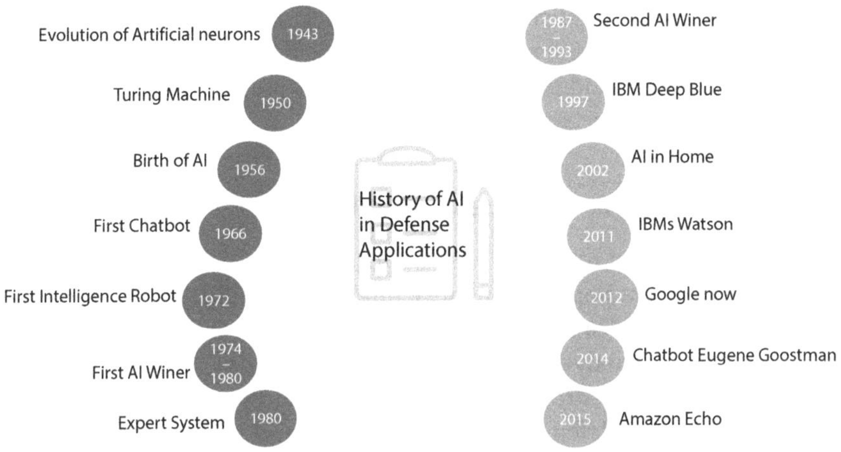

Figure 7.2 History of AI in defense applications.

cyberattacks. AI-powered cybersecurity schemes improve the pliability of security systems and structures. AI systems can analyze ancient and real-time information to envisage latent threats, evaluate hazards, and enhance resource provision. Predictive analytics can contribute to the prognostication of supply chain commotions, categorizing expanses disposed to skirmish, and enhancing security logistics which is illustrated in Figure 7.2.

AI permits precise and effective image and outline recognition, which is decisive for errands such as facemask recognition, article discovery, and goal identification. This competence improves the efficacy of investigation, goal procurement, and menace valuation, permitting AI schemes to comprehend and process human language. This ability is exploited to extents such as astuteness investigation, evidence mining from amorphous facts, and computerized transformation, easing announcement and data allotment in bilingual frameworks [15].

AI-based emulators and computer-generated training environment provide accurate circumstances for military employees to train and advance their assistance. These replications help advance decision-making facilities, strategic awareness, and situational awareness. AI enhances logistics and supply chain management in security operations. AI procedures [16] can analyze information to enhance path forecasting, catalog administration, maintenance setting up, and strength distribution, taming proficiency and dipping outlays. AI-powered conclusion care schemes assist military commanders in making knowledgeable choices. These schemes provide intuitions, setup displaying, and prognostic investigation to support tactical forecasting, menace valuation, and resource sharing. It is vital to note that the expansion and distribution of AI in security also advances moral, permissible, and strategic attention. Certifying accountable use, addressing predispositions, and preserving human lapse are decisive aspects of AI incorporation in the security segment.

7.4.2 AI in Defense Strategies in Industry 4.0

AI plays a significant role in defense strategies within Industry 4.0, leveraging advanced technologies to enhance military capabilities. Here are some specific applications of AI in defense strategies within Industry 4.0:

AI algorithms analyze vast amounts of sensor data, including radar, satellite imagery, and drone feeds, to provide real-time situational awareness. This enables defense forces to monitor and understand complex operational environments, identify threats, and make informed decisions. AI-powered predictive maintenance systems analyze data from sensors embedded in military equipment and machinery [17]. By detecting patterns and anomalies, these systems can predict equipment failures and optimize maintenance schedules, ensuring that defense assets are operational and mission-ready.

AI is exploited to identify and retort to cyber threats in real time. Machine learning procedures monitor network movement, recognize anomalous behavior, and preclude unapproved access. AI also assists in susceptibility assessments and threat intellect, firming the complete cybersecurity stance of security schemes. Industry 4.0 skills permit the temperament of self-governing automobiles in defense tasks. AI procedures control unmanned ground vehicles (UGVs), UAVs, and unmanned maritime vehicles (UMVs), permitting investigation, shadowing, and logistics procedures without imperiling humanoid lives.

AI supports intellectual capability and control structures by processing and analyzing data from numerous sources, including radars, satellites, and drones. This permits commandants to have a widespread consideration of the arena, make data-driven decisions, and quickly retort to altering situations. AI-powered decision support systems assist defense personnel in complex decision-making processes. These schemes analyze huge volumes of records, produce insights, and provide endorsements for tactical planning, resource allocation, and peril valuation. AI procedures enhance task forecasting by considering several aspects such as environment, enduring conditions, and accessible possessions. This aids in the effectual division of military resources, route scheduling, and mission achievement.

Swarm Intelligence [18]: AI assists the harmonization and association of self-directed systems, such as drones or robots, in a horde. Swarm intelligence procedures enhance the communal behavior of these structures, permitting them to be self-possessed for surveillance, target stalking, and other assignment intents. AI-driven drill and imitation systems afford accurate virtual environment for military workforces to enrich their services. These structures offer immersive and collaborative training circumstances, permitting warriors to rehearse tactical decision-making, conduct cyber exercises, and simulate accurate combat circumstances. Supply Chain Management: AI enriches defense supply chain management by analyzing records on inventory levels, plea designs, and logistics restraints. This aids in effectual attaining, dispersal, and preservation of military possessions.

Overall, AI in security strategies within Industry 4.0 enriches situational awareness, permits self-directed operations, supports decision-making procedures, reinforces cybersecurity, and enhances several aspects of military operations, causative to better-quality efficacy and success in defense schemes and tasks.

7.5 AI Applications in Defense Strategies in Industry 4.0

AI packages in protection tactics inside Industry 4.0 recognize a full-size preference for technology and competencies. Here are a few specific AI packages in protection regulations in the milieu of Industry 4.0:

- Smart Surveillance and Reconnaissance: By using AI algorithms, sensor records like photos and films sourced from drones, satellites, and different systems are analyzed to locate and discover items of hobby automatically. This procedure substantially assists in surveillance, reconnaissance, and goal acquisition efforts, presenting vital intelligence to enhance defense operations.
- Cyber Defense and Network Security: In the sector of cyber defense and network security, AI performs a vital function in detecting, preventing, and responding to cyber threats. Through device learning algorithms, community visitors may be analyzed to become aware of styles of malicious sports and anomalies. The usage of AI-powered cybersecurity structures bolsters the resilience of defense networks, ensuring the safety of touchy data and important infrastructure.
- Autonomous Vehicles and Robotics: The use of AI allows for the deployment of self-sufficient structures, along with

UAVs, UGVs, and self-navigating vessels. These structures are designed to function in difficult environments, conduct diverse missions like surveillance, logistics, and goal engagement, and ultimately enhance protection by lowering the exposure of human employees to risks.

- Predictive Maintenance and Logistics: AI algorithms examine sensor facts from military gadgets and cars to expect renovation desires and optimize logistics operations. This enables saving your gadget failures, lessens downtime, and enhances the performance of renovation and delivery chain processes.
- Intelligent Command and Control (C2): AI helps decision-making in command-and-manage structures by processing and analyzing massive volumes of data. This consists of real-time statistics from sensors, intelligence reports, and ancient data, supplying commanders with stronger situational focus and helping in making plans and execution of military operations.
- Threat Detection and Anomaly Recognition: AI algorithms can discover styles and anomalies in data, allowing the detection of potential threats and suspicious activities. This consists of spotting peculiar behavior in networks, identifying potential cyber threats, and detecting hidden styles in intelligence data [19].
- Natural Language Processing (NLP) and Language Translation: NLP strategies allow AI structures to recognize and method human language. This feature is important for responsibilities like intelligence analysis, records extraction, and language translation, enhancing communication and records sharing in multilingual protection environments.
- Simulations and Training: AI-powered simulations and digital training environments offer practical eventualities for military employees to educate and enhance their skills. These simulations can mirror complicated fight situations, permitting infantrymen to exercise decision-making, strategic planning, and teamwork.
- Predictive Analytics and Risk Assessment: AI algorithms examine historic and real-time information to perceive patterns, forecast events, and examine risks. This enables protection strategists to assume potential threats, optimize useful resource allocation, and make knowledgeable choices in complicated and dynamic operational environments.

➢ Biometric Identification and Authentication: AI structures can examine biometric data, including fingerprints, facial features, or voice patterns, for identity and authentication purposes. This complements security measures, access control, and employee monitoring within security organizations.

These AI packages in protection techniques inside Industry 4.0 contribute to progressed situational awareness, more desirable decision-making, optimized operations, and extended performance and effectiveness in protection missions.

7.6 Era of AI in Industry

The business generation of AI indicates an amazing transformation in how organizations feature and make use of the era to enhance efficiency, productivity, and decision-making. The speedy development of AI technology has facilitated the incorporation of smart structures and algorithms throughout numerous sectors. Here are a few key additives of the economic AI generation [37, 38]:

The usage of AI permits the streamlining of repetitive duties and processes, resulting in a reduced reliance on guide labor and development in general efficiency. Intelligent structures own the capability to examine facts, make knowledgeable decisions, and execute duties with pace and precision, in the long run, leading to expanded productiveness and value savings. Through the software of facts analytics and insights, AI algorithms can sift via sizable quantities of facts to find complex patterns, trends, and insights that will not be effortlessly discernible to humans. This empowers organizations to make facts-pushed decisions, optimize their operations, and pick out untapped commercial enterprise opportunities.

Predictive Analytics and Forecasting [20]: AI-powered predictive analytics fashions leverage ancient statistics and gadget learning algorithms to forecast destiny outcomes. This enables groups to count on marketplace trends, purchaser behavior, and call for patterns, permitting proactive decision-making and powerful useful resource allocation. Personalization and Customer Experience: AI permits groups to customize products, services, and reports primarily based totally on male or female purchaser choices and behavior. Machine learning algorithms analyze customer data to provide tailored recommendations, targeted marketing campaigns, and enhanced customer support, leading to improved customer satisfaction and loyalty.

AI optimizes supply chain operations by analyzing data related to inventory levels, demand forecasting, and logistics. Intelligent systems can optimize procurement, production, and distribution processes, reducing costs, minimizing waste, and improving overall supply chain efficiency. AI algorithms can analyze visual data and detect defects or anomalies in products or manufacturing processes. This helps businesses maintain quality standards, reduce errors, and improve product reliability. AI-powered decision support systems assist professionals in complex decision-making processes. By analyzing data, generating insights, and providing recommendations, these systems augment human expertise and improve the accuracy and efficiency of decision-making.

AI technologies drive advancements in robotics and automation [21], enabling robots to perform complex tasks with precision and adaptability. This enhances manufacturing processes, logistics operations, and other industrial tasks, leading to increased productivity and flexibility. AI enables NLP capabilities, allowing machines to understand and interact with humans through spoken or written language. This simplifies enhanced communication, customer service, and information retrieval.

Continuous Learning and Adaptability: AI structures can constantly research from new statistics and experiences, enhancing their overall performance over time. Machine learning algorithms permit adaptive structures that could adapt to converting conditions, optimize processes, and make self-sufficient choices primarily based totally on real-time information. The generation of AI in the enterprise is characterized by the mixing of sensible technology throughout diverse sectors, reworking enterprise operations, decision-making processes, and consumer experiences. AI-pushed improvements have the capacity to revolutionize industries, force financial growth, and form the destiny of work.

7.6.1 Era of AI Applications in Industry 4.0

The generation of AI programs in Industry 4.0 represents a massive development in the integration of AI technology with the commercial sector. Industry 4.0 refers back to the fourth commercial revolution characterized by the convergence of virtual technology, automation, connectivity, and data-pushed decision-making. Here are a few key factors of the generation of AI programs in Industry 4.0:

Data-Driven Decision-Making: AI programs in Industry 4.0 leverage big volumes of records generated through interconnected gadgets and sensors [22].

AI algorithms examine these records to extract insights, discover patterns, and make records-pushed selections in real time. Data will become a precious asset for organizations, permitting them to optimize processes, enhance efficiency, and force innovation. AI-powered automation and robotics play an imperative function in Industry 4.0. AI algorithms permit machines and robots to carry out complicated duties with minimum human intervention. These technologies enhance productivity, enhance precision, and decrease the hazard of mistakes in manufacturing, logistics, and different business processes.

Predictive Analytics and Maintenance: AI algorithms permit predictive analytics via way of means of analyzing ancient and real-time statistics to forecast destiny outcomes. In Industry 4.0, predictive upkeep structures make use of AI to display gadget performance, discover upkeep needs, and expect capability failures. This proactive technique reduces downtime, increases operational efficiency, and lowers upkeep costs. AI packages optimize production techniques and deliver chain control in Industry 4.0. AI-powered systems analyze data from production lines, sensors, and inventory management systems to streamline operations, improve resource allocation, and enable just-in-time manufacturing. This leads to improved productivity, reduced waste, and enhanced agility in response to market demands.

AI technologies, combined with robotics, enable cognitive robotics systems that can perceive and understand the environment, interact with humans, and perform complex tasks. This facilitates human-machine collaboration in Industry 4.0, where humans and machines work together to leverage their respective strengths, leading to increased efficiency and productivity. As Industry 4.0 relies heavily on interconnected systems and data exchange, AI plays a crucial role in cybersecurity. AI algorithms can detect and respond to cyber threats, identify vulnerabilities, and enhance defense mechanisms to protect critical infrastructure, data, and intellectual property. AI applications in Industry 4.0 enable personalized and customized experiences for customers. AI algorithms analyze customer data, preferences, and behavior patterns to offer tailored products, services, and recommendations. This enhances customer satisfaction and drives customer loyalty.

Autonomous Vehicles and Transportation [23]: Industry 4.0 incorporates AI technologies in autonomous vehicles, including self-driving cars, drones, and delivery robots. AI algorithms enable these vehicles to navigate, make decisions, and interact with the environment, transforming transportation and logistics operations with increased safety and efficiency.

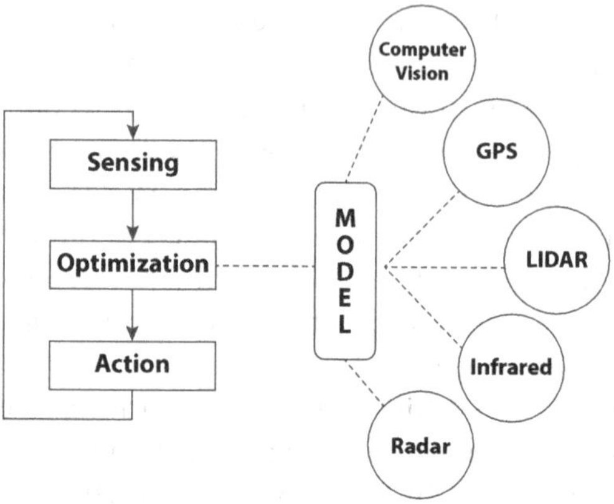

Figure 7.3 How AI of an autonomous system works.

Human-Machine Interaction: AI's NLP capabilities enhance human-machine interaction in Industry 4.0. Voice assistants, chatbots, and virtual agents utilize NLP to understand and respond to human queries, improving communication and facilitating seamless interaction between humans and machines. AI in Industry 4.0 enables continuous learning and adaptive systems. Machine learning algorithms can analyze data patterns, learn from past experiences, and improve performance over time. This allows systems to adapt to changing conditions, optimize processes, and make autonomous decisions based on new information as illustrated in Figure 7.3.

The generation of AI programs in Industry 4.0 brings forth transformative capabilities, revolutionizing industries throughout diverse domain names, including manufacturing, logistics, healthcare, and energy. AI-pushed technologies enhance efficiency, productivity, and innovation, using the virtual transformation of corporations in the fourth business revolution.

7.7 Importance of AI in the Defense Industry

AI performs an essential role in the defense industry, presenting diverse advantages and benefits. Here are a few key reasons highlighting the significance of AI in the defense industry:

Enhanced Situational Awareness: AI technologies, consisting of smart surveillance structures and sensor networks, allow protection forces to collect and procedure significant quantities of statistics in real time [34]. This complements situational focus by presenting correct and well-timed statistics approximately the battlefield, capacity threats, and operational environments. Improved Decision-Making: AI algorithms can examine complicated and various statistics sources, along with intelligence reports, sensor statistics, and historical statistics. This facilitates military commanders and decision-makers in making knowledgeable choices quickly and effectively, thinking about a couple of variables and scenarios.

AI-pushed automation and optimization permit protection groups to streamline processes, decreasing guide labor and minimizing errors. These results in progressed operational efficiency, decreased costs, and optimized useful resource allocation. Autonomous System: AI allows the improvement and deployment of self-sustaining structures, inclusive of UAVs, UGVs, and self-sustaining ships [24]. These structures can carry out responsibilities together with surveillance, reconnaissance, and logistics operations, decreasing dangers to human employees and increasing operational capabilities.

AI algorithms can detect, examine, and respond to cyber threats in real time. With the growing reliance on networked structures and statistics sharing, AI-powered cybersecurity structures assist guard protection networks, vital infrastructure, and touchy records from cyberattacks. AI-powered predictive renovation structures can examine sensor statistics from army devices and motors to discover renovation needs, save failures, and optimize logistics operations. This improves device availability, reduces downtime, and complements common operational readiness. AI algorithms can examine sensor statistics, historical records, and intelligence reviews to discover high-cost targets, expect their movements, and optimize weapon deployment for particular and powerful strikes. These result in stepped-forward accuracy, decreased collateral damage, and improved undertaking achievement rates.

AI technology allows rapid and green information processing, permitting protection corporations to examine and extract actionable insights from massive volumes of information. This is important for intelligence analysis, hazard detection, and selection aid in time-crucial situations. Training and Simulation: AI-powered simulations and digital training environments offer practical situations for army employees to decorate their abilities and readiness. These structures provide cost-effective and secure schooling opportunities, permitting infantrymen to exercise selection-making, strategic planning, and teamwork in simulated environments. Innovation and Technological Advancements: The security industry benefits from AI-pushed technological improvements and innovations. AI studies and improvements make contributions to improvements in robotics, independent structures, information analytics, and cybersecurity, fostering technological superiority and innovation in the protection sector.

Overall, the importance of AI in the defense industry lies in its ability to enhance situational awareness, improve decision-making, optimize operations, and increase efficiency and effectiveness in defense missions. AI technologies empower defense forces with advanced capabilities, ensuring they can adapt and respond to evolving threats and challenges.

7.8 Future of AI in the Defense Industry

The forthcoming integration of AI in the security industry holds significant potential and is expected to bring substantial progressions in several aspects of military operations. Here are some vital aspects that highlight the future of AI in the security industry:

Autonomous Systems: The expansion and disposition of autonomous systems will continue to advance. We can expect the development of more innovative and intelligent autonomous vehicles, drones, and machines for security procedures. These systems will possess enhanced supervisory capabilities, adaptability, and the ability to operate in complex environments with minimal human intervention. Swarm intelligence: AI-powered swarm intelligence will play a vivacious role in security operations. Hordes of autonomous vehicles or drones can exert influence collaboratively, leveraging AI procedures to connect, harmonize, and achieve complex tasks. This perception bids compensations such as amended situational awareness, improved pliability, and dispersed policymaking.
Intellectual Arena: AI will permit the construction of intellectual trenches where intellectual schemes can process and analyze huge volumes of facts from miscellaneous sources in real time. Intellectual schemes will afford military employees with improved situational awareness, prognostic analytics, and decision sustenance competencies, empowering quicker and further operative retort to lively frontline environments. The upcoming AI in security will focus on human-machine team-up, where humans and AI schemes slog collaboratively to influence their individual fortes. AI procedures will assist human machinists in policymaking, offer perceptions, and handle tedious errands, consenting employees to emphasize higher-level tactical thinking and complex problem-solving.
Cybersecurity and AI Security: As cyber threats continue to evolve [25], AI will play a decisive role in enhancing cybersecurity battlements. AI-powered schemes will advance menace recognition, glitch recognition, and retort competencies, permitting upbeat security against cyberattacks. Confrontational AI skills will also be established to thwart malicious

AI-based threats. Explainable AI as AI technologies become more innovative, and the capability to elucidate and comprehend AI results will become progressively vital in the security segment. Exertions will be made to advance explicable AI procedures and agendas that afford transparency and permit human machinists to realize the intellectual behind AI-generated endorsements and verdicts.

Quantum Computing: The initiation of quantum computing will have a substantial influence on AI in the security industry. Quantum computing's capability to unravel complex hitches and process immense volumes of information will improve AI competencies, permitting more innovative procedures, quicker replicas, and amended optimization for security bids. Artificial Data and Replication: The use of artificial facts and progressive replications will become more predominant in the security industry. AI procedures will engender artificial information to train and corroborate replicas, plummeting the confidence in real-life information and permitting further widespread and genuine replications for training, testing, and situation forecasting.

Ethical Contemplations and Ascendency: The future of AI in the security sector will also encompass speaking ethical contemplations and launching ascendency agendas. There will be a concentration on certifying accountable AI use, addressing preconceptions, and obeying permissible and moral canons in the expansion and disposition of AI technologies within security operations. Worldwide alliance gave the universal landscape of security encounters, intercontinental association in AI investigation, expansion, and canons will be decisive. Security organizations from diverse republics are probable to join forces to share proficiency, exchange familiarity, and create communal outlines to endorse the accountable and operative use of AI skills as shown in Figure 7.4.

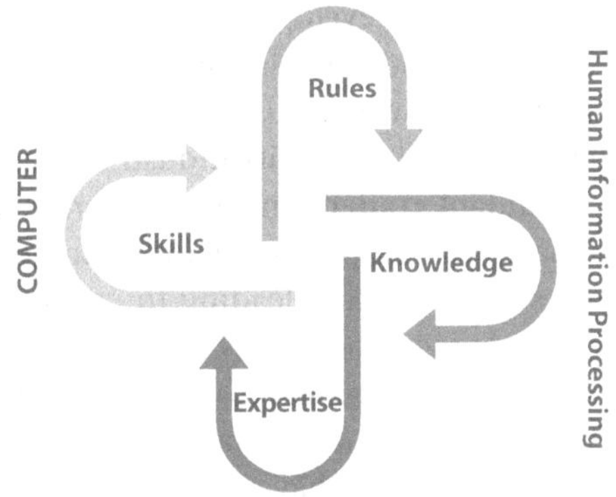

Figure 7.4 The relationship between uncertainty and skill, rule, knowledge, and expert reasoning.

The integration of AI in the security industry has the potential to transform military operations, making them more efficient, effective, and adaptive defense capabilities. However, it will also bring forth challenges associated with morals, ascendency, and intercontinental assistance that must be addressed to certify the accountable and advantageous disposition of AI in security.

7.8.1 Cyberattacks in Defense Industry

Cyberattacks in the security industry pose substantial threats as they can conciliate penetrating military information, disrupt operations, and destabilize nationwide safety. Here are some significant facts about cyberattacks in the security industry:

Several actors in the cybersecurity landscape may have various motivations for directing attacks against the security industry. These motivations can comprise state-sponsored replicated surveillance, cyber radicalism, hacktivism, or cybercriminals seeking financial gain. Realms are often engrossed in cyberattacks to expand military, scientific, or astuteness compensations.

Advanced Persistent Threats (APTs): Security organizations are often beleaguered by innovative tenacious threats, which are intelligent and enduring cyberattacks. APTs encompass tenacious exertions by accomplished adversaries to insinuate security grids, gain unauthorized access, and preserve existence for protracted epochs, producing exposure and extenuation exciting.

Targeted Information Cyberattacks: These attacks focus primarily on stealing confidential or sensitive information related to military operations, weapons systems, research and development data, and personal information about military personnel. Such evidence can be exploited for premeditated, financial, or politically aware lead.

Supply Chain Susceptibilities: The security industry relies on complex supply chains relating abundant traders and freelancers. Cyberattacks aiming at these supply chains can employ malicious encryption, conciliation mechanisms, or deed susceptibilities, leading to conceded schemes, data breaches, or unsanctioned access to security systems. The security industry is a prime target for industrial espionage, with adversaries attempting to gain insights into defense technologies, manufacturing processes, or military tactics. Such cyberattacks can have severe financial and nationwide safety implications.

The security industry comprises perilous infrastructure such as grasp and control systems, message systems, and supremacy lattices. Cyberattacks targeting these schemes can disrupt operations, undermine skills, and hinder military keenness. Insider threats within the security industry can stance significant risks [26]. Workforces or service providers with access to penetrating data may deliberately or inadvertently drip or misappropriate classified data, compromising security and enabling cyberattacks. Ransomware and Distraction: Outbreaks aiming at security administrations can have serious consequences. These outbreaks can disrupt critical systems, halt operations, and create significant financial burdens due to ransom payments, resulting in fiscal losses and operational delays.

Realm outbreaks, with advanced replication capabilities, frequently target the security industry as a part of their tactical ideas. These outbreaks can be extremely intelligent and obstinate and have enduring insinuations for nationwide refuge and security competencies. Security Industry Alliances: Given the embryonic landscape of replicated threats, the security industry alliance is decisive. Sharing information about cyber threats, best practices, and susceptibilities can help strengthen defenses, improve occurrence retort competencies, and alleviate the influence of cyberattacks.

To prevent cyberattacks in the security industry, vigorous cybersecurity trials, including system dissection, multi-factor substantiation, encryption, invasion recognition schemes, and systematic security assessments, are essential. Continuous monitoring, threat intelligence sharing, employee training, and collaboration with cybersecurity experts are also vital in building strong defenses against these sophisticated threats.

7.8.2 Trade-Offs of AI in Industry 4.0

Whereas AI brings abundant aids and progressions to Industry 4.0, some trade-offs and contemplations are prerequisites to be engaged in the interpretation. Here are some crucial trade-offs allied with the routine of AI in Industry 4.0:

Concealment and Data Security [27]: AI schemes frequently necessitate access to huge volumes of data to cram and make precise forecasts. Nevertheless, this advances apprehensions about concealment and data security. Administrations must ensure that suitable actions are in place to defend sensitive evidence and thwart illegal access or data breaches. Workforce Displacement: The automation capabilities of AI have the potential to displace jobs and cause changes in the labor market. While AI can modernize progressions and advance efficacy, it may also diminish the petition for certain categories of trades, requiring employees to attain novel aids or evolution to diverse protagonists.

Predisposition and Fairness: AI techniques are carried out on historical information, which can also additionally realize preconceptions and reproduce not unusual place preconceptions. If not carefully managed, AI schemes can hold or give a boost to those predispositions, leading to partial or bigoted consequences. Safeguarding impartiality and addressing predispositions in AI techniques are long-lasting assignments that require careful consideration. Ethical Contemplations: The use of AI advancements raises moral contemplations within Industry 4.0. For illustration, autonomous systems in protection or perilous infrastructure subdivisions can also additionally boost interrogations approximately accountability, human lapse, and the latent for inadvertent penalties. Administrations need to carefully ponder the ethical tips of AI and create appropriate outlines for responsible AI evolution and disposition.

Technical Limitations: Regardless of sizable advancements, AI technology nevertheless has limitations. AI fashions will not continually be correct or reliable, especially in complicated and dynamic environments. Interpreting the selections and information provided by AI, particularly in relation to the underlying reasoning, can be an intriguing endeavor, especially when it involves deep learning models.

Preliminary Speculation and Preservation: Instigating AI schemes in Industry 4.0 calls for large initial hypotheses in substructure, software program device, and capacity. Furthermore, maintaining and apprising AI schemes can be resource-intensive, necessitating investments in statistics supervision, technique enhancement, and device exaltations. Overreliance and Reliance: Trusting profoundly on AI schemes can result in reliance, building organizations vulnerable to device catastrophes, cyberattacks, or statistical predispositions. It is crucial to have contingency plans, redundancy tests, and human oversight strategies to relieve threats accompanied by overreliance on AI technologies.

Supervisory and Authorized Challenges: The hasty development of AI in Industry 4.0 stances tracking and permissible errands. Strategies and hints should maintain stride with AI revolutions to discourse troubles consisting of statistics confidentiality, algorithmic transparency, obligation, and accountability. Emerging right supervisory outlines that stability invention and patron fortification are crucial.

Human-AI Alliance: Conducting operative affiliation among human beings and AI schemes is a complex chore. Conniving unified boundaries, safeguarding colorful announcements, and addressing human conviction and the attractiveness of AI are critical contemplations. Finding the right balance between automation and human involvement is critical to harnessing the full potential of AI in Industry 4.0. Inadvertent Significances: The custom of AI in Industry 4.0 can lead to inadvertent significance. For instance, algorithmic policymaking may involuntarily emphasize prevailing predispositions or generate new social issues. Incessant monitoring, assessment, and moral valuations are essential to categorize and discourse any inadvertent significance of AI.

Distinguishing and extenuating these trade-offs are essential for effectively realizing the benefits of AI in Industry 4.0. Organizations and lawmakers must approach AI implementation with a comprehensive perspective, considering the moral, social, and financial insinuations to ensure the responsible and beneficial integration of AI technologies in industrial progressions.

7.8.3 Cyberattacks in Defense Industry 4.0

Cyberattacks in the security industry pose significant threats to national security, military operations, and critical infrastructure, especially in the context of Industry 4.0. As Industry 4.0 participates in advanced technologies and connectivity into defense systems, it also introduces new vulnerabilities that rivals can exploit. Here are some specific cyberattack trajectories and threats in the security industry within the milieu of Industry 4.0:

APTs are intelligent and targeted cyberattacks that involve persistent efforts by skilled rivals to insinuate security systems, establish a presence, and extract sensitive evidence over an extended period. APTs can exploit susceptibilities in associated schemes, common engineering systems, or zero-day susceptibilities to gain illegal access and conduct reconnaissance, or interrupt operations.

Supply Chain Outbreaks: The security industry depends on complex supply chains including abundant traders, outworkers, and cohorts. Rivals may target the supply chain to introduce malicious software or compromised hardware, allowing illegal access, data breaches, or distraction of defense systems. Weakness in the supply chain can be leveraged to gain access to classified data or conciliation perilous setup.
Intellectual Property [28] Theft: Security administrations invest heavily in research and development to create advanced technologies and defense systems. Cyberattacks aimed at the security industry often try to steal confidential or trademarked information, including intellectual property, trade secrets, and military skills. Theft of intellectual property can have severe financial and strategic implications. Operational Disruption Cyberattacks: Cyberattacks can interrupt security actions by negotiating command and control schemes, communication links, or perilous infrastructure.

Opponents may pursue to interrupt military operations, impair logistics, or hinder situational awareness by manipulating susceptibilities in associated schemes, disrupting network connectivity, or launching distributed denial-of-service (DDoS) outbreaks.

Espionage and Intelligence Gathering: State-sponsored cyber espionage targeting the security industry is prevalent. Opponents aim to gain insights into military strategies, intelligence capabilities [29], and security measures. They may target security outworkers, investigate foundations, or manage activities to attain confidential data, military diplomacies, or sensitive astuteness information. Weapon System Manipulation: With the incorporation of AI and automation in weapon systems, rivals may attempt to hack or disrupt these schemes. Cyberattacks that deploy targeting schemes, modify information ideas, or disable control mechanisms can lead to reduced accuracy, diminished effectiveness, or unintended engagement scenarios.
Insider Threats: Insider threats pose a significant challenge in the security industry. Workforces, service providers, or associates with authorized access to sensitive data may intentionally or inadvertently mismanage or leak confidential facts. Identifying and mitigating insider threats can be difficult, requiring robust security procedures, access controls, and effective awareness training [30]. Ransomware outbreaks can severely affect the security industry by encrypting critical systems and demanding ransom payment. The encryption of sensitive data can disrupt operations, compromise perilous facts, and create financial and logistical challenges for security organizations.

Cyber rivalry among countries with progressive cyber competencies may often lead to increased competition within the security industry. These outbreaks can be a fragment of broader geopolitical strategies aimed at achieving military or technological advantages, comprising perilous organization, or undermining national security proficiencies. Zero-Day Exploits: Defense systems often rely on proprietary or specialized software that may contain undiscovered vulnerabilities known as zero-day exploits. Adversaries [31] who discover and exploit these vulnerabilities can bypass traditional security measures and gain unauthorized access to defense networks or critical systems.

Addressing the cyber threats in the security industry within the milieu of Industry 4.0 necessitates a wide-ranging tactic. It encompasses instigating strong cybersecurity actions, such as network segmentation, invasion recognition schemes, encryption, regular security assessments, and incident response strategies [32, 33]. Collaboration among security organizations, management, and cybersecurity experts is crucial for sharing threat

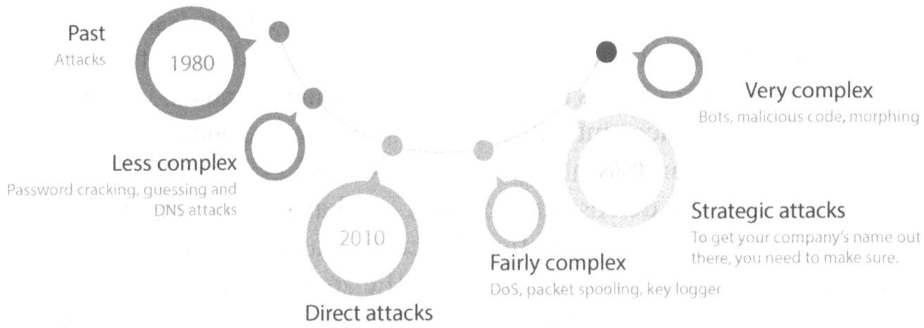

Figure 7.5 Evolution of cyberattacks in the defense industry.

intelligence, developing best practices, and creating effective security frameworks as shown in Figure 7.5. Moreover, unremitting intensive care, members of staff working out, and practical peril chasing can aid perceive and alleviate cyberattacks in a sensible way.

7.9 Conclusion

In conclusion, the amalgamation of AI in security strategies within the milieu of Industry 4.0 presents several breaks and challenges. Survivable AI in security tactics aims to improve military proficiencies, advance policymaking progressions, and fortify countrywide safety. By leveraging progressive skills such as autonomous systems, intellectual computation, and data analytics, AI permits quicker and further operative responses to embryonic threats. Nevertheless, the efficacious enactment of survivable AI in security approaches entails cautious contemplation of moral, lawful, and methodological aspects. Guaranteeing confidentiality and data safety, addressing biases and fairness in AI procedures, and upholding human oversight are vital for accountable AI arrangements. Moreover, the connection among security organizations, college circles, trade, and intercontinental assistance is critical to discourse tasks, stake exceptional applications, and create common canons. The future of survivable AI in safety strategies holds wonderful potential. Autonomous systems, swarm intelligence, and intellectual battleground perceptions will remodel military actions. AI-powered cybersecurity battlements might be beneficial sources to guard in contradiction of cyber threats, even as human-device teaming will enhance policymaking competencies. Dramatic advancement in computation and artificial data will further enhance AI's effectiveness in ensuring safety. Nevertheless, it is crucial to distinguish and navigate the trade-offs associated with using AI in safety applications. Issues such as employee displacement, methodological limitations, and the critical necessity for substantial resources and ongoing maintenance must be addressed. Ethical reflections, accountability, and monitoring agendas are critical to being advanced and without sophistication. By proactively discussing these challenges, the defense corporation can harness the transformative supremacy of AI to enhance national security, safeguard vital infrastructure, and enhance operational efficiency. The amalgamation of survivable AI in safety strategies in Industry 4.0 epitomizes a decisive segment in the direction of the building of a harmless and more resilient imminent.

References

1. Xu, M., David, J.M., Kim, S.H., The fourth industrial revolution: opportunities and challenges. *Int. J. Financ. Res.*, 9, 2, 90–95, 2018.
2. Kajanth, B., Industry 4.0: Securing the Future for German Manufacturing Companies, University of Twente, Enschede, Netherlands, 2016.
3. Rick, B., Adam, M., Stephen, L., Marty, H., Brenna, S., The smart factory; responsive, adaptive, connected manufacturing, 2017.
4. Liao, Y., Eduardo Rocha, L., Deschamps, F., Brezinski, G., André, V., The impact of the fourth industrial Revolution : a cross-country/region comparison. *Production*, 28, e20180061, 2018.
5. Deloitte, Industry 4.0: is africa ready for digital transformation?, 2016.
6. Naudé, W., Entrepreneurship, education and the fourth industrial revolution in Africa, Tech. Rep., Maastricht University, Maastricht, Netherlands, 2017, IZA DP No. 10855.
7. Daniel, L.M.N., Alencastro, V., Osvaldo, L.G.Q., *et al.*, Exploring industry 4.0 technologies to enable circular economy practices in a manufacturing context: a business model proposal. *J. Manuf. Technol. Manage.*, 30, 3, 607–627, 2019.
8. Lee, M., Yun, J.J., Pyka, A., *et al.*, How to respond to the fourth industrial revolution, or the second information technology revolution? Dynamic new combinations between technology, market and society through open innovation. *J. Open Innov.*, 21, 3, 1–24, 2018.
9. Chiarvesio, M. and Romanello, R., Chapter 14 industry 4.0 technologies and internationalization: insights from Italian companies, in: *Progress in International Business Research*, vol. 13, pp. 357–378, 2018.
10. Dorleta, I., Jaione, G., Juan, I.I., Business model innovation through industry 4.0: a review. *Procedia Manuf.*, 22, 4–10, 2018.
11. Stock, T. and Seliger, G., Opportunities of sustainable manufacturing in industry 4.0. *Procedia CIRP*, 40, 536–541, 2016.

12. Müller, J.M., Daniel, K., Kai-Ingo, V., What drives the implementation of industry 4.0? The role of opportunities and challenges in the context of sustainability. *Sustainability*, 247, 10, 1–24, 2018.
13. Pi-Shen, S., Janice, J., John, S., Ann-Louise, H., The Fourth Industrial Revolution : The Implications of Technological Disruption for Australian VET, NCVER, Adelaide, Australia, 2018.
14. Paravizo, E., Chaim, O.C., Braatz, D., Muschard, B., Rozenfeld, H., Exploring gamification to support manufacturing education on industry 4.0 as an enabler for innovation and sustainability. *Procedia Manuf.*, 21, 438–445, 2018.
15. Li, L., China's manufacturing locus in 2025: with a comparison of "Made-in-China 2025" and "Industry 4.0. *Technol. Forecasting Social Change*", 135, 66–74, 2018.
16. Zhong, R.Y., Xu, X., Klotz, E., Newman, S.T., Intelligent manufacturing in the context of industry 4.0: a review. *Engineering*, 3, 5, 616–630, 2017.
17. Schäfer, M., The fourth industrial revolution: how the EU can lead it. *Eur. View*, 17, 1, 5–12, 2018.
18. Günther, S., Reiner, A., Gausemeier, J., Michael, T.H., Wolfgang, W., *Industrie 4.0 maturity index*, Managing the Digital Transformation of Companies (Acatech STUDY Series), Acatech, Munich, Germany, 2017.
19. Gehrke, L., Rule, D., Bellmann, C., *et al.*, Industry 4.0. A Discussion of Qualifications and Skills in the Factory of the Future: A German and American Perspective, VDI and ASME Project, Düsseldorf, Germany, 2015.
20. Strandhagen, J.W., Alfnes, E., Strandhagen, J.O., Vallandingham, L.R., The fit of industry 4.0 applications in manufacturing logistics: a multiple case study. *Adv. Manuf.*, 5, 4, 344–358, 2017.
21. Morrar, R., Arman, H., Mousa, S., Schwab, K., The fourth industrial revolution (industry 4.0): a social innovation perspective. *Technol. Innovation Manage. Rev.*, 7, 11, 12–20, 2017.
22. Popkova, E.G. and Sergi, B.S., Will industry 4.0 and other innovations impact Russia's development?, in: *Exploring the Future of Russia's Economy and Markets*, pp. 51–68, Emerald Publishing Limited, Bingley, UK, 2018.
23. Sung, T.K., Industry 4.0: a Korea perspective. *Technol. Forecasting Social Change*, 132, 40–45, 2018.
24. Thoben, K.-D., Wiesner, S., Wuest, T., "Industrie 4.0" and smart manufacturing - a review of research issues and application examples. *Int. J. Autom. Technol.*, 11, 1, 4–16, 2017.
25. Mo, E., Centea, D., Singh, I., Wanyama, T., SEPT learning factory for industry 4.0 education and applied research. *Procedia Manuf.*, 23, 249–254, 2018.
26. Andrea, B. and Jiří, T., Requirements for education and qualification of people in industry 4.0. *Procedia Manuf.*, 11, 2195–2202, 2017.
27. Pereira, A.C. and Romero, F., A review of the meanings and the implications of the industry 4.0 concept. *Procedia Manuf.*, 13, 1206–1214, 2017.

28. Crnjac, M., Ivica, V., Banduka, N., From concept to the introduction of industry 4.0. *Int. J. Ind. Eng. Manage. (IJIEM)*, 8, 1, 21–30, 2017.
29. Mario, H., Tobia, P., Otto, B., Design principles for industry 4.0 scenarios: a literature review, Tech. Rep., Technische Universität Dortmund, Lukas Strasse, Switzerland, 2015, No. 01/2015.
30. Chen, B., Wan, J., Shu, L., Li, P., Mukherjee, M., Yin, B., Smart factory of industry 4.0: key technologies, application case, and challenges. *IEEE Access*, 6, 6505–6519, 2018.
31. Rani, S. and Koundal, D., An Optimized Framework for WSN Routing in the Context of Industry 4.0. *Sensors*, 21, 19, 6474, 2021, https://doi.org/10.3390/s21196474.
32. Centobelli, P. Department of Industrial Engineering, University of Naples Federico II, Naples, Italy; Cerchione, R., Determinants of the transition towards circular economy in SMEs: A sustainable supply chain management perspective, Department of Engineering, University of Naples, https://www.scopus.com/inward/record.uri?eid=2-s2.0-85115891651&doi=10.1016%2fj.ijpe.2021.108297&partnerID=40&md5=c354dd59ffdb0f03948a466e6434453c.
33. Singh, J., *et al.*, IoT Ecosystem Security via Distributed Ledger Technology (Blockchain versus IOTA): A Bibliometric Analysis Research. *J. Circuits Syst. Comput.*, 2430004, 2024, https://doi.org/10.1142/S021812662430004X.
34. Ramana, T.V., Ghantasala, G.S., Sathiyaraj, R., Khan, M. (Eds.), *Artificial Intelligence and Machine Learning for Smart Community: Concepts and Applications*, Springer, 2024, https://www.springer.com/gp/book.
35. Rajendran, S., Sabharwal, M., Hu, Y.C., Balusamy, B. (Eds.), *Artificial Intelligence for Autonomous Vehicles: The Future of Driverless Technology*, John Wiley & Sons, 2024, https://www.wiley.com/en-us/Artificial+Intelligence+for+Autonomous+Vehicles%3A+The+Future+of+Driverless+Technology-p-9781119757553.
36. Mohanty, A., Rahamathunnisa, U., Sudhakar, K., Sathiyaraj, R., Age of Computational AI for Autonomous Vehicles, in: *Artificial Intelligence for Autonomous Vehicles*, pp. 25–54, 2024.
37. Rajendran, S., Sabharwal, M., Ghinea, G., Dhanaraj, R.K., Balusamy, B. (Eds.), *IoT and Big Data Analytics for Smart Cities: A Global Perspective*, CRC Press, 2022.
38. Parameswaran, T., Reddy, Y.P., Nagaveni, V., Sathiyaraj, R., Era of Computational Big Data Analytics and IoT Techniques in Smart City Applications, in: *IoT and Big Data Analytics for Smart Cities*, pp. 1–22, 2022.

8

Industry 4.0 Based Turbofan Performance Prediction

M. Sai Narayan[1]*, Prajakta P. Nandanwar[2], Annabathini Lokesh[1], Bathula Lakshmi Narayana[1], Varun Revadigar[3], Judeson Antony Kovilpillai J.[1], Neelapala Anil Kumar[4] and D.M. Deepak Raj[1]

[1]*Department of Computer Science Engineering, Alliance University, Bangalore, India*
[2]*Department of Aerospace Engineering, Alliance University, Bangalore, India*
[3]*Department of Information Technology, Alliance University, Bangalore, India*
[4]*Department of Electronics and Communication Engineering, Alliance University, Bangalore, India*

Abstract
The turbofan engine is part of the critical fleet components driving its airlift aircraft. A stated design requirement for this engine provides thrust to perform various tasks, from astronaut training to scientific research missions. This engine requires periodic maintenance for safe and optimum operations. In this chapter, data science methods and machine learning algorithms are used for the accurate prediction of maintenance needs; and thus, the estimation of remaining useful life related to a turbofan engine. This chapter will cover an in-depth exploration of different measures of performance of machine learning models and random search to tune the parameters of the model until we find the best fit. Stream Lit will be used to deploy as an application. The ultimate result includes a.csv file along with the model's loss and accuracy by providing the outcomes of the prediction done by the model.

Many studies propose sophisticated planning models for predictive maintenance but assume general deterioration of the systems or components with fixed parameters instead of using component-specific data-driven RUL prognostics. This paper evaluates different techniques of feature extraction and activation function optimization to enhance the accuracy of the proposed predictive maintenance

**Corresponding author*: nsaiBTECH21@ced.alliance.edu.in

M. Thirunavukkarasan, S. A. Sahaaya Arul Mary, Sathiyaraj. R, G. S. Pradeep Ghantasala and Mudassir Khan (eds.) Artificial Intelligence and Machine Learning for Industry 4.0, (197–222)

model. The paper will investigate the efficacy of convolutional neural networks and recurrent neural networks in detecting a pattern indicative of an engine breakdown by analysis of historical operational data. This robust deep-learning programs optimizes the scheduling preventive maintenance for enhanced effectiveness in aerospace systems' operations.

This research has the potential to significantly enhance the efficiency of aerospace system operations by scheduling preventative maintenance based on actual engine health and reducing breakdowns in-flight while optimizing maintenance costs. The best-performing model is deployed, and users are allowed to estimate engine RUL and study model performance parameters like loss and accuracy via downloadable .csv files.

Keywords: Turbofan engine, remaining usable life (RUL), predictive maintenance, deep learning, aerospace

8.1 Introduction

The rationale for a predictive maintenance program for turbofan engines is strong. Turbofan engines are essential to the aviation industry, powering commercial and military aircraft. Maintaining their role is critical to passenger and crew safety, as well as mission success. The complexity of the system requires the coordination of all components as shown in Figure 8. 1, making routine maintenance less efficient.

Predictive maintenance, using advanced technologies such as data analytics and machine learning, is the best solution to address these challenges [1]. Engines are continuously inspected throughout the day and any issues can

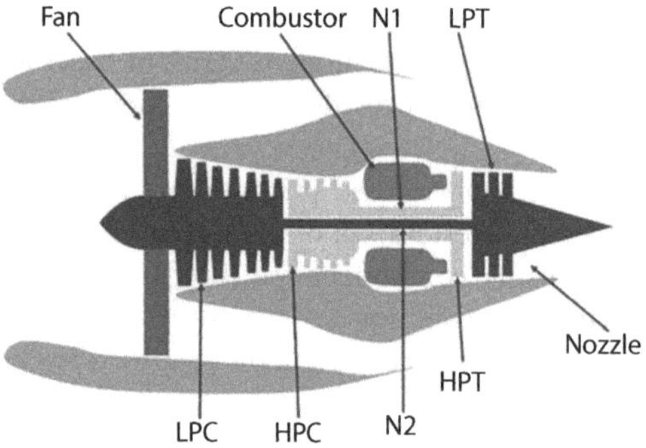

Figure 8.1 Shows a simplified diagram of an engine from the C-MAPSS, the Commercial Modular Aero-Propulsion System Simulation. N1 and N2 are the turbo axis; LPC, low-pressure compressor; HPC, high-pressure compressor; LPT, low-pressure turbine; and HPT, high-pressure turbine [3].

be captured early each day. Accuracy is key in aviation, so predictive maintenance is used to pinpoint engine problems and their remaining useful life. As it prevents aircraft failures and also acts as a shield against potential damage, this proactive approach has improved overall aviation safety [2].

Gas turbines (GTs) are key components in aerospace engineering that change fuel energy into mechanical power for flight. However, such harsh conditions constantly cause deterioration of parts, affecting overall performance, safety, fuel performance, and emissions. These six categories include predetermined, corrective, condition-based, predictive, and reactive maintenance. The airline industry has been evolving from the traditional fix it when it breaks the philosophy of corrective maintenance toward a model where nothing is allowed to fail in the first place called preventive maintenance. However, this has been hampered to some extent by its continued reliance on risk assessments. As preventive maintenance has become less effective, the company has started to move more towards monitoring the condition of equipment (condition-based maintenance) and predicting issues before they happen using real-time monitoring technology to improve maintenance schedules and performance [4].

Sensor technology has improved, and this makes it possible to carry out preventive maintenance supported by predictive maintenance, which involves around-the-clock engine health monitoring [5]. The diagnostic and prognostic capabilities of such techniques as blade tip timing (BTT) and biomimicry-inspired algorithms are leading to better insights into gas turbines' degradation activities. In addition, this report is interested in investigating these phenomena from the perspective of information acquisition techniques, processing techniques, and diagnostic methods generally used in gas turbine maintenance processes. On top of that, the complexity of aircraft turbojet engines poses greater safety issues, with higher likelihoods of fault failures that necessitate early detection.

Besides that, areas like deserts near or connected with water bodies, as well as offshore environments, have different types of impurities that lead to premature destruction of components in such mills. Although air filters serve their purpose, full filtration is impossible. To achieve a more flexible estimation method for users in gas turbines, this article will introduce a performance-oriented creep life assessment method whereby modes such as fouling and thermal barrier coating (TBC) deterioration would be considered in the estimation process [6]. This study focuses on how different degradation modes impact the lifespan of high-pressure turbine (HPT) blades [6, 8–10]. The intention is to enhance the aviation industry's maintenance facilities and to guide future research efforts. In more recent cases, maintenance strategies have passed to predictive maintenance. Advances in data technology and instrument analytics have spurred this shift. Predictive renovation makes use of statistics analytics and system studying algorithms to correctly predict preservation requirements and examine the remaining lifespan of turbofan engines. In the pursuit of improving turbofan reliability, numerous research have explored the efficacy of NASA datasets in making use of predictive protection techniques.

Guessing maintenance is super important for modern tech. It changes how we work complex systems like turbofans and engines to make sure they work right. In flying, where safety is most important, guessing and stopping costly downtime and big breaks is super key. Using smart AI to check and run engines, monitor temp, press, and shaking, and prevent big problems is very important [26, 27]. Smart AI predicts issues by analyzing lots of data from sensors in the turbofan engine. For instance, AI can spot small signs of parts failing and fix them fast. By noticing strange things in real-time, these systems help maintenance teams solve problems quickly [31, 36, 37].

By analyzing the impact of these degradation processes on high-pressure turbine (HPT) blade creep life, this study aims to help improve maintenance practices in the aviation industry and inform future research efforts Technologies and research increase provisioning by gaining mechanical efficiency [6, 11, 14, 18]. Many accessories try to be desirable on the turbofan. More research is needed to increase reliability-security-safety. We examined the effectiveness of NASA datasets in implementing the methods. It is important to anticipate turbofan engine problems early. This chapter examines the use of NASA data for prediction to improve reliability, examines strategies, challenges, and future directions. The aim is to provide stakeholders with insights focused on turbofan safety and aerospace engineering. Deep learning models can enhance predictive maintenance capabilities. Evaluating feasibility, effectiveness, and utility helps optimize program design. Predicting failures increases reliability, safety, and productivity [7].

Also, smart maintenance programs keep getting better by learning from old data and adjusting to different situations. They become more accurate at foreseeing potential problems as they process more information and face different conditions [19–21]. This skill is really useful in the changing airplane world, where things like weather and flight paths can seriously affect how engines work. Predicting maintenance not only makes flying safer and more dependable, but it also saves airlines and operators lots of money. By fixing or swapping out parts early based on these predictions, groups can dodge the expensive fallout of unexpected engine trouble, like unplanned fixes, cancelled flights, and customer payouts [22–24]. Plus, by planning maintenance better and using resources well, predictive maintenance cuts overall cost and makes the most of what's available [25].

8.2 Search Methodology

8.2.1 Sensor-Based Technique

Vibration analysis: measure movements which could cause abrasion or imbalance, or even lead it to failure.
Oil analysis: evaluating engine oil based on the wear debris, contamination and viscosity changes, to find out the internal components that are at fault.
Temperature monitoring: monitoring the vital indicators of engines such as temperatures to underscore issues in cooling systems, bearings, or combustion processes.
Performance monitoring: checks powerplant parameters (thrust, rate of fuel consumption, exhaust gas temperature) failure to the normal operating range with possible symptoms of engine deterioration and faults.

8.2.2 Data-Driven Approaches

Processing and sourcing data through sensors as well as other factors are key parts of data driven technologies in regard to predictive maintenance. The state-of-the-art turbo fan was endowed with a great many sensors such as temperature, pressure, vibration and fluid sensors that make continuous monitoring possible. These sensors produce 'live' data, which is highly advantageous in providing real-time information about realization and performance of the engine. Sensing surfaces are equipped with sensors that collect data in real time and the processed information is then obtained using methods such as signal processing and statistical analysis.

Acquiring of anomalies and failure footprints in real time for predictive maintenance systems is significantly facilitated by integration of ML algorithms into the system. These algorithms' ability to catch things that seemed only as small deviations from expected standard behavior, which may indicate impending machines' failure or degradation, will be a huge help. The AI is used for monitoring and analyzing the sensor data on a continuous basis. This allows the maintenance crews to take preventative measures by offering an early alert message when an issue is detected. This way, problems can be tackled earlier and there will be less chances of a full blown one.

In addition, the ML algorithms in the predictive maintenance systems are dynamic. They evolve through adaptation due to new input data they encounter. As time advances and more data are procured and examined, the programs will therefore become more effective and precise, thereby making accurate failure predictions and optimal maintenance strategies. Such an adaptive feature allows this strategy of predictive maintenance to be maintained valid even in an intricate and unpredictable situation in which numerous variables like flight conditions or patterns of engine usage are considered.

8.2.3 Benefits and Challenges of Machine Learning for PdM

Improved accuracy of failure prediction compared to traditional methods: Machine learning algorithms stand out from the crowd with the help of their highly developed ability to identify several complex patterns in data; therefore, they make it possible for the learning algorithms to predict the failures more accurately than traditional methods based on rules and/or threshold. Diagnosing these issues ahead of time, therefore, may not be a task for the traditional methods because the system analyzes huge amounts of data and considering multiple parameters and their interaction, the machine learning models detect those small markers of imminent failures which might go unnoticed by traditional methods.

Early detection of problems for preventive maintenance, minimizing downtime and safety risks: Machine learning models can detect early warning signs and hence, maintenance teams are able to perform a prompt action that vitalize in preventing the incidents from escalating to a complete failure. This is a preventive and business-oriented approach that involves planning the maintenance activities for long-term machines in the form of shutdown windows, rather than waiting for equipment to unexpectedly break down. The problems are also being tackled beforehand, and as a result, the risk of safety issues is curtailed decreasing the chance of accidents or operational disruptions.

Customization of models for specific engine types and operating conditions: Machine learning algorithms can be customized for different kinds of engines and operating conditions, which makes it possible for more precise forecasts and recommendations to be made across various ranges of data. When training models based on data of certain engine model or partial environment only, predictive maintenance systems may be able to account for unique performance factors and characteristics which dramatically influence the possibilities of failures and the requirements to maintenance.

8.2.4 Challenges

The data quality is, therefore, dependent on the amount and quality of available training data sets. If the sensor data output is incomplete or irregular, then this results in false alarms and a lower prediction accuracy. Ensuring that data quality is incorporated, and data are adapted effectively are major components instrumental to the success of a predictive maintenance system.

Computational cost: The development and utilization of a such complex machine learning models can be computationally demanding which might require quite a big load in the computation resources and processing power. This computational cost may be a source of a problem, especially when applications are natural for fast time reaction, and the predictions have to be made nearly instantaneously. Solutions such as optimization techniques and developments in hardware technologies that enable faster computing are being explored to address this problem.

Explainability: Scrutinizing the logic behind a supervised machine learning model prediction is one of the key factors in building the confidence and all the decision-making processes in maintenance area. Computers can learn much as humans, but every day, humans use classifiers, have a standard for class assigning and supervised learning: The historical data which is utilized in supervised learning is represented by two common operations which include the normal operation and known failures. Such data is normally labeled, and each class is associated with a specific label that may be either an indicator of a normal condition or a failure event. Through the performance on labeled data, supervised learning models can learn and recognize the patterns and weak indicators that were observed before failure events. One applied use is a predictive model that can derive faults in the future based on exposed patterns with the use of new sensor data Employing such a system 24/7 with continuous real-time monitoring of sensor data allows carrying the model to sense the earliest signs of faults before further escalations of maintenance cost, hence allowing for immediate taking of preventive actions.

Unsupervised Learning: To noisy and finicky maintenance, it is when can't get labeled failure data or it is limited utilized unsupervised learning techniques. While pre-labeled data are no longer the main reliance, unsupervised learning models can study the sensor data and find irregular functioning or abnormal operating patterns by this way. Those anomalies can be disturbing and serves as points of concern; thus, they call for more interest and closer examination. Unsupervised learning algorithms can create unique in-depth representations of typical, normal, and abnormal

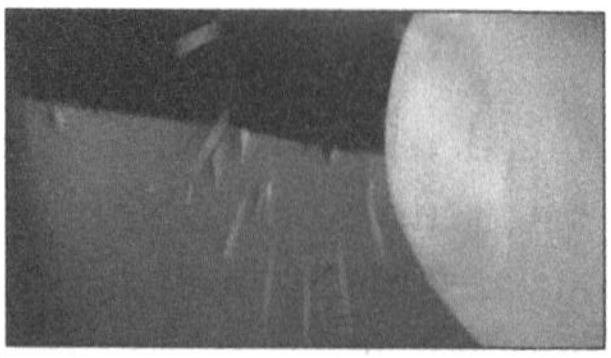

Figure 8.2 Scratches on engine blades.

engine behavior by analyzing the data distribution and detecting abnormal behavior which is out of the norm. Take, for example, an instance where the erratic deviations in temperatures or pressures such as those observed in the engine sensor may hint at existing issues with parts of the engine. The active anomaly detection via real-time monitoring feeds on the feedback loop, provoking proactive maintenance actions to stop failures by minimizing production loss.

However, many machine learning models, particularly complicated ones such as deep neural networks, are regarded as "black boxes" due to their intrinsic complexity. The main challenge is to transform the predictions and explanations provided by the model in a way that is understandable by domain experts and decision-makers, especially critical applications where transparency and reliability cannot be compromised. One of the most pursued areas in the field of model explainability and interpretability is techniques for plain talk around model definition and manipulation. Figure 8.2 showing visible scratch marks on the surface of a turbine engine blade.

8.3 Literature Review

PdM's foundation for turbofan engines is formed by several established techniques. One major player in this field is vibration analysis which monitors engine vibrations with sensors. Variations from regular oscillation patterns can serve as an indication of the component being worn off, having imbalances or approaching failure. Another technique is engine oil analysis that examines wear debris, contamination and changes in viscosity of engine oil samples. These pointers can indicate problems with internal components like gearboxes and bearings. Also important, temperature monitoring also acts as an indicator towards potential failures in the future. During temperature monitoring, key temperatures within the engine are tracked and abnormal temperatures may indicate either cooling system failures or bearing wears or even combustion processes not going on well. To conclude, performance monitoring which tracks thrust, fuel consumption and exhaust gas temperature among other parameter helps to identify deviations from expected values as well as detecting possible malfunctions in the system.

Leal *et al.* (2021) [12], Learning methods for remaining functional life prediction in a turbofan engine, present an overview of more recent approaches to research in the prediction of turbofan aircraft engines remaining helpful life, showing their applicability with convolutional neural networks, long short-term memory systems, and combinations. It noticed that one of the winners of the 2021 PHM Society data challenge utilized a deep convolutional neural network architecture, which could process variable-length inputs and pre-processed information through a feedforward neural network. In addition, other noted techniques include deep convolutional neural networks with residual architectures or autoencoder combined approaches. The whole text, therefore, highlights research and development on RUL prediction for turbofan engines.

Sabry *et al.* (2022) [13], Regression Analysis for Remaining Useful Life Prediction of Aircraft Engines, provides theoretically a method whereby the RUL of failing equipment could be forecasted, zeroing in on turbofan motors, to try avoiding unnecessary generation or utilization delays. The paper employments profound learning strategies propose a show that combines hereditary systems (GN) with a one-dimensional convolutional neural arrange (CNN) and long short-term memory (LSTM) organize with three thick layers and two dropout layers. The exploratory results indicate that the proposed model outperforms various machine learning and deep learning techniques in predicting the Remaining Useful Life (RUL) of turbofan engines.

Soualhi *et al.* (2022) used the following: Remaining Useful Life Estimation of Turbofan Engines Using Adaptive Fault Detection Learning. The paper highlights the importance of failure prognosis in advancing predictive maintenance for mechanical systems by providing crucial Remaining Useful Life (RUL) information. Hence, it highlights the challenge of accurately predicting RUL due to various degradation patterns, which result in varying failure onset times and corresponding RUL values for modeling. In this line, the paper proposes a flexible inconsistency discovery method that differentiates between blame event times and assigns appropriate RUL values for each disappointment direction. That thus allows for making a prognosis with higher precision. The strategy indicates progress in preparing the assignment for RUL expectations, particularly with cases featuring diverse erosion patterns. Execution of the proposed methodology is explained with a Long Short-Term Memory (LSTM) arrangement on quickened run-to-failure information from NASA turbofan motors, demonstrating its adequacy on RUL estimation.

Liu *et al.* (2023) [15], Remaining Useful Life Prediction Turbofan Engine Using SAE-TCN Model, point out that turbofan motors play a fundamental part in airship activity and the monitoring of well-being conditions for safe and stable flight. It reflects on how difficult it is to predict RUL for such motors given their high dimensionality and long duration of measured data. This paper presents a new residual life forecast model that combines autoencoder methods with transient convolutional organizers. An auto-encoder is used to reduce information dimensionality and extract features from motor observation information. At the same time, TCN is trained based on the resulting low-dimensional details to predict RUL.

Wang *et al.* (2023) [16], Remaining Useful Life Prediction of Aircraft Turbofan Engine Based on Random Forest Feature Selection and Multi-Layer Perceptron, has pointed out the intrinsic requirement for the prediction of remaining useful life of aircraft engines with better accuracy for improved safety and reduced maintenance costs. In the face of nonlinearities, high dimensionality, and complex distortion shapes of engine health monitoring parameters, a new approach will be presented. The strategy joins an arbitrary woodland calculation with a Bayes-refined multilayer perceptron. Above all, the arbitrary woodland calculation recognizes key highlights from verifiable observing parameters that influence motor lifetime activity. Currently, the single-exponential smoothing calculation is utilized for smoothing unique clamor impediments inside the extracted highlights.

Srinivasan *et al.* (2023) [17], Ensemble Neural Networks Remaining Useful Life (RUL) Prediction, states that support planning at the proper time is essential for giving accurate predictions on the health and deterioration of equipment—more specifically, expressed in terms of Remaining helpful Life. It states that most traditional data-driven methods for RUL prediction focus on single-point prediction and ignore entirely the probabilistic nature of failure. Various approaches utilizing neural networks for probabilistic RUL predictions decouple uncertainties related to the system and model parameters, addressing both aleatoric uncertainty and epistemic uncertainty. This de-coupling enables a clearer understanding of prediction confidence and its interpretation. The proposed strategy is assessed utilizing NASA's turbofan fly motor CMAPSS dataset and demonstrates its capacity to reveal instabilities and unravel the commitment of aleatoric and epistemic vulnerability.

8.3.1 Identification of Problem

When delving into the world of predictive maintenance on turbofan engines using NASA datasets and leveraging deep analyzing methodologies, it becomes obvious that expertise is paramount to the awesome goals of both customers and themselves. Customers, representing stakeholders and preference-makers in interior companies, prioritize reliability as their number one difficulty. They are attempting to find a guarantee that the turbofan engines will function seamlessly without sudden breakdowns or screw-ups, thereby minimizing high-priced downtime and operational disruptions. Furthermore, customers emphasize the importance of price-effectiveness in protection practices. They assume solutions that optimize preservation schedules and beneficial resource allocation, aiming to reduce needless expenses associated with each over-upkeep and sudden preservation.

Concurrently, the needs of clients, together with the upkeep of employees and engineers, are similarly important in the improvement and implementation of predictive maintenance solutions. These users require tools and structures that streamline protection techniques, ensuring that obligations are achieved effectively and correctly. They are trying to find intuitive interfaces and streamlined workflows that facilitate the well-timed, very last contact of preservation activities while maximizing useful resource utilization. Moreover, the client's area places a good-sized emphasis on protection, disturbing self-assurance inside the overall performance of the turbofan engines to mitigate the risks of accidents or malfunctions at some stage in operation. By addressing those diverse desires comprehensively, predictive protection answers utilizing deep analysis techniques on NASA datasets can provide superb service, enhancing operational reliability, rate-performance, and protection for each client and user alike.

8.3.2 Objectives

The core objective of this thesis is to design and deploy a deep learning-based system for health status prediction in physical activities based on data collected from multimodal meters. We provide a new method for estimating remaining usable life data. In learning the relationship between sensor data and health indices, the technique can predict RUL. Two datasets provided by NASA have been utilized during this study: the C-MAPSS dataset and the Challenge dataset. The challenge dataset contains two datasets—training and testing—while the C-MAPSS dataset comprises four datasets, further divided into two parts each, namely – training and testing datasets. Each row shows a snapshot of data gathered during one work session, with each column representing different variables.

Here, the first two columns indicate the number of units and launch duration in cycles, while columns three, four, and five include operational parameters. The remaining columns contain the sensor measurements. Then, this thesis aims to develop and evaluate a deep learning framework that predicts system health with a high accuracy rate. The results using the suggested technique on two different datasets have been clearly shown in this work on tables and figures. It simply conceptualizes the definitions and applications of machine learning and deep learning. Deep learning algorithms are, in this context, introduced comprehensively about their benefits and applications and a deep survey on many RUL prediction and classification strategies. The design and working methods of the proposed approaches are then explained in detail, together with data definition. It would review in detail the proposed deep learning and data preparation; then, present the results for RUL prediction obtained with the MATLAB program and a comparison with other approaches. Eventually, the report concludes with some recommendations for future research perspectives.

8.4 Methodology

The dataset, which was obtained from the internet-aid, pertains to the NASA turbofan engine degradation simulation facts. This statistic consists of sensor readings from several turbofan engines, along with temperature, strain, and rotational speed readings, like records of the engine's ordinary fitness and overall performance over time. This permits the improvement of machine-studying fashions capable of forecasting while preservation must be performed. The dataset encompasses both nominal and degraded engine conditions. Addressing null values was the first of many preprocessing steps applied to the dataset. Duplicate values have been then treated due to the fact that they were not useful inside the model's gaining knowledge of technique and had been eliminated from the dataset. To extract beneficial features from the unprocessed sensor facts, function engineering turned into finally implemented facts. This required calculating statistical capabilities for each sensor sign, consisting of mean, median, standard deviation, and skewness. It also involved the use of a histogram to determine the distribution of the sensor statistics, a field plot to identify any outliers in each sensor, and a time collection plot to display the performance of every sensor price over the years. To display which feature has a higher correlation, the characteristic correlation has been plotted the use of a heatmap. Following function identification, all the features were normalized to have an equal size and range using a standard scaler characteristic.

A variety of machine learning strategies were then adopted to predict the remaining usable lives of turbofan engines, including 'deep mastering' techniques: synthetic neural networks, and recurrent neural networks in conjunction with regression evaluation fashions along with ridge regression, support vector machines, and decision bushes. Model performance metrics, such as mean squared errors and r2 score, have been used to evaluate model efficiency. Then, a random search CV was used for fine-tuning the best quality-executing set of rules for higher accuracy. The saved model as a pickle record was put straight into user-friendly web software by the Python framework Streamlit. The application serves real-time entry for sensor records, where one can get forecasts of the engine's remaining useful life and diagnostic graphs with visualizations of trends in sensor statistics. Part of its flexibilities and configurability ensures that it simplifies smooth integration to other systems and information sources, improving further usability and flexibility.

Two main approaches exist within machine learning for predictive maintenance (PdM). Supervised learning refers to the use of past data with known failures. This information is usually used to train models which can pick up patterns in sensor readings that happen just prior to a failure. Thereafter, these models apply the ideas they have learned from the patterns and can make predictions about future malfunctions when new sensor data come. Unsupervised learning on the other hand uses an alternative method. Instead of utilizing the labeled datasets regarding failure, it detects anomalousness from sensors. By analyzing huge sets of information, these algorithms can learn what is considered as "normal" behavior of an engine. Any deviations from this behavior may indicate possible problems and thus enable maintenance personnel to perform actions before a failure happens.

The incorporation of machine learning has several advantages for PdM. ML models can understand intricate associations between sensor data and engine health; therefore, allowing more precise prediction of failures as compared to classical methods. Hence, timely detection of issues enables preventive maintenance leading to lesser downtimes and safety risks if any.

However, the application of machine learning to PdM is still faced with some challenges. ML models work well if they get much sensor data, and they have to be of high quality also. Flawed or inadequate data may result in wrong predictions. It might be difficult for some applications to train and run complicated ML algorithms that can consume much computing resources. Finally, there is explainability issue. Trusting a model or making maintenance decisions requires understanding why the model predicts

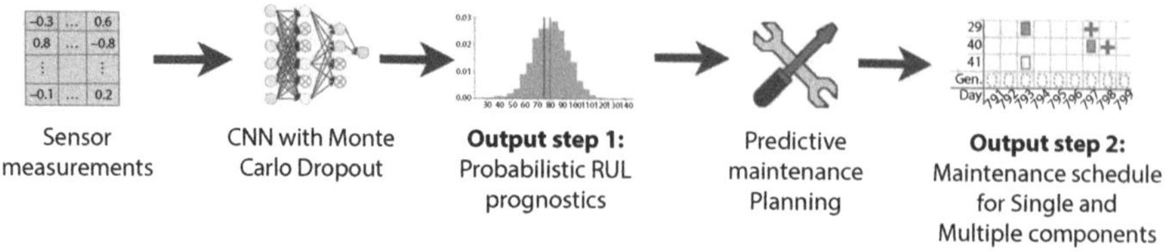

Figure 8.3 The roadmap outlines steps from raw sensor data to probabilistic RUL.

failure (failure). Some complex models can also be like black boxes and are hard to understand how they made their prediction. All these problems are being tackled by researchers who are enabling more effective and reliable PdM in the future.

Furthermore, such models could be calibrated against different types of engines under diverse operating environments which make them better than generic maintenance programs in terms of effectiveness. Figure 8.3 the steps involved in predictive maintenance process using remaining useful life with output steps.

To suit the version, the records were first pre-processed and then split into training and checking out sets. We then evaluated the capacity of different system mastering strategies to expect how lengthy the turbofan engines would stay operational. These consist of regression analysis fashions like ridge regression, lasso regression, support vector machines, selection bushes, random forests, and gradient enhance regressors, in addition to deep mastering techniques like synthetic neural networks and recurrent neural networks [28, 29, 32–35]. Several performance measures, which include implying squared mistakes, root suggest rectangular mistakes, and r2 score, were used to assess the fashions– a good way to decide which approach changed into quality for the activity.

The dataset obtained from internet sources contains crucial information pertaining to the degradation simulation of NASA turbofan engines. It encompasses sensor readings like temperature, pressure, and rotational velocity, along with indicators of engine fitness and overall performance over time. Through rigors preprocessing steps, including null value handling, duplicate removal, and feature engineering, meaningful insights have been derived from the raw sensor data. Statistical functions such as mean, median, and standard deviation have been calculated for each sensor signal to help identify outliers and conduct an overall sensor performance analysis. Furthermore, the data were standardized to ensure homogeneity in features before being split into training and testing. Various machine learning techniques were subsequently employed to forecast the remaining usable lives of turbofan engines. These include deep learning methods such as artificial neural networks and recursive neural networks, as well as regression analysis models such as ridge regression, support vector machines, and decision trees [30, 38, 39]. Mean squared error, r2 score for assessing model effectiveness, etc. Performance metrics were implemented, including fine-tuning the best-performing algorithm using a random sanch CV for increased accuracy. The resulting model, saved as a pickle file, was included in a user-friendly web application internally using the Streamlit Python program. This application enables users to input real-time sensor data and obtain predictions about the remaining engine's useful life, including diagnostic charts and visualizations of sensor data trends. Scalability and customizability allow for easy integration with other systems and data sources, making it usable and convenient. In terms of customer and user requirements observed from field visits and inspections, it is evident that a major issue arises in turbofan engine maintenance within expected timeframes and reduces the chances of faults or failures, which can result in significant financial and reputational risks. Thus, such solutions are needed to maintain the reliability, safety, and cost-effectiveness of turbofan engine operations in the dynamic operating conditions required to produce and implement a robust predictive maintenance system that can anticipate and meet maintenance needs. When these customer needs are translated into a product, it uses NASA data and advanced machine learning techniques to create customized maintenance plans that meet the requirements for reliability, efficiency, and cost-effectiveness. Customers are looking for high-performance engines that don't break down in accidents, efficient maintenance practices

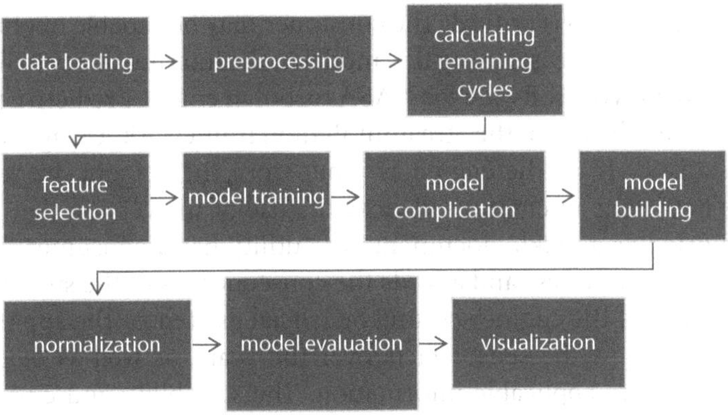

Figure 8.4 Flow chart of the model.

performed at optimal times, and cost-effective solutions that reduce costs while maintaining peak performance. Take lessons Take internal strategies and implement customized maintenance schedules to meet these needs in complete NASA datasets, ultimately leading to customer satisfaction and smooth engine operation. Figure 8.4 flow chart of the model the process of developing a predictive maintenance system for turbofan engines where it involves data loading, preprocessing, feature selection, normalization, model training, model evaluation and visualization.

Data Loading: import the datasets.
Preprocessing: Process of removing inaccurate values for data analysis.
Calculating Remaining Cycles: Estimate the time need for the further steps.
Feature Selection: Reducing Dimensionality, speed up the algorithm, Improving the accuracy prediction.
Model Training: Train the model on the processed data.
Model Complication: the process after defining the model architecture and before the model building.
Model Building Analyses data to make predictions.
Normalization: Transforming the data into more normal.
Model Evaluation: Helps to analyze the performance of the model, such as accuracy prediction, validation accuracy etc.
Visualization: Visualizing the results of the model such as violin plot, Boxplot, Correlation Heatmap, Graph etc.

To use the pre-educated version to directly forecast the records, the model is then saved as a pickle report. Next, using the Random Search CV characteristic, the superior parameters for the remaining best approach can be adjusted. To enhance the model's accuracy for the specific problem declaration, this step is critical. The consumer may be capable of obtaining the model's RUL forecasts using this model in the internet utility to forecast consumer data. Web software for NASA turbofan engine predictive preservation evolved the use of the Streamlit Python framework. Using real-time sensor statistics from the engine as input from the person, the software predicts how long an engine will close the use of the version that turned into imported as a pickle document. The utility has a consumer-friendly interface for facts access and affords the consequences of the studies, such as an estimate of the engine's closing beneficial existence. The app permits customers to view the sensor facts over the years, as well as diagnostic graphs and other applicable information. The scalability and customization functions of the software make it easy to integrate with other systems and record sources.

8.5 Experimental Results

NASA's Turbofan Maintenance Prediction experimental work typically involves several key steps to develop, test, and validate predictive maintenance models using relevant data sets. Here is an overview of the experimental process:

8.5.1 Data Preprocessing

Clean up the NASA turbofan maintenance data sets, addressing missing numbers, conflicts, and inconsistencies. Normalize or standardize numerical functions to ensure they are all on the same scale. Categorical variables are encoded using categorical variables when applicable. Divide datasets into training, validation, and testing sets.

8.5.2 Developing Models

This is the selection of proper machine learning algorithms or deep learning architectures. Data- and issue characteristic-driven RUL estimation, such as models created with TensorFlow, PyTorch, or scikit-learn, are considered. Tune hyper-parameters using Grid Search, Random Search, or Bayesian Optimization methods for better performance in the model.

8.5.3 Training and Validation

Test the developed models on the training data with appropriate loss functions and optimization algorithms. Monitor model performance on the validation set to avoid overfitting. Use early termination, learning rate time, and regularization techniques for better generalization and optimization. Avoid overfitting.

8.5.4 Evaluation

Test the models against test data to determine their performance on unknown data. Proper assessment measures will be used, such as mean absolute error, root mean squared error, and R-squared for regression projects. Examines how well the model works to decide on improvements.

8.5.5 Comparison with Baseline

Compare the performance of the developed models with that of base methods or traditional approaches in use for RUL forecasting. Consider benchmarks possibly set in literature reviews or even industry standards when assessing predictive maintenance models.

8.5.6 Sensitivity Analysis

Perform sensitivity analysis by evaluating the effects of various input characteristics on model predictions. Determine the robustness of developed models to variations in sensor data and operating conditions. Visualize and interpret the predictions of models by observing their RUL-i values. Interpret the importance of the various features and their effects on RUL prediction. Figure 8.5 the violin plot shows the distribution of values for different features it helps visualize the variability and central tendancy of each feature. Figure 8.6 this box plot shows the distribution of values for different features where it represents the range with the median indicated by a line with in the box. Figure 8.7 this distribution graph shows the count of occurrences for different labels. Figure 8.8 the correlation heatmap shows the pairwise correlations between sensors and operating conditions. Figure 8.9 this graph shows the training and validation accuracy of a model over 50 epochs where the training accuracy steadily increases while the validation accuracy initially increases. Figure 8.10 the histograms show the distribution of pixel brightness levels for different sensors. The distributions vary in shape and range, indicating different patterns in the sensor data.

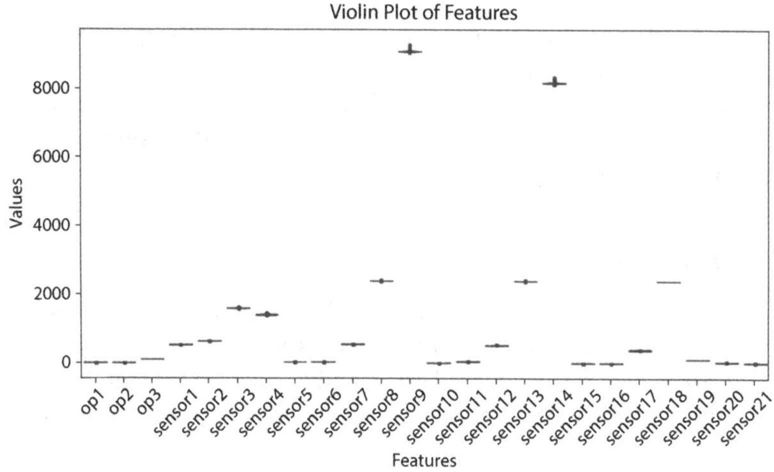

Figure 8.5 Violin plot of values vs features.

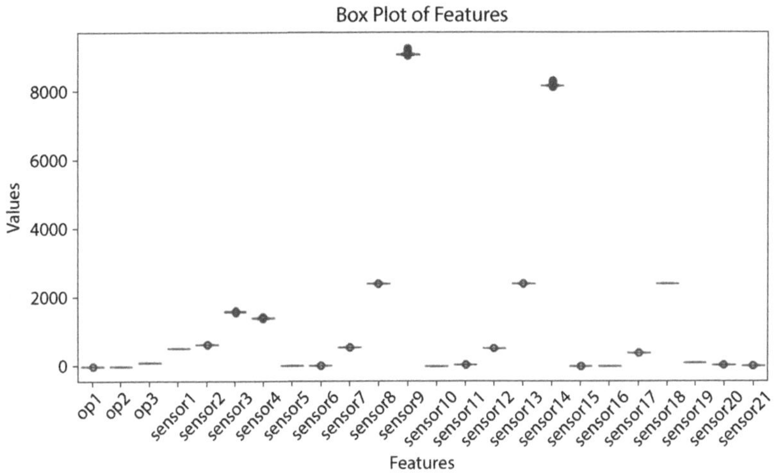

Figure 8.6 Boxplot of values vs features.

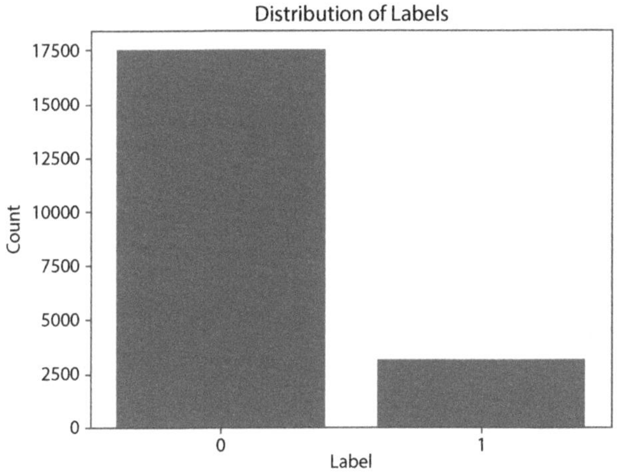

Figure 8.7 Distribution graph of count of occurrences vs labels.

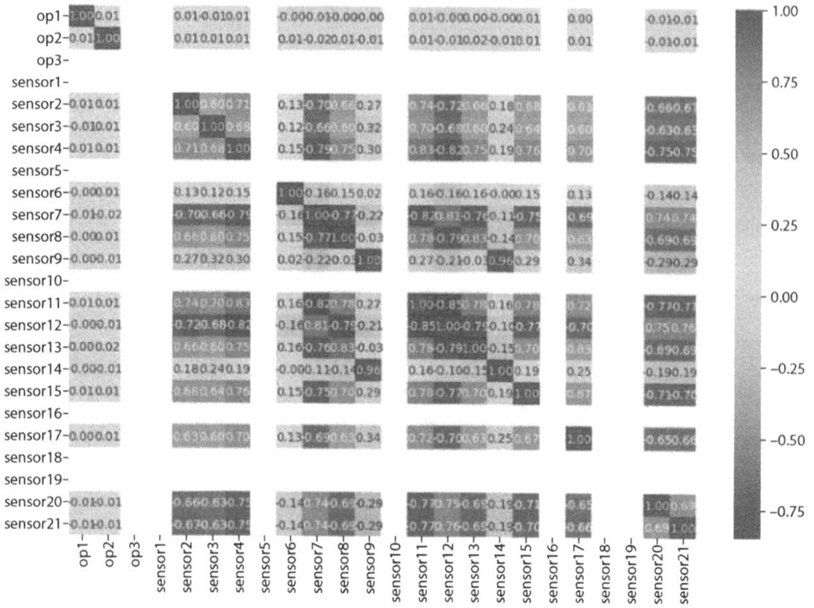

Figure 8.8 Correlation heatmap of failures.

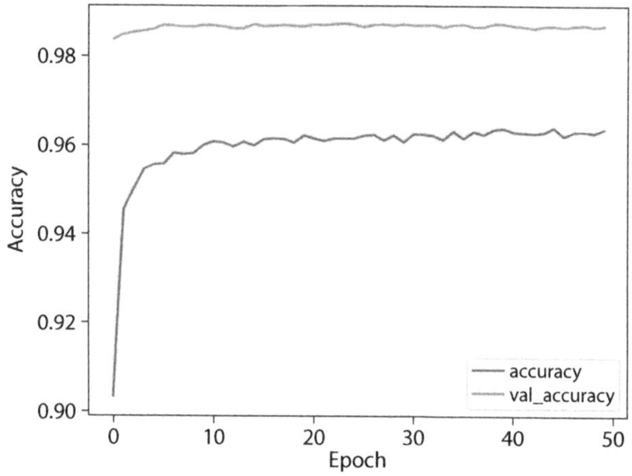

Figure 8.9 Training and validation accuracy vs epoch number graph.

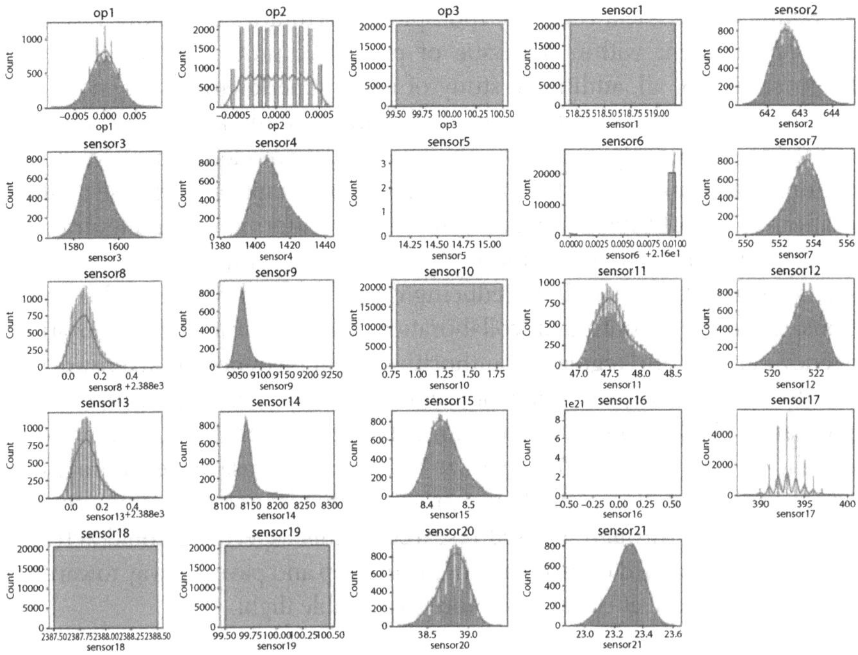

Figure 8.10 Pixel brightness level vs number of pixels having brightness.

8.6 Conclusion and Future Work

In the end, the development and implementation of a predictive safety device for turbofan engines, the use of NASA datasets, and deep analysis methodologies maintain significant value for several stakeholders inside the aviation organization. By leveraging superior technology like records analytics and machine learning, predictive upkeep structures can proactively show engine fitness, choose out capability troubles before they enhance, and optimize safety schedules, thereby improving operational reliability, protection, and cost-effectiveness. Through this study, we've explored the vital function of predictive protection in ensuring the clean operation of turbofan engines, specifically in high-stakes environments, which include agency aviation and military operations. Moreover, we have cited the diverse demanding conditions and methodologies concerned in developing such systems, in conjunction with record preprocessing, model choice, schooling, and validation. The experimental artwork noted on this record underscores the significance of thorough evaluation and assessment with baseline strategies to validate the effectiveness of predictive maintenance models.

Taking a step back, there are multiple opportunities for future research and development within the issue of predictive protection for turbofan engines. First of all, additional study of more superior tool-studying techniques, such as ensemble strategies and switch-gaining knowledge, may be needed to enhance the predictive abilities of safety models, especially in situations with constrained statistics availability or complicated engine configurations. Secondly, integrating real-time sensor information and leveraging the trouble computing era must allow extra-well-timed and responsive safety interventions, similarly reducing downtime and operational disruptions. Moreover, continued collaboration with commercial corporation agency partners and regulatory authorities might be important to ensure the scalability, reliability, and safety of predictive safety systems in actual-world programs. Finally, continued work on data super, accessibility, and interoperability is likely required to maximize NASA datasets use and encourage the wider implementation of predictive preservation technology over the course of aeronautics. Through focused research in this aspect, we could actively enhance the standard of turbofan engine upkeep and pave the way towards a more secure, more effective, and more sustainable flight.

8.7 Additional Considerations

Relevant Case Studies: Some typical demonstration of the predicted maintenance system (PdM) applied in the air transport industry are available. For example, predictive analytics for engines monitoring from General Electric (GE) Aviation can offer prompt maintenance and cut down unforeseen idle hours of flight. Through measuring and analyzing data from sensors which are embedded in an engine, GE Aviation can predict incidents of failure before they happen while the timely maintenance intervention can be applied leading to the reliability and safety of the engine. At Rolls-Royce, the use of predictive maintenance capabilities for jet engines relying on the latest analytics tools is practiced to ensure efficient maintenance planning and increase operational efficiency.

Regulatory Considerations and Industry Standards: Regulatory Considerations and Industry Standards: For the aviation industry, it is highly desirable to have internationally well-accepted regulatory agencies, such as the Federal Aviation Administration (FAA) and the European Aviation Safety Agency (EASA), which can introduce some basic standards and regulations in maintenance sectors related to predictive maintenance. However, there are no specific rules for predictive maintenance; existing regulations pertaining to maintenance, aircraft safety, and reliability should be preserved. Further, standards of industry best practice issued by the International Air Transport Association and the Society of Automotive Engineers, respectively initiate the implementation of previously designed and authorized activities.

Thereby, it improves reliability, security, balanced perspective and economy, but there is lack of certainty and has difficulties to overcome. The possibility of flawed machine-learning and analytics could still exist in computational approaches of predictive maintenance, and it might still confront issues such as false alarms, data quality, and computational complexity. Data validation and acquisition from reliable sources for maintenance experts with high level of expertise for interpreting and acting on the predictive insights are important for predictive maintenance effectiveness. On the other hand, predictive maintenance brings many advantages to the aviation industry, but sensibility on the different aspects is addressed to ensure the most accurate and effective implementation.

References

1. Mathew, V., Toby, T., Singh, V., Rao, B.M., Kumar, M.G., Prediction of Remaining Useful Lifetime (RUL) of turbofan engine using machine learning, in: *2017 IEEE International Conference on Circuits and Systems (ICCS)*, 2017, December, IEEE, pp. 306–311.
2. Basora, L., Olive, X., Dubot, T., Recent advances in anomaly detection methods applied to aviation. *Aerospace*, 6, 11, 117, 2019.
3. Kalyani, S., Rao, K.V., Sowjanya, A.M., A TimeImageNet Sequence Learning for Remaining Useful Life Estimation of Turbofan Engine in Aircraft Systems. *Struct. Durab. Health Monit.*, *15*, 4, 317, 2021.
4. De Giorgi, M.G., Menga, N., Ficarella, A., Exploring Prognostic and Diagnostic Techniques for Jet Engine Health Monitoring: A Review of Degradation Mechanisms and Advanced Prediction Strategies. *Energies*, 16, 6, 2711, 2023.
5. Azyus, A.F. and Wijaya, S.K., Determining the method of predictive maintenance for aircraft engine using machine learning. *J. Comput. Sci. Technol. Stud.*, 4, 1, 01–06, 2022.
6. Ogiriki, E.A., Li, Y.G., Nikolaidis, T., Isaiah, T.E., Sule, G., Effect of fouling, thermal barrier coating degradation and film cooling holes blockage on gas turbine engine creep life. *Procedia CIRP*, 38, 228–233, 2015.
7. Muneer, A., Taib, S.M., Fati, S.M., Alhussian, H., Deep learning-based prognosis approach for remaining useful life prediction of turbofan engine. *Symmetry*, 13, 10, 1861, 2021.
8. Kadre, S.S. and Paspula, R.G., Improved RUL Predictions of Aero-Engines by Hyper-Parameter Optimization of LSTM Neural Network Models.

International Journal for Research in Applied Science & Engineering Technology (IJRASET), 11(III), 2023, ISSN: 2321-9653.

9. Asif, O., Haider, S.A., Naqvi, S.R., Zaki, J.F., Kwak, K.S., Islam, S.R., A deep learning model for remaining useful life prediction of aircraft turbofan engine on C-MAPSS dataset. *IEEE Access*, 10, 95425–95440, 2022.
10. Karnik, R. and Pandya, K., Long-Short-Term Memory Model for Remaining Usable Life Estimation.
11. Leal, A.S., Berton, L., de Castro Santos, L.C., Learning methods for remaining useful life prediction in a turbofan engine, in: *Anais do XIX Encontro Nacional de Inteligência Artificial e Computational*, 2022, November, SBC, pp. 556–566.
12. Sabry, H.M. and El-Latif, Y.M.A., Regression Analysis for Remaining Useful Life Prediction of Aircraft Engines, in: *International Conference on Advanced Machine Learning Technologies and Applications*, 2022, April, Springer International Publishing, Cham, pp. 157–168.
13. Soualhi, M., Nguyen, K., Medjaher, K., Zerhouni, N., Remaining useful life estimation of turbofan engines using adaptive fault detection learning, in: *Annual Conference of the PHM Society*, 2022, October, vol. 14, no. 1.
14. Liu, X., Xiong, L., Zhang, Y., Luo, C., Remaining Useful Life Prediction for Turbofan Engine Using SAE-TCN Model. *Aerospace*, 10, 8, 715, 2023.
15. Wang, H., Li, D., Li, D., Liu, C., Yang, X., Zhu, G., Remaining useful life prediction of aircraft turbofan engine based on random forest feature selection and multi-layer perceptron. *Appl. Sci.*, 13, 12, 7186, 2023.
16. Srinivasan, A., Andresen, J.C., Holst, A., Ensemble Neural Networks for Remaining Useful Life (RUL) Prediction, arXiv preprint arXiv:2309.12445, 2023.
17. Mitici, M., de Pater, I., Barros, A., Zeng, Z., Dynamic predictive maintenance for multiple components using data-driven probabilistic RUL prognostics: The case of turbofan engines. *Reliab. Eng. Syst. Saf.*, *234*, 20, 109199, 2023.
18. Behera, S., Choubey, A., Kanani, C.S., Patel, Y.S., Misra, R., Sillitti, A., Ensemble trees learning based improved predictive maintenance using IIoT for turbofan engines, in: *Proceedings of the 34th ACM/SIGAPP symposium on applied computing*, 2019, April, pp. 842–850.
19. Düdükçü, H.V., Taşkıran, M., Kahraman, N., LSTM and WaveNet implementation for predictive maintenance of turbofan engines, in: *2020 IEEE 20th International Symposium on Computational Intelligence and Informatics (CINTI)*, 2020, November, IEEE, pp. 000151–000156.
20. Adryan, F.A. and Sastra, K.W., Predictive maintenance for aircraft engine using machine learning: trends and challenges. *Avia*, 3, 1, 20, 2021.
21. Zhuang, L., Xu, A., Wang, X.L., A prognostic driven predictive maintenance framework based on Bayesian deep learning. *Reliab. Eng. Syst. Saf.*, *234*, 109181, 2023.

22. Wang, Jiantai, W., Tan, L., Xiaobing, M., Kaiye, G., Heping, J., Li, Y., Prognosis-driven reliability analysis and replacement policy optimization for two-phase continuous degradation, *Reliab. Eng. Syst. Saf.*, vol. 230(C), Elsevier, 2023.
23. Ghadekar, P., Dargode, A., Deshmukh, J., Jaisinghani, A., Jadhav, M., Nimbalkar, A., Predictive maintenance on turbo fan dataset using deep learning. *AIP Conf. Proc.*, 2981, 1, AIP Publishing, 2023, December.
24. Soni, H., Kansara, A., Joshi, T., Predictive maintenance of gas turbine using prognosis approach. *Int. Res. J. Eng. Technol.*, *7*, 6, 4683–4691, 2020.
25. Stanton, I., Munir, K., Ikram, A., El-Bakry, M., Predictive maintenance analytics and implementation for aircraft: Challenges and opportunities. *Syst. Eng.*, *26*, 2, 216–237, 2023.
26. Ghantasala, G.P., Hung, B.T., Chakrabarti, P., Pellakuri, V., Machinery health prognostics: A systematic review from data acquisition to RUL prediction, *Mech. Syst. Signal Process*, 104, 799–834, 2018
27. Narayana, M.V., Rao, J.N., Shrivastava, S., Ghantasala, G.S., Ioannou, I., Vassiliou, V., A framework for identification of brain tumors from MR images using progressive segmentation. *Health Technol.*, *14*, 3, 539–556, 2024.
28. Sravanthi, J., Reddy, C.S., Mahendar, A., Kumar, V.R., Buragadda, S., Ghantasala, G.P., Gupta, G., Improve Accuracy in Healthcare Data Analysis using Competitive Ensemble Deep Learning Model, in: *2024 11th International Conference on Computing for Sustainable Global Development (INDIACom)*, 2024, February, IEEE, pp. 1792–1797.
29. Dilip, K., Ghantasala, G.P., Rao, D.N., Rathee, M., Bathla, P., ACO-Based Hyperparameter Tuning of a DL Model for Lung Cancer Prediction, in: *2024 IEEE International Conference on Computing, Power and Communication Technologies (IC2PCT)*, 2024, February, vol. 5, IEEE, pp. 883–887.
30. Reddy, A., Ramaiah, V.S., Ayyappa, R.M.K., Ghantasala, G.P., Kurra, M., Bathla, P., An Empirical Brief Analysis of Novelistic Approaches for Detection Of Bone Marrow Cancer Health Monitoring Through DL MODEL, in: *2024 IEEE International Conference on Computing, Power and Communication Technologies (IC2PCT)*, 2024, February, vol. 5, IEEE, pp. 1211–1214.
31. Ramana, T.V., Ghantasala, G.S., Sathiyaraj, R., Khan, M. (Eds.), *Artificial Intelligence and Machine Learning for Smart Community: Concepts and Applications*, CRC Press, Boca Raton, Florida, USA, 2024.
32. Ghantasala, G.P., Kunchala, A., Sathiyaraj, R., Raparthi, Y., Vidyullatha, P., Machine Learning Based Ensemble Classifier using Wisconsin Dataset For Breast Cancer Prediction, in: *2023 International Conference on Integrated Intelligence and Communication Systems (ICIICS)*, 2023, November, IEEE, pp. 1–4.
33. Kiran, C.C., Vidyullatha, P., Ram, V.V., Manish, T., Gopichand, K., Ghantasala, P., Graph Based Big Data Analytics on Unsupervised Machine Learning Framework, in: *2023 International Conference on Advancement in Computation & Computer Technologies (InCACCT)*, 2023, May, IEEE, pp. 732–737.

34. Mounika, C., Poojitha, K.V.V.M., Supraja, P.D.L.S., Vidyullatha, P., Priya, P.K., Gantasala, G.P., Advanced Graph Analytics Algorithms On Genre Based Recommending System, in: *2023 International Conference on Advancement in Computation & Computer Technologies (InCACCT)*, 2023, May, IEEE, pp. 738–743.
35. Ghantasala, G.P., Reddy, A.R., Arvindhan, M., Prediction of Coronavirus (COVID-19) Disease Health Monitoring with Clinical Support System and Its Objectives, in: *Machine Learning and Analytics in Healthcare Systems*, pp. 237–260, CRC Press, Boca Raton, Florida, USA, 2021.
36. Parameswaran, T., Reddy, Y.P., Nagaveni, V., Sathiyaraj, R., Era of Computational Big Data Analytics and IoT Techniques in Smart City Applications, in: *IoT and Big Data Analytics for Smart Cities*, pp. 1–22, 2022.
37. Rajendran, S., Sabharwal, M., Ghinea, G., Dhanaraj, R.K., Balusamy, B. (Eds.), *IoT and Big Data Analytics for Smart Cities: A Global Perspective*, CRC Press, Boca Raton, Florida, USA, 2022.
38. Vidyullatha, P., Reddy, V.D., Ram, K.D., Reddy, D.S., Shaik, A., Ramya, K.R., A Computer Vision based Facial Denoising Alignment using Convolution Neural Network Model, in: *2023 8th International Conference on Communication and Electronics Systems (ICCES)*, 2023, June, IEEE, pp. 841–848.
39. Vidyullatha, P., Prapulla, S.T., Saran, A.P., Ramya, P., Machine Vision based Object Detection using Deep Learning Techniques, in: *2023 3rd International Conference on Smart Data Intelligence (ICSMDI)*, 2023, March, IEEE, pp. 466–470.

9

Industrial Predictive Maintenance for Sustainable Manufacturing

Mohammed Rihan*, Ethiswar Muchherla, Shwejit Shri, Kushagra Jasoria, Judeson Antony Kovilpillai J. and G. S. Pradeep Ghantasala

Department of Computer Science and Engineering, Alliance University, Bangalore, India

Abstract

As industries have moved towards growth, the incorporation of advanced technologies is very crucial. One of the most important benefits of these technologies is the possibility of using them for scheduling, in particular, for the prediction of failures and the optimal planning of maintenance work. This chapter focuses on the impact of predictive maintenance in a variety of industries, and its value in reducing or avoiding costly breakdowns, increasing the profitability of the business, and increasing the overall performance indicator of industrial processes. Compared with traditional strategies, predictive maintenance is a completely different approach to perform maintenance.

Condition monitoring of equipment is done continuously to check on the equipment's state and if it is operating differently from the usual state, then it is time for equipment maintenance. After a particular equipment has been identified as likely to fail in the near future, it is possible to plan the maintenance at the best time that will not interrupt the production process while at the same time making the best use of the maintenance resources available.

A comparative analysis of different research works is also done to show the efficiency of predictive maintenance in various fields. Within manufacturing, one example showed a 30% improvement of the effective use of machines by applying IoT sensors and using machine learning models to anticipate the failure of key machines. The use of predictive maintenance has been implemented in the energy sector specifically in wind turbines, where it has cut the cost of maintenance by a quarter, besides increasing the lifespan of the turbines. Automotive manufacturing

**Corresponding author*: rimohammedbtech21@ced.alliance.edu.in

M. Thirunavukkarasan, S. A. Sahaaya Arul Mary, Sathiyaraj. R, G. S. Pradeep Ghantasala and Mudassir Khan (eds.) Artificial Intelligence and Machine Learning for Industry 4.0, (223–246)

has also been positively impacted as predictive maintenance has helped in detecting possible failures in robotic arms and other components; this has realized a 20% improvement in the overall equipment effectiveness (OEE) and cost savings. However, as is often the case with new methodologies, the introduction of predictive maintenance is not without its challenges.

Some challenges include high initial costs associated with the installation of IoT devices and sensors, integration of the predictive maintenance systems and architectures with the current system architecture, and the need for skilled personnel to manage as well as to analyze data from the systems. The chapter also describes the application and examples of using the predictive maintenance in practice and other industries, showing that this approach can provide tangible benefits and bring considerable improvements in companies' performance. The automotive industry has been able to use predictive maintenance in improving the operational efficiency of production lines and minimize equipment failure.

Keywords: Predictive maintenance, condition monitoring, IoT sensors, machine learning models, operational efficiency, sustainable manufacturing

9.1 Introduction

Maintenance is a cornerstone when we discuss the operations of industry setting where there is a need of continuous functioning of the machinery and equipment to ensure productivity and efficiency. Traditionally there has been a reactive response in cases of equipment failures, scheduled preventive measures to solve any potential issues and the emerging method of predictive maintenance that uses data driven methodologies to predict and prevent failures proactively [32].

Predictive Maintenance represents a huge shift in the philosophy of maintenance where it emphasizes a proactive approach as compared to reactive approach to equipment upkeep [1]. At the core of predictive maintenance, it relies in real-time monitoring of health of the equipment, leveraging the sensor data and IoT technologies to detect any anomalous behavior and predict the if any possible failures before they take place [33]. These maintenance models can identify equipment failure or degradation by analyzing the patterns in data collected through sensors; and hence, that allows us to intervene timely and take necessary actions. This approach minimizes unplanned downtime, disruptions of the production and maximizes asset reliability and lifespan of the equipment [2].

The machine learning techniques are very integral as to how effective the predictive maintenance strategies are. Machine learning algorithms allow the predictive models to reinforce from the historical-data and do proper predictions about the health and performance of the asset. By using advanced algorithms such as regression, classification, and anomaly detection, predictive maintenance models can identify the patterns and correlation within the data, hence improving predictive accuracy over time [34].

In industry 4.0, Predictive-Maintenance (PdM) has become a game changer in the field of industrial technologies which has completely transformed the process of machine maintenance. When PdM is combined with Internet of things (IoT) as it becomes the advanced approach that not only mitigates the risk of cost breakdown but also optimizes operational efficiency that reduces the expensive malfunctioning [3]. Now more concepts have been implemented with this new idea, e.g.; predictive maintenance which often has an important role in sustainable manufacturing and production by making machine maintenance which is the digital version [35].

This paper will provide the exploration of predictive-maintenance and machine learning techniques with their accurate comparisons. Through examination of these topics, we want to convey the transforming potential of predictive maintenance in today's industrial landscape.

9.1.1 IoT Internet of Things

Internet of Things (IoT) is a network of inter-connected devices that is integrated with sensors, actuators, and communications features. By this, devices collect, exchange data with the help of Internet that makes it possible to manage, optimize and monitor industrial processes and machinery in real time. By integrating IoT technologies into predictive maintenance strategies, organizations can enhance asset reliability, optimize maintenance and streamline operations.

9.1.2 Industry 4.0

The Fourth Industrial Revolution is referred to as "Industrial 4.0". The introduction of computers had a disruptive influence on Industry 3.0 through technology. Industry 4.0 mentions the networking of industrial machinery and computers to allow automated decision-making and communication without the need for human interaction.

9.2 Search Methodology

Multiple academic databases, including Google Scholar, IEEE Xplore, Applied Sciences, Science Direct, and ResearchGate, were searched using keywords such as 'predictive maintenance', predictive maintenance and IoT', 'PdM sensors' and 'PdM and machine learning'. The criteria for inclusion were peer-reviewed publications and conference papers published during the last five - seven years. The search approach was intended to find papers on IoT technology, predictive maintenance strategies, data gathering, machine learning techniques and analysis methods. The selected publications were critically analyzed to get knowledge on the methodology used for data collection, its analysis and predictive maintenance implementation, that served as the foundation for our review study.

9.3 Methodology

In the fast-changing environment of the IoT , where devices are interconnected, which are used in every aspect of modern life, the effective management and maintenance of these systems are important. With billions of devices interconnected, ranging from consumer gadgets to industrial machinery, ensuring their continuous operation, reliability, and performance is very crucial. Provisioning in IoT environments incorporates a variety of customized strategies to address various business challenges and improve the lifecycle of connected assets.

9.3.1 Types of Maintenance

Different types of maintenance strategies and techniques are used to prevent the failure of system. This increases the sustainability of the devices. Figure 9.1 illustrates the various types of predictive maintenance. These include:

a. *Reactive Maintenance*
Reactive maintenance, also known as corrective maintenance, refers to the strategy where maintenance is needed when an asset(device) has failed to

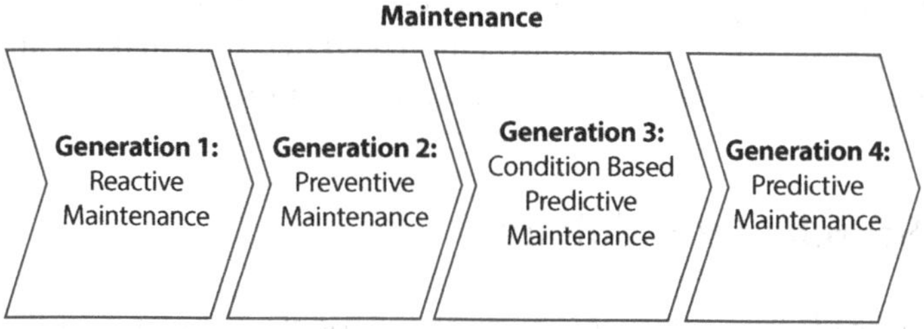

Figure 9.1 Types of maintenance.

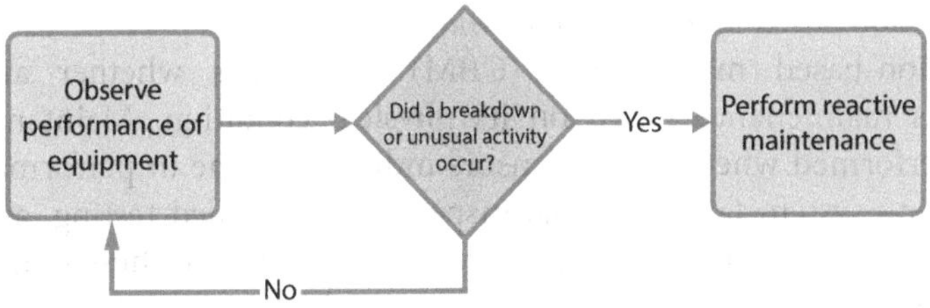

Figure 9.2 Reactive maintenance flow.

perform. The reactive maintenance approach is done when the costs sustained during asset failures are typically lower than that of maintaining the performance of asset. According to a study done by Plant Engineering 61% of manufacturing use reactive maintenance. Figure 9.2 depicts the workflow associated with reactive maintenance, showcasing the steps taken in response to equipment failures.

The main purpose of reactive type is to solve the problems when they take place. These activities take place when asset dysfunctions. If the asset can still work, it can be repaired and if it doesn't it will be replaced, e.g., do you change battery of a device before it stops working? The most - logical thing to do would be to stay put until battery completely drains out and to buy a new set of battery after that. This type of method is suitable for cheap products.

b. *Preventive maintenance*

In Preventative maintenance, the pre data collected is used to know when an asset the device is about to experience failure in its performance i.e., it explains about the life time of the device [36]. IoT smart sensors are built into assets such as auto-mobiles or infrastructure. These sensors collect data and send them to the database where human users can manage the data and deploy their maintenance resources more efficiently [43].

The types of data that can be gathered in preventive maintenance include,

- Vibration
- Temperature
- Voltage
- Humidity

By using IoT, assets can be controlled remotely. If an asset is about to malfunction, you can detect that and stop it. This improves worker safety and also prevents failures [4].

c. *Condition based Predictive Maintenance*

Condition-based maintenance (CBM) determines whether an asset requires maintenance based on its physical condition. Maintenance is only performed when certain sensors indicate decline in performance or upcoming system failure. Visual inspection, scheduled testing, and data about the performance are ways to evaluate a device for these indications. Then, status data can be collected continuously or at predetermined intervals. Non-mission assets can also benefit from maintenance-based status.

The best benefit of status-based predictive maintenance is the manufacturer-recommended oil change intervals found on vehicles. These intervals are determined by experience, years of business data, and production analysis. Nevertheless, instead of being determined by the actual level of oil in each vehicle, these intervals are based solely on a calculation. By using a condition-based oil maintenance method, the oil will be changed only when necessary and not according to a fixed schedule. There are other applications in oil analysis, as reflected in the use of technical instruments. The type, size, and shape of the metal fragments suspended in the oil can also be used to study behavior of the oil lubrication.

d. *Powered Predictive Maintenance*

Predictive Maintenance (PdM), a proactive maintenance methodology, uses machine learning and data analytics to predict machine failure before its occurrence. PdM systems are able to predict possible problems in the future by examining past data and real time sensor inputs. It enables potential issues, allowing industries to schedule maintenance activities and prevent expensive downtime. In recent years maintenance of the system has become important and it's increasing for product efficiency and continuity for long term [37]. Figure 9.3 outlines the sequential steps involved in the implementation process

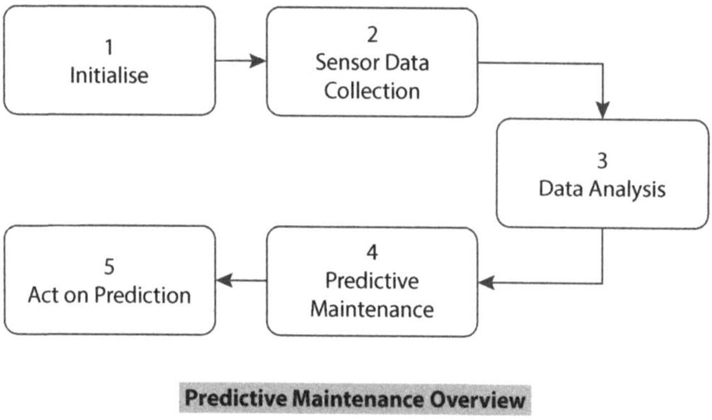

Figure 9.3 PdM overview.

of predictive maintenance. Table 9.1 summarizes the advantages and disadvantages of reactive, preventive, and predictive approaches.

Table 9.1 Advantages and disadvantages of different maintenances.

	Reactive maintenance	**Preventive maintenance**	**Predictive maintenance**
Advantages	• There aren't many upfront implementation costs. • Lowers labor expenses compared to proactive maintenance since it requires less labor. • Releases funds for other initiatives. • Doesn't need planning because tasks depend on their failure.	• Lessens the equipment down-time. • Even repeated usage can cause less failure. • Better contrivance.	• High productivity time for equipment. • High life period of the product. • High contrivance.
Disadvantages	• Unexpected downtime may have an impact on output. • Tough to plan a maintenance budget. • There's less time to get resources following a setback. If there is delay, losses take place. • Minimum repairs can again lead to failure.	• RUL of items is wasted, High cost to plan. • It is not capable to prevent unpredictable failures.	• Significant investment for prognostic and diagnostic product, partially immature technology

9.3.2 IoT Technologies for Predictive Maintenance

Collecting sensors and devices' data is a major reliance of predictive maintenance in embedded machinery and equipment. These sensors and devices, which are fundamental elements of IoT systems, make it possible to check the health conditions, as well as the functioning abilities of devices in real time [12]. Here we can explore different types of sensors and devices common to IoT systems to gather information with respect to predictive maintenance.

1. Predictive maintenance employs several sensors such as:

a. Vibration sensors: This type of sensor measures how much a machine vibrates to detect any abnormality or imminent failures. It can do this by detecting changes in bearing wear, among others.
b. Temperature sensors: They assist in monitoring device heat levels, i.e., these sensors determine when a device is overheating or has wrong temperature settings that could result in failure.
c. Pressure Sensor: This device detects liquid/ air pressure leaks or changes that are out of the normal range.
d. Acoustic Sensors: They measure balance discrepancies, anomalies and other anomalies related to sound characteristics.
e. Infrared sensors: By detecting hot spots or irregular heating patterns from a sample's emitted infrared radiation, we can use these infrared sensors for reactive fault repair approach.

Predictive maintenance sensors are embedded into data acquisition devices, including IoT things that include sensors and communication modules to pull and transmit data between these gadgets [27, 38]. These have batteries and can be used in hard-to-reach locations, which makes them suitable for medical applications and performance monitoring in remote areas.

2. The gateway:
It collects data from IoT node and forwards it to an edge device or cloud platform for processing and analysis [13]. Usually, power is received by the

gateways, hence local processing and filtering are done to minimize the amount of data sent over network on transmission.

3. Edge Devices:
These are more powerful than gateways making them capable of performing complex analytics algorithms thereby enabling them to provide insights at the edge. For this reason, they can do local data processing, reducing latencies as well as bandwidth requirements.

4. Communication Policy:

a. MQTT (message Queue Telemetry Transport): A low-bandwidth, high-latency subscription messaging protocol that is incredibly light-weight.
b. CoAP (Constrained Application Protocol): A lightweight, request-reaction protocol excellent perfect for low-strength, low-memory gadgets.
c. HTTP (Hypertext Transfer Protocol): is records switch protocol extensively used on the Internet and generally used for web-primarily based packages and cloud platforms [13].

5. Network architectures:
Network Architectures are extensively used in IoT systems, e.g. A famous person grid with an important node that communicates with all other nodes inside the grid and is right for packages that need a centralized system to manipulate and control the grid Another, grid architecture, has many nodes that talk decentrally, therefore, it's best for scalability and reliability in hybrid grids and ideal for packages that require a balance between centralized and decentralized networks [14].

6. Wireless Technology:
Wireless technologies including Wi-Fi, Bluetooth, ZigBee, and LoRa WAN are broadly utilized in generation to connect IoT devices [15]. Wi-Fi is a high bandwidth, excessive latency wi-fi technology, widely used in commercial packages; however, it isn't appropriate for low power, low memory gadgets. Bluetooth, however, is low electricity, quick time period ideal era for programs in which low strength intake, low -price and highly priced

ZigBee is a low-power technology used in industrial packages where battery lifestyles and fee are critical, period a LoRa WAN is a low-strength, lengthy-variety technology for low- and occasional- strength consumption programs.

7. Edge Computing and Cloud Platforms:
Edge computing refers records processing at the brink of the network, close to the facts supply, permitting actual-time processing and evaluation of sensor information, decreasing latency and bandwidth necessities [16]. Gateways, aspect servers and other edge devices have walking evaluating structures, going for walks and restructures insights at the brink, they may be used in collecting, filtering and processing sensor statistics, and exporting only applicable facts to cloud structures. Systems such as AWS IoT, Google Cloud IoT Core, and Azure IoT, are commonly utilized for gathering, storing, and analyzing sensor data at large scale, providing real-time information and predictive analytics. Considering the previous discussion, we are able to take a look at as IoT-enabled predictive protection structures sensor gadgets for statistics collection, over communication protocol and network layout for reliable and green statistics, and facet computing for information analysis and processing -wireless technology based on cloud structures, and past.

9.3.3 Predictive Maintenance Workflow

Step 1: Recognizing project's needs:
This step involves understanding of the properties of the business, problems, and projects. This step also involves the choice of IoT sensors that need to be installed. It is required to entirely understand the system/equipment and sensors used to solve the machine operation [30]. Figure 9.4 presents the workflow of predictive maintenance, highlighting its different stages.

Step 2: Gathering, comprehending, and preparing data:
Data collection: After the installation of sensors, it should collect real time data based on the parameters described for predictive maintenance. And then, the data should be transferred to the database.
Understanding: It analyses the data and identifies the data available and starts relating it to its meaning. By machine learning algorithms it identifies the patterns and trends. If it finds any issues in data, it is flagged for investigation [26].
Preparation: Preparation is the most time-consuming sub-step which includes related data; it integrates data by merging data; it helps clean the

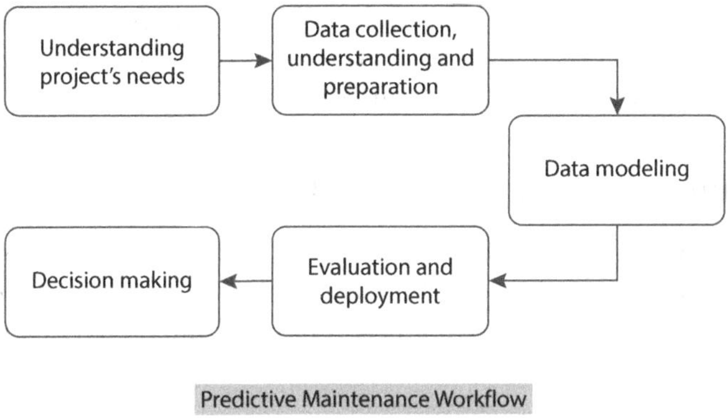

Figure 9.4 PdM workflow.

data, manages to predict missing values by deleting the wrong and missing data; and after all that, it forms the new features from the existing data. It assists in forming the intended structure and gets rid of extraneous columns and features.

Step 3: Data modeling:
The core idea of the data analysis process is data modeling. It creates the necessary output using the input from the previous phase. It's tough to choose the correct algorithm for problems like clustering, regression or classification. Model is complete by choosing different algorithms for testing.

Step 4: Evaluation and deployment:
Model Evaluation: This process evaluates the accuracy of the data and how it works, and whether the data given is relevant or not. The model generated should not be biased. It should have a balance between performance and generalization [30].
Model Deploying: At the end, evaluated model is implemented to the necessary format and channel. In PdM cycle it is the last step related to data. A failed step will impact the cycle and represent a waste if it fails to finish properly.

Step 5: Decision making:
Identifying the decision: In this phase the problem is recognized, and various scenarios appear related to cost and repair times.
Action and Review: Once the scenario has been identified, it is combined to find minimum cost and delay. After determining whether spare parts

are available, the repairs are scheduled. The most important phase is the review since it enables us to assess how well the decision was made. Review is a repetitive step, so it improves further interventions.

9.3.4 Predictive Maintenance Model

Predictive Maintenance Models are made to help industries according to their requirements, maintenance demands, and needs. Different PdM model types are available based on technological and digital maturity [29]. The subsections present three main models [30].

a. *Conditional-Based Maintenance*:
Conditional-Based Maintenance (CBM) is a proactive approach that maintains and keeps track of real time condition of the machine using equipment like sensors and monitoring devices. It is the maintenance solution based on data collected from monitoring, and it consists of three steps: data collection, data processing and decision-making. Three processes make up this maintenance solution, which is based on data gathered from device monitoring: data collecting, data processing, and decision-making. Alarms are set off in this extended form of Predictive Maintenance (PdM) in the event of a system failure. Reducing the expense of machine inspection and essential component repair is the aim of CBM. This process maximizes maintenance efficiency, avoids useless repairing by catching problems before it becomes critical [32].

b. *Prognostics and Health Management*:
Predictive maintenance using dynamic monitoring system state is part of Prognostic and Health Management (PHM). The process of prognostics is regarded as crucial. PHM is able to evaluate the emergence of a system of errors or future degradation [31]. It ensures that the system's functioning is an important step of maintenance scenarios used for predicting and preventing malfunctions. This enables the system to prevent accidents by taking preventative action. PHM is now widely used in an increasing variety of fields. PHM finds applications in multiple industries such as aerospace, manufacturing, automotive, and energy where maintaining health and reliability is essential for operational efficiency and safety.

c. *Remaining Useful Life*:
The period of time an item is expected to function before requiring repair or replacement is its Remaining Useful Life (RUL). This period can be stated in days, miles, cycles, or any other amount depending on the system

[28]. It offers signals of failure earlier. It prevents unnecessary downtime, maximizes operational efficiency and maintenance. RUL analysis accesses the current condition of the system through data collected from sensors or past maintenance records.

9.3.5 Data Collection Techniques

Techniques for collecting data entail compiling information from several sources to track and evaluate the state of machinery. These techniques include online monitoring, periodic inspections, and sensor networks.

a. *Online Monitoring*: It involves continuously gathering data from the sensors that are fixed inside the machinery or equipment. These sensors will measure various factors such as vibration, pressure, temperature, or fluid levels in real-time. Some of the frequently utilized systems for online monitoring include edge computing, IoT devices, and supervisory control and data acquisition (SCADA) systems.
b. *Periodic Inspections*: The equipment health checks are usually planned to be visual inspections, manual measurements or diagnostic tools sometimes. These tests allow for better insight into the state of the equipment in addition to online monitoring which can find faults, that the sensors cannot.
c. *Sensor Networks*: An array of connected sensory gadgets spread throughout an appliance or place, for better data gathering objectives across a large area, hence dealing with various parts. Wireless sensor networks (WSNs) having features including Zigbee or LoRa are used to economically and adequately retrieve data from large, disbursed assets.

9.3.6 Data Analysis Techniques

To understand equipment behavior and detect possible breakdowns, it is essential that data analysis techniques are utilized on the gathered data. Such techniques entail statistical analysis, machine learning algorithms as well as artificial intelligence models.

a. *Statistical Analysis*: To know how the machine functions, watch out for patterns and check if there is any anomaly. Regression analysis, descriptive statistics and time series analysis, are used for this technique. Control charts or statistical process control (SPC) method are good tools for monitoring long-term performance of one machine [25].

b. *Algorithms for Machine Learning*: Algorithms are used to perform predictive maintenance tasks such as discovering faults, estimating remaining useful life (RUL), and detecting variance. Deployment of algorithms such as decision trees, support vector machines, random forests, k-nearest neighbors and neural networks is a common practice. These algorithms learn from historical data so that they can predict the future actions of the equipment [5].
c. *Artificial Intelligence Models*: An example of deep learning AI models is Convolutional Neural Networks which are used for predictive maintenance using complex data. By using these models, it is possible to learn patterns and relationship in data which will make it easier to predict when the equipment would fail or require maintenance [38].

9.3.7 Predictive Analytics Algorithms

Using data analysis, predictive analytics algorithms may predict future problems, estimate useful life, and recommend the best course of maintenance. These algorithms include failure prediction models, prognostic models, and prescriptive maintenance models [39].

a. *Failure Prediction Models*: These models aid in predicting equipment failures by analyzing the historical data, catching failure patterns and forecasting when the system or components will possibly stop or malfunction. Survival analysis, considering time to event data and reliability-centered maintenance (RCM) methods are usually used for this purpose.
b. *Prognostic Models*: Prognostic algorithms determine the remaining useful life of the equipment by analyzing degradation patterns and predicting the time as to when the components possibly reach the end of their operational life. Techniques such as prognostic scoring, physics-based modeling and data-driven methods are generally used by these models to forecast RUL and thus optimize the maintenance schedules [6].
c. *Prescriptive Maintenance Model*: These algorithms suggest ideal maintenance actions based on predictive analytics

output, consideration of cost, operational constraints. These models basically determine the most cost-effective keeping strategies minimizing interruption and maximizing reliability on asset through techniques such as dynamic programming, Markov decision processes and reinforcement learning.

9.3.8 Machine Learning Techniques in PdM

Machine learning systems predict equipment failures and oversee maintenance schedules by utilizing both past data and current sensor data. Through identifying trends and anomalies in data, these techniques help prevent unexpected downtime and reduce maintenance costs [31, 33, 40].

a. *Random Forest Model*: Predictive maintenance makes extensive use of this adaptable technique. It builds several decision trees and outputs the mean regression or the class mode during training. Its primary benefit is its capacity to efficiently handle a large number of features of high-dimensional data. Also, it overcomes overfitting by aggregating the predictions of multiple trees, leading to robust performance [8, 9].
b. *Convolutional Neural Network*: It works by using convolutional, pooling, and fully connected layers to learn hierarchical representations of features. CNNs can also be applied in machine learning for feature extraction from sensor data and time-series data when used in PdM. It is therefore perfect for tasks such as fault identification and anomaly detection that require useful characteristics extraction from unprocessed data, because it has the capacity to extract automatically such features from raw data.
c. *Deep Learning Model*: The purpose why recurrent neural networks (RNNs) and convolutional neural networks (CNNs) are specially used for PdM is their capacity to deal with extra elaborate temporal and spatial enter patterns. While RNNs carry out nicely in regions like series modeling, CNNs are perfect for taking pictures spatial relationships inside data. Although those fashions have the capacity to analyze hierarchical functions automatically, they commonly require big datasets for the duration of training [7].
d. *Support Vector Machines (SVM)*: A powerful supervised gaining knowledge of approach for regression and type

obligations in PdM makes use of the Support Vector Machine (SVM) version. The set of rules unearths hyperplanes that maximize the margin among training and assigns factors to the one-of-a-kind training accordingly. It. These consist of fault detection, type in addition to RUL prediction [14]. This version is specifically beneficial for modeling each linear in addition to non-linear relationships among variables in data [10].

e. *Hybrid Approach Combining CNN and LSTM*: Using this combination of methods helps to combine long and short-term memorization abilities, LSTM, with spatial data extracted by CNNs to introduce temporal relations. In particular, it greatly benefits predictive maintenance tasks as together they ensure essential spatial as well as chronological characteristics' union. To increase identification accuracy rate concerning disorder occurrences, we employ CNNs for pre-handling data by extracting spatial characteristics that matter and rely simultaneously on time model dependencies offered by means of LSTM networks as suggested in this strategy [11].

f. *XGBoost, CatBoost, LightGradient*: The gradient boosting methods which are implemented in PdM because they are efficient when working with large-scale datasets are these. They include XGBoost or CatBoost or LightGradient which generate highly accurate predictive models by continually refining the predictions of weak learners. A complete list of other benefits that have made them suitable for PdM applications in sectors like manufacturing, energy and transportation includes automatic feature selection, handling missing data as well as outliers.

9.3.9 Comparative Analysis

Here is the table that shows a review of methods and techniques to predict and analyze failures in industrial systems. Table 9.2 presents a comparative analysis of different machine learning techniques employed in predictive maintenance. It is an analysis that has been conducted based on nine different experiments that used various methodologies with corresponding feature extraction techniques as well as data sets. The table also shows the accuracy of each study conducted since every review has its unique method/ approach used in this context. Some use deep learning

Table 9.2 Comparative analysis.

Sl. no.	Reference	Methodology	Feature extraction technique	Dataset	Accuracy
1.	[17]	Random Forest Model	Time-domain features, statistical features, and frequency-domain features	Case Western Reserve University (CWRU) Bearing Data Center	98%
2.	[18]	Deep Learning	CNN_LSTM	Dataset of industrial gearbox failures	97.3%
3.	[19]	Support Vector Machine (SVM)	Time-domain features	Industrial Valve Failure Dataset	93%
4.	[20]	Random Forest Model	Time-Domain Features	Industrial Pump Failure Dataset	95%
5.	[21]	ML techniques specifically SVM	Time-domain features, frequency-domain features, and statistical features	Dataset of industrial robot failures	93%
6.	[22]	Deep Transfer Learning	Time-domain features (e.g. RMS, kurtosis, skewness) and frequency-domain features (e.g. FFT coefficients)	Rolling bearing dataset from an industrial site	98.5% in fault diagnosis

(Continued)

Table 9.2 Comparative analysis. (*Continued*)

Sl. no.	Reference	Methodology	Feature extraction technique	Dataset	Accuracy
7.	[23]	Hybrid approach combining CNN and LSTM	Time-domain features (e.g. RMS, kurtosis, skewness) and frequency-domain features (e.g. FFT coefficients)	CRWU Bearing Data Center and NASA Prognostics Center Data Repository	99.6% for CRWU dataset and 98.5% for NASA dataset
8.	[24]	CNN	Time-domain features (e.g. RMS, kurtosis, skewness) and frequency-domain features (e.g. FFT coefficients)	CWRU Bearing Data Center	98.7%
9.	[25]	XGBoost	Sensor Data Fusion	Manufacturing Equipment Dataset	90-95%

techniques like CNN, Long Short-Term Memory use (LSTM) available, or hybrid methods combining CNN and LSTM. Others use techniques like Random Forest Model, Support Vector Machine (SVM), XGBoost, and Convolutional Neural Network (CNN). A study also uses a deep transfer learning approach. The methods for filtering Time-domain features, statistical features, and sensor data fusion are some of the extraction approaches employed in the research. Certain studies employ a combination of these methods.

Datasets used in the study include Case Western Reserve University (CWRU) Bearing Data Center, Industrial Gearbox Failure Dataset,

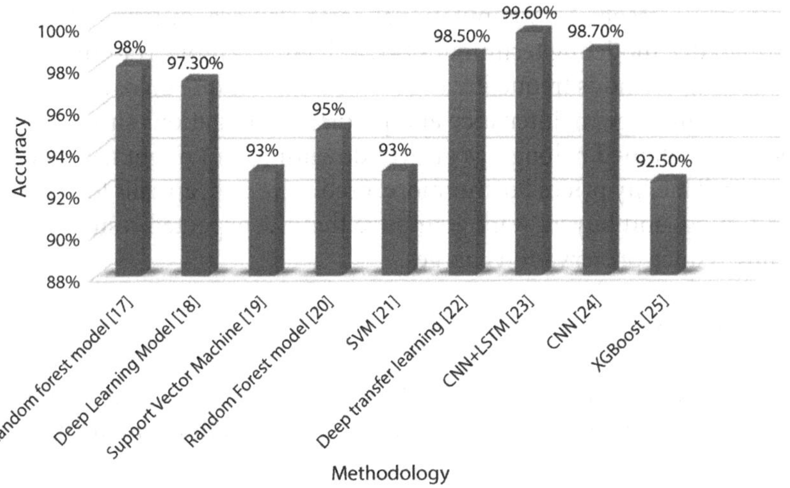

Figure 9.5 Accuracy achieved by different ML models used in predictive maintenance methodologies.

Indus-trial Valve Failure Dataset, Industrial Pump Failure Dataset, Industrial Robo-Data Center and NASA Forecasting Center data repository of failures data sets includes, rolling bearing data sets from industrial areas, CRWU bearings, and construction machinery data sets. The accuracy of the assessments ranged from 90% to 99.6%. Figure 9.5 provides a graphical representation of the accuracy levels achieved by different machine learning models employed in predictive maintenance.

Overall, the analysis makes it clear that deep learning models and hybrid approaches including CNN and LSTM together perform better in predicting and diagnosing failures in industrial systems, leading to higher accuracy rates.

9.3.10 Limitations and Considerations

Despite its benefits predictive maintenance has many limitations and considerations that need to be addressed. Cultural shifts occur throughout industries. The idea that predictive maintenance solutions are exclusively designed for maintenance management has to be changed immediately.

There are numerous boundaries inherent in the usage of predictive protection. One venture is the security concerns of Internet of Things (IoT) devices, as they're vulnerable to assaults as compared to different gadgets including computer systems or transportable gadgets Another drawback is excessive-level problems and records imbalances that cannot be comfortably resolved. Computational costs also are an issue while using cutting-edge modeling techniques [41, 42]. Furthermore, traditional fixing forecasting methods frequently use the equal technique upload up, making it hard to manage maintenance and predictive obligations simultaneously poorly maintained belongings growth downtime and might have an effect on overall facility prices Furthermore, predictive upkeep calls for financing and timing, and buyers want guarantee that the expected results will efficiently reduce preservation charges.

1. Limitations:

a. Data Accuracy: Ensuring high-quality data availability and avoiding incorrect data, which can cause failure, are the key challenges in predictive maintenance.
b. Equipment Architecture: This system struggles with complex machinery architecture.
c. High Price: Implementation of the predictive maintenance requires huge startup investments in sensors and analytic tools. For small-capped companies, this can be very difficult.
d. Skill: Developing and maintaining predictive maintenance models requires professional level skills in different domains such as machine learning, data analysis etc. complex machine learning algorithms user in predictive maintenance lack interpretability.

2. Considerations:

a. Data Accessibility: Organizations must ensure accurate integration of data for better performance of the system.
b. Monitoring: Predictive maintenance should be an ongoing process that requires continuous monitoring.
c. Risk Management: While predictive maintenance aims to prevent failures, organizations should also have other plans for the unforeseen circumstances.
d. Scalability and Regulatory Compliance: the predictive maintenance system should be scalable and needs to comply with relevant regulations of privacy.

9.4 Conclusion

This paper has delved into the dynamic world of PdM, it's application with the help of machine learning techniques, giving us insights into the transformative potential in the industrial world. Through the data driven approach of PdM we can understand it's importance in reducing downtime and increasing the reliability on assets and optimizing the maintenance of equipment. By using real time monitoring, sensor data and advanced analytics, PdM allows for early detection of equipment failures, hence timely intervention and preventive measures to disallow distributions in production process.

Moreover, combining machine learning algorithms in PdM has led to accurate predictions about equipment failures by empowering models to learn from past data. The significance of accuracy in evaluating predictive models cannot be neglected as it provides lot of insights into their reliability and real-world effectiveness. Predictive maintenance and machine learning together have the power to transform maintenance procedures and promote operational excellence.

This paper essentially functions as a call to action for scholars and industry professionals to fully and successfully harness the potential of predictive maintenance to optimize maintenance strategies. As such, it provides them with an understanding of the fundamentals of predictive maintenance as well as a comparative analysis of the different machine learning models commonly used in the field. Predictive maintenance, therefore, will lead industrial operations into new excellence and sustainability.

References

1. https://www.irantpm.ir/wp-content/uploads/2008/02/an-introduction-to-predictive-maintenance.pdf.
2. https://www.researchgate.net/publication/330217371_The_Predictive_Maintenance_Concept_in_the_Maintenance_Department_of_the_Industry_40_Production_Enterprise.
3. Lee, J., Kao, H.-A., Xiang, S., A cyber-physical system for adaptive predictive maintenance of machine tools. *J. Manuf. Sci. Eng.*, 136, 4, 041010, 2014.
4. Tian, Z., Jin, J., Wu, D., Song, P., Wang, P., Preventive maintenance scheduling with integration of online monitoring and periodic inspections, in: *2020 International Conference on Robotics, Automation and Mechatronics (RAM)*, 2020, June, vol. 3, IEEE, pp. 145–150.

5. Zhang, Y., Li, T., Xu, C., Wang, P., A review of fault diagnosis and prognosis techniques based on machine learning: New trends**. *IEEE Intell. Syst. Appl.*, 35, 6, 885–904, 2020.
6. Yan, W. and Yu, L., On prognostics of machine health based on Gaussian process and relevance vector machine**. *Reliab. Eng. Syst. Saf.*, 154, 401–408, 2016.
7. Sun, Y., Zhou, D., Guo, H., Li, Y., Deep learning framework for remaining useful life estimation of machinery using degradation data. *IEEE Trans. Ind. Electron.*, 67, 7, 5891–5900, 2020.
8. Li, Y., Li, G., Xiao, Y., He, S., A hybrid prognostics approach for machine health condition using random forests and extreme learning machines. *IEEE Trans. Ind. Electron.*, 65, 5, 4233–4241, 2018.
9. Zhu, S., Li, Y., Gong, X., E.-H. Han, X., Wang, C., Deep learning for remaining useful life estimation of machinery using multi-modal data. *IEEE Trans. Ind. Electron.*, 67, 7, 5880–5890, 2020.
10. Widodo, A. and Yang, B.-S., Support vector machine in machine condition monitoring and fault diagnosis**. *Mech. Syst. Signal Process.**, 21, 6, 2560–2574, 2007.
11. Xia, W., Shao, S., Yan, X., Lei, Y., A hybrid CNN-LSTM model for intelligent fault diagnosis of rotating machinery using continuous wavelet transform. *IEEE Access*, 8, 14727–14737, 2020.
12. Zhang, Y., Zhang, Y., Zhang, Z., A Review of IoT-Based Predictive Maintenance Systems for Embedded Machinery and Equipment. *IEEE Access*, 6, 16663–16681, 2018.
13. Alahi, M.E.E.,., Sukkuea, A., Tina, F.W., Nag, A., Kurdthongmee, W., Suwannarat, K., Mukhopadhyay, S.C., Integration of IoT-enabled technologies and artificial intelligence (AI) for smart city scenario: Recent advancements and future trends. *Sensors*, 23, 11, 5206, 2023.
14. Chen, X., Jiang, N., Wan, J., A Survey on IoT-Enabled Cyber-Physical Systems: Architecture, Communications, and Applications. *IEEE Access*, 8, 16352–16374, 2020.
15. Al-Fuqaha, A., Aledhari, M., Salah, K., Guizani, M., A review of the Internet of Things (IoT) for healthcare: Protocols, architectures and applications. *IEEE Access*, 3, 1567–1580, 2015.
16. Aburukba, E.A. and Rasheed, Å, A Survey on Cloud-Based Architectures and Services for IoT-Based Smart Cities. *J. Ambient Intell. Hum. Comput.*, 9, 10, 3159–3172, 2018.
17. Kulkarni, P., Patil, S., Kore, S., Predictive Maintenance of Industrial Bearings Using Machine Learning: A Review. *J. Tribol.*, 146, 2, 021001, 2024.
18. Wang, Y., Li, X., Zhang, J., Predictive Maintenance of Industrial Gearboxes Using Machine Learning: A Review. *J. Mech. Des.*, 135, 4, 041003, 2013.
19. Wang, Y., Li, X., Zhang, J., Predictive Maintenance of Industrial Valves Using Machine Learning: A Review. *J. Process Control*, 101, 123–136, 2023.

20. Kusiak, A. and Verma, A., Predictive Maintenance of Industrial Pumps Using Machine Learning: A Review. *J. Fluid Eng.*, 146, 2, 021201, 2024.
21. Kulkarni, P., Patil, S., Kore, S., Predictive Maintenance of Industrial Robots Using Machine Learning Techniques. *J. Intell. Manuf.*, 35, 1, 123–136, 2014.
22. Zhang, Y., Li, X., Wang, Y., A Predictive Maintenance Method for Rolling Bearings Based on Deep Transfer Learning. *Sensors*, 23, 12, 4567, 2023.
23. Li, X., Zhang, Y., Wang, Y., A hybrid approach for predictive maintenance based on convolutional neural network and long short-term memory network. *Sensors*, 23, 18, 4987, 2023.
24. Apeiranthitis, S., Zacharia, P., Chatzopoulos, A., Papoutsidakis, M., Predictive Maintenance of Machinery with Rotating Parts Using Convolutional Neural Networks. *Electronics*, 13, 2, 460, 2024.
25. Zhang, W., Yang, D., Wang, H., Data-Driven Methods for Predictive Maintenance of Industrial Equipment: A Survey. *IEEE Syst. J.*, 13, 4, 2213–2227, 2019.
26. Cachada, A., Barbosa, J., Leitão, P., Geraldes, C.A.S., Deusdado, L., Costa, J., Teixeira, C., Teixeira, J., Moreira, A.H.J., Moreira, P.M., Romero, L., Maintenance 4.0: Intelligent and predictive maintenance system architecture, in: *2020 IEEE International Conference on Industrial Engineering and Engineering Management (IEEM)*, pp. 1–9, 2020.
27. Leong, C.H., Poh, Y.Y., Pheng, L.W., IoT-based predictive maintenance for smart manufacturing systems. *Asia-Pacific Signal and Information Processing Association Annual Summit (APSIPA ASC)*, Kuala Lumpur, Malaysia, 2019, November.
28. Fernandez, J.R., Prasetyo, Y.T., Persada, S.F., Redi, A.A.N.P., Automation of predictive maintenance using internet of things (IoT) technology at university-based O&M project. *[IET Intell. Syst. Reference] *IJET**, 11, 7, 1727–1734, 2021.
29. Achouch, M., Dimitrova, M., Ziane, K., Sattarpanah Karganroudi, S., Dhouib, R., Ibrahim, H., Adda, M., On predictive maintenance in Industry 4.0: Overview, models, and challenges. *Sensors*, 12, 16, 8181, 2023.
30. Kaczmarek, M.J. and Gola, A., Maintenance 4.0 Technologies for Sustainable Manufacturing—An Overview. *IFAC-PapersOnLine*, 52, 91–96, 2019.
31. Çınar, Z.M., Nuhu, A.A., Zeeshan, Q., Korhan, O., Asmael, M., Safaei, B., Machine learning in predictive maintenance towards sustainable smart manufacturing in Industry 4.0. *Sensors*, 20, 19, 5641, 2020.
32. Samatas, G.G., Moumgiakmas, S.S., Papakostas, G.A., Predictive Maintenance - Bridging Artificial Intelligence and IoT, IEEE Explore, 2024, DOI: 10.1109/MIS.2022.3167561.
33. Paolanti, M., Romeo, L., Felicetti, A., Mancini, A., Frontoni, E., Loncarski, J., Machine Learning approach for Predictive Maintenance in Industry 4.0. *2018 14th IEEE/ASME International Conference on Mechatronic and Embedded Systems and Applications (MESA)*, Oulu, Finland, pp. 1–6, 2018, doi: 10.1109/MESA.2018.8449150.

34. Gama, J., Ribeiro, R.P., Veloso, B., Cao, L., Data-Driven Predictive Maintenance. *IEEE Intell. Syst.*, 37, 4, 27–29, July-Aug. 2022.
35. Cachada, A., *et al.*, Maintenance 4.0: Intelligent and Predictive Maintenance System Architecture. *2018 IEEE 23rd International Conference on Emerging Technologies and Factory Automation (ETFA)*, Turin, Italy, pp. 139–146, 2018, doi: 10.1109/ETFA.2018.8502489.
36. Yuting, J., Xiaodong, F., Chuan, L., Zhiqi, G., Research on preventive maintenance strategy optimization based on reliability threshold. *2014 Prognostics and System Health Management Conference (PHM-2014 Hunan)*, Zhangjiajie, China, pp. 589–592, 2014, doi: 10.1109/PHM.2014.6988240.
37. Pandey, S.C. and P, V.K., Predictive Maintenance Strategies for Internet of Things (IoT) Systems in, 2021, [Online], Available: https://www.publications.scrs.in/chapter/pdf/view/483. [Accessed: 07-Jun-2024].
38. Pech, M., Vrchota, J., Bednář, J., Predictive Maintenance and Intelligent Sensors in Smart Factory: Review. *Sensors*, 21, 4, 1470, 2021, https://doi.org/10.3390/s21041470.
39. Susto, G.A., Schirru, A., Pampuri, S., McLoone, S., Beghi, A., Machine Learning for Predictive Maintenance: A Multiple Classifier Approach. *IEEE Trans. Ind. Inf.*, 11, 3, 812–820, June 2015, doi: 10.1109/TII.2014.2349359.
40. Carvalho, T.P., Soares, F.A.A.M.N., Vita, R., Francisco, R.P., Basto, J.P., Alcalá, S.G.S., A systematic literature review of machine learning methods applied to predictive maintenance. *Comput. Ind. Eng.*, 137, 106024, 2019, ISSN 0360-8352, https://doi.org/10.1016/j.cie.2019.106024.
41. Mohanty, A., Rahamathunnisa, U., Sudhakar, K., Sathiyaraj, R., Age of Computational AI for Autonomous Vehicles, in: *Artificial Intelligence for Autonomous Vehicles*, pp. 25–54, CRC Press, USA, 2024.
42. Rajendran, S., Sabharwal, M., Hu, Y.C., Balusamy, B. (Eds.), *Artificial Intelligence for Autonomous Vehicles: The Future of Driverless Technology*, John Wiley & Sons, CRC Press, USA, 2024.
43. Ramana, T.V., Ghantasala, G.S., Sathiyaraj, R., Khan, M. (Eds.), *Artificial Intelligence and Machine Learning for Smart Community: Concepts and Applications*, CRC Press, USA, 2024.

10

Enhanced Security Framework with Blockchain for Industry 4.0 Cyber-Physical Systems, Exploring IoT Integration Challenges and Applications

P. Vijayalakshmi[1], B. Selvalakshmi[2], K. Subashini[3], Sudhakar G.[4], Kavin Francis Xavier[5] and Pradeepa K.[6]*

[1]*Computer Science and Engineering, Knowledge Institute of Technology, Salem, Tamil Nadu, India*
[2]*Department of Computer Science and Engineering, Tagore Engineering College, Chennai, Tamil Nadu, India*
[3]*Department of Information Technology, Tagore Engineering College, Chennai, Tamil Nadu, India*
[4]*Department of CSE, Sri Sai Ranganathan Engineering College, Coimbatore, Tamil Nadu, India*
[5]*M/S Muscat Engineering Consultancy Pvt. Ltd, Trichy, Tamil Nadu, India*
[6]*Department of Computer Science and Engineering, St. Michael College of Engineering and Technology, Kalayarkoil, Sivaganga, Tamil Nadu, India*

Abstract
The idea of "Industry 4.0" is revolutionary and has far-reaching effects on many different industries around the globe. Industry 4.0 uses new-generation, state-of-the-art engineering technologies and methodical adaptability to drive development as a technological accelerator. The Internet of Things (IoT), blockchain, Artificial Intelligence (AI), Augmented Reality (AR), printing in three dimensions, cloud computing and big data analytics are some of the key innovations that collaborate to realize the Industry 4.0 vision. A Cyber-Physical System (CPS) allows the exchange of information between physical things and a linked network of technologies and objects by combining computational and storage features with the physical objects. A novel distributed computing paradigm called blockchain

**Corresponding author*: pradeepa.k94@gmail.com

M. Thirunavukkarasan, S. A. Sahaaya Arul Mary, Sathiyaraj. R, G. S. Pradeep Ghantasala and Mudassir Khan (eds.) Artificial Intelligence and Machine Learning for Industry 4.0, (247–266)

offers a viable remedy for contemporary CPS applications. Strong options for CPS applications are offered by the natural combination of distributed memory and consensus techniques with cutting-edge security mechanisms. Blockchains in CPSs/IoT provide safe and preserved data for many industrial purposes and accomplish flexibility, procedure, and operational security, for instance, in activities related to production, logistics, medical care, and power.

Keywords: Cyberphysical systems, artificial intelligence, security framework, industry 4.0, IoT integration, blockchain, industrial internet of things, data protection

10.1 Introduction

The world has been living through Industry 4.0, the most recent version of the industrial environment, for the past ten years. Adoption of linked devices and methods is required for this fourth generation to satisfy the ever-increasing need for the security of systems [1]. The ultimate objectives of creating these computerized links include increasing income, cutting expenses, and improving efficiency. The information produced by edge sensors is essential for tracking production, anticipating repair requirements, and identifying abnormalities in the machinery. One crucial element is that any data-related operations would surely impact or stop the entire commercial environment if the information does not meet the safety requirements [2].

An advanced persistent threat (APT) aims to take over a computer connection as a stealthy threat actor following going extended periods without being noticed shown in Figure 10.1. Even while server-side vulnerabilities are the main aim of hackers, multiple instances have been reported in which the edge-side vulnerability was the cause. Industry 4.0 network

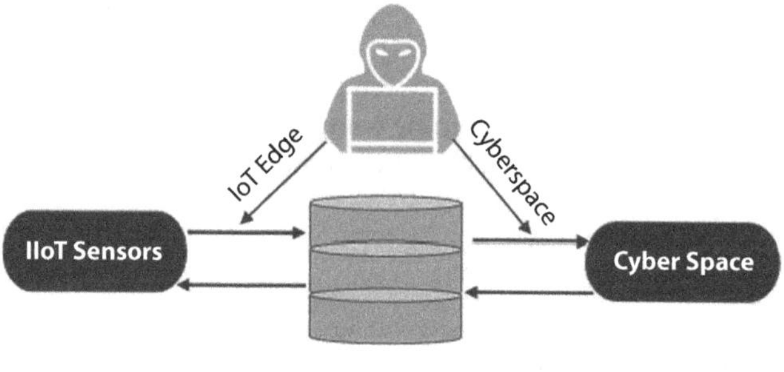

Figure 10.1 APT in industry 4.0 with CPS.

nowadays needs to address the issue of its border servers lacking an APT [3, 35].

Numerous methods concentrate exclusively on server-side security. Several studies use interactive machine learning to defend edge areas [4, 31]. It appears that current methods make use of sophisticated machine-learning techniques that need high processing power and are frequently not edge-compliant. Numerous studies have evaluated their proposed techniques might not be effective in other situations—using server-driven information [5].

The internet of services (IoS) includes contemporary service concepts that are put into practice using REST technologies or service-oriented architecture (SOA) [6]. The Internet of Things and Services (IoTS) was introduced by the IoS, which merges the IoT. Industry 4.0's primary facilitators are the IoT and CPS [7]. The concepts for implementing Industry 4.0 are outlined in the Six Sigma. In addition, anticipate, enact and enable are included in the Industry 4.0 three-stage procedure framework [8]. In Industry 4.0, the IoS, IoT, and CPS are interconnected, as illustrated in Figure 10.2.

Over the past few years, block chain technology and ML have been establishing their respective paths, with some modest overlapping. There appears to be an association between each technology in the form of information [9]. Nonetheless, research indicates that insurance and financial institutions would primarily steer clear of the relationship between distributed AI and blockchain technology in the years to come. The departure of many customers would simply be one of the many negative outcomes, and Industry 4.0 would be impacted by identical conditions [3].

Transaction times will be accelerated, safety and openness can be improved, and information administration will be streamlined by incorporating one or more blockchains into insurance and banking organizations. AI has advanced through the initial stages of technology in a different but comparable manner [10]. Its implementation has passed an important turning point as its application and acceptance have grown. As the fourth industrial

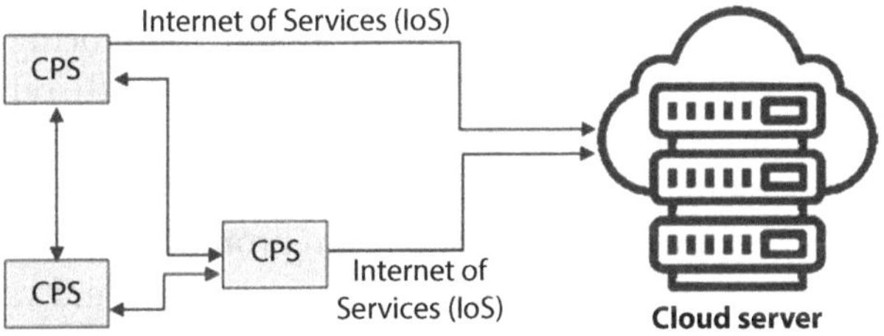

Figure 10.2 CPS, IoT, and IoS in Industry 4.0.

age approaches, blockchain technology and AI have a lot to offer each other. For instance, a chatbot will handle support inquiries if a consumer has a particular inquiry or requires an explanation on a certain topic. Chatbots rely on methods and artificial intelligence, their responses will surely be more expedient and relaxing [11].

As AI continues to advance, a channel will be needed to enable clients who are particularly interested in exchanging data and interacting securely. The AI revolution is fueled by the developments in massive amounts of data. It has enabled businesses to divide large datasets into manageable chunks that systems may process quickly [12]. The value of information has also spurred advancements in blockchain technology, as its distributed database offers a novel approach to storing information that is both distinct and efficient. Safety is one of the many areas wherein combining AI and blockchain might have an impact [13].

By combining both methods, knowledge and information transfer may be accelerated, facilitating quicker and more efficient customer-business interaction. Over the decades to come, products are going to become progressively tailored, and large companies' or businesses' systems for suggestions will proliferate [14]. Blockchain technology has demonstrated its ability to address several inefficiencies in current technology, and AI functions identically because of the current focus on data. The broad use of blockchain integration with AI might consequently result in some fascinating advances for Industry 4.0. Instead of only talking about programs, methods, robotics, machine learning, and technology, companies are now arguing more complicated concepts like disintermediation, deconstruction, and on-demand product creation and production [15].

10.2 Related Works

Corporations have been embracing technological change for the previous ten years, but until the COVID-19 pandemic-related force majeure in early 2020, the adoption of new technology platforms had not accelerated significantly [16]. IoT devices are capable of remote monitoring, actuation, and/or sharing information (directly or indirectly) with other gadgets and programs that are linked. Industry 4.0 refers to the industry's cyber-physical transformation. The phrase originated with the German administration's Industry 4.0 initiative, which aims to promote digitally connected and integrated production among businesses, industries, and various other endeavors [17].

The third happened when computers were introduced at the start of the 1970s to more fully automated machinery and production procedures. The intelligent factory and complete electronic manufacturing efficiency will be the pinnacle of the fourth industrial revolution idea. Even while it's still in its early stages and is happening in discrete methods all connected, and massive form is still a vision for the years to come [18]. It is expected that the industrial sector will see a radical, full-cycle digitization. The Industry 4.0 vision states that information will both guide and determine an approach to behavior, leading to a fully interoperable network of customers and devices across the chain of supply. It includes the evolution of information interchange technology and computerized systems in the commercial domains. Following the introduction of steam power and automated manufacturing in the eighteenth century, the start of technological advancement got underway [19].

Initially, the eight parts in the mechanical edition were created on just one whirling ring. The use of steam was widely recognized. The application of industry aims has represented many significant advancements in raising labor efficiency. Spinning looms can be powered by engines with steam as an alternative to electricity [20]. Improvements that could move massive distances faster, such as the steamboat or, approximately a century later, the steam-powered location, brought about further significant alterations. A whole vehicle was once constructed in just one facility; today, automobiles are manufactured in considerably quicker and cheaper phases on a conveyor belt [21].

From a safety perspective, blockchain technology may establish communicated safety differently from centralized systems. Blockchain's strong protection against manipulation of information helps prevent a rebel device from interfering with residential, industrial, or transportation networks through the infusion or transmission of malicious information. As blockchain technology is designed for decentralized administration, various verification and selection strategies developed on blockchains should be more adaptable than conventional ones [22]. Subsequent developments in electronics and wireless communication have transformed the IoT by enabling the creation of smaller devices that can manage and make use of data gathering and exchange. These main factors have facilitated the development of small, affordable, and more regulated multifunctional detection stages that are capable of verifying and exchanging many types of information in various industries, including automotive, medical care, and many more [23].

IoT strategy is used in conjunction with creative computation to extract a small amount of marketable information that may be useful for additional physical devices creating a CPS. The CPS is made up of a physical component and a cyber component connected by a network of communication [24]. This concept has enormous implications for the regenerative and healthcare industries and the industry at large. Variety of organizations are connecting CPS; blockchain has gained a lot of attention since it promises to provide safety, confidentiality, verification, and trust. However, the current blockchain-based solutions face some difficulties and are, therefore, not particularly relevant in the context of CPS [25].

By using detectors to connect data between electronics and physical parts, CPS extends beyond conventional presentation to dynamic framework models to comprehend physical consequences across the physical cyber interface [26]. CPS is a fundamental mechanism that connects the virtual and real worlds in industrial applications. CPS plan catalyzes the growth of many industries by creating untapped markets. Improved CPS performance will have a favorable impact on commercial applications' economic aspects. CPS is associated with the breakthroughs that enable physical items and electronic resources to communicate in ways that manage many supply responsibilities [27].

Public blockchain works well in situations when the security of an entirely untrusted network is required, but it is costly and sluggish. For instance, it is quite expensive to put up a strong mining node, and takes a significant amount of electric power to conduct the mining operations shown in Figure 10.3 [28]. Limited authentication speed of public blockchain renders it unsuitable for use cases like industry, where a high volume of immediate information exchanges is required. However, collaborative or permissioned blockchains, like Hyperledger (HLF), Quorum, and Corda, feature a selective structure in which participants who mutually trust one another—instead of random users—are only permitted to participate [29].

A manufacturing process reinforces the internet link and, in a way, the computerized digital replica networks. These enable interaction and the generation of private information with other establishments.

Public Blockchain	Consortium Blockchain
Rewards Costly, Energy intensive	Cheaper, miner cost & no-rewards
Check for new blocks slowly via TX	Faster Tx adding and verification

Figure 10.3 Industry 4.0 with blockchain.

The following development in industrial automation is this. Any form of connection results in "cyber-physical manufacturing structures," or "smart plants," where individuals, elements, and manufacturing processes connect virtually independently of one another via a system of networks [30, 32, 33]. When joined with these supporters, Industry 4.0 has the potential to significantly improve manufacturing environments. Manufacturers are becoming more digital, which affects the production, delivery, upkeep, and improvement of goods [31].

10.3 Industry 4.0 Elements

CPS incorporate mechanical operations, social networking, and computational tasks. Feedback cycles are used by networked machines for tracking and managing physical operations; the framework reacts physically and utilizes software to understand activities and monitor results. The concept centers on the integration of software and hardware into objects whose main functions are machine learning and activity loops rather than computation. IoT is a portmanteau for an ambitious concept. Networking all devices to the internet and each other is referred to as the IoT [34]. It depends on networks of gathering information devices and cloud computing; it is an adaptable, virtual, and instantaneous connection claims wired. The emergence of smart factories will be made possible by this connectedness, since machinery will use the information to efficiently create, transport, study, and learn at very fast rates. It is hardly hyperbole to say that

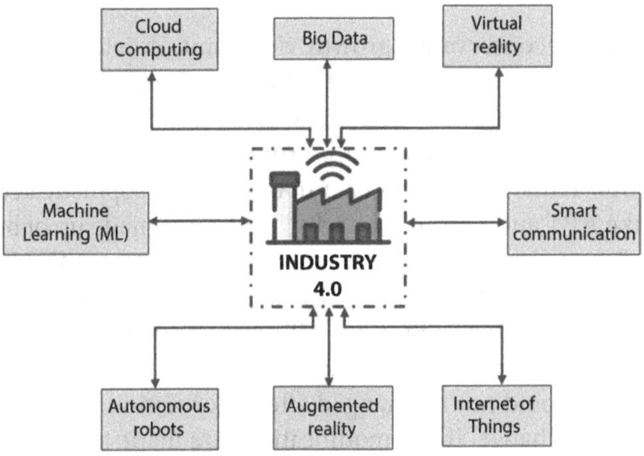

Figure 10.4 Industry 4.0 architecture.

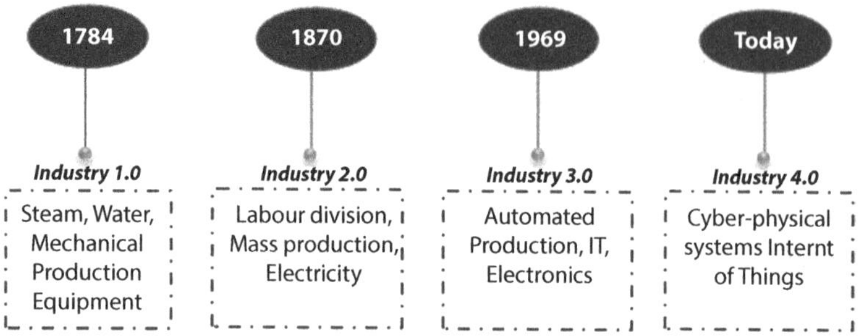

Figure 10.5 Evolution of industry modernization.

without the numerous advancements in artificial intelligence, Industry 4.0 architecture, shown in Figure 10.4, highlight Industry 4.0's capacity to generate information. There might be millions of connected gadgets interacting with one another and monitoring ecological conditions globally through a range of sensors, which means the information volumes will likely be enormous, shown in Figure 10.5. Large amounts of information will be produced by even small and constrained Industry 4.0 systems, like a smart factory, as a result of their daily activities. The large-data solutions are designed specifically to handle massive amounts of data. Although distributed ledger technologies (DLT) and blockchain are rarely discussed in discussions on Industry 4.0, researchers believe that these newly developed technologies might serve as the foundation for manufacturing that is automated.

10.3.1 CPS in Critical Industry 4.0

According to the conservative growth viewpoint, developing a system as important and decisive as this, calls for the use of tried-and-true methods as opposed to immature ones that might seem enticing at first. Even while BC technology drew a lot of attention from the public at first, Figure 10.6 illustrates how remarkable it was later in uncovering sophisticated security breaches like APT and Zero-day attacks. The CPS is made up of both physical and software elements that constantly communicate with one another while operating at various temporally and spatial levels. In reaction to those sophisticated attacks, BC with MS appears to be a viable substitute, as demonstrated by Figure 10.6(b), correspondingly.

As if a block could not be changed after information was captured, BC is impervious to change. If any modifications are made to the already submitted blocks, the connection between the next blocks breaks and requires

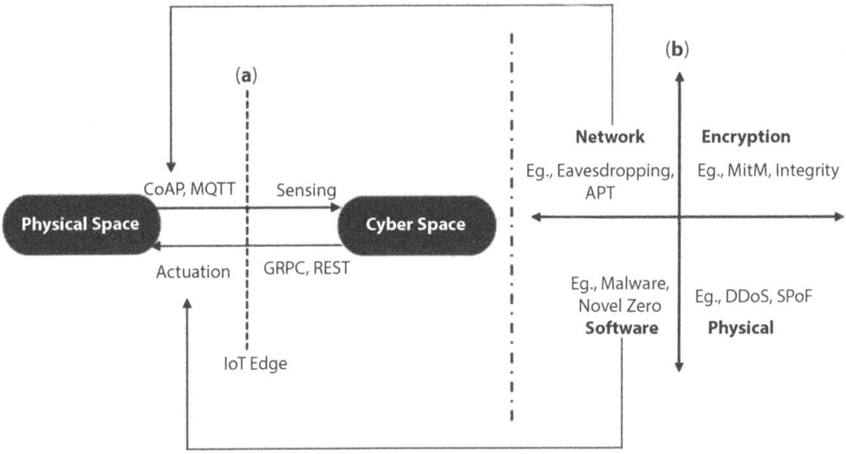

Figure 10.6 (a) Flow of CPS communication (b) Attacks on CPS.

consensus from all involved nodes. It is unmatched in the Bitcoin space, but because of its sluggish efficiency, it makes no sense for essential industries, such as the smart grid, food or medical facilities, traffic signals, etc. CBC systems, like Hyperledger or Quorum, include a selective configuration in which network access is restricted to authorized trustworthy users only. Since the new block confirmation does not necessitate the implementation of PoWlike consensus, CBC could make up for necessary incentives or benefits and avoid additional costs associated with establishing highly energy-intensive, modifying the consensus process for tolerance of faults, wherein the leader suggests the subsequent block to reduce award prices. Limiting the effect of potentially malevolent peers safeguards the structure from errors and, as a result, concludes an understanding of the latest deal without requiring numerous verifications. This makes it an attractive option for the proposed information security structure of the Industry 4.0 CPS.

10.3.2 Challenges in IoT Integration

Four perspectives are available for examining the issues facing CPS for production: technological advancement, standardized processes, dynamic reorganization, and improved output. Enhanced production encompasses the following elements: zero defect, security, hazards, efficiency, representation, surveillance, and delay in production, expenses, PLC, and enhanced automation. Dynamic reconfiguration includes a sensor network, procedure, equipment, labor, workforce, failures and repair administration, adaptability, and customer-focused item modification. Semantics, multilingualism, connectivity, safety, international exchange of information, integrating information, environmental responsibility, augmented and virtual reality, cloud computing, and other topics are also priorities for IT. The main goal of employing CPS in manufacturing is to create better products while reducing manufacturing times. To meet a uniform norm, automated and process/machine reconfiguring must be guaranteed dynamically. Computing technology also contributes to a smooth integration of all the elements. Various articles related to the three key components (HC, CC, and PC) are examined to determine the issues that are present or likely to arise. The integration of IoT into cyber-physical systems for Industry 4.0 poses numerous noteworthy problems.

Considering the rising number of devices that are connected, it is becoming more challenging to secure private information from cyberattacks and illegal access, making safety and confidentiality critical considerations. Another significant challenge is maintaining compatibility across various IoT systems and devices from various vendors and protocols. Flexibility is essential; as the number of IoT devices rises, managing and maintaining efficiency will require an adequate framework. The massive volumes of information produced by IoT devices also make the handling of information difficult and the need for efficient immediate monitoring, and storage techniques. Sustaining immediate operations and interactions requires keeping a network with dependable, fast, and low-latency connectivity. Another problem is how difficult it is to integrate IoT devices into current IT infrastructures and manufacturing procedures without seriously disrupting them. It is also necessary to address the high original and continuing expenses of establishing and upholding Internet of Things devices and connectivity. Compatibility problems resulting from a lack of standardization for IoT gadgets and standards might impede integration attempts. For battery-powered gadgets, in particular, energy conservation is essential to lowering operating expenses and mitigating adverse environmental impacts. IoT integration is further complicated by the need to navigate diverse and complex regulatory compliance requirements about safeguarding information, security, and sustainable development across various businesses and geographies.

10.3.3 Security Provided Through Blockchain

Three main steps may be used to simplify the operating concept based on the four levels of information. BC-based MS approach is used by the device's sensors to register and establish connections. This structure uses edge computing rather than computing in the cloud. The following arguments are presented before the stages within the proposed structure are explained. Sensors often lack computing power to malfunction when communicating with large storage nodes like the cloud. BC can swiftly implement smart edge computing with more organized memory shown in Figure 10.7.

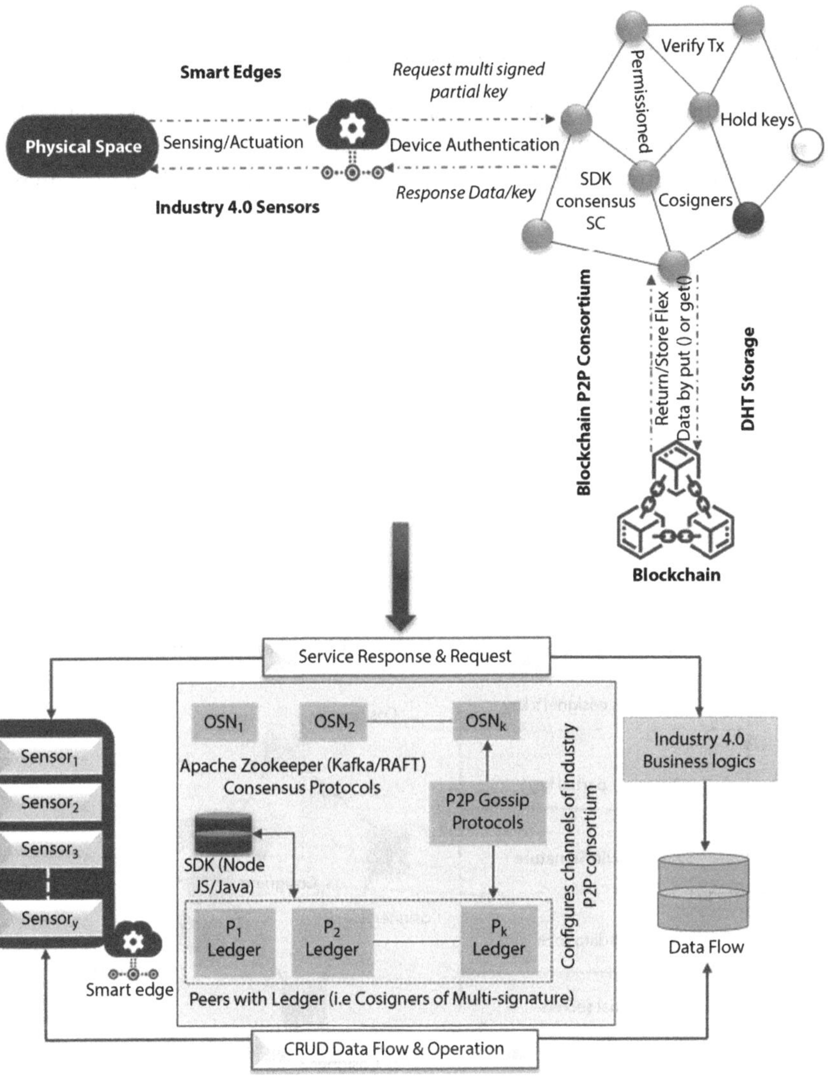

Figure 10.7 High level representation of proposed work.

The structure needs signatures; smart edge devices may safely solve cryptography problems that lightweight sensors cannot.

Within the proposed structure, the BC peers construct and then disperse key pairs where the private characteristics have been referred to as the partial key, based on the underlying system variables. It protects information traveling from the physical realm—that is, integrated machine sensors—to the virtual realm—that is, BC or DHT storage—to ensure cooperation and examine single-point reliance.

10.3.4 Blockchain Replaces the Certificate Authority

Assume that several industry participants have been working together using their public-private key combinations. Throughout the procedure, two distinct hashing methods generate corresponding text digests.

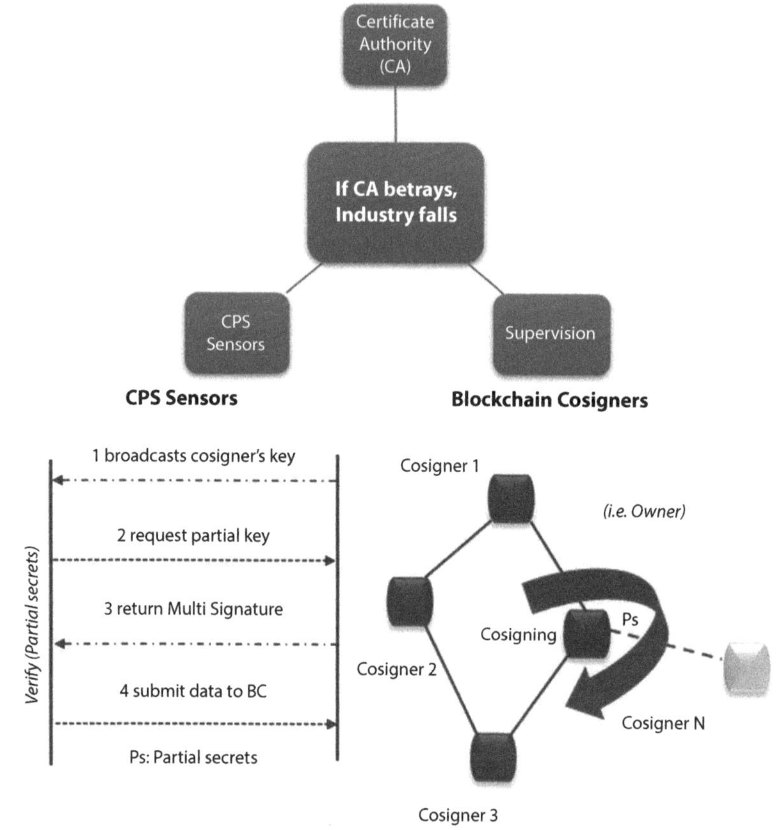

Figure 10.8 Certification authority and trust on smart industry 4.0 by proposed system.

To reveal the concealed values, a sensor runs through the safety variables set by the entire system, shown in Figure 10.8. After utilizing the combined public keys to encrypt it, it then transmits their identification (ID). The PS is generated, verified, and co-signed by all of the BC peers that are involved.

To identify the regulating and calculating processes and archive the capacity to carry out appropriate techniques for the functioning of computerized systems on the Internet, the design of CPS/IoT is an essential method for organizing and creating the structure of CPS systems that depend on connectivity to the Internet. Since the IoT encompasses items or things that use online networks while creating a CPS/IoT structure, simulation should take into account the advancement and portrayal of layering separately that seek after the elements and roles of non-specific multilayer architecture. Building services for smart infrastructures may be done using a variety of IoT designs. A straightforward IoT infrastructure for CPS is depicted in Figure 10.9.

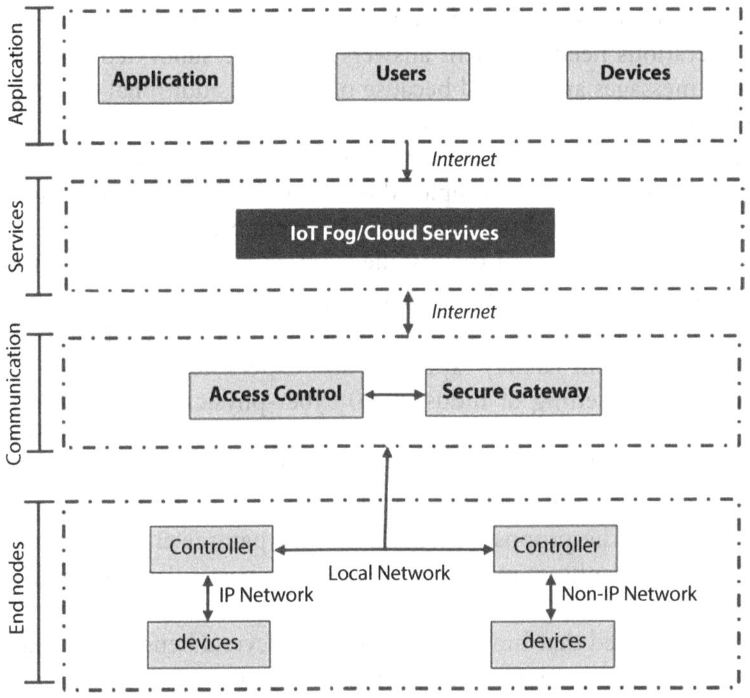

Figure 10.9 CPS-based IoT hierarchy simple architecture.

10.4 Results and Discussions

The cost estimations are approximations and might differ substantially depending on elements like hardware, software, repair costs, license fees, and the complexity of the deployment shown in Table 10.1.

The outcomes of the hyper ledger caliper benchmark demonstrate the efficiency determined by four measuring indicators: throughput and delay, utilization of resources for different evaluation scenarios, and accuracy (transactions properly committed against the provided request) shown in Figure 10.10. However, at peak performance, the process appears to have a larger throughput (up to 470 maximum) with a comparable accuracy frequency. Due to the requirement for writing to integrate OSNs on Apache Kafka, the mean latency seems to be half that of the WRITE latency. The conceptual approach demonstrates the consortium BC's considerable flexibility for a bigger number of nodes, and the benchmark assessment clearly shows that the established arrangement performs worse with greater numbers. Efficiency and delay are impacted by the local workload handling bottleneck, as was found. To prevent delay from increasing, HLF T_x flow operations need sufficient answers about the submitted transaction ideas. If messages are queued because of network additional costs, bandwidth constraints, or processor load, this might happen. The assessment for heavier workloads is slowed down by the general-purpose workstation setup. Utilizing the earlier completed READ and WRITE Operations, indicate that the outcome above illustrates the relationship between speed and capacity. The scalability of the installed system is reduced. In addition to strengthening the agreement on an appropriate MS system, other possibilities involve setting up an organization's standard system (512 GB or more RAM) to reduce the latency expense it now experiences.

In the larger setting of Industry 4.0 cyber-physical systems additionally IoT integration, this table offers a comparison study of certain indicators of success between the blockchain-enhanced safety standards and two current approaches shown in Table 10.2. Based on the two present structures and the proposed structure, every parameter is assessed. The corresponding rankings might change based on particular cases of use and technologies.

It is anticipated that Industry 4.0 will have several benefits. Intelligence will speed up the creation of new products by showing OEMs how customers use an item, compared to how it was intended to be utilized. Extremely flexible or modestly produced lines will be profitable; thanks to the technique of additive manufacturing. Numerous companies will be harmed due to the expensive nature of emerging technologies, even while few are

Table 10.1 Comparison of throughput, delay time and cost of proposed and existing systems.

System	Throughput (Mbps)	Delay time (ms)	Cost (USD)
Blockchain-based AI-IoT	100	55	$155000
Conventional AI-IoT	82	42	$125000
AI	N/A	22	$110000

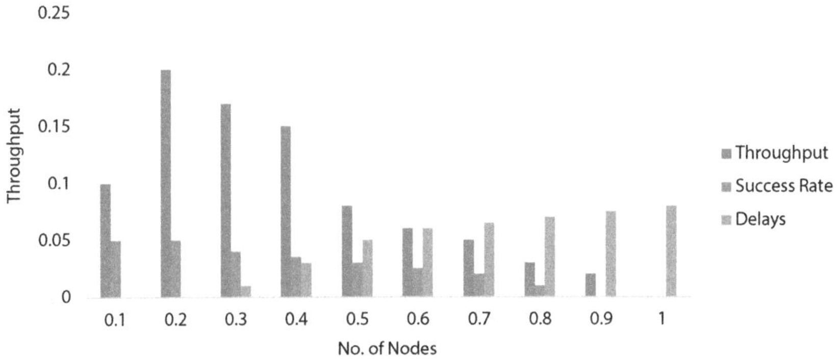

(**a**) Read operation

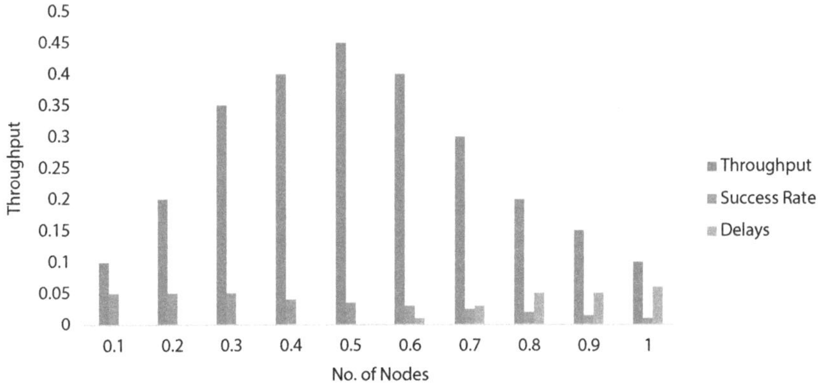

(**b**) Write operation

Figure 10.10 (a) Read (b) Write operations on comparison of throughput, success rate and delay time of proposed and existing systems.

Table 10.2 Comparison of performance measures.

Performance metrics	Blockchain-enhanced security framework	Conventional AI-IoT	AI
Throughput (Mbps)	100	82	92
Delay Time (ms)	55	62	72
Cost (USD)	$155,000	$125000	$135000
Security Effectiveness	High	Moderate	High
Scalability	Moderate	Low	Moderate
Interoperability	Moderate	High	Moderate
Energy Efficiency	Moderate	High	Moderate
Regulatory Compliance	High	Moderate	High
Data Integrity	High	Moderate	High
Privacy Protection	High	Low	Moderate
Network Resilience	Moderate	High	Moderate
Ease of Implementation	Moderate	Low	Moderate
Maintenance Complexity	Moderate	High	Moderate
Real-time Response	Moderate	High	Moderate

moving toward specific instances that show the great potential of Industry 4.0. Compatibility is a further obstacle preventing flawless information interchange between supply-chain parties.

10.5 Conclusions

As a result of the comparison, the proposed approach has several notable benefits over current methods when it comes to ensuring IoT integration in Industry 4.0 settings. Utilizing the blockchain system to guarantee exceptional levels of information credibility, safeguarding privacy, and compliance with regulations, the system shines in secure productivity. It outperformed present ones in these areas while displaying a reasonable level of scaling and compatibility, suggesting that it is suitable for handling the increasing complexity of the Internet of Things (IoT) landscape. The framework's strong safeguards and compliance with regulations make it worth spending money on, even with relatively greater expenditures for implementation, particularly for important uses in Industry 4.0 contexts. All things considered, the structure offers a viable way to deal with the particular safety concerns raised by the incorporation of IoT in Industry 4.0 cyber-physical systems, providing improved safety and reliability in a rapidly digitalized and networked workplace.

References

1. Chae, J., Lee, S., Jang, J., Hong, S., Park, K.J., A Survey and Perspective on Industrial Cyber-Physical Systems (ICPS): From ICPS to AI-Augmented ICPS. *IEEE Trans. Ind. Cyber-Phys. Syst.*, 1, 257–272, 2023.
2. Jeffrey, N., Tan, Q., Villar, J.R., A review of anomaly detection strategies to detect threats to cyber-physical systems. *Electronics*, *12*, 15, 3283, 2023.
3. Nair, M.M., Deshmukh, A., Tyagi, A.K., Artificial intelligence for cyber security: Current trends and future challenges, in: *Automated Secure Computing for Next-Generation Systems*, pp. 83–114, 2024.
4. Sarker, I.H., Multi-aspects AI-based modeling and adversarial learning for cybersecurity intelligence and robustness: A comprehensive overview. *Secur. Privacy*, *6*, 5, e295, 2023.
5. Haider, U., Nawaal, B., Khan, I.U., El Hajjami, S., AI-Based Secure Wireless Communication Technologies and Cyber Threats for IoT Networks, in: *Cyber Security for Next-Generation Computing Technologies*, pp. 70–83, CRC Press, London.
6. Jan, Z., Ahamed, F., Mayer, W., Patel, N., Grossmann, G., Stumptner, M., Kuusk, A., Artificial intelligence for industry 4.0: Systematic review of applications, challenges, and opportunities. *Expert Syst. Appl.*, *216*, 119456, 2023.
7. Tushar, W., Yuen, C., Saha, T.K., Nizami, S., Alam, M.R., Smith, D.B., Poor, H.V., A survey of cyber-physical systems from a game-theoretic perspective. *IEEE Access*, *11*, 9799–9834, 2023.
8. Rajagopal, M. and Ramkumar, S., Adopting artificial intelligence in ITIL for information security management—way forward in industry 4.0, in: *Artificial Intelligence and Cyber Security in Industry 4.0*, pp. 113–132, Springer Nature Singapore, Singapore, 2023.
9. Arulkumar, V., Kavin, F., Nagu, B., IoT Sensor Data Retrieval and Analysis in Cloud Environments for Enhanced Power Management. *J. Adv. Res. Appl. Sci. Eng. Technol.*, 38, 1, 77–88, 2024.

10. Bharathiraja, N., Pradeepa, K., Murugesan, S., Hariharan, S., Veeramanickam, M.R.M., A Novel Framework for Cyber Security Attacks on Cloud-Based Services, in: *2022 Fourth International Conference on Cognitive Computing and Information Processing (CCIP)*, 2022, IEEE, pp. 1–4, December, 2022.
11. Ullah, I., Adhikari, D., Su, X., Palmieri, F., Wu, C., Choi, C., Integration of data science with the intelligent IoT (IIoT): current challenges and future perspectives. *Digital Commun. Networks*, 2024.
12. Menaka, S., Harshika, J., Philip, S., John, R., Bharathiraja, N., Murugesan, S., Analysing the accuracy of detecting phishing websites using ensemble methods in machine learning, in: *2023 Third International Conference on Artificial Intelligence and Smart Energy (ICAIS)*, IEEE, pp. 1251–1256, February, 2023.
13. Awotunde, J.B., Imoize, A.L., Jimoh, R.G., Adeniyi, E.A., Abdulraheem, M., Oladipo, I.D., Falola, P.B., AIoMT Enabling Real-Time Monitoring of Healthcare Systems: Security and Privacy Considerations, in: *Handbook of Security and Privacy of AI-Enabled Healthcare Systems and Internet of Medical Things*, pp. 97–133, 2024.
14. Ullah, U., Usama, M., Muhammad, Z., Akbar, A., AI-enabled low-powered wireless area networks for quality air, in: *Low-Power Wide Area Network for Large Scale Internet of Things*, pp. 100–141, CRC Press, Boca Raton, Florida, USA.
15. Bimpas, A., Violos, J., Leivadeas, A., Varlamis, I., Leveraging pervasive computing for ambient intelligence: A survey on recent advancements, applications and open challenges. *Comput. Netw.*, *239*, 110156, 2024.
16. Marappan, R., Vardhini, P.H., Kaur, G., Murugesan, S., Kathiravan, M., Bharathiraja, N., Venkatesan, R., Efficient evolutionary modeling in solving maximization of lifetime of wireless sensor healthcare networks. *Soft Comput.*, 27, 16, 11853–11867, 2023.
17. Yadav, S.P., Yadav, S., Raj, P., de Albuquerque, V.H.C. (Eds.), *Advances in Fuzzy-Based Internet of Medical Things (IoMT)*, John Wiley & Sons, USA, 2024.
18. Chauhdary, S.H., Alkatheiri, M.S., Alqarni, M.A., Saleem, S., An efficient evolutionary deep learning-based attack prediction in supply chain management systems. *Comput. Electr. Eng.*, *109*, 108768, 2023.
19. Ravindhar, N.V., Sasikumar, S., Bharathiraja, N., Integration of cloud-based scheme with industrial wireless sensor network for data publishing in privacy of point source. *Int. J. Cloud Comput.*, 13, 2, 124–138, 2024.
20. Wang, S., Ko, R.K., Bai, G., Dong, N., Choi, T., Zhang, Y., Evasion Attack and Defense On Machine Learning Models in Cyber-Physical Systems: A Survey. *IEEE Commun. Surv. Tutorials*, 26, 2, 930–966, 2023.
21. De Azambuja, A.J.G., Plesker, C., Schützer, K., Anderl, R., Schleich, B., Almeida, V.R., Artificial intelligence-based cyber security in the context of industry 4.0—a survey. *Electronics*, *12*, 8, 1920, 2023.
22. Anand, M., Antonidoss, A., Balamanigandan, R., Rahmath Nisha, S., Gurunathan, K., Bharathiraja, N., Resourceful Routing Algorithm for Mobile

Ad-Hoc Network to Enhance Energy Utilization. *Wireless Pers. Commun.*, 127, Suppl 1, 7–8, 2022.
23. Javaid, M., Haleem, A., Singh, R.P., Suman, R., Towards insight cybersecurity for healthcare domains: A comprehensive review of recent practices and trends. *Cyber Secur. Appl.*, 1, 100016, 2023.
24. El-Hajj, M., Itäpelto, T., Gebremariam, T., Systematic literature review: Digital twins' role in enhancing security for Industry 4.0 applications. *Secur. Privacy*, 7, e396, 2024.
25. Saeed, S., Altamimi, S.A., Alkayyal, N.A., Alshehri, E., Alabbad, D.A., Digital transformation and cybersecurity challenges for businesses resilience: Issues and recommendations. *Sensors*, *23*, 15, 6666, 2023.
26. Epiphaniou, G., Hammoudeh, M., Yuan, H., Maple, C., Ani, U., Digital twins in cyber effects modeling of IoT/CPS points of low resilience. *Simul. Modell. Pract. Theory*, *125*, 102744, 2023.
27. Sobb, T., Turnbull, B., Moustafa, N., A Holistic Review of Cyber-Physical–Social Systems: New Directions and Opportunities. *Sensors*, *23*, 17, 7391, 2023.
28. Vinod, D., Bharathiraja, N., Anand, M., Antonidoss, A., An improved security assurance model for collaborating small material business processes. *Mater. Today Proc.*, 46, 4077–4081, 2021.
29. Dharmasiri, N.T.D., Nanayakkara, N.W.A.G.N., Abeyasinghe, U.I., Wisidagama, N.S., Karunarthne, M.L., Ranasinghe, D.M.M., Artificial Cognition-based Medical Diagnosis and Treatment Recommendation System: A Review, 2023.
30. Soni, T., Kaur, R., Gupta, D., Sharma, A., Gupta, G., The Cybersecurity Ecosystem: Challenges, Risk and Emerging Technologies, in: *2023 7th International Conference on Trends in Electronics and Informatics (ICOEI)*, IEEE, pp. 699–703, April 2023.
31. Ghantasala, G.P., Hung, B.T., Chakrabarti, P., Pellakuri, V., Artificial intelligence based machine learning algorithm for prediction of cancer in female anatomy. *Multimed. Tools Appl.*, 1–27, 2024.
32. Ramana, T.V., Ghantasala, G.S., Sathiyaraj, R., Khan, M. (Eds.), *Artificial Intelligence and Machine Learning for Smart Community: Concepts and Applications*, CRC Press, Boca Raton, Florida, USA, 2024.
33. Parameswaran, T., Reddy, Y.P., Nagaveni, V., Sathiyaraj, R., Era of Computational Big Data Analytics and IoT Techniques in Smart City Applications, in: *IoT and Big Data Analytics for Smart Cities*, pp. 1–22, 2022.
34. Arora, J., Singh, S., Sethi, M., Kaur, G., Ghantasala, G.P., Securing cloud data exchange related to IoT devices: key challenges and its machine learning solutions, in: *Hybrid Information Systems: Non-Linear Optimization Strategies with Artificial Intelligence*, p. 177, 2024.
35. Ramisetty, S., Ghantasala, G.P., Gupta, G., Prevention of Security Attacks at Wireless Network Layers using Machine Learning Techniques, in: *2024 11th International Conference on Computing for Sustainable Global Development (INDIACom)*, IEEE, pp. 1787–1791, February, 2024.

11

Integrating Artificial Intelligence and Machine Learning for Enhanced Cyber Security in Industry 4.0: Designing a Smart Factory with IoT and CPS

Kavin Francis Xavier[1], Subashini K.[2], Vijayalakshmi P.[3], Selvalakshmi B.[4], Sudhakar G.[5] and Pradeepa K.[6*]

[1]M/S Muscat Engineering Consultancy Pvt. Ltd, Trichy, Tamil Nadu, India
[2]Department of Information Technology, Tagore Engineering College, Chennai, Tamil Nadu, India
[3]Computer Science and Engineering, Knowledge Institute of Technology, Salem, Tamil Nadu, India
[4]Department of Computer Science and Engineering, Tagore Engineering College, Chennai, Tamil Nadu, India
[5]Department of CSE, Sri Sai Ranganathan Engineering College, Coimbatore, Tamil Nadu, India
[6]Department of Computer Science and Engineering, St. Michael College of Engineering and Technology, Kalayarkoil, Sivaganga, Tamil Nadu, India

Abstract

As a result of Industry 4.0, Fourth Industrial Revolution companies are now transforming into intelligent cyber-physical production systems (CPPSs) with complete supply-chain interconnectivity between people, products, and machines. Although streamlined, efficient, and rapid manufacturing are some of the many benefits of this digitalization. It also introduces several innovative methods of attack that endanger people's lives, manufacturing processes, and company services. In the framework of Industry 4.0, this article explores the detailed review of the integration of artificial intelligence (AI) with machine learning (ML) to strengthen cyber security precautions. The important objective is to construct a smart factory

**Corresponding author*: pradeepa.k94@gmail.com

M. Thirunavukkarasan, S. A. Sahaaya Arul Mary, Sathiyaraj. R, G. S. Pradeep Ghantasala and Mudassir Khan (eds.) Artificial Intelligence and Machine Learning for Industry 4.0, (267–286)

by integrating Internet of things (IoT) and cyber physical systems (CPS). Cyber risks, especially DDoS assaults, pose a major threat to the operational integrity of Industry 4.0 installations in the modern world. Intrusion detection systems (IDS) can successfully counteract such risks by utilizing ML and AI capabilities. The article addresses the process of merging the fundamental elements of an established industry to establish a smart production framework. An investigation into smart production using a drilling procedure is presented as an example of a simplified smart factory framework, and the investigation of the proposed model is discussed and confirmed through testing.

Keywords: Machine learning, intrusion detection systems, artificial intelligence, cybersecurity, cyber physical systems

11.1 Introduction

From the moment a purchase is shipped until the product reaches the final stage of meaningful use, digitization serves to enhance visibility throughout the entire production process. It permits production procedures to be quickly reconfigured and managed to timely reply to modifications in end user requirements [1]. Furthermore, it enables for the following and monitoring of completed end products even after they have been removed from the meeting track. The data can be gathered in real time for different types of frameworks with very less human intervention [2].

The security background of the industrial engineering location is quickly growing alongside with digitization. Initially, the air gap theory explored that the theory no longer grips for manufacturing industries that were conventionally isolated from the Internet [3]. Cyber physical protection systems (CPPSs) are slightly improving wireless networks and cloud services to link numerous participants along with supply chain by increasing their threat surface [4]. The industries depend not only on IoT devices with limited sources but also on formerly organized required equipment that lack safety procedures. Criminals may breech these liabilities to intrude the system and spread more severe issues [5]. Hence, constructing a strong IDS is important to protect the connections and enabling interaction among various nodes without granting unnecessary access mechanism guidelines [6].

The criminals hijack a significant number of devices to form a botnet or platoon of attackers. After forming the botnet, they launch synchronized large-scale intrusion among various connected targets that show less strength [7]. Criminals typically mask the actual locations of the compromised computers by falsifying their IP addresses. The distributed denial of service (DDoS) outbreak may target a communication channel or a hosting server. Consequently, the resulting attack is referred to as a bandwidth flooding threat or an endpoint flooding threat, respectively [8].

There is a growing demand among companies to become more adaptable and flexible to meet the evolving needs of consumers as modern innovations reshape marketplaces. Businesses are compelled to make significant adjustments to their manufacturing schedules, technology adoption, and management practices due to increased competition in global markets for efficiency, productivity, and quality [9]. The automation of tasks, technological advancements, artificial intelligence, sensors, data collection, expert systems, information and communication technology (ICT), IoT, vast amounts of data, cloud computing, and the unparalleled accessibility and power of computer have all enabled numerous sectors to enhance their efficiency and profitability [10].

CPSs represent technologies that merge digital and physical realms, intertwining computing, networking, and tangible resources to establish a communication bridge between virtual and real worlds [11]. The significant objective of Industry 4.0 adapts CPS and its achievement relies based on the efficient controlling of physical components and interconnected systems, leveraging the latest advancements in both domains as depicted in Figure 11.1 [12]. Since their inception, CPSs have been a significant focus of research and application in manufacturing technology. In the manufacturing sector,

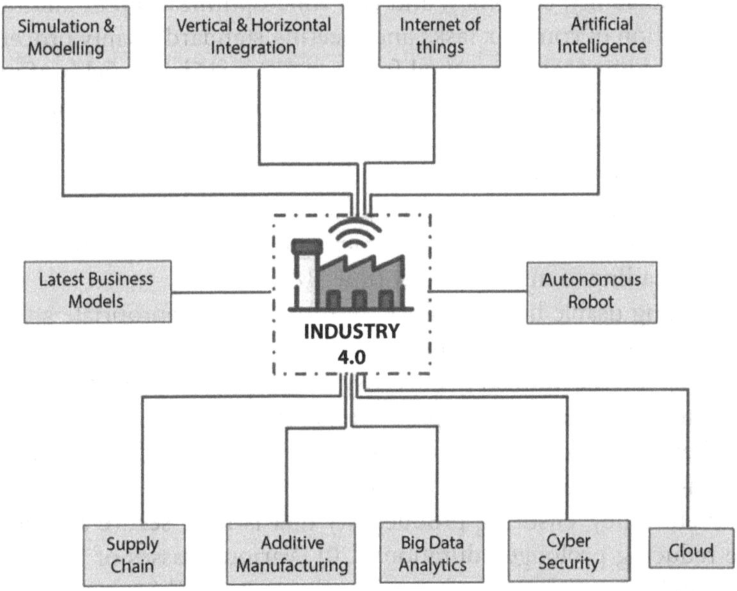

Figure 11.1 Pillars of Industry 4.0.

the latest advancements in computer science, communication, information technologies, and manufacturing science and technology are encompassed under the term CPPS. CPPSs have found applications across various sectors, including power, healthcare, and automotive industries [13].

11.2 Related Works

The integration of real and virtual aspects is facilitated by CPS. Physical components, such as computers, operator panels, and sensors, collaborate and exchange information to gather and transmit data to cyber-elements responsible for handling, analyzing, and making decisions [14]. IoT enables the secure and reliable connection of numerous items in real time, including devices, robots, sensors, and actuators. Communication networks supporting multilingual communication, such as Wi-Fi, cloud, fog, and edge technologies, as well as Machine-to-Machine (M2M) setups and Fifth-Generation (5G) systems, are fundamental to the IoT [15]. With these advanced technologies, Industry 4.0 aims to revolutionize the way industries currently manufacture goods and deliver services, benefiting workers, customers, and industry partners while promoting sustainable development [16].

Many requests are proposed within the design of Industry 4.0 with automation, tractability, efficiency, and real time optimization, in addition to the completion of complex tasks and meeting standard quality procedures in integrated physical and virtual functionalities [17]. The fields of manufacturing and manufacturing growth are predominantly encompassed by the relevant widespread applications. Defect identification, forecast, then management is an essential for the advancement of these developments. ML algorithms, capable of identifying faulty then malfunctioning portions or products in current environment, facilitate swift and accurate fault identification, leading to minimal downtime [18].

Remaining usable life and affects resulting in an appropriate and cost-effective service schedule that minimizes downtime due to problem occurrence [19]. In the Industry 4.0 ecosystem, human interaction remains integral to the manufacturing process; however, collaboration with robots and other machinery on factory floors presents significant challenges. Decision-making algorithms and human behavior detection enhance worker efficiency, ensuring productivity that is both secure and efficient while reducing prolonged durations [20]. Various classes of ML are outlined, emphasizing their key features in Figure 11.2. The main approaches

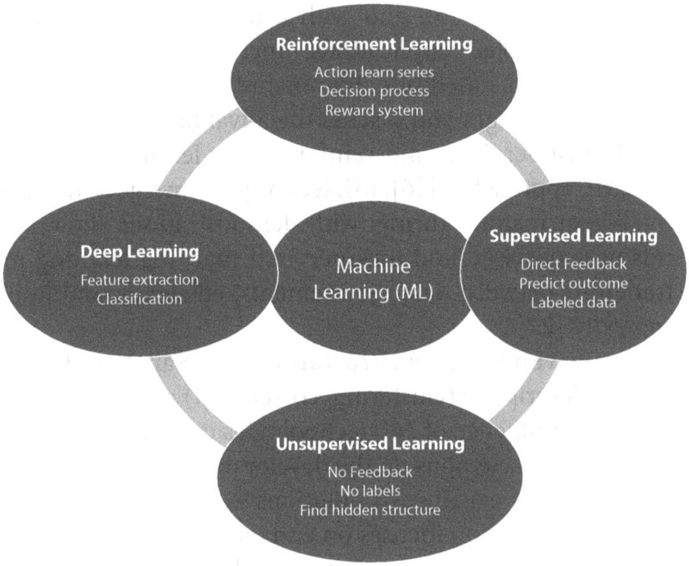

Figure 11.2 ML sub-classes.

of Industry 4.0 and ML models are increasingly being utilized to meet the demands of diverse industries [21].

One of the primary tenets of Industry 4.0 is automation, exemplified by robotics technology utilized in various applications within Industry 4.0, such as collaborative robots working alongside factory operators [22]. Recent advancements in robotics have significantly enhanced efficiency, flexibility, adaptability, configurability, and security in intelligent manufacturing facilities, positioning robotic machines as essential technology for automation and manufacturing. Modern robotics equipment finds application across diverse sectors, enabling the creation of innovative manufacturing cells using digital factory techniques [23].

The concept of IoT-aided robotics, frequently denoted to as the Internet of Robotic Things (IoRT), is a novel idea resulting from the integration of robotics with IoT technology. This integration is expected to unlock new product possibilities in both existing robotics and IoT systems. Developing flexible and adaptable systems will facilitate the production of mobile robots and autonomous robotics suitable for the wide array of applications required in Industry 4.0 [24]. Significant contributions have been made to the study of Industry 4.0, including surveys providing insights into CPS in IIoT contexts and offering detailed frameworks for managing systems and processes [25].

The big data analytics, IoT and with a taxonomy of ML techniques utilized in BDA-enabled applications, including self-prediction and self-configuration. ML methods for manufacturing systems address implementation challenges and discuss the advantages and disadvantages of supervised, unsupervised, and reinforcement learning (RL) methods, among other ML approaches [26]. ML techniques emerge as the most suitable for intelligent manufacturing, with demonstrations showcasing different kinds of supervised and unsupervised machine learning methods offering trade-offs between data requirements, efficiency, and implementation complexity [27].

Explorations delve into big data structures and CPS analytical approaches, evaluating both descriptive (clustering, correlation) and predictive analytical methods. The influence of ML technologies on machining operations is highlighted, with discussions on the development of deep learning (DL) and its advantages over existing ML solutions for handling highly complex data [28]. ML/AI utilization focuses on enhancing human-machine interaction (HMI) through knowledge-based ideal structures and leveraging relevant metadata across different levels of complexity [29].

11.3 Proposed Model

The key aspects of industries have emerged in response to growing digitization of numerous industries, particularly manufacturing, to harness the transformative potential of technological advancements to enhance profitability, efficiency, and effectiveness. Industry 4.0 indicates how the system can conceive and manage production processes. It advocates for a comprehensive and interconnected approach, where products, machinery, and people seamlessly interact within a unified environment, transcending traditional constraints of separate manufacturing processes and linear supply chains. The origins of Industry 4.0 can be viewed as a logical progression from earlier industrial revolutions, each characterized by significant technological advancements and profound socio-economic changes. The next revolution, propelled by the introduction of machine tools and power, revolutionized mass production and accelerated urbanization. The third revolution is digital revolution ushered in the digital age with the introduction of machinery and computers. Industry 4.0 leverages digital technology to propel industrial innovation and efficiency to unprecedented levels, shown in Figure 11.3. The concept of CPS, wherein physical components are equipped with integrated computing capabilities, enabling them to autonomously communicate with their surroundings.

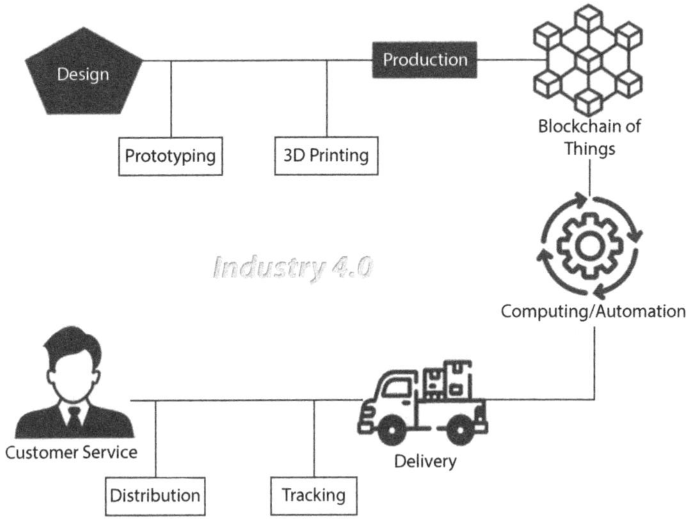

Figure 11.3 Industry 4.0 diagram.

11.3.1 Smart Factory

The smart business can be attained with the aims of Industry 4.0 through integrating vertical and networked industrial structures into manufacturing processes relying on the concept of the intelligent factory. The smart factory design illustrated in Figure 11.4 showcases the integration of the four layers interconnected at various levels to form advanced automation pyramids. This structure deviates from traditional designs by leveraging sophisticated computers, cloud computing, networking, and intelligent devices to enable seamless interaction and communication among the components of the manufacturing process hierarchy.

Figure 11.5 depicts the physical assets at the level of the intelligent manufacturing framework. It includes a drilling system, a PC equipped with multiple communication methods, several sensors, a universal web camera, and a PLC Siemens S7-1200. The intelligent production process, focusing on machining (drilling), involves moving the workpiece to a specified position where the PLC and webcam detect its presence. Once the correct location is identified, the pick-and-place robot selects the object and set it into the elected slot of the drilling part. Before commencing the drilling operation, a proximity sensor verifies its arrival at the drilling tables. Upon completion of the drilling procedures, the end switch is triggered, enabling the robot to transfer the data to the designated storage area. This sequence is repeated every period an item is placed in the initial space.

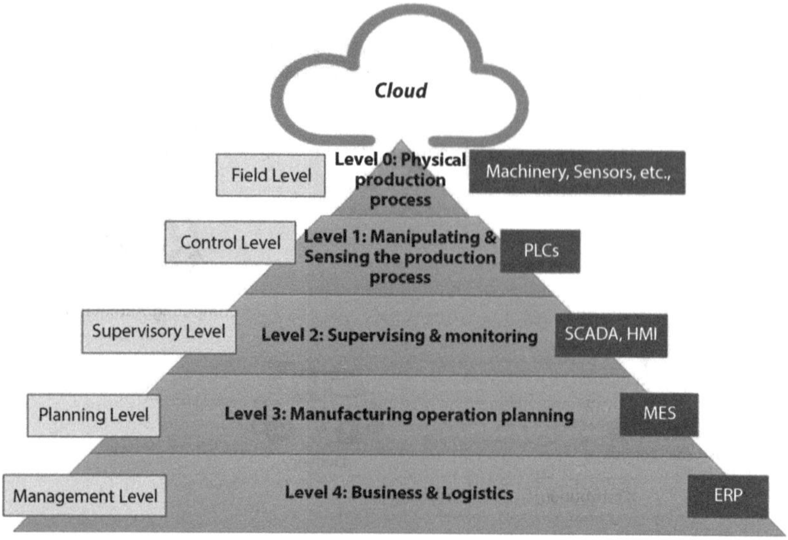

Figure 11.4 A smart factory's architecture.

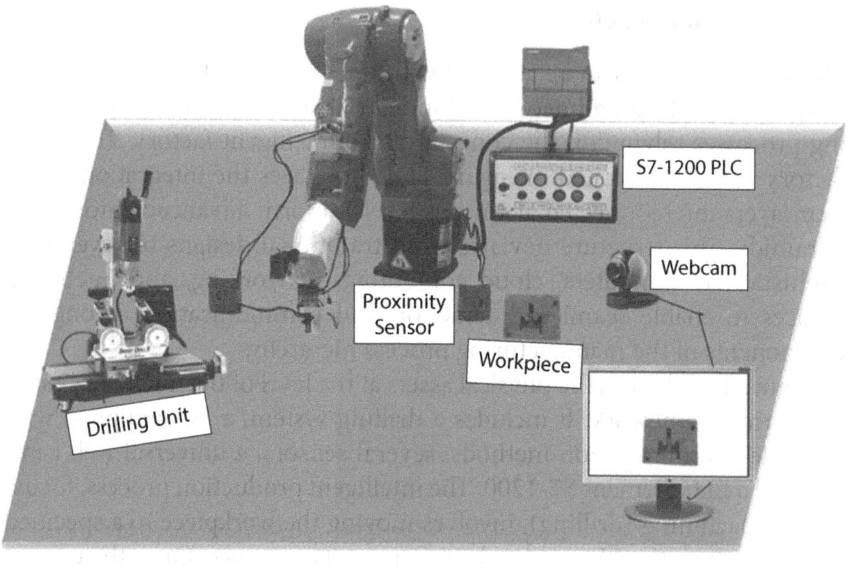

Figure 11.5 Smart factory installation.

11.3.2 The Mechanical Design

To establish a smart factory process, a horizontal drill was developed to select a sample after prearranged slots and transport it to a drilling stage.

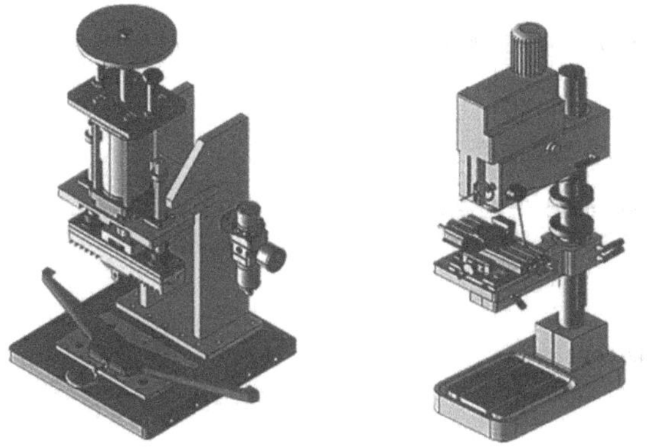

Figure 11.6 The drilling unit's proposed CAD model.

The drilling machine, utilized as a tool for creating openings in workpieces, consists of several components as depicted in Figure 11.6.

1. Technical elements include the drilling machine's base, supportive framework, beams, lead screwdriver, bearings, and other structural components.
2. Electrical System: The electrical infrastructure comprises controls and drive units for stepper motors.
3. Mechanism Control: It positions the drill point accurately and determines the cutting depth.

In Figure 11.5, a gripping device is attached to the drilling unit to protect the workpiece and ensure the constant operations through the drilling activities. The system secures the workpiece from both ends by incorporating a metal gripper (clamp) and a pneumatic piston on the base of the table.

11.3.3 Proposed IDS Architecture

Characteristics such as size of packet, transport layers guidelines, measurement of incoming and outgoing packets, inter-arrival time of packet and flow duration are among the attributes extracted. This mapping information is then directly fed into the identification engines, which, upon detecting an unauthorized network traffic pattern, trigger an alarm. The dataset generated by the feature selection modules is managed in a storage area and periodically utilized to update the ML methods employed in the identification system, as the definition of benign activity may evolve as shown in Figure 11.7. The alert manager analyzes the results from the monitoring

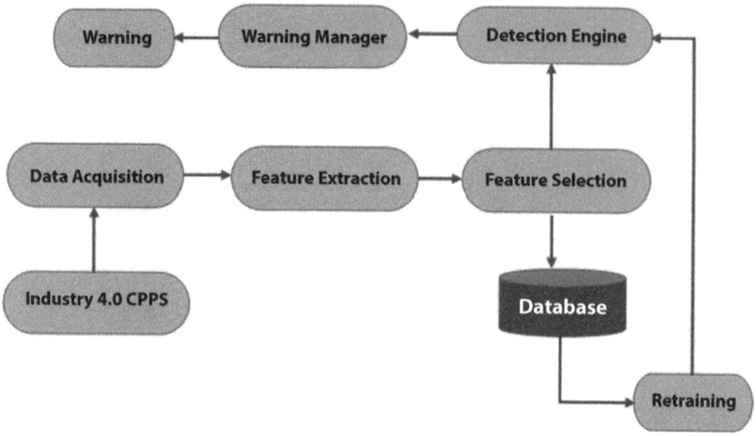

Figure 11.7 DDoS attack in Industry 4.0 process.

engine and triggers an alarm if the likelihood of an intrusion reaches a predefined security threshold set by the client, such as when multiple consecutive alerts are detected.

11.3.4 IDS in CCPS

CCPS, an online technology amalgamating physical components and computer systems to deliver AI-based solutions, has undergone rapid

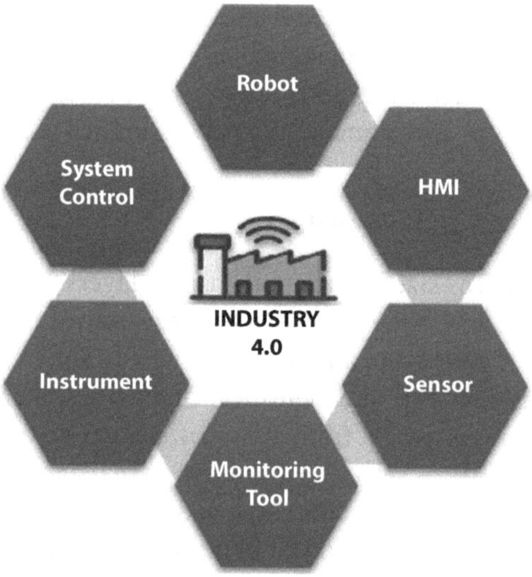

Figure 11.8 Smart manufacturing Industry 4.0.

transformation in recent times. Employing neuroscience to integrate ML or AI, CCPS is pivotal in the development of intelligent systems and holds significant importance in commercial computing, shown in Figure 11.8.

CCPS applications in the Industrial Revolution have led to the appearance of smart industries driven by the technological advancements of Industry 4.0. Data analysis, cloud computing, interconnected devices, and AI are utilized across various domains such as healthcare systems, smart homes, robotic systems, and autonomous driving systems, enabling further automation of processes. These enabling technologies empower autonomous decision-making, data connectivity, accessibility, and technological assistance. Figure 11.9 illustrates how CPS manages IDS.

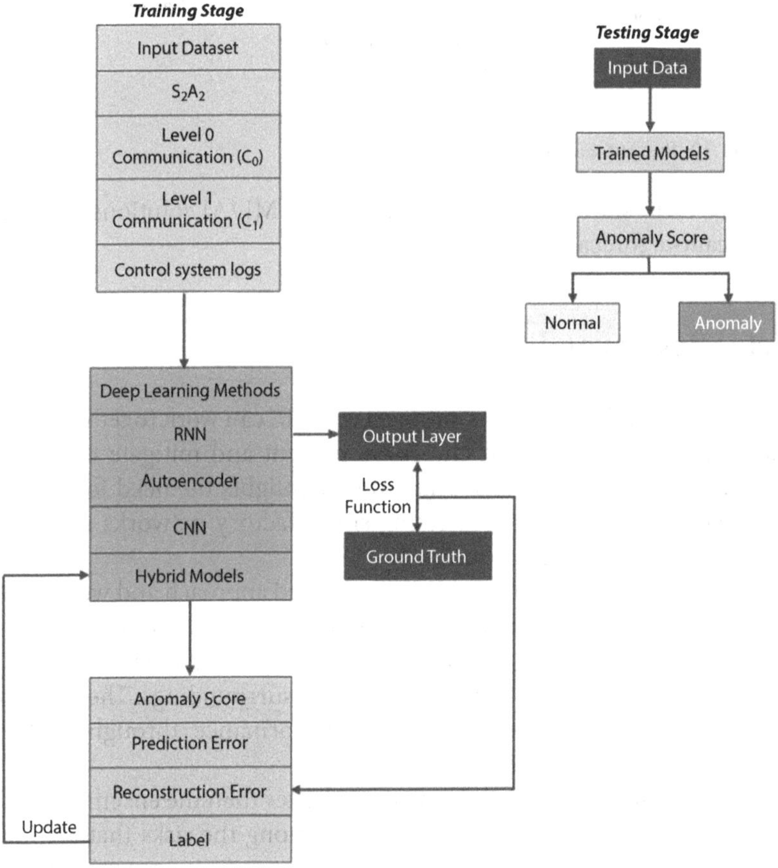

Figure 11.9 IDS in CPS.

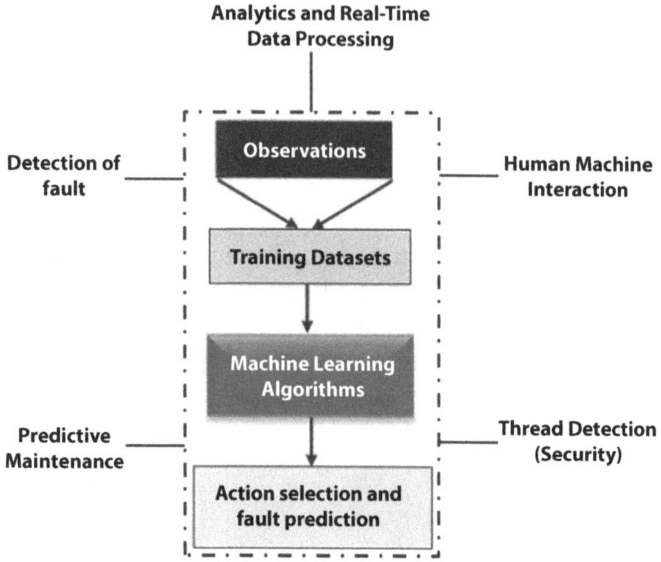

Figure 11.10 Prevent and fault detection in Industry 4.0.

Figure 11.10 showcases various examples of ML/AI solutions for defect identification, forecasting, and prevention.

11.4 Results and Discussions

The research studies explore how the AI and ML can work together to construct a strong IDS that can effectively prevent and mitigate cyber hazards including DDoS assaults. This study highlights the need for an early and proactive approach to protecting smart factory networks despite an unchanged cyber threat environment.

The decision to choose between the proposed approach and well-known models like RNN, CNN, or combination models depends on specific needs such as precision, rapidity, limitations on resources and the kind of threats experienced in Industry 4.0 intelligent factory surroundings. The proposed ML/AI-based IDS may offer superior performance throughout these parameters shown in Table 11.1.

The final results of proposed system are better than the ensemble model that indicates the fewer false positives are among the risks that are identified. Comparison of performance measures precision, sensitivity, specificity, and F1-score is shown in Table 11.2 and Figure 11.11. Multiple variables, including the complexity of the information, the type of cyber

Table 11.1 Comparison of performance measures (accuracy, FPR, FNR, detection time, and response time).

Performance measure	Proposed model	CNN model	RNN model	Ensemble model
Accuracy	96	93	92	95
False Positive Rate (FPR)	4	6	5	3
False Negative Rate (FNR)	3	4	3	2
Detection Time	0.6	1.1	1.1	0.7
Response Time	1.1	2.1	2.1	1.1

Table 11.2 Comparison of performance measures (precision, sensitivity, specificity, and F1-score).

Performance measure	Proposed model	CNN model	RNN model	Ensemble model
Precision	0.96	0.93	0.96	0.95
Specificity	0.95	0.89	0.90	0.94
Sensitivity	097	0.95	0.87	0.96
F1 Score	0.96	0.94	0.91	0.95

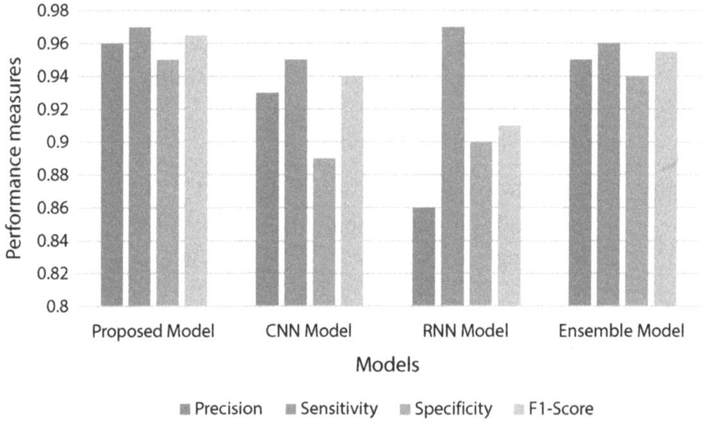

Figure 11.11 Comparison of performance measures.

threats, and the optimization approaches employed during learning and assessment, might affect every model's particular success in these domains.

The proposed model's effective use of resources and capacity to grow with the size of the network makes it more scalable overall. All models' robustness based on the diversity of training dataset, however, ensemble models often have a higher level of robustness since they combine a range of models, shown in Table 11.3. The proposed model's flexibility is demonstrated by its capacity for continuous learning and its capacity to adjust to novel and changing cyber threats. Ensemble models combine several models and may learn from different sources; they also show flexibility.

Table 11.3 Comparison of scalability, robustness and adaptability.

Performance measure	Proposed model	CNN model	RNN model	Ensemble model
Scalability	Scales well with increasing network size and efficient resource utilization.	If the size of the network expands, then more resources and processing powers are required	If the size of the network expands, then more resources and processing powers are required	Generally scalable due to combination of multiple models
Robustness	Robust against varying network conditions and noisy data.	Robustness depends upon the diversity of training data	Robustness depends upon the diversity of training data	Generally robust due to a combination of diverse models
Adaptability	Adaptable to new and evolving cyber threats through ongoing learning and updates.	Limited adaptability to new cyber threats without retraining or significant adjustments.	Limited adaptability to new cyber threats without retraining or significant adjustments.	Adaptable due to the combination of multiple models and the ability to learn from diverse sources.

The lower MAE is often achieved by the combined and proposed models, suggesting reduced mean errors between reality and anticipated quantities. RMSE of the combined model and the proposed model tends to be lower, indicating fewer total differences between the anticipated and actual outcomes and, thus, more precise predictions as shown in Table 11.4 and Figure 11.12.

Both the ensemble approach and the proposed model often attain high training accuracy, demonstrating their proficiency with the initial data set and efficient acquisition of the fundamental trends. Both the combined model and the proposed model often have high validating reliability. CNN models frequently attain high validation reliability, shown in Table 11.5 and Figure 11.13.

When errors in the initial training information are properly minimized throughout training, the proposed model and combined model often achieve low learning loss. Low loss of validation is another characteristic of the proposed model and ensemble approach that suggests they are also functioning well on untested data, shown in Table 11.6 and Figure 11.14.

Table 11.4 Comparison of performance measures (MAE and RMSE).

Performance measure	Proposed model	CNN model	RNN model	Ensemble model
MAE	0.06	0.09	0.08	0.05
RMSE	0.08	0.2	0.10	0.07

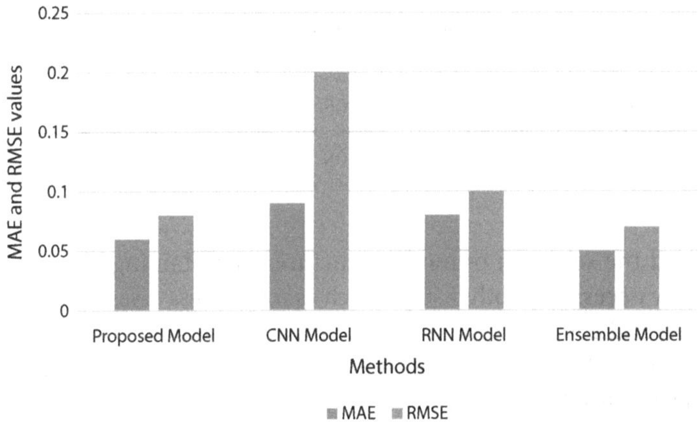

Figure 11.12 Comparison of performance measures (MAE and RMSE).

Table 11.5 Comparison of performance measures (training and validation accuracy).

Performance measure in accuracy	Proposed model	CNN model	RNN model	Ensemble model
Training	0.98	0.98	0.97	0.98
Validation	0.96	0.95	0.89	0.97

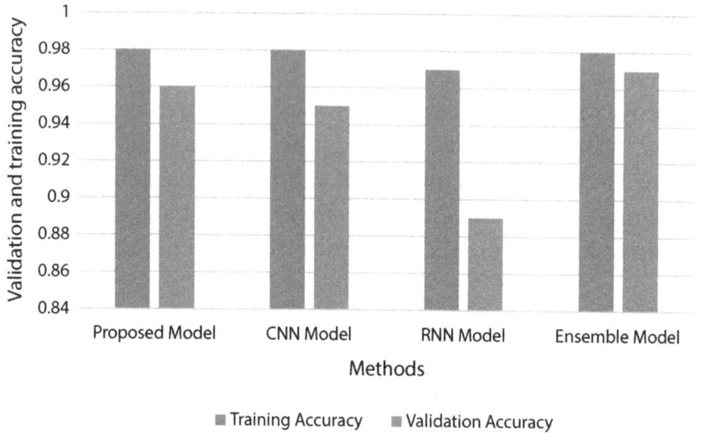

Figure 11.13 Comparison of performance measures (training and validation accuracy).

Table 11.6 Comparison of performance measures (training and validation loss).

Performance measure	Proposed model	CNN model	RNN model	Ensemble model
Training Loss	0.06	0.05	0.07	0.05
Validation Loss	0.09	0.08	0.13	0.07

Beyond the selection of model structures, maintaining excellent safety frequently necessitates other steps, such as robustness assessment, frequent upgrades, and commitment to safety standards. Table 11.7 shows that multiple variables like license fees, maintenance expenses, and adaptability may affect cost-effectiveness calculations.

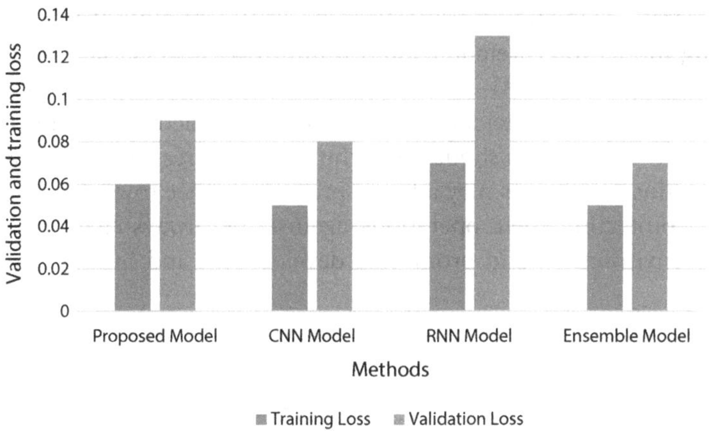

Figure 11.14 Comparison of performance measures (training and validation loss).

Table 11.7 Comparison of performance measures (security, resource utilization, and cost-effectiveness).

Performance measure	Proposed model	CNN model	RNN model	Ensemble model
Security	High	Moderate	Moderate	High
Resource utilization	Efficient	Moderate	Moderate	Efficient
Cost-effectiveness	Cost-effective	Moderate	Moderate	Cost-effective

11.5 Conclusions

In response to the development of smart automated production factories, Industry 4.0 has become a major area of interest for manufacturing companies. These settings can identify, evaluate, and react to cyber threats in real-time by using powerful ML/AI methods, especially in the form of IDS. Through integration with the IoT and CPS, AI and ML-enabled systems may make use of the huge amount of data gathered by connected components, the massive amounts of data generated by networked devices to detect abnormalities that could be signs of impending assaults. By taking a proactive approach, the security posture of smart factory infrastructures is improved and the likelihood of operational interruptions and data breaches are reduced. Nevertheless, there are additional difficulties associated with this integration, including protecting the confidentiality of information, handling model interpretability, and minimizing adversarial assaults. So, to further improve ML/AI-driven cyber security in Industry 4.0 and eventually open the door for safer and more resilient manufacturing environments, subsequent study efforts should concentrate on addressing these obstacles. By doing this, businesses may adopt a proactive stance toward information security, protecting their operations against the always-changing online security environment and promoting development and innovation in the digital age.

References

1. Alowaidi, M., Sharma, S.K., AlEnizi, A., Bhardwaj, S., Integrating artificial intelligence in cyber security for cyber-physical systems. *Electron. Res. Arch.*, *31*, 4, 1876–1896, 2023.
2. Chen, G., Wang, P., Feng, B., Li, Y., Liu, D., The framework design of smart factory in discrete manufacturing industry based on cyber-physical system. *Int. J. Comput. Integr. Manuf.*, *33*, 1, 79–101, 2020.
3. De Azambuja, A.J.G., Plesker, C., Schützer, K., Anderl, R., Schleich, B., Almeida, V.R., Artificial intelligence-based cyber security in the context of industry 4.0—a survey. *Electronics*, *12*, 8, 1920, 2023.
4. Kaur, G., Bharathiraja, N., Singh, K.D., Veeramanickam, M.R.M., Rodriguez, C.R., Pradeepa, K., Emerging trends in cybersecurity challenges with reference to pen testing tools in Society 5.0. *Artif. Intell. Soc. 5.0*, 196–212, 2024.
5. Khan, I.H. and Javaid, M., Role of Internet of Things (IoT) in adoption of Industry 4.0. *J. Ind. Integr. Manage.*, *7*, 04, 515–533, 2022.
6. Marappan, R., Vardhini, P.H., Kaur, G., Murugesan, S., Kathiravan, M., Bharathiraja, N., Venkatesan, R., Efficient evolutionary modeling in solving maximization of lifetime of wireless sensor healthcare networks. *Soft Comput.*, *27*, 16, 11853–11867, 2023.
7. Menaka, S., Jonnalagadda, H., Philip, S., John, R., Bharathiraja, N., Murugesan, S., Analysing the accuracy of detecting phishing websites using ensemble methods in machine learning, in: *2023 Third International Conference on Artificial Intelligence and Smart Energy (ICAIS)*, IEEE, pp. 1251–1256, 2023.
8. Pandithurai, O., Bharathiraja, N., Pradeepa, K., Meenakshi, D., Kathiravan, M., Air pollution prediction using supervised machine learning technique, in: *2023 Third International Conference on Artificial Intelligence and Smart Energy (ICAIS)*, IEEE, pp. 542–546, 2023, February.
9. Ravindhar, N., Sasikumar, S., Bharathiraja, N., Kumar, M.V., Secure integration of wireless sensor network with cloud using coded probable bluefish cryptosystem. *J. Theor. Appl. Inf. Technol.*, 100, 7438–7449, 2022.

10. Shankar, G., Kaur, G., Gill, S.K., Security and privacy challenges in IoT system resolving using blockchain technology, in: *Convergence of IoT, Blockchain, and Computational Intelligence in Smart Cities*, CRC Press, pp. 136–161, 2023.
11. Song, Y., Yu, F.R., Zhou, L., Yang, X., He, Z., Applications of the Internet of Things (IoT) in smart logistics: A comprehensive survey. *IEEE Internet Things J.*, *8*, 6, 4250–4274, 2020.
12. Zheng, P., Wang, H., Sang, Z., Zhong, R.Y., Liu, Y., Liu, C., Xu, X., Smart manufacturing systems for Industry 4.0: Conceptual framework, scenarios, and future perspectives. *Front. Mech. Eng.*, 13, 137–150, 2018.
13. Rath, K.C., Khang, A., Roy, D., The role of Internet of Things (IoT) technology in Industry 4.0 economy, in: *Advanced IoT technologies and applications in the Industry 4.0 digital economy*, CRC Press, pp. 1–28, 2024.
14. Abosuliman, S.S., Deep learning techniques for securing cyber-physical systems in supply chain 4.0. *Comput. Electr. Eng.*, 107, 108637, 2023.
15. Adel, A., Unlocking the future: Fostering human–machine collaboration and driving intelligent automation through industry 5.0 in smart cities. *Smart Cities*, *6*, 5, 2742–2782, 2023.
16. Amara, F.Z., Djezzar, M., Hemam, M., Tiwari, S., A real-time semantic based approach for modeling and reasoning in Industry 4.0. *Int. J. Inf. Technol.*, *16*, 1, 507–515, 2024.
17. Anand, M., Antonidoss, A., Balamanigandan, R., Rahmath Nisha, S., Gurunathan, K., Bharathiraja, N., Resourceful routing algorithm for mobile ad-hoc network to enhance energy utilization. *Wireless Pers. Commun.*, 127, Suppl. 1, 7–8, 2022.
18. Arulkumar, V., Kavin, F., Nagu, B., IoT sensor data retrieval and analysis in cloud environments for enhanced power management. *J. Adv. Res. Appl. Sci. Eng. Technol.*, *38*, 1, 77–88, 2024.
19. Chennam, K.K., Taranum, F., Hijab, M., An overview of cyber-physical system (CPS) security, threats, and solutions, in: *Convergence of deep learning in cyber-IoT systems and security*, pp. 415–433, 2022.
20. Eckhart, M. and Ekelhart, A., Digital twins for cyber-physical systems security: State of the art and outlook, in: *Security and quality in cyber-physical systems engineering: With forewords by Robert M. Lee and Tom Gilb*, pp. 383–412, 2019.
21. Haldorai, A., A review on artificial intelligence in Internet of Things and cyber-physical systems. *J. Comput. Nat. Sci.*, *3*, 1, 012–023, 2023.
22. Kumar, R. and Sundaramurthy, S., AI and IoT in manufacturing and related security perspectives for Industry 4.0, in: *Artificial Intelligence and Cyber Security in Industry 4.0*, pp. 47–70, Springer Nature Singapore, Singapore, 2023.
23. Naphade, M., Banavar, G., Harrison, C., Paraszczak, J., Morris, R., Smarter cities and their innovation challenges. *Computer*, *44*, 6, 32–39, 2011.

24. Ravindhar, N.V., Sasikumar, S., Bharathiraja, N., Integration of cloud-based scheme with industrial wireless sensor network for data publishing in privacy of point source. *Int. J. Cloud Comput.*, *13*, 2, 124–138, 2024.
25. Sedjelmaci, H., Guenab, F., Senouci, S.M., Moustafa, H., Liu, J., Han, S., Cyber security based on artificial intelligence for cyber-physical systems. *IEEE Netw.*, *34*, 3, 6–7, 2020.
26. Vinod, D., Bharathiraja, N., Anand, M., Antonidoss, A., An improved security assurance model for collaborating small material business processes. *Mater. Today Proc.*, 46, 4077–4081, 2021.
27. Wang, X., Wang, Y., Yang, J., Wang, X., Meng, Z., Liu, Z., Wang, F.Y., A paradigm shift for modeling and operation of oil and gas: From Industry 4.0 in CPS to Industry 5.0 in CPSS. *IEEE Trans. Ind. Inf.*, 20, 7, 9186–9193, 2024.
28. Xia, L., Semirumi, D.T., Rezaei, R., A thorough examination of smart city applications: Exploring challenges and solutions throughout the life cycle with emphasis on safeguarding citizen privacy. *Sustain. Cities Soc.*, 98, 104771, 2023.
29. Azambuja, A.J.G., Giese, T., Schützer, K., Anderl, R., Schleich, B., Almeida, V.R., Digital twins in Industry 4.0–Opportunities and challenges related to cyber security. *Procedia CIRP*, 121, 25–30, 2024.

12

Application of AI and ML in Industry 4.0

V. Vinaya Kumari[1], G. S. Pradeep Ghantasala[2], S. A. Sahaaya Arul Mary[3], M. Thirunavukkarasan[3] and Sathiyaraj. R[4]*

[1]Department of Computer Science and Engineering, Malla Reddy Engineering College for Women, Hyderabad, India
[2]Department of Computer Science and Engineering, Alliance College of Engineering and Design, Alliance University, Bengaluru, India
[3]School of CSE, Vellore Institute of Technology, VIT University, Vellore, India
[4]GITAM School of Technology, GITAM University, Bangalore, Karnataka, India

Abstract
The emergence of Industry 4.0 marks a transformative alternative in commercial practices pushed through the convergence of cyber-physical structures, the Internet of Things (IoT), and superior computing technology. Artificial intelligence (AI) and Machine Learning (ML) are at the core of this commercial revolution, playing a pivotal role in making production techniques extra green, productive, and innovative. This chapter explores the huge variety of packages of AI and ML within the Industry 4.0 paradigm and explains their effect on diverse components which include predictive upkeep, great management, deliver chain optimization, and the improvement of self-reliant structures. Predictive upkeep makes use of AI and ML algorithms to investigate records from gadget sensors and expect gadget disasters earlier than they occur. This not only minimizes downtime but also reduces upkeep expenses and extends the carrier existence of the gadget. Quality management makes use of AI-powered imaginative and prescient structures and ML fashions to discover defects and anomalies in real time, ensuring better product requirements and lowering waste. Additionally, AI and ML facilitate delivery chain optimization by reading big quantities of records to expect demand, manipulate inventory, and optimize logistics. This technology permits organizations to reply quickly to marketplace changes, enhancing operational agility and patron satisfaction. Another key application, self-reliant operations, is seeing the

**Corresponding author*: rsr026@gmail.com

M. Thirunavukkarasan, S. A. Sahaaya Arul Mary, Sathiyaraj. R, G. S. Pradeep Ghantasala and Mudassir Khan (eds.) Artificial Intelligence and Machine Learning for Industry 4.0, (287–306)

combination of AI and ML in robotics and clever factories, permitting machines and structures to self-organize and adapt to special manufacturing wishes without human intervention. The integration of AI and ML in Industry 4.0 additionally enables the introduction of virtual twins (digital replicas of bodily assets) that allow superior simulation, monitoring, and optimization of techniques. These virtual representations enhance decision-making and operational performance by presenting a deep perception of the device's overall performance and ability issues. This evaluation highlights the transformative effect of AI and ML on Industry 4.0 and emphasizes their position in riding shrewd production, shrewd automation, and human empowerment.

***Keywords*:** AI and ML, IoT, cyber-physical systems, supply chain optimization

12.1 Introduction

The industrial landscape is undergoing a profound transformation with the advent of Industry 4.0, the term that summarizes the fourth industrial revolution [2]. This new era is characterized by the integration of digital technologies, cyber-physical systems and the Internet of Things (IoT) into traditional industrial and manufacturing operations in Figure 12.2 and Table 12.1. At the forefront of this revolution are artificial intelligence (AI) and machine learning (ML), which are key enablers of the smart factories and connected systems that define Industry 4.0. AI and ML technology are revolutionizing the way industries operate, providing cutting-edge solutions that improve efficiency, productivity and decision-making. These technologies enable machines and systems to process large amounts of data, learn from those data, and make informed decisions without human intervention [1]. The applications of AI and ML in Industry 4.0 are diverse and wide-ranging, including predictive maintenance, quality control, supply chain optimization, and automated systems development. Predictive maintenance uses AI and ML algorithms to monitor equipment health and predict failures before they occur, significantly reducing downtime and maintenance costs. When it comes to quality control, AI-based systems can detect defects with high accuracy, thereby ensuring superior product quality and minimizing waste. Supply chain optimization leverages AI and ML to analyze data and forecast demand, manage inventory, and optimize logistics, leading to more responsive and efficient operations.

Additionally, the advent of automated operations powered by AI and ML enables the creation of intelligent systems capable of self-organizing and adapting to changing production needs. These systems improve flexibility and reduce the need for human intervention in routine tasks, allowing

Table 12.1 Minimum, maximum and average for advanced IoT agriculture 2024.

S. no.	Advanced IoT agriculture 2024	Minimum	Maximum	Average
1	Average of chlorophyll in the plant (ACHP)	33.08	36.30	34.33
2	Plant height rate (PHR)	45.59	67.07	57.24
3	Average wet weight of the growth vegetative (AWWGV)	1.10	1.36	1.17
4	Average leaf area of the plant (ALAP)	981.46	1284.25	1142.10
5	Average number of plant leaves (ANPL)	4.00	5.02	4.83
6	Average root diameter (ARD)	15.96	16.99	16.29
7	Average dry weight of the root (ADWR)	0.76	1.72	1.37
8	Percentage of dry matter for vegetative growth (PDMVG)	18.39	31.42	20.90
9	Average root length (ARL)	17.32	20.85	19.70
10	Average wet weight of the root (AWWR)	2.75	2.97	2.89
11	Average dry weight of vegetative plants (ADWV)	0.20	0.44	0.25
12	Percentage of dry matter for root growth (PDMRG)	27.90	57.65	47.24

workers to focus on more complex and creative aspects of production. The integration of digital twins, which are virtual replicas of physical assets, further illustrates the transformative potential of AI and ML in Industry 4.0 [3]. These digital models enable advanced simulation, real-time monitoring and optimization, providing insights into system performance and potential problems.

The commercial panorama is the present process of a profound transformation with the arrival of Industry 4.0, the period that summarizes the fourth commercial revolution. This new generation is characterized via way of means of the mixing of virtual technology, cyber-bodily structures and the Internet of Things (IoT) into conventional commercial and production operations. At the vanguard of this revolution are synthetic intelligence (AI) and device learning (ML), which can be key enablers of the clever factories and related structures that outline Industry 4.0. AI and ML generation is revolutionizing the manner industries operate, imparting modern answers that enhance efficiency, productiveness and decision-making [5]. These technologies permit machines and structures to process huge quantities of facts, examine those facts, and make informed decisions autonomously without human intervention. The programs of AI and ML in Industry 4.0 are various and wide-ranging, which include predictive preservation, great control, deliver chain optimization, and automatic structure improvement. Predictive preservation makes use of AI and ML algorithms to display gadget fitness and is expecting screw-ups earlier than they occur, notably decreasing downtime and preservation costs. When it involves great control, AI-primarily based total structures can stumble on defects with excessive accuracy, thereby making sure advanced products are great and minimizing waste. Supply chain optimization leverages AI and ML to investigate facts and forecast demand, control inventory, and optimize logistics [4] leading to more responsive and efficient operations.

Additionally, the advent of automated operations powered by AI and ML enables the creation of sensible structures able to self-organize and adapt to converting manufacturing needs. These structures enhance flexibility and decrease the want for human intervention in recurring tasks, allowing employees to be conscious of greater complicated and innovative factors of manufacturing [6]. The integration of virtual twins, which can be digital replicas of bodily assets, also illustrates the transformative capacity of AI and ML in Industry 4.0. These virtual fashions permit superior simulation, real-time tracking and optimization, imparting insights into machine overall performance and capacity problems. Additionally, AI and ML enhance human-device collaboration by enabling more intuitive and green interfaces [7]. For example, AI-primarily based total analytics can provide employees with actionable insights through an augmented reality (AR) interface, facilitating higher decision-making on the shop floor in manufacturing. Additionally, ML algorithms can customize schooling packages primarily based totally on every employee's overall performance, selling ability improvement and adaptability [9]. This phase units the degree for a complete exploration of the vital function AI and ML play in Industry 4.0. By examining their programs and impacts, this article aims to highlight how these technologies are driving the evolution of modern industries toward a connected, intelligent and more efficient future [8]. It can even cope with the demanding situations and issues related to deploying AI and ML in commercial environments, which include facts security, moral concerns, and the want to upskill the workforce. quantity of labor. Through this exploration, we intend to offer a complete knowledge of the transformative capacity of AI and ML within the context of Industry 4.0.

12.2 Application of AI and ML in Industry 4.0

Predictive upkeep

Predictive upkeep leverages AI and ML algorithms to research facts accrued from sensors embedded in business equipment. By figuring out styles and anomalies, those technologies can be expected while a gadget is probable to fail. This proactive technique allows groups to plot upkeep technique earlier than issues occur, substantially lowering unplanned downtime and related upkeep charges [10]. Additionally, predictive upkeep extends the operational lifespan of equipment and improves protection with the aid of averting potential malfunctions that would result in accidents. For example, General Electric (GE) makes use of predictive upkeep to reveal its reactor fleet [12]. AI algorithms examine sensor facts to avoid viable mistakes, lowering downtime and upkeep charges. Similarly, Siemens makes use of a predictive upkeep technique for its wind turbines, with gadgets mastering fashions predicting thing screw-ups and allowing proactive upkeep, minimizing downtime and ensuring turbines to operate efficiently [11].

Quality management

In first-rate management, imaginative and prescient structures powered with the aid of AI and gadget-mastering algorithms are revolutionizing the manner defects are detected and managed [13]. These structures take snapshots of merchandise and use AI to research them in actual time, figuring out defects with excessive accuracy. This guarantees advanced first-rate management and minimizes waste with the aid of detecting defects that inspectors may in any other case miss [14]. For example, inside the car industry, AI structures inspect vehicle components for defects, ensuring high-quality and protection standards. In electronics production, AI detects mistakes in circuit forums and components, stopping faulty merchandise from reaching consumers. Machine mastering fashions are constantly skilled on massive datasets of product snapshots, enhancing their potential to differentiate between perfect and faulty items. This results in constant and dependable first-rate guarantee processes [15].

Supply chain optimization

AI and ML are crucial for optimizing delivery chains through stepped-forward calls for forecasting, stock control, and logistics optimization. By studying historic income facts, marketplace tendencies and outside factors, AI can expect future calls with remarkable accuracy [16]. This allows businesses align manufacturing schedules with forecast calls, avoid over-production or stockouts, and hold the choicest stock levels, thereby lowering garage charges and waste [17]. AI-powered stock control structures robotically tune stock levels, expect future stock needs, and streamline the replenishment process. In the logistics sector, AI optimizes delivery routes and shipping schedules, resulting in value savings, quicker deliveries, and higher patron satisfaction. The capacity to research and adapt to actual-time schedules allow deliver chains to react quicker and greater efficiently in Figure 12.1.

Operate autonomously

The improvement of automated operations represents a considerable development to AI and ML. Automated robots and automated guided vehicles (AGVs) can carry out complicated obligations without human intervention, running constantly and with excessive precision [18]. These structures enhance productiveness by operating continuously and enhance protection by eliminating hazardous tasks. Additionally, self-organizing and adaptive structures use AI to evolve in actual time to convert manufacturing requirements [19]. They can reorganize workflows and adapt seamlessly to new merchandise or manufacturing volumes, presenting flexibility and maximizing efficiency. For example, in production plants, AI-primarily based totally robots carry out repetitive and unique obligations, while AGVs deliver materials, ensuring a streamlined and green manufacturing process [20].

Digital twins

A virtual dual is a digital replica of a bodily asset created by the usage of AI and ML to simulate and optimize actual global processes. These virtual fashions allow actual-time overall performance monitoring, diagnostics and optimization. By presenting insights into the device's overall performance, virtual twins facilitate knowledgeable choice-making and proactive upkeep [21]. AI and ML accumulate and examine records from bodily belongings to create correct virtual representations, which may be used to expect results and optimize processes. For example, in manufacturing, virtual twins can simulate manufacturing traces to become aware of bottlenecks and optimize workflows. In the strength sector, virtual twins

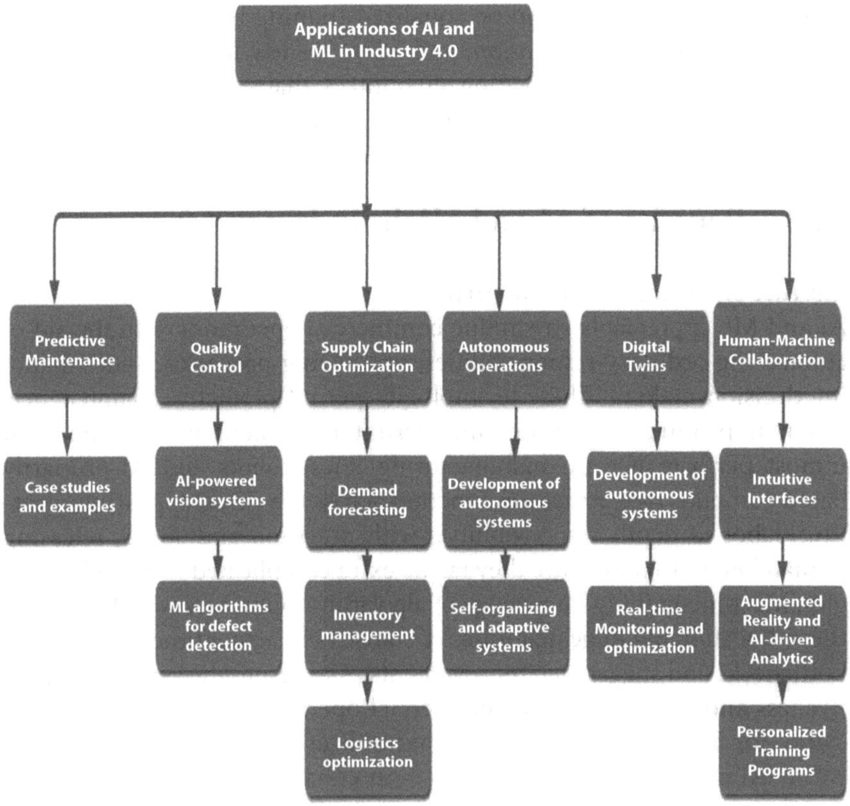

Figure 12.1 Application of AI And ML.

monitor energy plant overall performance, expecting capability-issues, and optimize upkeep schedules [22].

Cooperation among people and machines

AI improves human-device collaboration by presenting intuitive interfaces, augmented reality (AR), and customized schooling programs. AI-primarily based total interfaces, inclusive of voice assistants and natural language processing (NLP) systems, make generation greater reachable and user-friendly, facilitating higher interactions with complicated devices. AI-powered augmented truth systems overlay digital information onto the real world, assisting employees to carry out complicated duties and providing real-time guidance and insights [23]. This is especially beneficial in maintenance and repairs, wherein AR can guide technicians through complicated procedures. Additionally, ML algorithms analyze individual performance data to develop personalized training programs, boost skill development, enhance retention, and adapt to new technology and processes. This tailor-made training guarantees that employees are highly organized to fulfil the needs of AI-pushed commercial environments [24].

12.3 Benefits of AI and ML in Industry 4.0

Increase efficiency and productivity

AI and ML appreciably streamline commercial operations with the aid of automating ordinary responsibilities, optimizing processes, and enhancing decision-making. These technologies permit predictive maintenance, lessen unplanned downtime, and permit equipment to function with utmost performance. In manufacturing lines, robots and AI-primarily based computerized structures function across the clock, appearing repetitive, labor-in-depth responsibilities with precision and speed, releasing human beings to make sure they tackle extra complicated roles and strategies. Machine-gaining knowledge of algorithms optimizes workflows with the aid of studying huge quantities of statistics in actual time, figuring out bottlenecks and suggesting improvements. As a result, the general productiveness and performance of commercial operations will increase appreciably, for better output and higher aid utilization. Improve and decrease waste: AI and ML play a vital position in enhancing product exceptional and decreasing waste. Vision structures primarily based totally on AI and device-gaining knowledge of algorithms enhance exceptional manipulation with the aid of detecting mistakes with excessive accuracy. These structures constantly look into merchandise all through manufacturing, figuring out and putting off faulty objects earlier than they reach the market [25]. This reduces waste and guarantees that the simplest excessive exceptional merchandise is added to customers. Additionally, AI can optimize manufacturing parameters to minimize variations and maintain consistent quality. The capacity to locate and accurate mistakes in actual time approach much less transform and scrap, for productive use of substances and resources.

Improved operational flexibility

AI improves operational agility by means of permitting organizations to reply quickly to converting marketplace situations and demands. Machine mastering fashions examine marketplace trends, client preferences, and different outside elements to appropriately forecast demand. This permits groups to regulate manufacturing schedules, manipulate stock tiers, and quickly regulate delivery chain operations. AI-primarily based total structures additionally facilitate speedy reconfiguration of manufacturing traces to deal with new merchandise or adjustments in manufacturing volumes. This flexibility is critical in dynamic marketplace environments, wherein the capacity to evolve quickly can offer a massive aggressive advantage. By leveraging AI, organizations can maintain excessive tiers of responsiveness and adaptability.

Cost savings and return on investment

The economic blessings of AI and ML in Industry 4.0 are huge, mainly due to huge price financial savings and return on investment (ROI). Predictive preservation facilitates fewer fees related to surprising device screw-ups and downtime. Optimizing production methods and delivery chain control facilitates lessening running fees with the aid of lowering waste, enhancing aid utilization, and improving logistics efficiency. AI-powered automation reduces exertion fees even with growing productivity. Additionally, the insights generated with the aid of using AI and ML assist groups make extra knowledgeable choices that result in worthwhile strategies. The cumulative impact of those upgrades is an excessive ROI due to the fact investing in the AI and ML era will supply tangible economic blessings [26].

Make better decisions

AI and ML empower business companies with statistics-pushed insights and predictive analytics, permitting higher decision-making in any respect stages of the organization. By reading substantial quantities of statistics in real time, AI algorithms can become aware of patterns, trends, and correlations that human beings may also overlook. This permits decision-makers to gain deeper insights into marketplace dynamics, consumer behavior, and operational performance, permitting them to make knowledgeable choices with extra confidence. Additionally, AI-powered predictive analytics allow agencies to expect future trends, risks, and opportunities, permitting proactive decision-making that drives strategic boom and aggressive advantage. By leveraging AI and ML technology, business companies could make smarter choices that optimize performance, mitigate risks, and force a sustainable boom inside the virtual era. The advantages of AI and ML in Industry 4.0 are multifaceted and far-reaching [27]. From expanded performance and productiveness to greater excellent and decreased waste, progressed operational agility, value savings, and higher decision-making, AI and ML technology are revolutionizing the economic landscape, using innovation, and permitting businesses to thrive in the virtual age.

12.4 Challenges and Considerations in Adopting AI and ML in Industry 4.0

The integration of synthetic intelligence (AI) and gadget learning (ML) technology in Industry 4.0 gives many possibilities for innovation and growth. However, it additionally poses a chain of demanding situations and concerns that agencies need to cope with to ensure a successful implementation and adoption. This phase delves deeper into those demanding situations and offers records on how agencies can efficaciously cope with them [28].

1. Data security and privacy

In the Industry 4.0 era, in which information is the lifeblood of operations, ensuring robust information safety and privacy measures are paramount. Industrial groups acquire massive quantities of touchy information, which includes proprietary designs, production processes, and patron information. Protecting this information from unauthorized access, manipulation or robbery is critical to maintaining commercial enterprise continuity, safeguarding intellectual property and maintaining customer trust.

Measures to ensure data security: The use of encryption strategies to stabilize records in transit and at rest, making sure that although records are intercepted, they stay incomprehensible to unauthorized customers [29]. Access Control: Implement strict get right of entry to manipulate and consumer authentication mechanisms to restrict get right of entry to touchy records to legal customers only. Intrusion detection structures: Deploy intrusion detection structures that screen community site visitors and discover and reply to capacity protection breaches in actual time. Regulatory Compliance: Comply with records safety policies which include the General Data Protection Regulation (GDPR) and industry-unique requirements to make certain compliance and avoid highly-priced penalties.

2. Ethical concerns

The huge adoption of AI and automation generation in Industry 4.0 increases moral concerns around task displacement, group of workers effect, transparency and fairness. While AI and robotics provide the capacity to enhance productiveness and efficiency, additionally they pose demanding situations associated with task loss, converting roles, and capacity bias in decision-making.

Resolve moral issues: Mitigate task losses Implement proactive measures which include reskilling and upskilling packages to equip people with the abilities wanted for brand new roles and limit the effect of automation closer to employment. Transparency and fairness: Ensure transparency in AI structures by means of supplying visibility into how choices are made and what elements are considered. Implement fairness measures to limit bias and discrimination in algorithmic decision-making [30].

3. Improve workforce qualifications
As AI and automation reshape the commercial landscape, businesses face the assignment of making ready their body of workers for the virtual future. Rapid advances in generation require the improvement of the body of workers' competencies and talents to correctly adapt to an AI-pushed environment.

Workforce development strategy: Comprehensive schooling applications Invest in complete schooling applications to equip personnel with the technical skills, virtual literacy, and area information to thrive inside the surroundings of AI support. Culture of Continuous Learning: Cultivate a lifestyle of non-stop getting-to-know and innovation to inspire personnel to stay updated with rising technology and adapt to converting activity roles. Collaborate with instructional establishments: Collaborate with instructional establishments to increase specialized schooling applications tailor-made to the wishes of Industry 4.0 and create possibilities for life-long getting-to-know and expert improvement in Figure 12.1.

12.5 Case Studies and Examples of AI and ML in Industry 4.0

1. Predictive Maintenance in Manufacturing
Company: General Electric (GE)
Industry: Manufacturing

Implementation: GE implemented AI and ML algorithms to predict equipment failures in their manufacturing facilities. By analyzing sensor data from industrial machines, such as turbines and compressors, GE's AI system can detect anomalies and predict maintenance needs before equipment failures occur.
Outcome: This predictive maintenance approach has enabled GE to reduce downtime, optimize maintenance schedules, and extend the lifespan of

industrial equipment. As a result, GE has seen significant cost savings and improvements in operational efficiency.

2. ***Quality Control in Automotive Manufacturing***
Company: BMW Group
Industry: Automotive Manufacturing

Implementation: BMW Group utilizes AI-powered vision systems to inspect vehicle components for defects during the manufacturing process. Machine learning algorithms analyze images captured by cameras to identify defects such as scratches, dents, and misalignments.
Outcome: By automating quality control processes with AI and ML, BMW Group has improved product quality, reduced manufacturing defects, and enhanced customer satisfaction. This has led to higher production efficiency and cost savings for the company.

3. ***Supply Chain Optimization in Retail***
Company: Amazon
Industry: Retail

Implementation: Amazon leverages AI and ML algorithms to optimize its supply chain operations, including demand forecasting, inventory management, and logistics optimization. By analyzing vast amounts of data, such as historical sales data, market trends, and customer behavior, Amazon's AI system can accurately predict demand and optimize inventory levels.
Outcome: Through AI-driven supply chain optimization, Amazon has achieved faster delivery times, reduced inventory holding costs, and improved customer satisfaction. The company's ability to fulfil customer orders quickly and efficiently has contributed to its success in the highly competitive retail industry.

Lessons Learned and Best Practices

1. ***Start with clear goals:***
Defining clean dreams and using instances is important to efficiently deploy AI and ML in Industry 4.0. Organizations must pick out precise regions wherein that technology could have the maximum considerable impact, consisting of predictive upkeep to decrease downtime, fine management to enhance fine merchandise and deliver chain optimization to enhance operational efficiency. Beginning with clean dreams, groups can focus efforts and sources on projects that align with strategic priorities and supply tangible enterprise value.

2. ***Data quality is essential:***
High-first-rate facts are vital for the fulfilment of AI and ML projects. Organizations have to make certain that the facts used to teach AI and ML fashions are clean, relevant, and diverse. This consists of facts preprocessing steps to take away noise, outliers, and inconsistencies, in addition to facts augmentation strategies to enhance the range of the facts set. By prioritizing facts first-rate, groups can increase correct and dependable algorithms that generate actionable insights and power knowledgeable choice-making.

3. ***Collaborative and cross-functional teams:***
Collaboration throughout cross-purposeful groups is vital for the successful implementation of AI and ML projects. By bringing together information scientists, area experts, and IT professionals, these groups can leverage various views and understanding to expand revolutionary answers that deal with complicated commercial enterprise challenges. Cross-purposeful groups ensure alignment between technical answers and commercial enterprise goals, facilitating the adoption and integration of AI and ML technology throughout the organization [31].

4. ***Continuous improvement and iteration:***
Implementing AI and ML is an iterative manner that calls for regular monitoring, evaluation, and refinement. Organizations need to set up mechanisms to screen version overall performance, accumulate stakeholder feedback, and iterate on answers to force non-stop improvement. This may also include undertaking everyday version testing, reading overall performance metrics, and incorporating end-person feedback to enhance the set of rule's accuracy and performance over time.

5. ***Ethical Considerations and Transparency:***
Ethical concerns and transparency are paramount in AI and ML implementations to ensure equity, accountability, and trustworthiness. Organizations need to proactively perceive and cope with ability, biases, discrimination, and privacy issues related to AI and ML algorithms [32]. This consists of accomplishing bias exams, equity audits, and privateness effect exams to perceive and mitigate moral risks. Additionally, corporations ought to enforce transparency measures, which include explainable AI strategies and algorithmic transparency frameworks, to offer visibility into how AI and ML fashions make decisions [33]. By prioritizing moral concerns and transparency, corporations can construct beliefs with stakeholders, mitigate reputational risks, and foster accountable AI and ML adoption.

These extra insights into the classes discovered and pleasant practices offer corporations a complete framework for efficiently imposing AI and ML in Industry 4.0. By beginning with clean objectives, prioritizing information quality, fostering collaboration among cross-useful teams, embracing non-stop development and iteration, and addressing moral concerns and transparency, corporations can unencumber the entire ability of AI and ML technology to force innovation, efficiency, and competitiveness inside the virtual era.

12.6 Emerging AI and ML Technologies in Industry 4.0

The future of Industry 4.0 could be fashioned through a wave of rising AI and ML technology that promises to revolutionize production and business processes. One such generation is "reinforcement getting to know", which permits machines to study through trial and mistake and make self-reliant choices in dynamic environments. "Reinforcement getting to know" gives the capacity to optimize complicated production processes, including robot meetings and logistics, through constantly adapting to converting situations and enhancing performance [34].

Another rising generation is "federated getting to know", which permits AI fashions to learn collaboratively through allotted side gadgets at the same time as retaining information privateness and security. "Federated getting to know" allows corporations to leverage information from a couple of resets without centralizing touchy information, beginning up new opportunities for decentralized AI programs in clever factories and IoT environments industry. Additionally, advances in herbal language processing (NLP) and conversational AI are poised to convert human-system interplay in Industry 4.0. Chatbots, digital assistants and voice-activated interfaces powered through NLP generation will allow seamless verbal exchange among people and machines, enhancing the productivity and performance of producing operations.

Potential future applications and innovations:

The future of Industry 4.0 holds the tremendous ability for transformative packages and improvements pushed through AI and ML technologies. One ability utility is the call for forecasting primarily based totally on predictive analytics, which makes use of superior ML algorithms to appropriately expect client calls for patterns. By predicting future calls for trends, producers can optimize manufacturing schedules, decrease stock costs, and make certain on-time product delivery to fulfil client expectations. Another innovation on the horizon is AI-powered independent robots geared up with superior sensors and laptop imaginative and prescient capabilities. These robots can carry out complicated obligations appropriately and efficiently, consisting of cloth handling, inspection, and maintenance, without human intervention. Automated robots will revolutionize production processes, allowing agile, bendy and adaptive production structures to respond quickly to converting marketplace demands [35].

Additionally, AI-primarily based virtual twins are anticipated to play a key position in Industry 4.0 by means of developing digital copies of bodily assets, processes, and structures. The virtual dual leverages simulation fashions and real-time data to monitor, examine and optimize commercial operations, allowing predictive maintenance, manner optimization and overall performance monitoring. real-time overall performance. By offering insights into asset condition, overall performance and productivity, virtual twins permit agencies to make data-pushed choices and power non-stop development at some point of the chain. manufacturing value. The potentiality of IoT in agriculture is depicted in Figures 12.2 and 12.3.

Predictions of industrial landscape:

Industry experts and analysts predict that AI and ML technology will continue to reshape the future industrial landscape, driving innovation, efficiency and competitiveness. The adoption of AI in manufacturing is predicted to accelerate rapidly, with AI-based automation and optimization becoming widespread in smart factories and industrial environments [36].

Furthermore, the convergence of AI with different rising technologies, inclusive of 5G, facet computing and blockchain, is anticipated to open up new possibilities for business transformation. 5G networks will permit ultra-low latency communications and high-pace information transfers, facilitating real-time choice-making and far-off tracking of business assets. Edge computing will carry AI processing towards the information technology source, permitting quicker inference and decreased latency for time-vital production programs [37]. Additionally, the blockchain era will enhance information security, integrity, and transparency in Industry 4.0 by means of imparting an immutable and tamper-evidence ledger to file and affirm transactions throughout the scattered networks. By combining AI with those rising technologies, agencies can create intelligent, interconnected ecosystems that power innovation, flexibility and resilience throughout the business landscape. The future of Industry 4.0 might

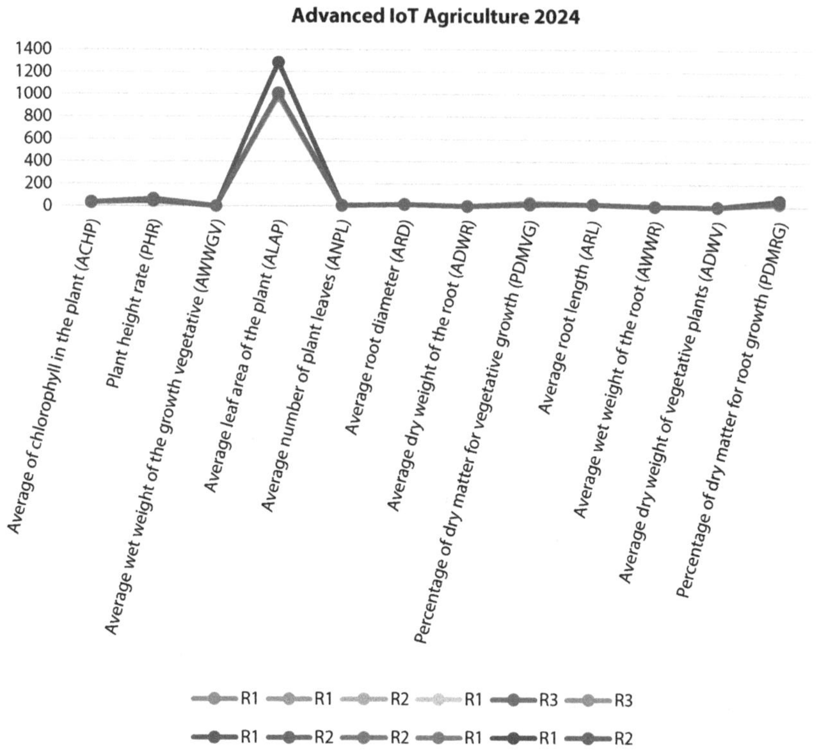

Figure 12.2 Advanced IoT.

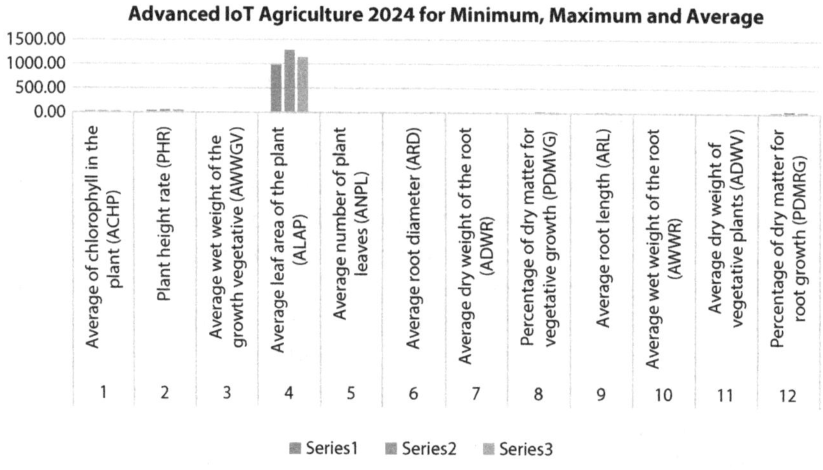

Figure 12.3 Advanced IoT minimum, maximum and average.

be characterized by massive adoption of rising AI and ML technologies, transformative programs and improvements that propose to revolutionize production and business processes. By embracing those traits and developments, agencies can live in advance of the curve, power virtual transformation and open up new possibilities for increase and competitiveness in an evolving enterprise landscape.

12.7 Conclusion

The transformative effect of AI and ML technology on Industry 4.0 highlighted their function in riding innovation, efficiency, and competitiveness in numerous sectors. During the discussion, numerous key factors emerged that spotlight the significance of leveraging those technologies to unencumber new possibilities and deal with complicated demanding situations in business environments. We commenced exploring programs of AI and ML in Industry 4.0, together with predictive maintenance, pleasant control, deliver chain optimization, self-sustaining operations, virtual twins, and human-system collaboration. These programs display the various ways AI and ML are revolutionizing conventional business processes, allowing organizations to enhance operational efficiency, enhance product pleasantness, and supply world- class client experiences. Additionally, we explored the demanding situations and issues related to imposing AI and ML in Industry 4.0, together with facts on safety and privacy, moral concerns, and a group of workers' upskilling. By proactively addressing those demanding situations and imposing suitable measures, organizations can lessen dangers and ensure accountable and moral use of AI and ML technology. We additionally mentioned instructions found and quality practices for a hit AI and ML integration. We begin with clear goals, prioritize facts, foster collaboration among cross-useful teams, inspire non-stop development and iteration, and contain moral issues and transparency.

References

1. Chui, M., *et al.*, Artificial intelligence: The next digital frontier?, 47, 3, 6, 6–8, McKinsey and Company Global Institute, 2017.
2. Kusiak, A., Smart manufacturing. *Int. J. Prod. Res.*, 56, 1-2, 508–517, 2018.
3. Gaiardelli, P., *et al.* Product-service systems evolution in the era of Industry 4.0. *Service Business*, 15, 177–207, 2021.

4. Bughin, J., *et al.*, *Artificial intelligence: The next frontier in productivity and innovation*, McKinsey Global Institute, 2017.
5. Sharma, R., *et al.*, Applications of artificial intelligence techniques in Industry 4.0: A comprehensive review. *Comput. Ind. Eng.*, 113, 333–351, 2017.
6. International Data Corporation (IDC), *IDC FutureScape: Worldwide Manufacturing 2022 Predictions*, IDC FutureScape, 2021.
7. Iansiti, M. and Lakhani, K.R., *Competing in the age of AI: Strategy and leadership when algorithms and networks run the world.* Harvard Business Review Press, 2020.
8. Geissbauer, R., Vedso, J., Schrauf, S., *Industry 4.0: building the digital enterprise.* Price Waterhouse Coopers, 2016
9. Schindler, J., *et al.*, Artificial intelligence in logistics and supply chain management: A systematic literature review and research agenda. *Transp. Res. Part E Logist. Transp. Rev.*, 141, 102035, 2020.
10. Brown, S., *et al.*, *World Economic Forum: The future of jobs report 2020.* (2020).
11. Varshney, K.R., *et al.*, Artificial intelligence and robotics. *IEEE Trans. Sys. Man Cybernetics Part C (Applications Reviews)*, 42, 6, 1203–1213, 2012.
12. Cao, M., *et al.*, Internet of things, blockchain and shared economy: The next revolution. *Engineering*, 5, 5, 858–866, 2019.
13. Agrawal, Mayank, *et al.*, *Industry 4.0: Reimagining manufacturing operations after COVID-19.* McKinsey & Company, 1–11, 2020.
14. Lee, G.S., *et al.*, Industry 4.0: A review of enabling technologies and challenges. *IEEE Access*, 6, 49–64, 2018.
15. Deloitte, I., *Industry 4.0: Are you ready?*, Deloitte Review 22.1, 2018.
16. Grieves, M., *et al.*, Digital twin: Mitigating unpredictable, undesirable emergent behavior in complex systems. *CIRP J. Manuf. Sci. Technol.*, 22, 6–9, 2018.
17. Atzori, L., *et al.*, The Internet things A survey. *Comput. Netw.*, 54, 15, 2787–2805, 2010.
18. Agrawal, A., Gans, J., Goldfarb, A., Power and prediction: The disruptive economics of artificial intelligence. Harvard Business Press, 2022.
19. Accenture, How AI boosts Industry profits and Innovation. 2017.
20. Raj, P., *et al.*, A survey on applications of machine learning techniques in smart manufacturing: Industry 4.0. *J. Manuf. Syst.*, 53, 261–279, 2020.
21. Grieves, Michael W., Virtually intelligent product systems: Digital and physical twins. 175–200, 2019.
22. Tchouganov, A., *et al.*, Industry 4.0 and its application in lean construction. *J. Clean. Prod.*, 256, 120486, 2020.
23. Al-Turjman, F., *et al.*, Blockchain for Industry 4.0: A comprehensive review. *IEEE Access*, 8, 143140–143163, 2020.
24. Servent, Ariadna Ripoll. The European Parliament after the 2019 elections: Testing the Boundaries of the 'cordon sanitaire'. *J. Contemp. Eur. Res.*, 15, 4, 331–342, 2019.

25. Morathi, Lerato Perseverence. Millennial perceptions of the 4th industrial revolution in an information technology company. Diss. North-West University (South Africa), 2020.
26. Leaders, Young Global. World economic forum annual meeting 2016 mastering the fourth industrial revolution. 2016.
27. Bloom, Gedare, *et al.*, Design patterns for the industrial Internet of Things. *2018 14th IEEE International Workshop on Factory Communication Systems (WFCS)*, IEEE, 2018.
28. Hogan, M., Piccarreta B., Interagency International Cybersecurity Standardization Working Group. *Interagency report on status of international cybersecurity standardization for the Internet of Things (IoT)*. No. NIST Internal or Interagency Report (NISTIR) 8200 (Draft). National Institute of Standards and Technology, 2018.
29. Hofmann, E., *et al.*, Industry 4.0 and the current status as well as future prospects on logistics. *Comput. Ind.*, 89, 23–34, 2017.
30. Ashton, K., That 'internet of things' thing. *RFID journal* 22.7, 97–114, 2009.
31. Kalpaka, A., Sörvik, J., Tasigiorgou, A., Rissola, G., Digital Innovation Hubs as policy instruments to boost digitalisation of SMEs. 2020.
32. Singh, J., *et al.*, Industry 4.0: A perspective on opportunities and challenges of industrial internet of things. *Procedia Comput. Sci.*, 132, 991–998, 2018.
33. Toffler, A., *The Third Wave*. Bantam Books (US), 1980.
34. Lu, Y., *et al.*, Internet of Things (IoT) for Industry 4.0: State-of-the-art and prospects. *IEEE Ind. Electron. Mag.*, 14, 1, 5–17, 2020.
35. Adamson, G., Havens, J. C., Chatila, R., Designing a value-driven future for ethical autonomous and intelligent systems. *Proceedings of the IEEE*, 107, 3, 518–525, 2019.
36. Wang, W., Electronic Information Technology in the Internet of Things in Smart Cities. In: *Journal of Physics: Conference Series*, vol. 2037, no. 1, p. 012079, IOP Publishing, 2021, September.
37. Sackey, Mensah, S., Bester, A., Industrial engineering curriculum in Industry 4.0 in a South African context. *S. Afr. J. Ind. Eng.*, 27, 4, 101–114, 2016.

About the Editors

M. Thirunavukkarasan, PhD is an assistant professor in the School of Computer Science and Engineering at the Vellore Institute of Technology with over 15 years of research and teaching experience. He has published papers in several international conferences and journals and given keynote speeches at many international conferences. His research interests include Internet of Things (IoT), wireless sensor networks, wireless communication, cloud computing, artificial intelligence, and machine learning.

S. A. Sahaaya Arul Mary, PhD is a professor in the School of Computer Science and Engineering, Vellore Institute of Technology with over 29 years of teaching and over 15 years of research experience. She has over 70 publications in various reputed journals and conferences and reviewed over 35 papers in addition to mentoring aspiring PhD students. Her research includes software engineering, data mining, machine learning, and artificial intelligence.

Sathiyaraj. R, PhD is an assistant professor in the Department of Computer Science and Engineering at Gandhi Institute of Technology and Management University in Bangalore, India. He has contributed to two books, served as lead editor for an additional two books, and published five patents and over 20 articles in various international journals and conferences. His research interests include machine learning, big data analytics, and intelligent systems.

G. S. Pradeep Ghantasala, PhD is a professor in the Department of Computer Science and Engineering, at Alliance University with over 16 years of academic experience. He has contributed to internationally published books, chapters, patents, and numerous papers in journals and conferences. He also serves as an editor and reviewer for several journals. His research interests include machine learning, deep learning, healthcare applications, and software engineering applications.

Mudassir Khan, PhD is an assistant professor in the Department of Computer Science at King Khalid University with over ten years of teaching experience. He has published over 25 papers in international journals and conferences and one patent. He is a member of various technical and professional societies including the Institute for Electrical and Electronics Engineers and Computer Science Teachers Association. His research interests include big data, deep learning, machine learning, eLearning, fuzzy logic, image processing, and cyber security.

Index

Also of Interest

Check out these other related titles from Scrivener Publishing

Controller Design for Industrial Applications, Edited by Arindam Mondal & Souvik Ganguli, ISBN: 9781394287079. *Controller Design for Industrial Applications* is essential for anyone looking to master the advanced techniques of intelligent controller design, enabling you to effectively tackle the complexities of modern industrial processes and optimize performance in an ever-evolving landscape.

Special Electrical Machinery, Edited by Dr. Jigneshkumar P. Desai, ISBN: 9781394193912. This book is a comprehensive guide to specialized motors, covering everything from switched reluctance motors to axial flux ironless PM motors, giving in-depth information on their operating principles, applications, and controls.

DESIGN, MODELING AND RELIABILITY IN ROTATING MACHINERY, Edited by Robert X. Perez, ISBN: 9781119631682. This broad collection of current rotating machinery topics, written by industry experts, is a must-have for rotating equipment engineers, maintenance personnel, students, and anyone else wanting to stay abreast with current rotating machinery concepts and technology.

MAINTENANCE, RELIABILITY AND TROUBLESHOOTING IN ROTATING AND PROCESS MACHINERY, Edited by Robert X. Perez, ISBN: 9781119631644. For Rotating equipment professionals, maintenance personnel, project engineers, process engineers, mechanical engineering students, and anyone working around critical rotating equipment.

Troubleshooting Rotating Machinery: Including Centrifugal Pumps and Compressors, Reciprocating Pumps and Compressors, Fans, Steam Turbines, Electric Motors, and More, by Robert X. Perez and Andrew P. Conkey, ISBN: 9781119294139. A must-read for anyone whose job depends on operating or maintaining safe, reliable, and efficient machinery in a process facility, this volume shows the newcomer and veteran alike how you can start troubleshooting rotating equipment problems immediately by implementing this book's common-sense methodology. *NOW AVAILABLE!*

Operator's Guide to Process Compressors, by Robert X. Perez, ISBN: 9781119580614. The perfect primer for anyone responsible for operating or maintaining process gas compressors. *NOW AVAILABLE!*

Operator's Guide to General Purpose Steam Turbines: An Overview of Operating Principles, Construction, Best Practices, and Troubleshooting, by Robert X. Perez and David W. Lawhon, ISBN: 9781119294214. A must-read book for anyone operating or maintaining general purpose steam turbines in a process setting, this is a practical reference that includes a collection of field-tested procedures aimed at ensuring safe general purpose steam turbines start-ups, shutdowns, and over-speed tests. *NOW AVAILABLE!*

Dictionary of Industrial Terminology 2nd Edition, by Michael D. Holloway and Emma Holloway, ISBN: 9781119363446. Greatly expanded and revised, this second edition is the most comprehensive and in-depth dictionary of industrial terms available, a must-have for any engineer, scientist, technician, or operator working in industry. *NOW AVAILABLE!*

Basic Electrical and Instrumentation Engineering, by P. Sivaraman, C. Sharmeela, A. Thaiyal Nayagi, and R. Mahendran, ISBN: 9781119764465. Offering the most up-to-date coverage on the subject available, this new volume provides detailed concepts of AC circuits and power systems, transformers, DC machines, AC machines, measurement and instrumentation, and many other practical concepts for the engineer or engineering student. *NOW AVAILABLE!*

ELECTRIC VEHICLE DESIGN: Design, Simulation and Applications, Edited by Krishan Arora, Suman Lata Tripathi, and Himashu Sharma, ISBN: 9781394204373. This book will serve as a definitive guide to conceptual and practical knowledge about the design of hybrid electrical vehicles (HEV), battery electrical vehicles (BEV), fuel cell electrical vehicles (FCEV), plug-in hybrid electrical vehicles (PHEV), and efficient EV charging techniques with advanced tools and methodologies for students, engineers, and academics alike.

INDUSTRIAL CONTROL SYSTEMS, Edited by Vipin Chandra Pal, Suman Lata Tripathi, and Souvik Ganguli, ISBN: 9781119829256. This volume serves as a comprehensive guide in the journey of industrial control systems with a multidisciplinary approach to the key engineering problems in the 21st century.

MODERN AUTOMOTIVE ELECTRICAL SYSTEMS: Theory and Applications, Edited by Pedram Asef, Sanjeevikumar Padmanaban, and Andrew Lapthorn, ISBN: 1119801047. Presenting the concepts and advances of modern automotive electrical systems, this volume, written and edited by a global team of experts, also goes into the practical applications for the engineer, student, and other industry professionals.

NANODEVICES FOR INTEGRATED CIRCUIT DESIGN, Edited by Suman Lata Tripathi, Abhishek Kumar, K. Srinivasa Rao, and Prasantha R. Mudimela, ISBN: 9781394185788. Written and edited by a team of experts in the field, this important new volume broadly covers the design of nano-devices and their integrated applications in digital and analog integrated circuits (IC) design.

DESIGN AND DEVELOPMENT OF EFFICIENT ENERGY SYSTEMS, Edited by Suman Lata Tripathi, Dushyant Kumar Singh, Sanjeevikumar Padmanaban, and P. Raja, ISBN: 9781119761631. Covering the concepts and fundamentals of efficient energy systems, this volume, written and edited by a global team of experts, also goes into the practical applications that can be utilized across multiple industries, for both the engineer and the student.

Printed in the USA/Agawam, MA
September 16, 2026

910661.100